ALSO BY MARC FISHER

AFTER THE WALL: GERMANY, THE GERMANS
AND THE BURDENS OF HISTORY

CONTENTS

✳ THE MAGIC OF RADIO

THE SUMMER I WAS TWELVE, I spent hours walking along the beach on Long Island, transistor radio in my hand, listening to the most popular station in the nation. I didn't much care for the songs on WABC; I particularly despised Gilbert O'Sullivan's "Alone Again (Naturally)," a whining ballad that somehow swelled my adolescent frustrations and made me want to hurl the radio into the sea. But I couldn't do that. Nor did I turn the dial on the cream-colored plastic box—notched black dials for volume and tuning, smooth ribs of plastic over the speaker, a single nine-volt battery inside, the whole package a bit larger than a pack of Marlboros. That radio stayed with me all day; each night, I slipped it under my pillow.

I kept that radio tuned to the Top 40 station because the next song might be Billy Paul's "Me and Mrs. Jones," which I couldn't get enough of, even if I hadn't the slightest idea what the song was about. I kept the radio tuned to Musicradio 77 because I was twelve, this was America, and that was what I was supposed to do. I listened because the deejays were fast and fevered, because there was nothing else moving at the frenetic pace of my mind and emotions. In the voice of my favorite deejay, Dan Ingram, in his six-second antics sandwiched between ads and pop songs, I heard freedom and passion, everything a kid wants to think is out there somewhere, just beyond his reach.

In New York City, where I grew up, WABC was the sound that poured out of car windows, storefronts, beach blanket transistors, and even some of those hip hi-fi stereos the older kids were buying so they could play their albums—albums WABC assuredly did not spin. Every big city had a similar station—WLS in Chicago, KHJ in Los Angeles, WRKO in Boston, and on and on across the land, the deejays shouting, the hits repeating, the jingles and contests and promotions and ads flying out of the speakers, a locomotive of a generation.

Nobody talked much about radio then; it was just there. The songs and jingles embedded themselves in our memories, linking to moments magical and painful, connecting to events, places, people. Americans who grew up in the 1950s, '60s, '70s, and into the '80s received the blessing (and the curse) of a common soundtrack, not only in popular music but across all of radio's programming—the rock and the pop, the deejays and the news, the all-night talkers and the FM fringe.

For a few brief decades, pop culture brought the nation together into a sense of belonging, a deep belief in the great American myth that had powered the nation to victory in World War II and propelled the economic dynamo of the 1950s and '60s—the deeply felt conviction that we were one community, one generation. We grew up dancing and dreaming to the same soundtrack, and we were therefore somehow united. That sense of belonging molded our expectations in politics, work, home, and school. Until the Great Unraveling of the late 1960s and early '70s, this shared pop culture was a meeting ground for our nation, a commons that we only years later realized we had lost.

Radio—at least in its traditional AM-FM incarnation—has seemed like a fading technology of late, but it's a big piece of how we got to be who we are. And if the history of changing technologies teaches us anything, we should know better than to write radio's obituary. Listening to Americans talk about radio over the past few years, I've heard one story after another about the voice, program, or music that changed a life. Almost everyone has a radio story—of a road trip on which they first heard the blues or zydeco, of an all-night talk show that lured them into the mysteries of the JFK assassination or the deep unknowns of cosmology, of a deejay who talked them through a teen romance gone bad. When I met Michael Freedman, who rose to the

SOMETHING IN THE AIR

Radio, Rock, and the Revolution That Shaped a Generation

 RANDOM HOUSE | NEW YORK

SOMETHING IN THE AIR

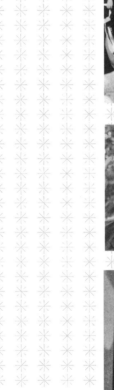

MARC FISHER

Published in the United States by Random House,
an imprint of The Random House Publishing Group,
a division of Random House, Inc., New York.

RANDOM HOUSE and colophon are registered
trademarks of Random House, Inc.

ISBN 978-0-375-50907-0

LIBRARY OF CONGRESS CATALOGING-IN-PUBLICATION DATA

Fisher, Marc.
    Something in the air: radio, rock, and the revolution
that shaped a generation/Marc Fisher.
        p.   cm.
    Includes bibliographical references and index.
    ISBN: 978-0-375-50907-0
        1. Radio broadcasting—United States—History.
I. Title.
  HE8698.F47 2007
    384.540973—dc22   2006047353

Printed in the United States of America on acid-free paper

www.atrandom.com

9 8 7 6 5 4 3 2 1

FIRST EDITION

*Title page photographs courtesy of (clockwise from top left)
Bruce Morrow, Fred W. McDarrah, Robert Altman,
Richard Fatherley, and Jim Marshall*

Book design by Barbara M. Bachman

to my mother and father,

and to Julia and Aaron

top of CBS Radio News, he pulled open his desk and cradled in his hand the transistor radio he had kept under his pillow decades ago to listen to the ball games and newscasts that shaped his future. George Michael, the great Philadelphia and New York Top 40 deejay who later became a nationally syndicated sportscaster, reached into his top drawer and let me hold the stopwatch he used four decades ago to time the introductions of each pop hit so he could talk right up to the first syllable of the song's vocals. I've been taken into basements to see treasured jukeboxes, into back offices to hear an old tape of a cherished but long gone Top 40 station, into kitchens to pore over scrapbooks of concert tickets, programs, and song surveys featuring the swinging all-American deejays of one boss rocker or another. Each visit brings back my own memories in rushes of sound muffled by the passage of time: the velvet tones of Clarence Rock, the all-night newsman on all-news WINS; the wild conspiracy theories and classic carny pitches of all-night talker Long John Nebel; the tinny tunes of distant AM pop stations as I faded to dreamland.

Radio lends itself to nostalgia, to a pining for the innocence of a summer's night listening to baseball from a far-off city, the signal fading in and out, the crack of the bat sometimes lost in the sizzle of static from a distant lightning bolt. Or the longing could be for radio's lost edge, for that moment when you first heard a certain Dylan song, or the whole A side of *Sgt. Pepper's,* or National Public Radio's coverage of the fall of the Berlin Wall, or Art Bell's midnight conjuring of too many coincidences surrounding the official explanation of Area 51.

But far more than nostalgia, the story of radio is the story of imagination in American popular culture. It is Richard Dreyfuss in *American Graffiti* picturing Wolfman Jack as a pirate of the airwaves holed up in some Mexican hideaway, illicitly pumping out the cruising tunes that kept the Strip hopping each night. It is Rush Limbaugh thumping his desk and grandiosely describing his vast Excellence in Broadcasting Network headquarters even as he delivers his talk show from the luxurious splendor of his South Florida home. It is thousands of college kids playing radio, summoning a fantasy world of their own, as I did in the late 1970s, when I took listeners to my all-night show on an aural tour of a towering "Holder Broadcasting Complex," "twelve great stories of radio," with live reports from our beleaguered weatherman calling in from his outdoor perch, our stentorian but oft inebriated sports reporter, and our officious and incompetent newsman—all me, of course. Finest moment: a listener called and asked if tours were available of the "complex," which was actually a decrepit studio in the sodden basement of an ancient, deteriorating dormitory.

Radio, not even a century old as a mass medium, has already evolved from plaything of hobbyists and tinkerers to source of the first truly national pop culture (the Golden Age of radio network broadcasting in the 1930s and '40s) to its first brush with death (when TV hit a majority of U.S. homes in the early 1950s) to bonding agent for a generation of American youth (the Top 40 era and the rise of rock and roll) to messenger of the counterculture (the rise of the FM band and free-form radio) to vanguard of niche specialization (the triumph of market research and the perfection of satellite technology) and finally to this moment, in which radio is widely groused about and dismissed, yet remains a constant companion for nearly all Americans—in the car, at home in the morning, in the background at the office. Like most old media, radio defies predictions of its death at the hands of new technologies. American radio—like the pop culture it has helped to create, like the country it speaks to—is ever adapting. As it ages, radio absorbs the new, co-opts the rebellious, and reinvents itself every step of the way.

THE FIRST NATIONAL BROADCAST reached a relative handful of homemade radio sets on July 2, 1921, when RCA arranged for a live description of the heavyweight boxing championship bout between Jack Dempsey and Georges Carpentier. The match took place in Hoboken, New Jersey, where a commentator's remarks were transcribed and telegraphed to KDKA in Pittsburgh. Around the country, boxing fans and the plain old curious paid a few pennies admission to gather in firehouses and social halls where volunteer radio hobbyists had set up their receivers.

"Never before has anyone undertaken the colossal task of simultaneously making available a voice description of each incident in a fight to hundreds of thousands of people," wrote the RCA house magazine, *Wireless Age*. The event was deemed so important that each person who set up a receiver and pulled in the broadcast could receive a certificate—signed by Jack Dempsey and Franklin Roosevelt, a former assistant secretary of the Navy who was then president of the Navy Club, which helped organize the fight—thanking the listener for his role in "the successful promotion of amity between the nations."[1]

Within a few months, radio had so captured the American imagination that a song swept the nation—on sheet music, of course. People called it simply "The Radio Song":

> *I wish there was a "Wireless" to Heaven,*
> *And I could speak to Mama ev'ry day,*
> *I would let her know, by the Radio,*
> *I'm so lonesome since she went away.*

Radio became a truly mass medium after the first reasonably affordable sets came on the market in 1927. The Sears catalogue that year featured a $34.95 table radio and advised that "no family should be without its untold advantages." A catalogue from the Radio Specialty Corp. made the Sears pitch seem shy: "When the forces of the Almighty Creator of the Universe and the skill and genius of Man so combine to bring you untold blessings which may be yours to enjoy without even the asking, we ask you in all seriousness why you should not at once show your gratitude and appreciation and accept that which is so freely offered?"[2]

Radio quickly became essential to daily life. The dance bands and other musical acts of the 1930s gave way during the war years to a more ambitious menu of news, dramas, comedy, and variety shows. The great networks—huge concerns created in the late 1920s to link the nation's local stations by phone lines—had symphony orchestras and creative staffs teeming with serious playwrights and fine actors. Radios were the new hearth, their baroque design reflecting the importance of the object and the hours that families spent with it. Radio inspired new kinds of communities, liberated from geography—clusters of Americans who shared the same musical taste, political philosophy, or sense of humor. In a country with distinct regional sensibilities, radio was something universal.

Franklin Roosevelt was the first president to understand how to marry the listeners' imagination to a distant voice. When citizens visited their president's home each week for his fireside chats, they had little concrete sense that Roosevelt's hands shook as he stood before crowds, or that braces held him up on legs crippled by polio. On the air, there were no tremors: Roosevelt's voice was clear and strong, and he used radio as an instrument of power.

During and after World War II, radios expanded beyond the living room to every corner of the house. With more and more urgent news coming over the air, Americans wanted to be near a radio. Clock radios came on the market, and soon the radio was waking commuters for the workday. Kitchen table radios meant that news and music became companions while dinner was cooking. By 1940, there were even rudimentary "portable" radios, bread-box-sized units that looked like small suitcases and weighed more than five pounds. In 1946, playwright Norman Corwin wrote a script for CBS called "Seems Radio Is Here to Stay."[3]

THE CLEAREST WAY to understand a culture, Marshall McLuhan said, is to examine its tools of conversation. Radio, from its start, was something magical, a stunning turn in the popular culture from centuries of writing and reading back to the roots of human communication: voice and listening. All of a sudden, one could speak to many—unseen, unknown. The broadcaster could be whoever he chose to be, and the audience assumed new identities too. The president might call you "my fellow Americans." A commentator such as Walter Winchell might address "Mr. and Mrs. America and all the ships at sea."[4] At home, you could say to yourself, That's me he's talking to.

At first alone, and then in ever larger communities, listeners bonded through their appreciation of characters, shows, phrases, songs, all the bits and pieces of sound that add up to a shared culture. The tools were ancient, biblical—repetition, formulaic expressions, parables—but they were adapted to the new medium in the form of jingles, hit songs, time and temperature, slogans, radio storytellers, and midnight talkers. The result was a people with a common set of references, ideas, and beliefs.[5]

Then came television. Whenever a new communications medium arrives, the first wave of hype informs us that the old ways are history: radio will kill off newspapers, television will eliminate radio, the Internet will obviate the need for TV, bloggers will supplant professional journalists. But the real story of how media evolve is much more interesting than any on-off switch model of replacement. It is a story of belonging, of how we cope with being alone in a crowded world.

TODAY, RADIO SEEMS CLUELESS. One-third of the recorded music sold in this country falls into categories that barely exist on the radio—jazz, classical, Broadway, bluegrass, zydeco, trance, New Age, the vast spectrum of American sound. An Andrea Bocelli CD outsells Elton John five to one but is not heard on the radio. The Welsh classical singer Charlotte Church outsells Sheryl Crow three to one; again, radio silence. The soundtrack from the Coen brothers' movie *O Brother, Where Art Thou?* wows the buying public and sweeps the Grammys, but listeners turned on to bluegrass find no place on the radio to sample the genre. Some of the top-grossing concert acts each summer are Jimmy Buffett and Steely Dan; it takes patient dial-scanning to find the specialized station that might perhaps play one or two of their biggest hits.[6]

Radio's audience has been in decline for more than a decade, as the advertising load each hour soared toward the thirty-minute mark. Among Americans age eighteen to twenty-four, the folks advertisers most love to reach, radio listening has dropped by more than a quarter just since the turn of the century. How did something that meant so much to so many become such a neglected corner of the popular culture? How could such an intimate medium come to be governed by impersonal and corporate forces? Why have we allowed radio, which brought together the most influential generation of the past century, to splinter into so many niches that it now divides us from each other more than it binds us in song or any sense of common cause?

For all our technological prowess, we seem to be moving back toward the kind of lives our great-grandparents led in the days before radio—apart, atomized, in our own worlds, Googling in countless different directions. Technology and culture went micro, and now each of us has access to our own portal, our own America. That is surely a grand gift, but something is missing. America's sense of unity through mass media started with radio. Radio popularized the idea of being part of a generation. When radio lost its way, those grand, enveloping ideas seeped out of our cultural vocabulary. The bonds that radio seemed to cement were always artificial, taking on different meanings in each individual. But radio gave us a starting point for conversations about community. For all its artifice, its deejays with fake names, its sameness and phony familiarity, radio gave Americans what his job and the road gave Willy Loman in Arthur Miller's *Death of a Salesman:* a persona, a foundation. This book is about what that time of community felt and sounded like, how it came to be, why it all collapsed, and what we will listen to next.

PART ONE

SURVIVOR

TODD STORZ, 1956

Chapter 1

✳ OMAHA MORNING

I N 1949, ROBERT STORZ, the owner of Omaha's leading brewery, bought his boy a toy. Todd Storz was twenty-five and something of a disappointment to his father. The heir to the Storz beer fortune had spent much of his childhood in his room, discovering another world. At eight, he built himself a crystal set and spent his evenings scanning the airwaves, listening to voices that spoke of a world beyond the flatlands of Nebraska, a world of crowded ballrooms and swell gents and ladies who could dance all night. At sixteen, he qualified for a ham radio license—permission to scan the airwaves and chat with strangers in faraway places—and suddenly, he was both alone in the far reaches of the Storz mansion and aloft, flying around the Midwest, his voice calling out to other anonymous amateur broadcasters on the prairie. Todd and his fellow hobbyists didn't talk about much other than the fact that they were talking to each other. Marveling at the machinery they had put together with their own hands, they were enraptured by the mere fact of their contact. Todd was a loner, but his radio granted him the courage to reach out to strangers. In that room, he could step away from the shadow of his father. In there, he could reach beyond the expectations that his family and community had for him. In there, he could be someone who was not merely the brewer's son.

Taking over the family business was the last thing Todd wanted to do. He craved something more than the stultifying life of upper-crust Omaha. Todd went away to Choate, the New England boarding school where the nation's leading families sent their sons to be groomed for power, and there, his passion for adventure blossomed. He retired each night to his ham radio, listening in on a world of people who yearned to connect with each other. Todd's hunger for the wider world led him, following a year at the University of Nebraska, to join the U.S. Army Signal Corps. It wasn't a military career that he sought, but rather the chance to be part of an operation that seemed to have no borders.

When his stint was up, Todd returned to Omaha intent on finding a place on the radio. He soon found work at Omaha's Mutual network affiliate, KBON. Assigned the late-night deejay slot, Storz scrapped the swing and bebop, playing instead the most popular records of 1947—the sweet crooners and lush instrumentals of a period of pop music that would never make it to any latter-day oldies station. Todd soon switched to a sales job at another station in town, but he was smitten with radio's power.[1]

In 1949, when the *Omaha World-Herald* put its hometown radio station on the market for $75,000, Robert Storz made his boy a deal. Dad would put up $30,000; if Todd could raise $20,000, the family would borrow the rest and Todd would have himself a station. Todd mortgaged an Iowa farm that he owned, and father and son created the Mid-Continent Broadcasting Co., owner of KOWH, a money-losing, low-rated station that aired the usual mix of chatter for house-wives, hillbilly shows, sweet music, light classics, jazz, and religious programs. The common wisdom of the day was that radio wasn't going to make anybody rich. Commercial spots sold for $1 each—"a dollar a holler," the salesmen would say. But Todd Storz believed that even if that TV thing that was just starting up ever made it big, radio was far from over. Storz's instincts told him that a mass audience could still be found, even if Americans decided they'd rather watch their favorite shows than listen to them.

This was not a widely shared view.

"IS RADIO DOOMED?" *Life* magazine asked in 1949. Jack Benny, Bing Crosby, Johnny Carson, the Goldbergs, the Lone Ranger, Superman—

they'd all seen the writing on the home screen and bid radio adieu. From 1949 to 1953, the number of TV stations in the nation rocketed from 97 to 550.² You could sit in New York or Los Angeles and listen to radio fade. The assumption in Manhattan was that if technology was destiny, television would do to radio what radio itself had done to sheet music, home pianos, and vaudeville halls.

TODD STORZ, AGE SIXTEEN, AS A HAM RADIO OPERATOR IN OMAHA, 1940 *(Courtesy Richard Fatherley)*

But most Americans that summer assumed that radio was the same as ever, something permanent and satisfying, like Schlitz, Schaefer, Storz—all those beers sponsoring all those cracks of the bat. After twenty-one years on the air, the *Amos 'n' Andy* comedy serial remained in the top ten, week after week. When Todd Storz bought KOWH,

108 of the programs on network schedules had been on the radio for a decade or more; twelve had been anchors of American entertainment since the dawn of network broadcasting. Radio network revenues were steady, year after year, an astounding $200 million a year in 1948, '49, and '50.

But the networks were starting to pump some of that revenue into the new technology. Television had been under development since the twenties, but the medium's rollout had been delayed by bureaucratic wrangling over which technical standards to adopt, by war and the diversion of engineers to military work, and by skepticism in the broadcasting industry about whether TV would catch on.

In 1948, TV was up and running in New York and Los Angeles, but most big cities had only one channel, and in much of the country, the medium remained a distant rumor. Still, where TV entered the scene, life changed quickly and dramatically. In 1951, movie attendance held steady in cities without TV but plummeted by 20 to 40 percent where TV provided an alternative to going out.[3] Movie theaters closed by the hundreds. Jukeboxes, nightclubs, professional sports, bookstores—all reported declining business in TV cities. Radio felt the heat. First audience numbers sagged, then sponsors started fleeing to the new medium. Finally, radio lost its programming.

The old network standbys fell down. Bob Hope's radio ratings died like a bad joke, from a 23.8 percent share of the audience in 1949 to 12.7 the next year and 5.4 the year after that. Radio's stars and top shows migrated to TV: Milton Berle, Jack Benny, Groucho Marx, *Gunsmoke, Captain Midnight.* TV's early successes were direct copies— and sometimes simulcasts—of radio's hits: Ed Sullivan's *Toast of the Town* variety hour, *Philco Playhouse*'s serious dramas, Lucille Ball and Sid Caesar's comedy sketch shows, and Arthur Godfrey's personality chat show, a carbon copy of his radio program. Talent rushed out radio's door in a panic—writers, directors, salesmen, technical workers.

TV's rise was stunningly swift: In 1950, 9 percent of American homes had a set. Three years later, half the households had TV. At the same time, a youth explosion swept the nation: the baby boom topped out in 1957, when 4.3 million children, still a U.S. record, were born.

The national radio networks that Todd Storz had grown up with suffered first and hardest. When the big stars and their shows migrated to TV, so did national advertising for cars, gasoline, cigarettes, and household products. Radio station owners woke up without their programming or their old revenue stream. Network advertising receipts plummeted from $131 million in 1950 to $64 million in 1955. Station owners had to find some other source of income—fast. Storz instinctively knew where to turn. He might have yawned at the idea of following in his father's footsteps, but the son had absorbed the role Storz beer played in Omaha—he understood the intricate web of relationships among beer distributors and local bars, restaurants, shops, and families. Storz knew that the local grocer, car salesman, and clothier needed to form and maintain that kind of emotional bond with their customers. That was the American way, and radio—local radio— could make the connection. Television's national programming might suit the big cigarette companies and automakers, who sold to the entire country, but the corner store would want to get its message across through the cheap time available on radio shows with purely local appeal.

Storz took pride in being open to whatever was new, especially if it was something that the old establishment in Omaha hadn't yet cottoned to. During all those hours he spent alone as a kid, Storz developed a sharp eye and keen ear, and his travels had persuaded him that the country was changing. He saw young people leaving the cities and farms for suburbs where life revolved around the car, and radio, he figured, would become the nation's clock, waking us in the morning, accompanying us to work and back home again, babysitting the kids after school, lulling us to sleep at night. The burgeoning suburbs would alter the American day: now, in addition to work time, evening, and bedtime, there would be "drive time," and the only entertainment medium that had a pipeline into the American auto was radio. Storz watched the demise of network radio and concluded that families would never again gather around in the living room, sitting together to stare at a talking wooden cathedral. But he had a hunch that radio could take on an even more intimate, if less obvious, role: it would just

be there, always on, in the background, serving not as the main entertainment of the evening, but as the soundtrack of American life.[4]

Storz was open to all this in ways that veterans of the Golden Age
of radio could not be. He had no special allegiance to the old serials
and variety shows, no nostalgia for the networks in New York and California. In the heartland, Storz wanted to sell radio the way his family
had always sold beer—in massive quantities, with Prussian efficiency,
to local people who knew, trusted, and enjoyed his product in part because it was well made, but also because it was native to Omaha. It was
theirs.

Even as TV began to capture the national imagination, radio was
changing too. Thanks to ever smaller tubes and batteries, radios were
shrinking. Handheld radios were still a few years off, but "portables"
the size of a small overnight bag came on the market, and automakers
were offering far more cars equipped with radios. The radio was
emerging from the living room. By 1953, nearly one in three Americans used the radio to wake up in the morning.

But what would they listen to? Storz wasn't sure what he wanted to
put on KOWH, but he knew what he didn't want. He started killing
off the "minority programs"—the classics and country tunes that he
believed appealed only to small clusters of listeners, and the fifteen-
minute music remotes from New York nightspots, a bit of Harry
James, a quick set from Peggy Lee.

The way Storz told the story, he hit on the replacement for those
programs back when he was a cryptographer in the Signal Corps. The
answer was sitting in every jukebox in every diner and nightspot. As
Storz watched customers plunk coins into the machines at his hang-
out, "I became convinced that people demand their favorites over and
over. . . . The customers would throw their nickels into the jukebox
and come up repeatedly with the same tune." Fascinated, Storz would
stick around until after the front door was locked. "Let's say it was
'The Music Goes Round and Round.' After they'd all gone, the waitress would put her own tip money into the jukebox. After eight hours
of listening to the same number, what number would she select?
Something she hadn't heard all day? No—invariably she'd pick 'The

Music Goes Round and Round.' Why this should be, I don't know. But I saw waitresses do this time after time."[5]

In the annals of radio history, there are as many variations on this tale as there are stations on the dial. By some accounts, Storz was at that restaurant night after night because he was dating the waitress who loved her song; in other tellings, the inspiration for radio's future was an anonymous woman in white. Sometimes, Storz's revelation comes to him alone; other times, he is with his future sidekick in radio management, Bill Stewart, on Sixteenth Street in Omaha or over lunch at the Omaha Athletic Club.

To be sure, Storz was generally in the market for a comely waitress, but he was too single-minded about radio to adopt a business plan picked up in a diner. The less dramatic but more accurate version of the story finds Storz reading everything he could get his hands on about radio listening. In 1950, a University of Omaha researcher brought Storz the results of an industrial testing project that asked people what they listened to on the radio. Storz eagerly read that KOWH's only top-rated programs were music shows and that listeners wanted to hear their favorite songs, over and over.

If repetition of top music hits was what it would take to salvage radio, Storz was more than happy to dump the remaining hours of network programming, as well as Aunt Leana's homemaker show, the *Back to the Bible Hour,* and the third-rate soap operas he had been importing from England on jumbo-sized transcription discs. He started in 1951, adding a 9 A.M.–11 A.M. hit parade show for housewives. The gospel in radio in those days was that no tune ought to be repeated within twenty-four hours of its broadcast—surely listeners would resent having to hear the same song twice in one day. But Storz now instructed his announcers to blend some of the songs played on *Your Hit Parade,* the long-running weekly network show, into KOWH's morning program.

Over the next several months, Storz extended music to more and more of the broadcast day. The idea was simple—music and news, each presented as a purely local product, with announcers who knew Omaha and worked its daily rhythms into their patter: what was happening at the high school, this day's price of wheat and corn, those new houses going up on the edge of town. A traffic report, the latest tornado watch, a pancake breakfast at the Jaycees' next meeting. And above all, the same songs, repeated a few times each day, simply because they were the most popular tunes in town, as measured by sales at local record stores. By the end of 1951, KOWH's share of Omaha listeners shot up from 4 percent to 45 percent.[6]

Those who knew Storz highly doubt whether he ever read Sigmund Freud, but the father of psychoanalysis had focused on the essential human need for repetition half a century earlier. Freud's "repetition compulsion" theory said it is human nature to try to repeat childhood traumas in order to work through them. As Storz ordered up repeated spins of hit records in an Omaha studio, psychologist Harold Mendelsohn stretched Freud's ideas about repetition into a theory about the essence of pop culture. The pleasure people get from mass entertainment comes in good part from the simple repetition of actions, sounds, and situations that connect to emotional tensions in our own lives, Mendelsohn said.[7]

Bud Armstrong, who ran the station Storz bought in Kansas City, put it more simply. In his instructions to deejays who balked at playing the same records over and over, Armstrong said: "About the time you don't like a record, Mama's just beginning to learn to hum it. About the time you can't stand it, Mama's beginning to learn the words. About the time you're ready to shoot yourself if you hear it one more time, it's hitting the Top Ten."[8] Thus was the course of modern radio set.

Many in radio dismissed the idea entirely. "They all laughed at him because you couldn't get ratings with just forty records," said Ruth Meyer, who parlayed her work for Storz in Kansas City into a position running Top 40 WMCA in New York City. Others inside and outside the industry derided Storz as a purveyor of pap, cheapening the culture and filling the air with meaningless trifles.

He pleaded no contest: "I do not believe there is any such thing as better or inferior music. If the public suddenly showed a preference for Chinese music, we would play it."[9]

—

UNTIL TV CAME ALONG, the music played on the radio consisted almost entirely of live performances. From early in radio's history, music publishers demanded royalties for any records played on the air, a powerful incentive for stations to stick to live performances of the classics and other material in the public domain. And in those early years, it wasn't easy to transmit decent sound quality from records to home radio sets. Even when sound quality improved, radio's overseers favored live programs; beginning in 1922, the Department of Commerce made it clear to applicants for radio licenses that proposals for live programs would be favored over broadcasts of records.[10] From early on, the FCC mandated that stations divulge on the air whether programs were live or recorded. Not until 1940 did the agency relax that rule to the point that one announcement per half hour would suffice to warn listeners when music wasn't live. Even then, the feds, who saw the public's airwaves more as a community-building tool than as a profit center, made it clear that radio was for live performance: the FCC promised accelerated approval of licenses for applicants who pledged not to air any recorded fare during their first three years of operation.[11]

There was also a legal barrier to playing records on the air. Bing Crosby and other top crooners of the day, fearful of giving away their product, regularly had their records stamped "Not Licensed for Radio Broadcast." Their lawyers backed them up with suits against stations that dared to play their tunes. But in 1940 a federal court ruled that once a record was sold, artists had no further claim to control how or where it was played. Stations were free to spin any records they cared to.[12]

Still, the bias against canned music persisted. In the excitement of a new medium, playing recorded music seemed tacky, lacking the grandeur of a live band. So the first deejay shows on radio sought to dress up the simple act of spinning a record with a zesty mix of show biz magic and pure hokum: in 1933, Al Jarvis launched his *Make Believe Ballroom* program on KFWB in Los Angeles, using sound effects and dramatic descriptions of the "action" to mimic the sound of a live concert. Jarvis became the star of the show—not just an announcer in a studio spinning records but the host of a make-believe concert.

Martin Block picked up Jarvis's idea in New York two years later, and his *Make Believe Ballroom* on WNEW added an informality of speech that Block stole from FDR and Crosby. No more stentorian announcer booming out introductions as if he were calling out to a crowded theater; Block realized that the president's fireside chats worked because of their intimacy, because of the illusion that this was one person speaking to one listener at a time.

"And now, just for the record [hint-hint], here's Benny Goodman and the band swinging out for all Ballroom patrons with 'The 10 O'Clock Jump.' Take it, Benny," Block intoned one night. And then, after the record: "Thanks, Benny, that was great. I never heard the band sound better, and I really mean that, fella." Did the audience at home really believe that Goodman and his band were in the WNEW studios—in Block's "ballroom"—at that moment? Most likely, few listeners thought it through; what they loved about Block's show was that it sounded fresh and personal. It connected. As Block's nightly sign-off said: "For you and you—and *especially* for you."[13]

Radio executives doubted whether an audience would be loyal to programs of spinning shellac discs. Sponsors wondered why people would turn on the radio to hear the same records they could play on their home Victrola. One WNEW sponsor decided to test Block's appeal. Smack in the middle of a snowstorm, the company went on the *Make Believe Ballroom* to offer refrigerators at a deep discount—but only if listeners came immediately to the store. One hundred and nine customers showed up right away. The sponsor was sold. By 1941, the Block show had a waiting list of advertisers.

Yet deejays remained second-class citizens in radio until the final battle against recorded music was waged in the form of a legal face-off between broadcasters and music publishers. The National Association of Broadcasters had created Broadcast Music Inc. (BMI) in 1939 to break the monopoly held by the American Society of Composers, Authors and Publishers (ASCAP), which required station owners to pay 2½ percent of their revenue for blanket permission to use music copyrighted by its members. When ASCAP sought to raise its fees, station owners decided to go their own way—both to save money and to open the airwaves to songwriters who weren't part of ASCAP. Suddenly, stations had access to all sorts of music barely represented in ASCAP's offerings—especially country and western and also rhythm and blues, then known as "race music."

In 1941—the year *Variety* coined the term "disc jockey"—ASCAP's demand for a 70 percent boost in royalties resulted in a ten-month-long boycott of ASCAP music by virtually all of the nation's radio stations. Limited to the golden oldies in the public domain and the less mainstream numbers that dominated BMI's music library, stations and networks exposed listeners to all manner of new music, such as blues, bebop, and bluegrass (and way too much very old, very cheap stuff—musty Stephen Foster knockoffs from the nineteenth century). More important, radio stations established new relationships with small labels, record promoters, and record shop owners—the grassroots music industry that would eventually bring the new sounds of R&B, rock, and country to the nation's airwaves.

A year later, the American Federation of Musicians union demonstrated just how far performers would go to halt stations from playing records on the air: the union called a strike, ordering its members to refuse to make any recordings. The union was determined to avoid its nightmare scenario, in which radio would consist largely of deejays playing records, and musicians in radio orchestras and bands would be fired by the hundreds.

The union was right about radio's future and right about losing those jobs but completely missed the enormous impact that playing records on the air would have on the sales of tunes performed by its members. The battle finally ended in 1944—after more than a year with hardly any records made in the United States—when record companies and other employers agreed to pay higher royalties and set up a benefits fund for musicians.

Labor peace opened the way for the deejay revolution that would be radio's response to the triumph of television. Stations played more and more records to fill time between network shows. In a few big cities, by the end of the 1940s, the deejays spinning those records were becoming big names—Dave Garroway, Mike Wallace, and Hugh Downs in Chicago, Bill Cullen in Pittsburgh, Arthur Godfrey in Washington, Soupy Sales in Cleveland. In the vacuum left by star performers who had forsaken radio for the home screen, these voices passed for celebrities.

TODD STORZ'S GOAL was to win. He wanted the profits, of course, and the ratings, but to get there, he first had to catch up with the nation's quickening pace. He was obsessed with radio and everything new, collecting every gadget that came on the market. He remained a ham operator, checking in with other early adopters across the land. He traveled the country to listen to unknown stations in hopes of gleaning a new idea or discovering a bright new personality.

A thin, energetic man with piercing brown eyes, close-cropped brown hair, and a luminous smile, Storz came off as something of a radio geek, but those who worked closely with him saw another side. His frequent travels to visit his stations were also a quest for extracurricular social engagements. "He was always running around," said Dale Moudy, a Storz protégé who ran several stations around the country. "His wife once called my wife and me to their house in Fair Acres and told us, 'Todd's not a real husband.' He was a real cocksman."

Storz encouraged his managers to work hard and play hard. At a program directors meeting in Houston once, Storz managers were playing poker when the boss walked in with a rented gal on his arm. "He didn't come to play," Moudy said. "He needed cash, for the girl. I loaned him $40."

Storz had his managers tearing their hair out over his weakness for razzle-dazzle. He would hire itinerant carnival workers to swoop into a city and drop in on businesses that weren't advertising on his station, enticing potential sponsors with ridiculously cheap ad rates and a visit from a scantily clad female carnival performer. The carnies would then show up at the station and hand over half the cash they'd raised—the other half was their fee—leaving station sales managers to deal with the damage to their pricing schemes and to attempt to reinstate less dramatic relationships with local merchants.

"Todd had a very simplistic view of things—he led by instinct," said Steve Labunski, who worked for Storz in Kansas City and Minneapolis before going on to run NBC Radio in the 1970s. "He cared very little about sales, never went to sales meetings. He cared about programming. He listened constantly to tapes of his stations and others. He'd come to town a day early and not tell you, so he could listen and make sure you were doing everything right."

Identifying and repeating the top hits was only the first ingredient in the Storz formula. A showman at heart, he concocted a blend of stunts, promotions, and dependable program structure designed for the accelerating pace of American life. In a nation that was now on the road, speeding along to work and play, Todd Storz's Top 40 stations— by the mid-1950s, he had expanded to Kansas City, New Orleans, Minneapolis, and Miami—gave Americans a little extra gas.

He wanted his deejays to display more energy, more personality. In the boss's teachings, a Storz jock had "to use his own talent. If he sings, let him sing. He is left completely free to talk as he feels best."[14] Storz didn't want refined voices introducing music. Storz stations played the hits, but they also made it clear who was playing those hits. In the new world of Top 40, the deejay was the star, and to young men around the country, the prospect of spinning the dreams of a nation on the go was intoxicating. Most of Storz's staff was as young as or younger than he was; together, they scoffed at the old standards of radio—dramas, variety shows, advice for housewives, big-band remotes. To work for Storz was to be in the presence of a "god of radio," as Bill Armstrong put it.

Armstrong, who would go on to be elected a U.S. senator from Colorado, decided in 1948, at the age of eleven, that he wanted to be on the radio. His voice had not yet broken, a source of constant humiliation. But Bill went to his dad and asked for a job on the radio.

Sorry, the father said, no can do. But I can tell you how to find one. So Bill Armstrong found himself down at the office of KORN—"The Golden Buckle on the Corn Belt"—in Fremont, Nebraska, making himself useful. On Saturday afternoons, for no pay, he played records on the 3:30 music program. As a high school junior, he moved up to full-time duties during school vacations. The job was hardly glorious: mostly, Armstrong took metal transcription discs containing *The Gloria DeHaven Show* or the Red Seal RCA Victor Classics Library and played the music—classical one hour, country the next, then a bit of polka, then some sports headlines.

After high school, Armstrong set out to join the Storz revolution. "Every young disc jockey in America was trying to go work for Todd Storz," he said. Many of them could, because, as Armstrong said, "all the adults were leaving radio and going to TV." Armstrong, seventeen, interviewed with Storz himself and landed a job as an announcer at KOWH in Omaha. His first assignment was the sweet music show at 4:30 P.M. each day. There was nothing special about the music Armstrong selected, heavy on Montovani and other lush pops, and nothing particularly entertaining about what he said between tunes. But there was something distinctive about KOWH's emerging sound. Storz required his deejays to say the station's name frequently, not only at the top and bottom of the hour, as tradition dictated. He had them announce the time and temperature incessantly. He gave them one-liners to say, pronouncing KOWH "the world's greatest radio station." He told them to lighten up, be themselves—drop the stuffed-shirt voice with the elocution right out of the NBC Announcers' Guide. He commissioned singing station breaks (jingles). He added fanfares to introduce each element of every hour—the sports report, the weather, the news (broadcast at five minutes before the hour, just to be different, just to be first).

Everything was to sound planned and purposeful, even if it was just showbiz sparkle. "Top 40" sounded like the records were scientifically selected; in fact, forty was just the approximate number of songs a deejay could play in a three-hour shift. Market research barely existed, so KOWH managers invented ways to justify their Top 40 selections. Station salesmen cut barter deals with local music stores, trading one free advertising spot a week for lists of the top sellers at each store.

But there was more to producing successful radio than simply picking the most popular songs. Storz executives quickly learned that the fewer songs they played, the higher their ratings would soar. If they quietly cut their lists down to thirty or even twenty-five songs, the audience numbers responded immediately, always up.

IN NEW YORK, STORZ'S success was greeted with a big harrumph. Radio networks clung to the old model. "We refuse to operate like a jukebox," the ABC Affiliates Advisory Board declared in an advertisement in a trade magazine in 1956. A few months later, ABC network executive Robert Eastman announced that "there is no good reason why a network should ever play phonograph records." Instead, ABC served up live musical programs "for the on-the-go housewife who's busier than ever," starring Merv Griffin and Jim Backus as emcees for shows of light pops and big-band tunes.

The networks tried to plow ahead with their standard menu of variety, comedy, and drama shows. But Americans could get that fare on TV—with the bonus of actually seeing the performers. So gradually, the networks gave in. They returned to the evenings of dance bands that had filled the airwaves back in the 1930s—Guy Lombardo, Lawrence Welk, and the Dorsey Brothers all had their own national shows once more. But this time, sponsors weren't buying. The networks tried giving top singers their own fifteen-minute shows; Kate Smith, Frank Sinatra, legendary bandleader Paul Whiteman, and others would spin some of their own records and make a few remarks. The networks prayed that star appeal would draw listeners and sponsors. It didn't. CBS even tried to turn the stars of *Amos 'n' Andy* into deejays, recasting the longtime comedy show as *The Amos 'n' Andy Music Hall* in 1954. No go.

That year, television advertising sales surpassed radio's sales for the first time. It would never be close again.

In 1956, NBC Radio made a last-ditch attempt to revive its network by launching *Bandstand,* a weekday morning big-band show featuring the music of Benny Goodman, Louis Armstrong, Harry James, and the like. The host, Bert Parks, finished reading his script one morning at Studio 6A in NBC's Rockefeller Center headquarters and reminisced with the sparse studio audience about his glory days as a radio announcer for huge national hit shows such as *Camel Caravan* and *Stop the Music!* Parks knew *Bandstand* was dying—it would be off the air less than a year after its debut. He asked the audience, "Did you ever get the feeling that the whole business is sliding into a lake?"[15]

NOT THE WHOLE BUSINESS. Storz knew his stations would not be the only ones on the dial serving up hit music. So he installed equipment that made his stations sound louder. They played the clatter of a Teletype machine underneath their newscasts. They paid $10 for listener tips to breaking news stories. They took listener requests for songs (though the disc jockeys went right ahead and chose the music, announcing listener requests only as they happened to match deejay choices). They filled every corner of empty airtime with sound effects and jingles. Above all, Storz set his deejays loose on a candy-coated trail of contests and promotions unlike anything anyone had ever heard on the radio. Free money was always just around the corner.

In October 1951, Storz had cash hidden in secret locations around Omaha. KOWH broadcast clues leading to those locations, and listeners reacted with some of the largest traffic jams the city had ever experienced. Storz, touring the city to revel in what he had wrought, was pleased to be arrested on a charge of failing to stay in the line of traffic. The incident brought the station enormous publicity, and Storz developed an insatiable appetite for more.

In March 1952, deejay Jim O'Neill climbed a tree and began tossing cash to passersby, drawing a wild crowd and a squad of exasperated police. Over the next few years, in each new city where Storz acquired a station, his programmers kept listeners gleefully glued to their radios with an ever-changing roster of gimmicks. In Minneapolis, WDGY drew two hundred thousand people to search for two hidden checks for $105,000 each; no one found them. In New Orleans, the combination of free money and gravity—comedy's favorite physical force—resulted in a near-riot when a WTIX deejay started tossing dollar bills off the rooftop of a downtown building. After police hauled the deejay off to jail for paralyzing traffic, the station encouraged listeners to bail him out. A thousand listeners showed up at the jail. The station shot up from eleventh to first in New Orleans within a year after Storz bought it; ad billings were up 3,000 percent over the same period.[16]

In Omaha, Storz launched what became a regular game on his stations, the Lucky House Number: the deejay would turn to a random page of the local phone directory, read out an address, and if the person at that address phoned the station within a minute, he'd win the jackpot, which increased by $10 each day it was not claimed. After Storz bought KXOK in St. Louis, deejay Richard Fatherley became the station's "Millionaire," cruising the city in a stretch limousine, handing out cash to random strangers.

On a Sunday afternoon in 1955, Ruth Meyer, then a young copywriter for Storz's WHB in Kansas City, was chosen to hide the final clue in the station's first big treasure hunt. She had already written the clues that had been broadcast for weeks leading up to the event, luring thousands of listeners to gather in Loose Park on this day. Now, her job was to plant the last piece of the puzzle, a number she had written in nail polish on the back of a turtle. "But there were so many people in the park searching for the clue that I couldn't plant it," she said. "My only job was to let the turtle go, but people were following me everywhere."

By the time Meyer managed to sneak away and put the turtle down, the traffic surrounding the park had grown so paralyzing that Kansas City's police chief threatened to ban station promotions. Storz declared the mess a huge success.

In 1956, Storz had his men hide prize checks inside six books in the Omaha public library and announce the treasure hunt on the air. Thousands of listeners stormed the library and tore up ninety books in their mad search. Storz, thrilled to have to reimburse the library $565 for the damage, stuck by KOWH's story: the stunt had been staged "to encourage better patronage of the Omaha Public Library."[17]

Storz knew his stations had to connect to a public that now had choices. When Omaha suffered what became known as its Flood of the Century in 1951, KOWH got FCC permission to stay on the air past its usual sundown sign-off and broadcast flood coverage around the clock, without commercials.

One year later, Storz found a way to both remind listeners of that public service and prove to advertisers that his audience would stay loyal to a station that merely played records. On the first anniversary of the flood, KOWH rebroadcast the emergency announcements from the previous year. Though the streets were dry and safe, the station's switchboard jammed with responses, hospitals called in off-duty nurses, offices around town reported workers leaving in droves, and dozens of men showed up at the station to volunteer their help. The station eventually explained that it had rerun the old news to "keep people awake to the ever-present danger of an emergency."[18] Much of Omaha may have been momentarily perplexed or appalled, but advertisers got a vivid illustration that the whole city was listening to Top 40 KOWH.

Everywhere Storz went, the ratings were stratospheric. In Kansas City, WHB attracted 52 percent of the audience; three other stations split the rest. Competitors tried to portray Storz's listeners as youngsters who didn't buy advertisers' products: "If you want the whole family, it's KCMO radio," read one Kansas City competitor's ad in a trade journal. But Storz responded with ads quoting from ratings showing huge, dominant numbers for his station even during school hours. "When the youngsters are away, Kansas City radios stay with WHB," the Storz response read.

Determined to erase any doubts the competition might have instilled in the minds of advertisers, Storz launched a new stunt: deejays would announce a Secret Word of the Day, usually a person's name. End of stunt. The name would sweep the town and, so the theory went, potential sponsors would hear the name everywhere—at work, at Little League games, at bridge parties, at the service station. It worked so well, it became a staple of Storz stations around the country.

The FCC, perturbed by Storz's more disruptive stunts, accused the broadcaster of bribing listeners with giveaways. When Storz sought to buy WQAM in Miami in 1956, federal regulators said they were reluctant to grant a license to a man who would litter the airwaves with contests that constituted "a deterioration in the quality of service" to the public. Storz got the license only by promising to refrain from giveaways. No matter: three months after Storz took over, without a single contest but with a blizzard of promotional buzz, and with the unique Storz sound—a dose of electronic reverberation that made deejays sound like God Himself—WQAM soared to first place in the Miami ratings.

By 1956, the keys to Storz's success were no secret. Other companies sent emissaries to cities with Storz stations. "They'd come and stay in a hotel room and listen for days and write down what they heard and take it home," Dale Moudy recalled. Although Storz had standing orders to his managers to say nothing about his formula, the gospel of Top 40 spread nonetheless. "We all stole from Storz," said David Segal, who got out of the Army in 1944 and drove around the South and West, buying up small radio stations. "We were losing our ass after TV came in, but we all heard about Storz. I sent one of my boys to Omaha, gave him motel money and a radio and a tape machine. And he got down the records they were playing. We got those forty records and we played the #1 tune on the hour and the #2 on the half hour. People complained like crazy but we played the hell out of that rock and roll, and it worked."

In Miami, WFUN, emboldened by Storz's semi-voluntary ban on contests, took on the fast-rising WQAM by upping the ante on wild promotions, stunts, and ingenious programming tricks. Miamians woke one morning to hear this announcement: "WFUN offers for your swimming pool a very real, very much alive, authentic ocean shark, and she can be yours. In 25 words or less, write 'Why I Want a Shark for My Very Own Swimming Pool Pet.' Send your entry to Shark, in care of your fun station, WFUN Miami Beach." Whereupon followed a jingle, more a rap than a song: "A shark you'll win from FUN, to grace your pool, a streamlined fin."

The competition was so intense that Rick Shaw, a Miami radio legend who was one of WQAM's top deejays, recalls two of his station's jocks spending a night in jail after they were caught rifling through the trash cans outside the WFUN studios, searching for memos about new promotions the upstart station might be planning.[19]

Bud Connell, WFUN's manager, was determined to make his station the talk of the beach. One day, Connell walked in on deejay Bill Dean and—in front of a live microphone—said in his gravest tone, "Bill, you shouldn't have said that."

"I'm sorry, sir," the deejay replied hesitantly, warming to the stunt as Connell stormed out of the studio. Within seconds, the calls came pouring in: "What'd you say, Bill?"

The phones wouldn't stop blinking. Finally, Connell came back on the air and told the deejay, "Bill, I have to take you off the air." The next day's Miami papers headlined the story: "Deejay Canned on Air." Which gave WFUN the opportunity to put the question to a vote of the listeners. When the public overwhelmingly demanded Bill Dean's return, the station launched a "Where's Bill?" promotion, a massive manhunt propelled by the offer of $1,000 to the lucky listener who brought him in. Dean got a brief vacation out of the deal and the station got yet more buzz.

Connell, who was barely out of his teens when Storz first hired him in Omaha, had learned well at the foot of the master. Connell once bought twenty-five thousand plastic Easter eggs and had them stuffed with candy, money, and clues directing the recipient to listen to the station for more clues. Then he sent staffers out in a convertible to deposit the eggs on front lawns all over the city.

"Everything was promotion and personality," Connell said. "The music was secondary." But of course listeners thought they were tuning in for the music, and Connell had his tricks there too. He had engineers wrap a small amount of Scotch tape around the spindles of the station's turntables, which made the 45 rpm discs spin just a bit faster, about 46½ rpm. "So our music sounded a little brighter, and when people heard the same music on WQAM, it sounded draggy," Connell said.

Within fifty-seven days of Connell's arrival, WFUN took the #1 rating away from Storz's WQAM. Not long after that, Connell got a telegram from Storz: "OK, I give up." Storz offered his protégé a job running programming at his largest station, KXOK in St. Louis. Connell was twenty-five. He took the job. In Miami, the Storz station came roaring back, and the rivals battled on through the Top 40 era.

In most cities in the early years of Top 40, only one station in a market tried the new format. And in the South, if Storz had no station in a city, it was a fair bet that Top 40's other major pioneer, Gordon McLendon, would be there. McLendon, like Storz, was the son of a local business magnate with a knack for judging popular taste. In McLendon's case, Dad owned a booming chain of movie theaters in Texas. Like Storz, McLendon came out of school and the military with one great passion—radio. McLendon and his father bought a small station in Palestine, Texas, in 1947 and soon parlayed that into a license to build a new station in Dallas. That tiny, daytime-only station, KLIF, had no network affiliation, so McLendon had to fill time without the programming staples listeners had come to expect.

A showman with a love for the novel, McLendon had a parrot trained to say "KLIF" (the bird was locked in a room in which a recording of the call letters was played fifteen thousand times), and listeners were treated to the spectacle of KLIF The Parrot going live with the station ID—and the constantly hyped possibility that he might break into "a rash of Portuguese cuss words."[20] Like Storz, McLendon would try anything—at various points, he experimented with the nation's first all-news station and even a short-lived all-advertising outlet.

But McLendon also added substance to his lineup. After Major League Baseball barred stations near minor-league cities from broadcasting major-league games, McLendon subverted the ban by launching a network that distributed re-created baseball games to stations all over the South. McLendon himself, known as the Old Scotchman, would handle the "play-by-play." He mixed sound effects of crowd noise and cracking bats with liberal expansions upon the skimpy game updates he received via Teletype from fans he paid to sit in out-of-town stadiums. Les Vaughn, who handled the effects for KLIF's baseball re-creations, said McLendon could cover almost ad infinitum for any lapse in the Teletype accounts of the game: "When the ticker tape fouled up, he would fill it in with a fight in the stands or a dog on the field. Once he had somebody fouling off 58 pitches. That would give him time to fix the tape."[21] McLendon's re-creations lasted only a few years before baseball put him out of business, but in the interim, he had built up a network of four hundred stations and identified radio's desperate craving for showmanship.[22]

It wasn't until 1954 that McLendon adopted Storz's approach and dropped varied programming for a total concentration on hit music. McLendon, who by then had acquired several stations, concluded that there were "only two things that radio could do either as well as or better than television: music and news."[23] His news would sell the station to its community—he had his managers collect the names of hundreds of local leaders of business, government, and community groups, then ordered them to work those names into newscasts as frequently as possible.

McLendon studied each Storz innovation and had his men rev it up. Whenever a McLendon station switched to the Top 40 format, a deejay would stage an on-air takeover, barricading himself in the studio and playing the same record over and over for hours. At WNOE in New Orleans, Bill Stewart played Joe Houston's 1953 hit, "Shtiggy Boom," 1,349 times straight over two and a half days, drawing an FCC inquiry and visits from both the police and the song's composer.[24] The stunt always generated powerful word of mouth and, if managers were lucky, a police response.

When KLIF hired a new deejay and dubbed him Johnny Rabbit (McLendon created the radio tradition of economizing by keeping the same deejay names even as he hired new announcers; that way, he didn't have to pay to have new jingles recorded), the owner planted overturned autos along highways outside of Dallas. Painted on the bottom of each vehicle was the message "I just flipped for Johnny Rabbit."[25] McLendon's finest giveaway was a contest in which listeners competed to win a mountain. McLendon operatives had found and purchased a tall hill on three acres in southeastern Texas, where land was cheap; one lucky listener won title to the land. McLendon fancied himself the P. T. Barnum of radio. Like Storz, he believed in branding his station's call letters onto the consciousness of a community. So he hired planes to seed clouds during droughts, bought mobile broadcast units so his newsmen could cover events from the scene, and set his deejays loose on their cities to host record hops, appear in golf tournaments, race donkeys for charity, or stage concerts at firehouses and parks.

When the Shrine Circus came to Houston, managers at McLendon's KILT asked morning deejay Joel Spivak if he'd be willing to fly with the trapeze artist. "You've got to be crazy," replied Spivak, noting that he had a young child and a wife to support.

"We'll insure your life with Lloyd's of London for $1 million," the manager offered.

Spivak caved. He went on the air and started dropping remarks about how the circus was coming to town and any bozo could do the trapeze act. Harold "Tuffy" Genders, one of the Flying Wards, then called in and challenged Spivak to join him at the top of the tent. Fifteen thousand fans packed the arena to watch their favorite deejay face death, or at least total humiliation. Spivak, dressed in tights decorated with green sequins, daydreaming about his wife collecting a cool million, was nervous enough even before the clowns drew him aside and asked if he was quite sure he wanted to do this. Finally, the clowns chased the deejay up the rope ladder, Spivak reached the top, and somewhere in the depths of his mortal fear, he heard Genders shouting instructions at him: "Yell 'Drop,' let go, arch your back, and fall to the net."

He grabbed on to the trapeze and swung out over the silent crowd. "I tried with all my strength to let go, and I did not," Spivak said. On the second swing, he somehow willed himself to loosen his grip and sailed through the air—"it was maybe the most exhilarating feeling in my life." He bounced safely onto the net below as the crowd cheered, and walked off the floor to his waiting boss, who promptly informed Spivak that Lloyd's had refused the station's application for an insurance policy.

BY THE MID-1950S, Top 40 stations in many cities were the soundtrack of a mobile life—heard at the drive-in, in the breezeway of the new Park 'n' Shop strip malls, in the high school parking lot, on the counter at the insurance agency, in nearly every kitchen on the block. Storz's stations and their imitators routinely pulled in 50 percent to 70 percent shares of the audience. But Storz faced a growing suspicion that despite the huge numbers his stations scored, his audience consisted largely of teenagers, because who else could stand the banging beat and primal howls that were popping up on Top 40 radio?

Storz's agnostic approach to the type of music his stations played—just the hits, ma'am—meant that increasingly playlists reflected the thump and grind, the adolescent energy of "race music" and its offspring, a new sound from a white kid in Memphis. Parents sensed a visceral connection between the black leather jackets and dark attitudes their kids were donning and the music they heard on the radio. In many cities, stations resisted climbing onto the Top 40 bandwagon for fear of alienating adult listeners with the new tunes that had the kids hopped up and hopping.

Storz always packaged his programming as something for the entire family. He wanted his stations to stay out of politics, out of anything divisive. He just played hits and entertained people, he'd say. Like generations of popular culture executives to come, Storz argued that radio had no obligation to promote better taste. "We follow the trend; we do not try to lead it," he said. "The hit tune is the common meeting ground."

But Storz could not silence the cultural backlash from worried parents. And his attempt at enforcing a corporate neutrality about the content of his programming threatened his bottom line: the new music that arrived on Storz's stations after 1957 led some advertisers to believe that only teenagers could be listening, and advertisers had no interest in talking to twerpy teens.

"A babysitting society has taken over the musical programming of hundreds of American radio stations," an outraged ad executive, Ernest Hodges, wrote in a trade journal. "Rock and roll as an art form is of no interest to our agency. We are not concerned in a corporate sense with the problems of a group of juveniles who require constant noise as a background to nearly every waking moment."[26]

Even within the Storz empire, some doubted the new music. "Many of the old-line guys didn't want to run into all the static we got from playing rock 'n' roll," said Storz executive Steve Labunski. "And it was hard, because you had to dominate the market for it to work. If you had 60 percent of listeners, you had lots of adults in there. But if you had 15 percent of the audience, those were just kids and you were in trouble." Luckily for Storz's philosophy, "if you played the music often enough in the household, the parents would hear it and get curious and then you'd have them. The key was frequent repetition of the music."

Some of Storz's competitors, such as Gerald Bartell's Milwaukee-based group of stations, tried to hold the line against rock and roll. "We speak out against the flagrant invalidity of the pulpy, sensational approach," Bartell said in 1958. His stations would cater instead to housewives, young couples, and baseball fans with "happy musical entertainment . . . , pleasant reminiscences, games for family fun, interesting revelations, and a constant, never-ending joining of hearts and spirits."[27]

It didn't fly. Bartell came to see that Top 40 worked only if it reflected whatever was popular, with no regard to highfalutin ideas about quality. Bartell credited Storz, "a man who really understood beer and beer packaging," with seeing that what mattered was the ingredients. Only the most popular ingredients would win over the largest audience.

But much as he maintained a brave front in public, Storz was shaken by the backlash. At one point, he became so frustrated by advertiser skepticism that he had his stations send doctored airchecks—the tapes that gave potential sponsors a taste of the station's sound—to New York ad agencies, deleting some teen tunes and splicing in Sinatra and other more adult numbers. "All of a sudden, the music was a little sweeter," Labunski said. "It was part of a never-ending struggle to get big-name accounts."

McLendon tried a different approach. In 1955, he ordered all of his stations to offer advertisers actual numbers of listeners, broken down by age and sex. The survey methods of the time made McLendon's numbers suspect—the ratings services, Hooper, Pulse, Nielsen, and Arbitron, dealt in total audience figures and would not start breaking down their samples by demographic characteristics until the 1960s. But McLendon had opened the door to the demographics revolution that would soon sweep through radio and then much of American industry.

Madison Avenue was not alone in its wariness toward Top 40 and the concept of a format aimed at only a slice of the potential audience. Storz's notion of a station that pumped out the same brand of programming around the clock was also an assault on the federally approved notion of what a station should be. Federal regulations required stations to dedicate specified percentages of their airtime to public affairs, educational, religious, and agricultural programs. Storz and McLendon squeezed a few such programs into hours when no one was awake—4 A.M. on Sundays was (and remains) station owners' preferred time for public affairs and religious programming.

But McLendon took on the regulators, denouncing the FCC's demand that stations serve the "broadest possible community need." No, he said, such a requirement "defies all laws of the free marketplace and, in doing so, throttles radio. . . . The only public interest is what interests the public."[28] Slowly but surely, the FCC backed off. In 1960, when Chicago's WLS went Top 40, the station dramatized its break with the past by staging the smashing of a ceramic bull's phallus, a symbol of the farm reports that would no longer be aired.

Parental discomfort with radio's new sound would not vanish so easily. The rock revolution is often recalled as an overnight pivot in the popular culture, but it was an anguished struggle that played out over a decade. Top 40 radio was designed to reflect what had been widely accepted, not to showcase anything avant-garde. But across the country, a revolution was brewing, racial lines were starting to buckle, and a huge new generation of young people was beginning to flex its demographic muscles. Todd Storz had pumped pop music into the vacuum TV had created on the radio; now that music was morphing into something beyond Storz's control, something that would change the nation. The beat and howls and rebellion that Storz sold on his stations was an answer to what Jack Kerouac ached for in *On the Road* as he walked through a black part of town, "wishing I were a Negro, feeling that the best the white world had offered was not enough ecstasy for me, not enough life, joy, kicks, darkness, music, not enough night."[29]

Chapter 2

✳ *HARLEMATINEE*

S AN ANTONIO WASN'T MUCH of a city back in the 1930s; the night sky was still dark and clear enough so a boy could lean out the window and lose himself in a field of stars. And if you turned on your AM set

HUNTER HANCOCK DEEJAYING A RECORD HOP FOR KPOP
IN EAST LOS ANGELES, 1960

after dark, that clear sky delivered voices from halfway across the continent. Stations in Dallas, St. Louis, even Chicago pumped southward the sounds of another planet, a lush, rich place where gentlemen and ladies stepped out each night, flitting from one hotel to another, dipping into ballrooms where the finest bands in the world served up jazz so hot you could dance till dawn. On a steamy Texas night, Hunter Hancock loved to close his eyes and plant himself in those ballrooms high atop the Ritz or the Royale, listening to Basie and Benny, the Duke and the Dorsey Brothers. He savored the swashbuckling baritones of the announcers who invited him into the big-band shows, and he imagined that through the gentle static, he could hear the sweet murmurs of the lovers who buzzed in the background as the announcer set the stage for the next number.

And then, when Hunter opened his eyes and was back in his bedroom in San Antonio, he told himself that he could be in those bands, he could ride the rails day after day, stopping each evening in a new city, tying his bow tie just right and making an entrance splashy enough to attract the perfect lady, the one who would wait for him till the gig was over and off they'd go, to one club and another, stopping only when the sun burned off the mystery of the night. He'd roam the country from coast to coast, New York, Chicago, Hollywood. He'd know the greats (and they'd know him)—the bandleaders and the broadcasters, the golden-tongued gents who clued in rubes like him, lying on the floor in dark living rooms in towns that knew nothing of the glories of the city at night.

Hunter Hancock had just enough musical talent to make his fantasy convincing. After graduating from high school in 1934, he got a few paying gigs as a drummer and singer in a vaudeville troupe, and off he went—anywhere but San Antonio, thank you. There was even a brief, memorable stint at a burlesque club in Massachusetts. But the Depression was on, and the allure of the road turned out to be shallow. Hancock soon found himself back home in Texas, his drum set tucked in a corner. Man had to eat, and Hancock bounced from job to job— bank clerk, chauffeur, vacuum cleaner salesman. It wasn't Hollywood, not by a long shot.

He had no real sense of where he might end up until World

War II, when he was classified 4-F by the draft board because of hernias left over from a childhood operation. Suddenly, Hancock was a marketable commodity—a man who was not heading off to war. His resume didn't matter nearly as much as his physical presence. If he wanted to be the voice on the radio, and if his only previous experience in front of a microphone had been announcing the day's sale items as a department store floor man, no one was going to sneer at his paucity of on-air hours. Hancock approached KMAC in San Antonio, got a job as a deejay, and within a few weeks won a promotion and a $5-a-week raise: he was sent to his company's station in little Laredo, where he would be program director and chief announcer. But Hancock hated the small town, and after three months, he decided to make his big move. He would try his luck in Hollywood.

In the spring of 1943, Hancock arrived in the glamour capital of the West, joining a veritable battalion of other 4-Fs in search of work in the dream factories. After three months at a tiny station out in the desert, word of an opening at an L.A. station brought Hancock to the front steps of KFVD. Early one morning, Hancock accosted the program director as he arrived for work. By noon, Hunter had a spot as the weekend announcer.

A downtown L.A. clothing shop that catered to black workers had just bought an hour of Sunday airtime and wanted the show to have a distinctly black appeal. Hancock didn't know a thing about black tastes in music, so he stuck with jazz hits that were popular across racial lines. Hancock's *Harlem Holiday,* with a theme song by Ella Fitzgerald, became reasonably popular, drawing a racially mixed audience. By design, nothing on the show was overtly black; nothing remotely threatened to alienate white listeners.

By 1947, things were moving smoothly enough that the station, renamed KPOP, gave Hancock a daily jazz show, *Harlematinee.* But black taste had shifted. "Race records," the industry term for black artists' pop-tinged tunes with a heavy beat and lyrics packed with sexual innuendo, had displaced jazz tunes as the musical passion of black Los Angeles. A few days after Hancock started that afternoon jazz gig, Jack Allison, a salesman for Modern Records, dropped in to see him.

"You're playing the wrong records," Allison told the deejay. "If you want to reach a huge Negro audience, you should be playing race records." Allison handed over a list of the records that were biggest on jukeboxes in black bars and clubs in the South.

Hancock had no idea what Allison was talking about. His own tastes ran toward Tchaikovsky and Beethoven, but Hancock decided to take Allison's word for it. He immediately played two of the records—produced by Modern, of course. The first was a song by Hadda Brooks, "a real sexy broad," Hancock recalled. "She was dating the white guy who owned the record company."

Brooks played boogie-woogie piano and sang ballads. She had won her recording contract after a chance meeting with Jules Bihari, a juke-box operator just starting out in the record business. After one local hit with Brooks, Bihari launched Modern Records, which went on to record B. B. King, Etta James, and many other black stars. Hancock later forgot which Brooks record he played first, but it was likely "Out of the Blue," her first Top 10 hit and the theme from a movie of the same name, in which Brooks appeared.

Though he played only two R&B numbers that first day, Hancock felt the impact of his shift instantly. "By the end of that week, every R&B distributor in town had a stack of records on my table," he said. Within a few days, Hancock's show was 100 percent race music. Knowing nothing about the music, Hancock left the choices to record promoters and record stores.

Sponsors came rushing to KPOP, wanting a piece of the Hancock show. The station expanded the program, first by half an hour, then again and again until he was on for three and a half hours each afternoon, plus his Sunday jazz hour. Hancock's switch to race music had created a pop phenomenon and a palpable sense of pride across black Los Angeles. What the black newspapers called "our music" was finally on the radio. Through Hancock's show, the music won a new respectability inside the radio and records industries. Black deejays were popping up on the air across the country, but this was the first time a white announcer had dedicated himself to these sounds.

Change would come at a breathtaking pace. New labels blossomed to serve the increasing number of stations willing to play the music. In 1946, *Billboard* magazine added a "race music" chart of hits; three years later, it changed the chart's name to "rhythm and blues." And starting in 1949, white deejays in other cities began to adopt Hancock's approach, slipping a few race records into the usual mix of standards and sweet songs. In Memphis, not long after WDIA soared to the top of the ratings by catering to a black audience, white deejay Dewey Phillips at WHBQ took the cue and added race music to his mix of blues and country sounds. And in Cleveland in 1951, a classical announcer named Alan Freed let a local record store owner talk him into playing some R&B—a change that would lead to the rock revolution.

But in 1948, black Los Angeles knew nothing of the nationwide cultural ferment that was soon to come. The Hancock show—and the man who delivered it—was presumed to be a black thing. It all added up—the tunes, the sponsors, the patter. Surely no white deejay would play this music. Hancock's energy and easy style sounded irresistibly rebellious, even dangerous to listeners accustomed to the standard baritone and stilted formality of radio announcers. The hedonism of the music he played, combined with Hancock's slight touch of a black dialect, pulled many listeners into what felt like an illicit zone, the place Norman Mailer described as "the infinite variations of joy, lust, languor, growl, cramp, pinch, scream, and despair."[1]

Hancock took his cues from the music; he let his voice rise and fall with the wail of the saxophones and the rumble of the boogie-woogie. Coming out of a song called "Hi-Yo, Silver," Hancock squeals like a pig, then drops down low to correct himself: "Oh—Silver was a horse." And immediately he spins into a pitch for a Christmas benefit concert featuring Dinah Washington, Johnny Otis, and the Trenier Twins, "and, of course, ol' H.H. is going to be there to emcee the program, that's one I wouldn't miss." He's emceeing a concert sponsored by the

Sentinel, L.A.'s black newspaper. He writes a column in the *Sentinel.* He is the voice of black music in Southern California. His on-air side-kick, Margie Williams, is a well-known local black singer. His sponsors are products such as Manischewitz wine, which H.H. pitches as "one sweet, great, rich wine that is made for people—so delicious [and Hancock shoots his voice way high, almost like a minstrel actor] it just makes my mouth water to think of it."

On tape, ol' H.H. today sounds almost stereotypically white. How could listeners not have known Hancock's true racial identity? Hancock himself always wondered why the myth of his race was so persistent. After all, he made plenty of personal appearances; he'd sit onstage at dinners, dances, record hops, white as can be, in front of a microphone and two turntables. Still, for a long time, much of the radio audience took Hancock for black. At least they did until *Harlematinee* and Hancock's later show on KGFJ, *Huntin' with Hunter,* became #1-rated programs in Los Angeles, eliciting the inevitable invitation to host a TV show.

On his first day on the tube, Hancock, a slender, somewhat shy presence with oversized horn-rims and a Dick Clark–like baby face, greeted his audience with these words: "So now you know what ol' H.H. looks like." The crowd roared.

In the end, the issue was not so much the pigmentation of Hancock's skin but what he represented—a break with the formality of the past, a gift to a new generation eager for an identity of its own, and an endorsement by a powerful social institution, the media, of the freedom, sexuality, and fun that had been dismissed and derided as something only for subjugated blacks. The voice that delivered these tunes was offering the holy grail of American pop culture—freedom from respectability.

White reaction to Hancock's programs was mixed. He fielded a steady stream of threatening calls and letters, from those early days right on up to the Watts riots in 1965, when Hancock resorted to carrying a rifle to work for fear of whites who considered him a race traitor. But to much of Los Angeles, white or black, Hancock was the source of a sound so forbidden and illicit that the mere act of listening made you feel like part of a secret society.

"Good huntin', everybody," his show would start in the mid-1950s. "This is Hunter Hancock, ol' H.H., getting ready to do a little huntin' around with some of the very best of rhythm and blues records, featuring principally the greatest and most popular Negro musicians, singers, and entertainers in the world. You'll hear music which runs the gamut from bebop to ballads, swing to sweet, and bluuuuues to boogies."

Ol' H.H. was hip, but he was no political activist. In 1950, driving down to San Diego with a black quartet whose music he'd been playing on the radio, Hancock was stopped by police. "The cop wanted to know what the hell a white guy was doing with four black guys in his car," he recalled. "Maybe I was a drug dealer. He asked my name and I said, 'Hunter Hancock,' and he said, 'I know you, I've heard you on the radio.' "

The cop pulled Hancock aside and told him in a low, serious voice, "Don't do this again, because if any of those guys had drugs on them, I'd have to take your car."

Hancock wrapped up the story like this: "And so, I never did again."

"I deliberately stayed away from talking about race on the air," he said. "You just didn't do it. That wasn't our job."

Although KPOP never hired a black deejay, Hancock's last station, KGFJ, became more and more black-oriented, and by the late 1960s, Hancock was one of only two remaining whites on the air. He retired in 1968, when a doctor told him his heart was so weak he might not live out the year.[2]

Thirty-five years later, I found him in a retirement home, voice thinned but mind still huntin'. Shows such as *Harlematinee* and *Huntin' with Hunter* "made white people realize that black people had something to offer and made blacks realize that whites were accepting them, in some degrees at least," Hancock concluded late in life. To my twenty-first-century ear, Hancock sounded like a white guy, far more midcentury midwestern than black hipster. But in Los Angeles at that pivot point in American pop culture, Hunter Hancock's daring forays into someone else's music amounted to a leap across a fortified racial boundary, an opening that let a generation see

HUNTER HANCOCK
WITH DUKE
ELLINGTON, 1955
(Courtesy Art Lewis)

HAL JACKSON
(holding bottle)

itself in a new way. Listeners both black and white could be excused if they thought they were hearing the future—a black man on white radio.

—

ALTHOUGH JAZZ HAD been at the heart of radio's first and most dramatic surge of popularity, the medium's first decades provided hardly any place for blacks. There were no black owners, managers, deejays, or announcers, even if many of the most popular performers on radio were black jazz artists. That contradiction set the stage for an anguished evolution in which black music was rejected, then replaced by pale white imitations, then tentatively accepted, then embraced. This sequence unfolded repeatedly, in the 1920s and '30s with jazz, in the '50s and '60s with rhythm and blues and rock, and, to a lesser degree, in the '80s and '90s with hip-hop.

In 1924, radio's first color barrier fell when New York's WHN ran a wire into the Club Alabama on Forty-fourth Street and aired performances by Fletcher Henderson's big band. Soon, stations and networks were airing remote broadcasts from hotel ballrooms and nightclubs in many big cities, making national stars out of Louis Armstrong, Benny Carter, and other jazz greats. But the intended audience of those shows, like the audience at those clubs, was white.

As blacks migrated to northern cities, they brought a musical tradition more varied than the big-band sound that whites had found so danceable. The move from field to factory created large urban ghettos, and as blacks from different parts of the South gathered, their musical forms blended and evolved. Blues and gospel combined with jazz to produce a more urban beat—the music that became known as R&B. In big cities, that music found its way onto the air at stations whose owners found profit in selling program time to black preachers and others who wanted to talk to their community. The time slots were usually late at night or on weekends, when white advertisers weren't buying.

The first such programs were a comedy sketch show in Washington in 1925 and *The All-Negro Hour*, which debuted on WSBC in Chicago in 1929. Both were the work of Jack Cooper, a onetime bellhop and newsboy who started out at Washington's WCAP using the minstrel dialect that whites then expected of black entertainers.[3] By the time he reached Chicago, where the black population soared by a hundred thousand in the years immediately before the Depression, Cooper had decided to out-white the Man. He adopted an exaggerated form of the stylized diction that shouted "announcer" to an audience already accustomed to voices straight out of elocution class. *The All-Negro Hour* featured comedy bits, gospel songs with Mahalia Jackson, and other live musicians. One day in 1932, the show's female pianist walked out of the studio just before airtime to protest Cooper's refusal to give her a raise. Cooper improvised: he hauled out a record player, held a microphone up to it, and gave birth to the deejay era in black radio.

Back in Washington, a young black sports nut named Hal Jackson was trying everything he could think of to get on the air. As a kid, Jackson finagled his way into Washington Senators games by volunteering to clear trash during games. Once inside Griffith Stadium, he made his way to the broadcast booth, where he'd watch Senators announcer Arch McDonald do the play-by-play. When Washington's Negro League team, the Homestead Grays, were in town, Jackson was there too, and by the late 1930s, he occasionally substituted for stadium announcer Sam Lacy, narrating the game to the Griffith crowd from the roof, where he perched with his microphone because stadium management would not let blacks in the press box.

But Jackson's true hunger was to be on the radio. There were no broadcasts of Negro League games in Washington, so in 1939, Jackson went to the offices of WINX, then owned by *The Washington Post*, introduced himself to the station manager as the stadium announcer for the Grays, and made the case for putting games on the air.

The manager's response: "No nigger will ever go on this radio station." Later that day, the manager called a staff meeting, invited Jackson along, and, evidently amused, announced: "Can you imagine, this nigger is talking about going on this radio station?"

Incensed, Jackson resolved to find a back door to his dream. He would buy time from WINX through the sales department and avoid the programming executives entirely. Jackson rounded up a sponsor, C. C. Coley, who owned half a dozen barbecue joints in town, and wrote up a proposal to buy a nightly fifteen minutes to present *The Bronze Review,* a program of entertainment, interviews, and news.

Working incognito through a white advertising agency, Jackson purchased the 11–11:15 P.M. slot on WINX Monday through Saturday for $35 a show. Nothing in Jackson's proposal indicated that the show would be run by a black man. The white executives were clueless about the fact that *bronze* was then the classy term for *Negro* in Washington's black community. Time slot in hand, Jackson took to the streets to promote his show. He handed out flyers all along Washington's U Street—the Black Broadway, as it was known. He used a bullhorn to call out to passersby from a car roof on Seventh Street Northwest, the retail heart of black D.C.

On the appointed night that November, Jackson arrived at WINX to launch his *Bronze Review.* His first guest was to be Mary McLeod Bethune, President Roosevelt's director of Negro affairs. The two waited in a car outside the station's downtown building until fifteen minutes before airtime to minimize management's opportunity to bar them from the air. When Jackson and Bethune walked in, shocked staffers tried to call the general manager to stop the program. The manager couldn't be found in time, however, and the show went on, devoted that first night to a discussion about Washington's blighted black neighborhoods. *The Bronze Review,* with guests such as Eleanor Roosevelt, Lena Horne, New York congressman Adam Clayton Powell, and Whitney Young, became a nightly must for black Washington, which credited the Meyer family, owners of the *Post,* with an unusually enlightened racial sensibility—not knowing that the station had sold the airtime unwittingly. "I knew the station was getting flak for letting me on," Jackson recalled, "but they liked that money they were making."

Having slipped in through an unwatched door, Jackson now found it easier to talk WINX into airing both Negro League baseball and Howard University football, with Jackson as announcer. By the mid-1940s, Jackson was doing sports and his nightly talk show on WINX and spinning race records during morning drive time on WOOK up the road in Silver Spring, Maryland. Jackson called his show *The House*

That Jack Built and introduced each record by pretending that the musicians were set up to perform in a different room of his house. He performed his commercials in rhyme and involved his audience in his Good Deed Club, collecting toys and books for hospitals and other charities.

Before long, Jackson took on two more radio jobs, a midday show at WANN in Annapolis and an evening gig at Baltimore's WSID. Working virtually around the clock, and driving hundreds of miles a day, Jackson became the voice of black Washington. His appearances at benefit concerts drew thousands, his charity drives raised unprecedented sums. He was recognized everywhere he went, sought after as a speaker, advisor, socialite, diplomat.

Though Jackson still considered himself a sportscaster, his prominence pushed him into a role in the nascent civil rights movement. Congressman Powell and Jackson made a habit of meeting for lunch at whites-only restaurants. "He'd call and say, 'Hal, we're going to lunch,'" Jackson recalled, "and when we got there, they had to bow, had to let us in because he was the congressman. He loved it. I loved it."

In 1949, Jackson organized a protest and picket on Connecticut Avenue, the city's most prestigious shopping boulevard, against retailers who sold to black customers but refused to let them use the dressing rooms or restrooms. Managers at WINX grumbled about Jackson's foray into politics but took no action against him. Later that year, however, Jackson went over the line: he led a strike by radio employees seeking higher pay and union recognition. WINX told Jackson to take his act elsewhere.

Within months, he was on his way to New York, where he would become a radio institution.

"FROM THE TOP O' THE HILL stood the mellow frames, there's Sue from Vine Nine, Rocket Kitty and O'Wee Fine, Dottie Dee, Mabel and Jan, the Martin Sisters with their terrible tan. All the cats are hipped to the tip and draped on down—here are a few of the crazy cats who came to town. There's Daddy Rabbit with the do-rag habit, and Ice Cube Slim in his porkpie brim. My man Jivin' Joe with Charlie the Blowtop, check out Frantic Fred and Heavy Hiphop."

Dr. Hepcat ruled the night in Austin, Texas, in the late 1940s, moving the tradition of neighborhood house parties onto the airwaves on KVET, describing the crowd at a local dance to his radio audience, picking out neighborhood fixtures—kids desperate to hear themselves named on the air, couples who reached up to the stage with their names scrawled on scraps of paper—all delivered in a lilting patter that generations later would morph into chanted song called rap: "Jumpin' Jills and jivin' cats, upstate Gates in Stetson hats, lace your boots and tighten your wig, here's some jive, can you dig? I'm Dr. Hepcat, on the scene, with a stack of shellac in my record machine. I'm hip to the tip and bop to the top, I'm long time coming and I just won't stop. It's a real gone deal that I'm gonna reel, so stay tuned while I pad your skulls."

Blacks and whites alike could quote that opening jive that Hepcat—real name Lavada Durst—laid down each night. The son of a bricklayer and a nursemaid for rich whites, Durst was a high school athletic director whose true love was his sideline as the public address announcer at Disch Field, where he delivered the play-by-play of semi-pro black baseball games—in rhyme. At one of those games in 1948, John Connally, the future governor of Texas and owner of KVET, enraptured by Durst's delivery, offered him the late-night shift at the station, making him the first black deejay in Texas. Durst was barred from the station building by day, but at night, he became one of the first crossover hits.

Hepcat's jive lingo became such a phenomenon that he collected his finest lines in a glossary that has stayed in print for half a century. His classic bit is his jive version of the classic children's prayer: "I stash me down to cop a nod. If I am lame I'm not to blame—the stem is hard. If I am skull orchard bound, don't clip my wings, no matter how I sound. If I should cop a drear before the early bright—when Gabe makes his toot—I'll chill my chat, fall out like mad with everything allroot."[4]

Helped along by the success of stars such as Durst, black deejays could be heard on late-night radio in many cities by the late 1940s. Though blacks first found a way onto the radio through religious programming, ever more stations were willing to sell time to programs that featured the local musicians who drew the biggest crowds to juke joints and black theaters. Playing race music on the air was controversial, but it was also cheap: most race records weren't in the ASCAP catalogue, so stations were free to play them without worrying about the exorbitant fees that the music licenser demanded.

Black radio had another big edge—the freedom to speak to a defined audience. Network programming was the ultimate in *broad*casting—jokes, stories, and newscasts aimed at everyone had to be bland and simple enough to reach any and all. On black shows, deejays could speak to one neighborhood, one crowd, an audience in which everyone knew the same places, institutions, and lingo. The voice on the radio could bring them together in a new community of the air.

IN STRICTLY SEGREGATED MEMPHIS, which was 40 percent black in the late 1940s, John Pepper and Bert Ferguson were white radio executives stuck with a weak-signaled daytime station that had flopped with country and classical formats. The duo had already put their station, WDIA, on the market—asking price a modest $70,000—when they gingerly decided in 1948 to try something that had never before been done: all-black radio. Ferguson had a strong hunch that the format would sell; he knew that radio ads for black-oriented products—hair care items, patent medicines of highly suspect utility, sweet wines, and malt liquors—had raked in profits for stations that dared to nudge the color barrier late at night. But Ferguson and Pepper could not have known that by taking this dramatic leap, they would one day reach much of the black South, make the careers of legendary bluesmen such as B. B. King and Bobby "Blue" Bland, inspire a white country boy named Elvis Presley, build a cadre of black political leaders who would serve Memphis for generations to come, and trigger a local civil rights campaign that would help launch a national revolution.

Ferguson and WDIA's program director, Chris Spindel, had re-

cently attended a broadcasters convention at which the looming prospect of competition from television had made radio's uncertain future
topic A. The solution, the conventioneers had heard, was to stop trying to reach everyone and pick their audience: "Whether it's teenagers
14 to 16, or older folks 39 to 95, the man was saying that you need to
gear your program for one group," Spindel recalled.[5]

Ferguson figured that group might just be blacks. A year after
Jackie Robinson integrated baseball, Memphis still had separate black
and white teams. The city's newspapers refused to capitalize the *N* in
Negro, and black men who were deemed important enough to men-
tion in the paper were denied the honor of a *Mr.* in front of their
names. But there were a few whiffs of change. Memphis's post office
hired its first black clerks in 1948, and the police department brought
on its first black officers, though they were not permitted to arrest
whites; they had to hold a white suspect and call in for a white
officer.[6]

The black police were the big story on the day WDIA put its first
black announcer on the air. Bert Ferguson had served a decade earlier
as announcer at a black vaudeville revue in Memphis; there, he had
met Nat D. Williams, a charismatic young high school history teacher
who also wrote a column—called "Dark Shadows"—for the city's
black weekly and served as emcee of Amateur Night shows at the
Palace Theater on Beale Street. Those shows, broadcast on another
station in town, had made Williams a household name even before he
became WDIA's first black deejay. Williams would host the morning
show each day, teach social studies at Booker T. Washington High,
then return to the studio for his afternoon program.

Like Hal Jackson in Washington, Williams crossed paths with
blacks in every walk of life in Memphis. He introduced them to new
music on the radio, taught their children in school, judged their
singing talents down at the Palace. In his newspaper column, he entertained them with yarns about his down-country characters named
Swampy and Swilly, and he campaigned against segregation and black
self-loathing. Williams's *Tan Town Jamboree,* opening with the deejay's
huge, rolling guffaw, became appointment radio, a 4 P.M. break from

the station's otherwise soporific lineup of sweet music, light classics, country crooning, and preacher shouting.

For putting black voices on the radio, WDIA's owners received bomb threats, hate mail, and silent stares. Still, over the next year, Ferguson shifted one program after another to black announcers. At first, for fear of galvanizing accusations of Negro-loving from the city establishment and E. H. Crump, Memphis's powerful boss of all things political, the station brass limited deejays to music that would play well with blacks and whites alike—Duke Ellington, Count Basie, the crooners of the time. But before long, management acceded to the deejays' desire to play race records, and especially the bluesy products of small, Southern labels, eventually including recordings made in WDIA's own studio.

WDIA didn't use the word *black* or *Negro* to describe its programming; instead, the shows soft-pedaled their identity with names such as *Tan Town Coffee Club*, *Sepia Swing Club*, and *Brown America Speaks*. Ferguson assured the FCC in his license renewal application in 1949 that "by necessity, we are proceeding slowly and carefully along this uncharted course."[7]

Despite such reticence, black Memphis had never heard anything quite like this. WDIA's early-morning man, Brother Theo Wade, played gospel at dawn, but mostly he was the whole city's jovial black uncle. He shouted, he whooped, he cajoled, he virtually shook the town awake: "Get up outta that bed, children," he'd command at four-thirty in the morning, "and put them clothes on. I know you want to go back to sleep, but you can't do that. Don't worry me now. Don't aggravate me. Y'all hear me?"[8]

Deejay Rufus Thomas started off his shows with a declaration of independence: "I'm young, I'm loose, I'm full of juice. I got the goose, so what's the use? We're being engaged, but we ain't got a dollar. Rufus is here, so hoot and holler!" Thomas was talking to black Memphis, but he knew the white side of town was listening closely. Most nights, he could count on a crowd of young whites gathering outside his studio. "They came, they saw, they danced," he said. And they knew their parents "didn't want their precious white kids to listen to this black music, this N-word music, devil's music, dirty, filthy music."[9]

Not long after WDIA started its adventure in black, a young blues singer walked several miles in his Army fatigues from the city's Greyhound bus terminal to the storefront studios of his favorite radio station. The young man inquired within about getting his music on WDIA; he got an instant audition—on the air. Nat Williams put the visitor on that afternoon for ten minutes of song. The singer returned day after day to perform his own tunes and to sing the advertising jingle for Peptikon, one of WDIA's big patent medicine sponsors. By the following April, B. B. King had a daily fifteen-minute show of his own, and he had his own sponsor, Lucky Strike cigarettes—probably the first time a major national advertiser had invested in a local black program.

King built himself an audience through his radio show, and by 1953, he was ready to make his way as a touring performer. He always credited WDIA not only with launching his career but also—and more important—with showing all of Memphis a way out of the Delta, out of the ghetto. "Everybody who worked for WDIA, when we got into the radio station, we thought, 'Freedom,' " King said. "I used to think of it kinda like an embassy in a foreign land. When you were in there, you were secure."[10]

Bert Ferguson's experiment paid off. The station rocketed to #2 in the market within a few months of Nat Williams's debut. Then, after one year of black radio, WDIA knocked the CBS affiliate off the top perch. That fall of 1949, WDIA's success inspired imitators: WEDR in Birmingham adopted an all-black sound, and WERD in Atlanta became the nation's first black-owned station.

WDIA's success taught station owners and the nation that there was a lot of money to be made by giving businesses a way to reach the black audience. But the industry still feared backlash from white advertisers and listeners. In 1949, *Sponsor*, a broadcasting trade journal, published "The Forgotten 15,000,000," which called for "Negro appeal radio" but warned stations to pay attention to advertisers' concern that if they sponsored black programs, their products might become "black-identified."

WDIA's appeal was far more than financial. In a strictly segregated society, the station let blacks hear themselves as arbiters of what was good music and what was worth talking about. After WDIA vastly increased its broadcasting power in 1954, becoming the first 50,000-watt black station in the nation, its signal covered much of the South. R&B's new stars gained an audience stretching from Texas to Alabama.

WDIA dominated the Memphis airwaves through the 1950s. But in 1957, Ferguson and Pepper sold the station to Sonderling Broadcasting, a white-owned New York outfit that bought black-oriented stations and fitted them to a uniform, nationwide template of hit songs and interchangeable deejays. The station remained popular but never again played the same intimate role in the life of black Memphis.

LISTENING TO WDIA at his desk at a small music company called Memphis Recording Service ("We Record Anything—Anywhere—Anytime"), Sam Phillips knew there was music out there that could change America's idea of entertainment. Phillips had had some success recording and selling the blues as sung by WDIA deejay Rufus Thomas, but if he was going to make the big score, it would have to be with a different approach. Phillips became convinced that "if I could find a white man who had the Negro sound and the Negro feel, I could make a billion dollars." Phillips's talent search led him to a truck driver named Elvis Presley, one of the station's many white listeners.[11]

Presley had once dropped by the studio to record two tunes as a birthday present for his mother. A year later, in June 1954, Phillips invited the kid back in for an audition at his company, now called Sun Records. The session didn't go very well, but when Elvis and Phillips's studio musicians started fooling around with an up-tempo version of a blues number called "That's Alright, Mama," Phillips heard the blend of black blues and white country music that he'd long wanted to sell.

Before the week was out, Sam Phillips got his friend and ex–business partner, deejay Dewey Phillips, to spin that first Elvis record on another Memphis station, WHBQ. Dewey played "That's Alright, Mama" fifteen times that first night. WSM's *Grand Ole Opry* in Nashville booked Presley that October, and his version of Bill Monroe's bluegrass number "Blue Moon of Kentucky" rocked listeners in twenty-five states. In 1956, Presley's "Blue Suede Shoes" became the first country hit to cross over to the pop charts, and in September of that year, he appeared on Ed Sullivan's CBS-TV variety hour, swinging his hips and shaking things that had not yet been shaken on the home screen.

Now the solid line that had divided black and white radio was really blurring. The illicit sound of the new music drove radio further and further from the innocence of TV America and the pretense of racial separation. Hancock and a few other white jocks around the country helped turn Bill Haley's "Rock Around the Clock" into a #1 hit in 1955, and soon deejays were tromping all over the color line.[12]

Throughout the entertainment business, it was clear that whites were very curious about the emotion, energy, and beat of race records. Deejays saw the mix in the crowds that gathered when they emceed dances or spoke at store openings. The music industry first realized something was happening in 1945, when bandleader Woody Herman won big sales with a cover version of Louis Jordan's black hit "Caledonia." Then, when a court ruled that musical arrangements could not be copyrighted, the floodgates opened: white labels started remaking black tunes without credit or payment.

The new fascination with race records coincided with a powerful boom in the music industry. Record sales spiked from $48 million in 1940 to $200 million in 1946, and that figure would double in the next decade, as two new formats—45 rpm singles and 33 rpm long-playing albums, both introduced in 1948—altered the character and extended the reach of American music. The relationship between the music industry and radio was also changing dramatically, as record companies recognized the natural connection between airplay and record sales.

Not until after World War II did music companies focus on winning radio airplay. Until Todd Storz's repetition revolution, itinerant song pluggers would visit radio stations to push singers and bands to use their sheet music during radio appearances. Now, in a Top 40 world, record sales became the measure of success: a song played over and over on the radio generally became a song that customers demanded at the record store. That made the deejay a powerful fellow. And the more audiences attached themselves emotionally to deejays, the more freedom station managers gave their announcers to express their personality and pick their own records.

But what if those deejays chose to play race music, or its nearly as explosive white alternative, Elvis? Storz had never contemplated playing race music on his stations; the very concept of targeting a slice of the audience violated his belief in mass pop culture. But when Elvis broke through with his appearance on the Sullivan show, Storz faced a choice. The public was polarized—wild enthusiasm set off against raw disgust—and almost immediately, that split was mirrored on the radio. The decision at Storz stations seemed simple at first. The boss in Omaha told his programmers to do the only thing he knew how to do: play the hits.

Storz stations spun as much Elvis as the audience seemed to want, spreading the rock-and-roll craze. But other Top 40 stations held back. And some stations that did experiment with rock got hit with heavy backlash from listeners and advertisers, prompting a quick retreat to the sweeter, less controversial sounds of Doris Day and Andy Williams.

As protests mounted against the sexual suggestiveness of Elvis and other rock acts, stations around the country dumped their rock records in public displays of revulsion. In 1958, Milwaukee's WISN went "non-rock, anti–Top 40" by playing five hours of rock tunes, then burning the whole lot of them in the station's courtyard. In St. Louis, KWK manager Robert Convey ordered all rock records to be played once more and then snapped in half on the air.[13]

The reaction against rock was not just a directive from the executive offices. Even deejays were appalled by the new hits. Mitch Miller—a Columbia Records music executive better known to the public for his "follow the bouncing ball" *Sing Along with Mitch* TV show and records—won a standing ovation from a Storz-sponsored convention of disc jockeys with a blistering attack on Storz's Top 40 formula: "You carefully built yourself into the monarchs of radio and abdicated—abdicated to the corner record shop, to the eight- to fourteen-year-olds, to the pre-shave crowd that makes up 12 percent of the country's population and zero percent of its buying power, once you eliminate the ponytail ribbons, Popsicles, and peanut butter." Miller was an accomplished musician—he'd played oboe in an orchestra featuring George Gershwin, and he was a favorite of conductor Leopold Stokowski's. As a record executive, Miller scored huge hits in jazz, country, gospel, and folk. But he drew the line at rock. It wasn't that he considered the music immoral. What drove Miller nuts about rock was its generational, exclusionary appeal, and the seedy business practices that grew up around the music. He could not stomach the idea of paying deejays to play records (even though record companies had long paid distributors and record shops to get their products into customers' hands). Miller was appalled at what he saw radio doing to the record business. Radio was pushing rock 45s, and it was mainly kids who bought singles. The albums Miller generated at Columbia were not getting much airtime, and it was mainly adults who bought albums. How, Miller demanded, could radio turn its back on adult America?[14]

Deejays loved Miller's rant because they saw the rise of rock as a challenge to their ability to mold the public's tastes. They feared that rock would narrow their audiences to just kids, exactly the nightmare that advertisers had warned about. Strict adherence to Storz's ideas about playing the hits now meant that stations would play white and black bands alike, bluesy tunes, and even some country music. Many deejays didn't see that as democratization. No, they saw it as a dive into the muck, an abdication of their personal responsibility to be tastemakers. Deejays—at least the older, more established ones who attended broadcasters conventions—were no rockers. As late as 1959, their confab at the Americana Hotel in Miami Beach featured not a single rock or R&B act; the deejays entertained themselves instead with the swinging Count Basie Band, Peggy Lee, Connie Francis, and Patti Page.

But though he paid for the deejays convention and catered to their belief in themselves as showmen who could steer public preferences, Storz was unrepentant about his tolerance of rock, questionable lyrics, and anything that sold in mass numbers. "It seems like nobody likes our programming but the people," he said. To make things perfectly clear, Storz banned Columbia's albums from the deejays convention where the label's Mitch Miller delivered his blast against radio.

The objections might be phrased otherwise—"junk music," "kiddie rot"—but this cultural divide was largely about race. Miller didn't use the word, nor did many of the radio executives who tried to pull their stations back from the rock abyss. The issue was framed instead as a matter of raunchy lyrics—as early as 1951, Billy Ward and His Dominoes' "Sixty Minute Man" ("I rock 'em, roll 'em all night long / I'm a sixty minute man!") was banned on station after station even as the record climbed the sales charts.

The campaign against rock and roll struggled to hold back a wave of social change, to keep the airwaves white. The enemy was not WDIA or the handful of other stations that appealed to black America, but rather the rebel deejays who breached the color line, bringing black music to white teens.

When white deejays put black acts onstage in front of white audiences, and white deejays were buddies with black musicians, and white deejays went out of their way to talk and walk like black men, the reaction ranged from queasy discomfort to unchecked rage. Asa Carter, the executive secretary of the Alabama White Citizens Council, announced that the "obscenity and vulgarity of the rock and roll music is obviously a means by which the white man and his children can be driven to a level with the 'Nigra.' "[15] Even when the cultural rebels were white—like the motorcycle gangs, delinquents, and leather-jacketed thugs in the teen menace movies of the period—they were assumed to be under the influence of black pop culture. Those who felt assaulted by the new tempo and beat of young America saw their Supreme Court force integration on the nation's schools and heard music and deejays on the radio that sounded black and out of control. Self-appointed guardians of the old (white) ways concluded that black popular culture was being forced on America's children, and radio deejays were among the chief culprits.

In the first rush of change after Hunter Hancock started playing race records, a few stations stepped forward and tried to defuse the color wars. In 1954, Nathan Straus, who owned WMCA in New York, lured Hal Jackson away from Washington to create the city's first integrated air staff. Jackson's *All-American Revue,* advertised as a program of "top artists of all races, creeds and colors," was designed to appeal to both black and white listeners with the music of Duke Ellington, Frank Sinatra, Sarah Vaughan, and Xavier Cugat. Straus instructed Jackson to steer clear of the jive talk and hip mannerisms that jazz jocks used on other stations. "He wanted me to be known as a person, not as a black man," Jackson said. "He said we'll never be a community until people get beyond black and white."

Straus had commissioned a study, "New York's Negro Market," which found that one million blacks spent $1 billion a year and that the city's black population had tripled in the previous decade. Those families were going to buy cars, clothing, and furniture, and Straus wanted a piece of that action. But he feared losing white listeners or sponsors. So he gave Jackson the task of appealing to the entire audience; ideally, blacks would know that the deejay was black, and whites would not.[16] Jackson was thrilled to be able to play white artists, something his bosses on black-appeal stations had forbidden. And he was happy to sign a deal that gave him a cut of the ad revenue he brought to the station. He got a particular kick out of doing spots for Parks sausages ("More Parks sausages, Mom—please?"), making a black-owned company a success in white parts of town, perhaps for the first time.

Jackson used his evening show on WMCA to create a dual existence, as Straus had envisioned. He was a hero on the streets of Harlem, where he was best known for his afternoon show on black-oriented WNJR. He was a token but accepted black in Manhattan's white power circles, where he was recognized for his work on WMCA and on the ABC network's all-night show, on which Jackson interviewed musicians, white and black, who played at Birdland—Dinah Washington, Tina Turner, Stan Kenton, Miles Davis. Working virtually around the clock, as he had in the nation's capital fifteen years earlier, Jackson added a TV kiddie show that featured the city's first integrated studio audience.

And when Irving Rosenthal, the owner of Palisades Amusement Park, asked Jackson to join WABC's Cousin Bruce Morrow as host of the weekend concerts at the theme park, the deejay found his face plastered on billboards throughout the New York area. "My shows drew white kids and Hal's drew black kids," Morrow said. "But then it started mixing, because I played black acts and he played white acts and as the music blended, so did the audiences, in one continuous groove."

That groove got scratched pretty quickly. While white deejays were expected to keep their noses out of politics, black listeners relied on their deejays—often the only blacks in town widely recognized by both races—for leadership on civil rights. On Atlanta's black-owned WERD, Jack "The Rapper" Gibson—working closely with Martin Luther King Jr.'s Southern Christian Leadership Conference, which had offices in the same building as the station—advised listeners about which stores discriminated against them and which deserved their business. In Detroit, police and school leaders called on Martha Jean "The Queen" Steinberg, the deejay who broke many of Motown's first hits, to calm street disturbances and mediate between rival gangs.[17]

Jackson had always accepted that fame carried responsibility, and when black listeners asked why he worked for an amusement park that did not permit black customers to use its heavily advertised saltwater swimming pool, he felt compelled to act. Jackson went to see Rosenthal and asked how someone who sought black business could maintain this racist policy. "Oh, no, no, no," Rosenthal protested. "The pool is open to everybody." The next day, Jackson lined up fifty black visitors and marched them right into the pool.

A guy who played records on the radio changed the racial calculus that day—and many other days in the 1950s and '60s. Deejays worked in a deeply segregated medium—to this day, radio joins the church and barber and beauty shops among the most racially divided places in America. So no one was shocked when, a couple of years after Hal Jackson launched his color-blind show in New York, sponsors became scarce: "They were happy to buy time on both white and black stations, but they wanted them separate," Jackson said. "They wanted to know exactly who they were buying."

WHITE DEEJAYS FELT the heat even more keenly. What Hunter Hancock unwittingly started in Los Angeles in 1948 turned into a real cultural threat in Cleveland on March 21, 1952, when Alan Freed, the deejay who owned the night on WJW, invited all of the city's youth, black and white alike, to his Moondog Coronation Ball.

Freed had spent most of his deejay career as a classical music announcer. But in the spring of 1951, Leo Mintz, owner of the Cleveland music shop Record Rendezvous, asked Freed to host a show he was going to sponsor on the station to feature the rhythm-and-blues numbers that were selling startlingly well at his store.

Freed was reluctant at first—the classics really were his passion. But after a time, enchanted by the music's energy and eager to be in on something hot and new, he agreed. He needed the extra work. Freed started off in July 1951 playing blues and up-tempo swing, mixing in some tunes with a heavier beat and racier lyrics. Freed wouldn't play Elvis—that was hillbilly music as far as he was concerned—but he was open to just about anything else that sounded illicit.

That evening show turned into *Moondog House*, a title taken from "Moondog Symphony," a tune by a blind New York City street performer that Freed adopted as his theme. Freed decided to have fun with the new music. He began to mold his patter to the songs, hooting over the introductions. "Howl it out, baby!" he'd shout, ringing a cowbell and keeping the beat by banging on a phone book on the studio table. Unlike Hancock, Freed set out to make himself sound stereotypically black—he had a naturally gravelly voice, and he started extending his vowels and dropping the final *g*'s from the ends of words. He mimicked the voices of black artists whose discs he was spinning, but he was careful not to talk *about* them or about race. Indeed, he never called the music he played "rhythm and blues," instead using the term "rock and roll"—the old blues metaphor for sexual intercourse—as a euphemism.

Freed's show quickly became everything Todd Storz had feared: a cult phenomenon, a magnet for a narrow section of the audience, young whites and young blacks. The whole idea of playing the hits— Storz's belief that nearly everyone wants to hear the hot songs of the moment and that advertisers want to buy time on the station everyone is listening to—was being turned on its head. Freed's show wasn't about reaching the largest possible audience; it was about exciting and satisfying one or two pieces of the demographic pie.

Executives at WJW, raised on the Storz approach, didn't know quite what to make of their station's increasingly popular evening program. Sure, the town was talking about this *Moondog* thing. But would it sell? Would it alienate adults and advertisers? Freed heard the grumbling from upstairs and decided to take his act to Cleveland's largest arena, in part to help his bosses see that *Moondog* was no fringe phenomenon. Freed lined up some black acts he'd been playing on the radio and announced that he would crown a new King of the Moondoggers at a Coronation Ball. Though Cleveland Arena held only ten thousand people, Freed sold more than seven thousand tickets in advance, then thousands more at the door. The throng, racially mixed but mostly black, grew angry at the impossibility of getting inside. People pushed at the doors, police pulled back from their positions, and the crowd went wild—fights, knives, kids storming the stage. The concert was stopped, the evening a disaster.

Except, of course, that it was no such thing. Freed milked his audience for support, announcing on the air that the Coronation Ball debacle had left him in danger of losing his job. He needed his audience to let management know that they were "with the Moondog." Letters, calls, and telegrams bombarded WJW's offices. Far from sacking Freed, management extended the hours of his show. Word spread across the nation about the turnout at the arena and the popularity of the Moondog radio show.

In 1954, Freed made the move to New York, stardom, and big money—$75,000 a year to spin discs on WINS. There—thanks to a court ruling in favor of Louis "Moondog" Hardin, the street performer from whom Freed had taken his trademark—the deejay had to give up the Moondog shtick and find a new one. He renamed his show *Alan Freed's Rock and Roll Party* and, to avoid further court trauma, applied for a copyright for the term "rock and roll."[18] The party on the radio attracted a huge audience, and once again Freed took his show on the road. Freed would run onto the stage of Brooklyn's Paramount Theater, spin around to show off his glaring plaid sport jacket, shout "Go man go!" to the audience, and introduce Fats Domino, Joe Turner, and other black bands to a crowd that was half black and half white.

Freed would never win the numbers that Storz's Top 40 stations collected with far less controversial fare, but by 1957, he was syndicating his show to a handful of stations across the land. The music he played, and the message those choices sent, would shape not only radio's future but that of the young people who were emerging as a cultural force.

To sell himself to stations worried about the backlash against black music, Freed tried to separate his show from the public's increasing association of rock with evil and delinquency. Hollywood hired the deejay to star in a movie based on Haley's "Rock Around the Clock," and Freed spiced the script with sermonettes on the benefits of rock, which he said kept kids off the streets and occupied them with harmless fun. But when the flick hit theaters, the newspapers filled with reports of vandalism and mini-wildings by movie-going kids hopped up on the beat, the freedom, and the disapproval of their elders.

Freed's pleas on behalf of the innocence of the music clashed with his persona on the air. He was the first white deejay who really did sound like the music. Freed melded with the soul and energy of the relatively anonymous R&B artists whose records he played. Freed's name was always posted in the biggest letters on the marquee of the

Paramount Theater in Brooklyn; the dozen or so acts who appeared at his Rock and Roll Parties seemed mere cogs in his PR machine.

So when Freed's concerts turned sour—notably a 1958 show in Boston that ended with white boys surging onto the stage, Chuck Berry fleeing from the wild fans, fights in the arena, and violence outside—it was the deejay who became fixed in the minds of many adults as an incitement to corrupted minds and riotous behavior.

In the imaginations of young people across the country, Freed and deejays such as Hound Dog Lorenz in Chicago and Wolfman Jack (Bob Smith) from his mysterious platform somewhere across the Mexican border were a revelation, private guides who delivered the authentic R&B stuff—the raw blues, the howls in the night.

The kids who were cruising the Strips in the new suburbs were hip to this strange, sexually charged soundtrack. In *American Graffiti*, George Lucas's 1973 film about 1962 Modesto, California, the real Wolfman Jack is an icon in the fluorescent midnight of a transmitter site on the edge of suburbia.

"I just love listening to the Wolfman," says the Mackenzie Phillips character, a preteen desperate to fit in with the older kids. "My mom won't let me at home, because he's a Negro. I think he's terrific. Do you know that he just broadcasts from a plane that flies around in circles all the time? Do you believe that's true?"

And the ultra-cool drag racer who got tricked into carting this girl around town can only smile a kid's smile, because he has his own Wolfman in his mind's eye too, and it's not even close to this little girl's Wolfman. But is he tough enough to share the Wolfman in his imagination with another living soul? No way.

Every car on the Strip has Wolfman on the radio. He cries out not only from Richard Dreyfuss's radio or Ron Howard's or Harrison Ford's but from all of them at once, and from every car on the street. The gang toughs, the nerds, the losers, the intellectuals, all bouncing along Modesto's Strip and every other Strip in California and the Southwest, all listening to the howl and the growl, the Wolfman's funny phone calls and leering teases, all latching on to something in the deejay's wit, daring, and fabulous otherness.

On the air, the Wolfman dissects an officious telephone operator, reducing the everyday transaction of a person-to-person call to an opportunity to show that kids rule, that you *can* fight the machine.

"You tell her, Wolfman," a little gang tough shouts as the bit comes to an end. "He's my man," the tough tells his fellow troublemakers. "When I graduate, I'm going to be a Wolfman. You know, he broadcasts out of Mexico someplace?"

"No, he don't," the leader of the gang replies. "I seen the station, right outside of town."

"No, that's just a clearing station, man. So he can fool the cops. He blast that thing all around the world. It's against the law, man."

It hardly matters that Bob Smith—the Wolfman—was a white guy from Brooklyn, or that his station was perfectly legit, or that the kids in *Graffiti* discover the Wolfman doing a shift in a barren little shack on the outskirts of town, bored and alone in the dark, sucking down Popsicles to fight off the heat while the 45s spin. No, what's important is that in the first fires of the American cultural revolution, Wolfman Jack and a slew of other improvisers ignited the imagination of a nation, burning off the patina of conformism and lighting the way toward the 1960s. The disillusionment of discovering that the Wolfman was not really in Mexico, that there was nothing illegal about him, made him no less essential to those kids' story of their own lives, to their fantasies and dreams. He was still their Wolfman, their challenge to parents and everything adult. He was theirs to keep.

Chapter 3

✳ THE TRANSISTOR UNDER THE PILLOW

Can't you hear that groovy beat now, baby?
Don't you want to tap your feet now, baby?
Come on, let's go, go, go,
What a groovy show,
Come on and go, go, go,
With Cousin Brucie!
Go, go! Go, go, go, go!

THE THEME SONG WAS A gift to Cousin Bruce Morrow from Frankie Valli and the Four Seasons, a thank-you for playing the band's records. The gift was also recognition that one big kid from Brooklyn, sitting in a dark Manhattan studio, had gotten a fix on the coordinates of a generation. When that song's syncopated shouts rang through the dime-thick speakers inside millions of palm-sized transistor radios under millions of sound-muffling pillows in bedrooms from Maine to the Mississippi, the young Americans listening knew that even as each of them remained alone in bed, pretending to fall asleep, others were out there somewhere, rocking with their Cousin Brucie.

Morrow wasn't the kind of guy who spent his life trying to relive high school; he'd liked it fine, but he'd been eager to get out into the world of work. Now, some mystical connection to his school days was kicking in each evening as he stood behind his microphone and took calls from what seemed like every kid in the eastern half of the United States. In the solitude of the dark studio, Morrow heard from teens who thought he was the coolest cat on the planet. Station executives

BRUCE MORROW ON AIR AT WCBS-FM, 1990s

(Courtesy Bruce Morrow)

didn't understand the phenomenon, but they knew what to do with it: their evening man was a star, so the twenty-three-year-old dynamo was put out on the road every day and every weekend evening, appearing at every high school dance and shopping center opening the station could book. Bruce Morrow didn't have the best radio voice—there was still plenty of husky Brooklyn in his delivery. He didn't have the funniest shtick—he didn't really do bits at all. He didn't break new musical ground—WABC just played the records that sold big, and played them, and played them.

But Cousin Brucie was the kids' own. Somehow, he came off as one of them. In a way, he was: when he could well have afforded to move to Fifth Avenue, he instead bought two apartments on the top floor of a building on Ocean Parkway in Brooklyn, to stay close to the sounds and rhythm of his native borough.[1] He liked their music, he got their pace. And when kids phoned in, he listened. Determined to be the love courier of the New York night, carrying messages between lovesick kids, Brucie listened to their awkward banter and studied the topics that broke the ice in the stilted talk between boy and girl. He knew that girls could jabber at each other for hours about when and whether they might call the station to dedicate a song to a particular boy.

In the studio, Morrow waited through each call, teased out who was interested in whom, and delivered the goods: "This song goes out to Bobby and Mike in Rego Park. It's from Patty and June. Oh, you lucky, lucky guys. Here's 'I'm Leavin' It Up to You,' by Dale and Grace." The next morning, Morrow knew, the girls would meet up at school and scream, "Oh my God, Cousin Brucie played it! I'm going to die! Oh my God, I'm going to die! If he asks me to the dance next week, I'll die!"[2]

Morrow did not invent this. Alan Freed read telegrams from boy to girl and girl to boy on his early R&B shows in Cleveland. In St. Louis, Stinky Shafer's evening show on KXOK was a community bulletin board for teen passions and jealousies: "Bob and Nancy are crazy about Sean and Mary, so why can't Sean and Mary be crazy about Bob and Nancy?" Shafer asked before playing a song for the love-torn foursome. Before serving up the weather forecast, he warned: "Barb of Hillsboro, keep your hands off of Eddie, or Sharon's going to step in and knock Barb out of the world."

Morrow, like Johnny Holliday in Cleveland and San Francisco, or Larry Lujack in Chicago, or Rick Shaw in Miami, turned the simple spinning of records into a collective statement of unity and rebellion. The radio was becoming a clubhouse, a semi-private hideaway for kids who saw themselves as different from their parents.

Cousin Brucie's clubhouse was, by virtue of WABC's 50,000-watt powerhouse signal, the biggest of them all. Brucie's exhortations to "go, go, go" wafted over thirty-six states, the magic of the night and the mysterious action of sunspots extending AM radio waves far beyond their intended audience. In Durham, North Carolina, four hundred miles from Manhattan, George Dennis did homework with the radio on, with Cousin Brucie and the other WABC jocks. "You felt like you knew them and they knew you," Dennis said. "I was in the Cousin Brucie Fan Club. Cousin Brucie was the big city to me. And he was a *cousin*—it was a magical thing."

New Yorkers in the 1960s hung on the Cousin's every word, followed his every direction. In his Bronx apartment, Ira West listened on a plastic eight-transistor set—under his pillow at night, while he did his homework, through his twisted-wire earplug as he walked to Junior High School 135. West loved the music—"Build Me Up, Buttercup," Sammy Davis, Jr., the Beatles, of course—but what kept him glued to the radio was the Cousin. "He had a strange way of knowing what kids were interested in, what we were talking about," West said. "At a time when it was difficult for most adults to identify with teens, Brucie talked about love and things that sounded significant to us. If you go back and listen to the tapes, there's really nothing going on at all, but we thought he was the maestro of the show. He was the center of the action. He never really said anything probing, but you felt like you were missing something if you weren't listening."

West, whose father was an inspector in the New York City Fire Department, began going downtown to the WABC studio to wait outside until Morrow finished his show at 10 P.M. His parents would stay in the car on West Sixty-sixth Street while Ira and his brother, Marty, exchanged a quick hello with the deejay, who plied them with Big M (for Morrow) Fan Club membership cards and invitations to come see Cousin Brucie's weekend shows at Palisades Amusement Park across the Hudson River in New Jersey.

There, Morrow—dressed in his trademark leopard-skin suit and matching shoes, trailed by his leopard-skin-jacketed poodle, Muffin—presented the great lip-synchers of the age. Motown girl groups, Frankie Avalon, Bill Haley and His Comets, R&B shouters, and second-tier British groups—anyone who wanted his records played on WABC was only too happy to appear at Palisades. (The crowds seemed oblivious to the lip-synching, with the possible exception of the time Tony Bennett was "singing" "I Left My Heart in San Francisco" and the record skipped. Morrow ran onto the stage and announced that "the equipment in Studio 3B is a little finicky today.")

Ira made it his business to be there as often as possible and then report back on the fabulous doings to his friends at school. By virtue of his occasional contact with the Cousin himself, Ira became a semi-celebrity at Junior High School 135 and later at Columbus High. As president of his school's chapter of the fan club and Morrow's "duly empowered representative," he was charged with recruiting new members and had the privilege of signing Morrow's name to membership cards and, later, to Official WABC Beatles Fan Club cards, the ones that said "Welcome to America from the All-Americans," the station's collective name for its deejays in their sleek black suits and oh-so-thin ties. "Brucie made me feel so involved," West said. "I'd call him up and tell him stories of what happened in school that day, and he'd listen. All these kids are calling him and he's gracious as hell. It was incredible validation. And somehow I was in the biz."

THE HOURS AFTER SCHOOL were time for Captain Midnight, *Lux Radio Theater,* and the Lone Ranger, the heroes and tales the kids would be talking about the next day. But on this April afternoon in 1945, Bruce Meyerowitz walked home from his after-school punchball game at P.S. 206 in Brooklyn, turned the corner onto East Twenty-sixth Street, and immediately knew something was amiss. There were Mrs. Bloom and Mrs. McGuire, Mrs. Ionucci and Bruce's own mom, Minna, all outside on the sidewalk, crying. Bawling. Usually at this time of day, the mothers were in their kitchens, preparing dinner. But on this April afternoon, they were gathered around an RCA radio perched in someone's front window, listening to a CBS announcer, his voice grave and deep.

The president of the United States was dead. Each bulletin from Warm Springs, Georgia, produced a new wave of grief. Franklin Roosevelt had been president for nine-year-old Bruce's entire life. It had not quite dawned on the boy that another person could be president. But what stayed with Bruce from that day forward was that his mother and her friends were reduced to tears by what they had heard on the radio. "Right then and there," he remembered, "I gave up my desire to become a gynecologist."

At Madison High School, Bruce found a place as an actor in radio dramas produced by the All City Radio Workshop, which culled the most promising young voices from around New York, grooming them for careers onstage and in the studios of the great networks. Bruce spent his evenings glued to Alan Freed's rock-and-roll party on WINS. Bruce decided he belonged behind the microphone, alone in a studio from which he would command the attention of the audience he imagined when he closed his eyes. He practiced honing his voice for radio, imitating the deejays and announcers he heard each night. This would be better than the stage—the whole world might be listening, each person connecting to Bruce, one at a time, lying on the living room floor, a single voice directing their imaginations.

But first, he would need a radio name, something with broader appeal than Meyerowitz. He explained this one day while visiting his friend Paula Waksmon, whose mother pulled down the phone book and turned to the *M*'s, because Bruce should at least keep the initials his parents gave him. Mrs. Waksmon paged through and let her finger land on "Morrow." Bruce accepted the gift and went home that day to his house on Twenty-ninth Street to tell his mom and dad that he was now Bruce Morrow.

Decades later, when he was a senior citizen still known to all of New York as Cousin Brucie, the radio Peter Pan who had chaperoned their adolescent evenings of dreams and frustration and introduced teenagers to the Beatles and a world of rebellion and freedom, Morrow would explain it all to himself by recalling that afternoon when the rock-solid moms of Twenty-ninth Street wept for a man they had only heard on the radio.

FDR's voice connected adults to places and events—the White House, the war—they had only read about. Cousin Brucie took young people to a world that felt utterly new and vaguely illicit. He mesmerized teenagers in city apartments and especially in the new suburbs that were rising on top of Long Island potato fields and upstate apple orchards. Kids who had been separated from the family and friends they knew back in their old city neighborhoods tuned in and heard a voice that sounded like home, a deejay who talked about streets and schools and stores more familiar to them than the treeless cul-de-sacs and brand-new shopping strips of Levittown and East Setauket, Staten Island and Rockland County. As a kid in the Bronx, I remember visiting the home of my parents' friends who had recently moved to a freshly constructed suburb an hour outside the city. The family's teenage girls retreated nightly into a bedroom, locked the door, turned on Cousin Brucie, sneaked a cigarette, doused their ashes in a fishbowl of water, and wept about the friends and routines they'd left behind. Bewildered by their new surroundings, they found solace and adventure in their Cousin's nightly evocation of the names and passions of kids who sounded just like them.

Morrow—not much more than a gawky, frenetic kid himself—envisioned exactly such scenes. "I could feel what people were doing after 7," he said. "I could feel the night shift at work. I knew about the cops taking a break in a diner and the kids in their rooms doing everything but their homework."[3]

Ira West was far from alone in making the pilgrimage into midtown Manhattan to see his Cousin. There was a constant stream of visitors to the studios. In 1959, when Morrow was still at WINS, New York's first rock-and-roll station, an old and weary black woman came in one night and asked if she could sit down. Morrow figured the woman was there to hit him up for some cash. She sat for a time. He cautioned her to be quiet when the red light went on, indicating that the microphone was live.

Finally, she asked, "Do you believe all people are related?"

"Yes, I do, I really do," Morrow replied.

"Well, cousin, can you give me fifty cents please? I want to get home to the Bronx."

Morrow handed over two quarters and the visitor left. Driving home through the Brooklyn Battery Tunnel that night, Morrow kept reliving that moment. The word *cousin* stuck with him. He was going to be *Cousin* Brucie. His listeners were going to be family. The general manager of WINS thought that was just about the corniest idea he'd ever heard, and New York was no place for corn. Morrow insisted: "I know New York, and this city is cornier than any place on Earth."

A cousin, Morrow figured, is someone you want to hang out with, family without the feud. He went on the air and introduced himself as "your Cousin Brucie, and for all you cousins everywhere, I have what you want: the music, the magic and the message."[4]

IT WAS ALL ABOUT FREEDOM. The suburbs gave the postwar generation places of their own—houses empty of parents, grandparents, and the extended families of the old city neighborhoods. The car opened a road to new careers and distant jobs for veterans who had helped themselves to college degrees and new homes—no money down—courtesy of the GI Bill. ("You're a lucky fellow, Mr. Veteran," the ads for Levittown houses proclaimed.) The new highways that President Eisenhower built sped travel across the continent, shattering geographic limits.

You could go where you wanted, do what you felt like doing. And if you were young and American, the new music you heard on the radio was telling you that you were free to rock around the clock and cruise the streets and let your baby know that you only have eyes for her. Music, like almost everything else in America, was suddenly portable. The new 45 rpm records fit onto plastic record players that opened up like a suitcase, perfect for carrying over to a friend's house. And beginning in the late 1950s, the transistor radio gave young people the means to orchestrate their lives, to carry the beat anywhere they wished, no matter what their parents said.

The goal of a handheld radio had eluded engineers throughout radio's Golden Age. The barrier was the size of the tubes inside the console radios of the 1930s and '40s. But in 1948, at Bell Labs, physicist William Shockley led a team of scientists who laid two wires next to each other on a crystal of silicon, which conducted sound without tubes—transistors. The new technology was first used in hearing aids, but by 1952, Western Electric engineers had cobbled together a wrist radio, just like the one sported by Dick Tracy, the comic book detective. The engineers even gave their first wrist radio to Chester Gould, who drew the Tracy strip.[5]

At first, many radio executives doubted whether there would be a market for handheld radios. But the looming prospect of atomic war in the mid-1950s created an opening. In 1954, an Indiana company marketed the Regency TR-1 radio—the size of a three-by-five card and weighing only twelve ounces—the appeal of which was grounded in, to coin a phrase, homeland security. The radio's dial featured tiny triangles marking the frequency of civil defense broadcasts that would be activated in the event of nuclear attack. But the Regency cost $50, required a hefty battery, and was incapable of reproducing music in recognizable form. It flopped. Except that one customer loved the device: Thomas J. Watson, chief executive of IBM, bought hundreds of TR-1s to hand out to his engineers to push the notion that computers should be built with transistors, an idea much of his staff had been resisting.[6]

The first transistor radio to find an American market was also the first Japanese electronics product to dominate in this country. On a trip to the United States in 1952, the co-founder of Sony, Masaru Ibuka, learned that he could license AT&T's new transistor technology for just $25,000. Ibuka persuaded Japan's Ministry of International Trade and Industry (MITI) to pay the fee, and Sony developed a radio small enough to fit in a shirt pocket. While the first models were expensive, by 1959, dozens of smaller Japanese companies had copied Sony's work and were flooding the U.S. market with cheaper versions. Many consumers had no idea that the radios they could pick up for $20 were made in Japan. After all, the names sounded American: Crown, Monarch, Universal, Global, even Trans-American and Americana.[7] Five million Japanese-made transistor sets—half of Japan's production—were sold in the United States in 1959, and almost twice that many in 1960. By 1965, the radios were ubiquitous and so cheap—less than $10—as to be virtually disposable; 21 million of them were sold that year.[8]

To the surprise of manufacturers and retailers, the radios found their way largely into the hands of teenagers and children. The number of fifteen-year-olds in the United States shot up by 500,000 between 1955 and 1960, and by another 700,000 between 1960 and 1965. They were, Morrow said, "the royalty of the country. The nation revered the young and radio was the kingdom that belonged to them."[9]

Parents loved the idea of the earplug, which promised to spare them the painful noise now emanating from the same stations that had once brought them their favorite soap operas and detective shows. Kids saw the radio—many with ultra-cool space-age design, gleaming in silver or gold, with blue-mesh metal stretched over the top or a sleek raised V framing the dial—as a badge of independence and freedom, a pipeline to a whole new world created just for them. Cousin Brucie shouted greetings to "every young person out there in Radioland," but they were listening, as often as not, in the only absolute privacy many of them could find, afforded to them by a thin, "flesh-colored" wire.

Half a century later, Bruce Morrow—still a loud, fun, fast-talking, boyish presence, a man on Social Security who introduces himself as "Cousin Brucie"—palmed his own black and gold Zenith, kept in a display case in his living room, and remembered: "You carried this on your shoulder and you walked with an attitude. This is what made us portable and brought us together. This gave us the youth movement. It was something young people had that was all our own. It gave us secrecy."

The masters of Top 40 quickly figured out that radio was being heard in completely different places, in an entirely new way. "I literally was in their ears," said WABC jock Dan Ingram.[10] Stations ordered up new jingles urging listeners to "take us along wherever you go, take us along whatever you do." Now deejays were talking to people lying on the beach, picnicking in the park, working the factory line, manning the cash register. In 1962, when New York's WMCA commissioned the first psychological study of listening habits, the Psychological Corporation's Harold Mendelsohn reported that transistor teens were comforted by a "blanket of sound that keeps them apart from the world they walk through." (Later psychologists would have a field day interpreting the get-offa-my-cloud meaning of 1970s boom boxes and the leave-me-alone statement made by Sony's 1980s Walkman.)

Adults were in on the new portability too, because just as transistor sets took radio onto the sidewalks, car radios transformed the daily commute. The first car radio, an option in the 1922 Chevrolet, was the Westinghouse Radio Sedan, a $200 extravagance with an antenna that covered the car's entire roof, batteries that filled the space under the front seat, and huge horn speakers erected behind the seat. The first built-in car radio appeared in 1934, and the first push-button station selector followed in 1939.[11] But radios remained rare in cars; to most drivers, the idea of playing music in the car was an unwanted and dangerous distraction from the serious business of motoring.

In the faster-paced, multi-tasking 1950s, however, radio was a welcome addition. Suburbia's newly restructured day, with the addition of morning and evening commutes, created a yearning for entertainment in the car. The development of the transistor pushed the price of car radios way down and allowed a far less cumbersome fit in the dashboard. In 1946, only 40 percent of cars were equipped with radios; by the early 1960s, that number had jumped to more than two-thirds of new cars. In 1957, for the first time, more than one-third of radio listening occurred in the car.[12] And by 1961, half of the boys in the senior class of American high schools had cars.[13]

Radio adapted quickly to the changes. An early 1950s ad campaign urged Americans to have "A Radio in Every Room," but by decade's end, the focus was on each member of the family taking radio everywhere—to school, to work, to the bathroom. You could rent radios at the beach. Detroit designers did their part: in the early 1960s, Cadillac installed the ultimate tool for impressing a date, a button on the floor that a cool driver could tap to change the station—a guy could sell it as "magic," and a girl might just choose to be wowed.

Programming changed to serve the newly mobile audience. Stations added traffic reports. News headlines aired more frequently. Radio's biggest audience shifted to mornings, on the way to work, rather than evenings, when families now settled in front of the TV.

Ratings services had to change the way they measured the audience, dropping home radio meters for less reliable diaries in which listeners were asked to note exactly when they'd tuned in to which station as they traveled through their day.

Together, the portable transistor set and car radio liberated the medium from the living room and kitchen. Radio became part of the background, unseen, even unnoticed, yet omnipresent. People were doing other things—driving, cooking, working, making love—while listening, NBC's analysts noted in their 1956 report "Future for Radio."[14]

Todd Storz and the other Top 40 explorers led the way into the zippy new world. Storz recognized that fast-paced programming tended to attract the younger half of the population, especially toward the end of the 1950s, when rock and roll started pushing Perry Como and Patti Page out of the hit parade. The new technology and Storz's Top 40 format led the music industry to a new way of writing and packaging its product. Producers and bands created songs to fit the Top 40 sound. A hit song had to be instantly recognizable, like station jingles. The new songs were repetitive, with catchy hooks taking precedence over longer melodies. Hits came with instrumental lead-ins, so deejays could talk over the introductions. And songs were written to be perishable, with a shelf life of a few weeks or months; they no longer aimed to be the kind of standards that had emerged out of Tin Pan Alley in the 1930s and '40s. Above all, songs were shorter, a result not only of the pace of Top 40 radio but also of the latest technology from the record industry, the 45 rpm single, which premiered in 1949 and won wide acceptance in the mid-'50s.

To Todd Storz, the music and its form of delivery hardly mattered. It was the attitude and spirit of his format that sent the real message of freedom and rebellion.[15] To weave a web of media seduction, Storz unleashed his deejays to make a show of their American individualism. What no one had foreseen was how America's young people would hear that message of freedom and rebellion as a personal invitation. What even Storz didn't realize was that the game had changed: the kids were heading off on their own.

—

TALKING FASTER, CREATING a nonstop frenzy of action—song, jingle, commercial, temp and time, joke, song, stunt, headline, weather, song, commercial, jingle—all while juggling records and leaping across the studio from one turntable to the other: this was not your dad holding up the wall at a cocktail party, martini or Schlitz in hand. This was life move-move-moving with pow-pow-power. Deejays were purveyors of emotional punctuation, "shouting joy boys drowning in their own adrenaline," sometimes helped along by some speed or a joint, entertaining with bits that went by so fast you'd have to call up your friend to ask, "Did you catch what Ingram said?"[16] Dan Ingram on New York's WABC had his Honor Word of the Day ("Solid!" "Humdinger!" "Rococo!"); Jerry Blavat, Philadelphia's "Geator with the Heater," tossed out words from his Hiptionary; and always the trick was to keep it churning, to number everything (Twin Spin, Twofer Tuesday, Hit Number Four, #1 Dance Craze), make it spin madly, all hopped up, like the music, like the cars, like the girls (in the boys' dreams), everything fast, on the road, the hip and the hop, at the hop, in the air.

Cousin Brucie wanted to sound like the kids he was talking to, like "a kid with energy to burn, with a voice as frantic as the passage of puberty felt."[17] WABC engineers would literally set Morrow's commercial copy aflame as he raced to recite the spot before the last words turned to ash; savvy listeners knew when that game was in play because Cousin Brucie would end an ad with "Boy, it's getting hot in here, cousins!"[18] Deejays tried to crack each other up on the air by tossing water-filled condoms at the man on the live mike, slamming their fists down on ketchup packets aimed at the deejay, anything for a cackle.

Radio's new identity—fun, fast, frenetic—led Americans to pick a station and stick with it all day, hoping not to miss the moment everyone would be talking about tomorrow. No longer did listeners tune to a particular program, no longer did stations think in terms of programs. Instead, stations adopted personas, even changing their call letters to become KING, WINK, WARM, KFOG, WSUN, WFUN. Call letters became songs, jingles to hum along to.

At the red-hot core of adolescent rebellion, disc jockeys became folk heroes, pied pipers of the new music and role models for a generation that was rising out of the postwar baby boom. These guys would do anything—even the stuff Mom told you never to do. In Peoria, of all places, deejay Stan Major staged a Stay Awake Marathon, going 210 hours without sleep and sparking a nationwide competition among jocks. The marathons involved no protest, no charity drive. They were the perfect Top 40 stunt: renegade behavior in service of nothing in particular except the doing. The kids loved it.

This was the era of deejays swallowing goldfish and locking themselves in the studio, refusing to come out until they'd played their favorite new song a thousand times in a row. In Beloit, Wisconsin, in 1957, deejay John Gregory sat on a flagpole for twenty-one days. The next year, in San Francisco, Don Sherwood decided that he, his flying weatherman Hap Harper, and thousands of KSFO listeners would mount an aerial attack on the innocent denizens of the town of Stockton. With the vague goal of returning Stockton to its roots as a red-light district and the explicit aim of increasing the region's fun quotient, the Sherwood-Harper Liberation Expeditionary Force of the Greater Bay Area commissioned 15,000 listeners as admirals and generals, sent them buttons to wear, printed up 100,000 phony $1,000-and-a-half bills of Sherwood Invasion Dollars to fund the invasion, and dropped 30,000 "Consider Yourself Bombed: Surrender—or Else" leaflets on the streets of Stockton.

All summer long, General Sherwood devoted his show to preparations for the assault. On September 21, Sherwood borrowed a Sherman tank and led a column of listeners supported by 163 light planes and units of the Air National Guard on the invasion. Thousands of listeners followed the tank into town in their own cars. The brigade rolled downtown to the cheers of a huge crowd of locals waving handkerchiefs. Stockton had surrendered, unconditionally. Sherwood appointed himself king, a peace treaty was signed, and the deejay got himself a raise, to more than $100,000.[19]

The stunt had no purpose other than to demonstrate the power of KSFO to generate listener solidarity. But that was purpose enough. The stunts would not last; in 1962, the FCC banned the "repetitious playing of one record" because it was not "inventive or in the public interest," and in 1966, the feds outlawed radio treasure hunts because of their tendency to paralyze entire cities.[20] But radio's ability to rally this generation into collective action would not be forgotten. In just a few years, revolutionaries on the FM band would use radio to sell the causes of peace, civil rights, drugs, sex, and cultural change.

That shift had its roots in Top 40's heyday, when radio challenged the adult world with wacky contests, coded humor, and music that dared to hint at the splendors of sex. From Storz's stations in the Midwest to the All-Americans at WABC, Top 40 stations promoted themselves with stunts designed to win over young people expressly by mystifying their elders. The more meaningless the task, the better, because the only thing that mattered was that their parents knew nothing about this world.

Like any Top 40 station, WABC ran contests—when the *Mona Lisa* visited New York, the station offered $100 each to the listeners who created the best, worst, smallest, and largest copies of Leonardo's masterpiece, as judged by Salvador Dalí. Nat King Cole sang the jingle that promoted the contest every hour. Thirty thousand entries poured in, and so did the rain on the open-air judging session at the Polo Grounds stadium, but Dalí pushed ahead and honored the dripping Mona Lisas. In a city of 8 million souls, WABC handed out 14 million buttons that said "WABC Musicradio 77," the ticket to a $25,000 payout if the station's button spotter saw you wearing the ad on your shirt.[21]

But nothing compared to the Principal of the Year contest the station launched in 1962. The drill was simple: the school that mailed in the most votes for its principal won. "We thought we'd get, like, ten thousand ballots," Morrow said. "Well, we were mistaken." They came in by the truckload, by the millions. Schools kept students after hours so they could write out entry after entry. The idea was to create what WABC program director Rick Sklar called "forced listening. Someone could copy the music, but you couldn't copy our jocks. It was all about incentives to listen."[22]

The next year, the station repeated the stunt, but while WABC executives had spent the intervening months concentrating on other promotions, hundreds of schools had been preparing all year for the next principal election. Inundated with more than 100 million votes, the station had to hire eighty college students, substitute teachers, and street drifters to sit in St. Nicholas Arena for two months to count ballots. In West New York, New Jersey, a candidate for superintendent of schools accused a rival principal of keeping students after school and forcing them to fill out tens of thousands of ballots.[23] WABC hyped the near-hysteria, hiring a helicopter to fly Morrow to suburban high schools in New York, New Jersey, and Connecticut to promote the contest, landing on football fields, on rooftops, and in a principal's backyard.

"We sat in shifts at Hofstra in the cafeteria, writing over and over the president's name to win the college dean award," said Sue Ronneburger, who grew up on Long Island listening to WABC and went on to work at the station. "All day, we sat there, writing the name on slips of paper, one name after another."

The prize: a color television set.

WHILE TELEVISION, on *The Donna Reed Show* and *Father Knows Best,* presented adults with an idealized, sanitized, separate-beds view of their lives, radio slipped young people plenty of winks and nods toward the subject of sex, though still heavily sugarcoated. No one at WABC had to tell Cousin Brucie that "politics was verboten. That was a given. Religion was also absolutely verboten. Sex wasn't what parents wanted and it wasn't what the station owners wanted, but we could touch on it if we didn't spell it out. We did it with our voices, with expression, with music. We were very aware of being a bridge between the adult world and the teen world. The adults listened because they thought we understood their kids' world."[24]

Deejays did everything they could to heighten young people's sense that they were different from their elders, that they were special. In Chicago and Los Angeles, Dick "The Wild I-tralian" Biondi gave his young listeners on-air shaving lessons, "bay-bee." At KYA in San Francisco, Johnny Holliday drew 60 and even 70 percent of the audience with nothing more threatening than the Fabulous 50 top songs and a daily recitation, with listeners standing at attention, hands on their hearts, of the pledge of "allegiance to the station we adore, from the halls of Tamalpais to the San Francisco shore."

But Top 40 jocks were always conscious of the need to reach the audience beyond the kids. The trick was to bring in the adults without making kids think you'd sold out or gone square. Morrow made parents happy by going on the air with appeals for runaway kids to "just call and talk to your Cousin Brucie." He made moms and dads believe he was an ageless, trustworthy babysitter, that despite the questionable lyrics and unsettling beat of the music he played, he was essentially a Good Guy, an all-American.

Once parents were made reasonably comfortable, deejays had to pivot and make the young folks believe they were being addressed in some secret code. In many cities, parents, principals, police, and politicians heard deejays speak in a lingo ostensibly designed to prevent old fogies from figuring out what was going on. But, of course, the stations knew that young adults were listening too, if perhaps not in the same room as the kids, and that everyone wanted to be in on the code, part of the fun. Thanks in part to the first psychological study of radio listening, some radio managers understood that kids and young adults sought pretty much the same thing: they wanted at once to belong and to rebel.

The answer to that customer demand came in the form of jocks who rhymed and jocks who sang, jocks who howled and jocks who moaned. At the dawn of the space program, there was an epidemic of blastoffs and echo chambers and rocket ships to the moon. On stations in New York and Washington, Murray the K (Murray Kaufman) combined pseudo-black patter with his own code to call himself "Mee-euz-aray the Kee-euz-ay." Listeners to his *Swingin' Soiree* could pop over to the local record shop to pick up a pamphlet that spelled out how to talk like the K. With just enough of a leer in his voice to get his message across, Murray narrated nightly "submarine races," which could only be viewed while necking in the backseat of a car. In Los Angeles, the Real Don Steele signed off his *Fractious Friday* show on KHJ by calling out to everyone hip enough to understand: "What do we know and believe?" That cued a recording of a passionate young woman shouting with ecstatic joy that "Tina Delgado is alive, alive!" The bit aired every week for years, without the slightest explanation. Steele took the solution to the mystery to his grave, and still the words are pregnant with meaning for nearly anyone who grew up in Southern California in the 1960s and '70s.

Dan Ingram, probably the fastest wit ever to spin records on American radio, won enormous ratings in St. Louis and then New York with a daily thumbing of his nose at authority. "Twenty-two before three on the Ingram Travesty, the program designed to belt the Establishment," he said one afternoon in 1962. The listener was "Kemosabe" and the deejay was the Lone Ranger, galloping through the hits on his daily "Ingram Mess" or "Ingram Atrocity," spraying one-liners at sponsors, station managers, and even the musicians the audience supposedly loved.

Frankie Valli sang "My Eyes Adored You," and Ingram added, "But my wallet couldn't afford you." Gene Pitney's tune "It Hurts to Be in Love" prompted Ingram to say, "Then you're doing it wrong." He answered Jimmy Ruffin's Motown classic "What Becomes of the Brokenhearted" by remarking, "They bleed to death." The Chords' "Sh-Boom" won this introduction: "And now, the song of the exploding librarian." Ingram edited the copy of an ad for the sofa store Castro Convertibles to offer "chairs that convert into beds and ottomans, which convert into an entire empire." When a supermarket spot offered a special on iceberg lettuce, Ingram helpfully added, "You know it's iceberg lettuce because two-thirds of it is under the counter."[25] Pushing "fresh lamb from American farms" for A&P supermarkets, Ingram assured listeners that this was "none of this Chinese communist lamb, this is *patriotic* lamb."

Ingram could push the boundary of what was acceptable. He once signed off his Easter show by noting, "It's my opinion that all religions are just different commercials for the same product." But his barbs blazed by so fast that the listeners most likely to be offended spent their time muttering, "What did he just say?" He was Letterman to Cousin Brucie's Leno.

In some cities, trying to figure out what the deejay just said was the whole point of the shtick. Pittsburgh's Porky Chedwick was, despite his squeaky-clean behavior, "so cool, I could make the Statue of Liberty drool," as he said in his daily sign-off. "This is your Daddio of the Raddio, the platter-pushin' papa, Pork the Tork, the Boss Man, Porkalating and getting you Porkified with my groove Porkology," he'd say to kick off his show on WAMO. Chedwick, for many years the only white on all-black stations, railed against drink, drugs, and delinquency. He took pride in reciting his Teen Commandments, ten exhortations to his listeners to respect their parents, be kind to one another, and steer clear of bad influences. He set up youth baseball leagues and took in wayward boys assigned to him by the juvenile court—and still he was deemed authentic enough to pack the Pittsburgh Civic Arena for his Porky Chedwick Groove Spectaculars, featuring the likes of Jackie Wilson, Bobby Vinton, Bo Diddley, the Marvelettes, and the Drifters. But the music he played and the hip patter he taught sent a different message, many parents believed: they accused Chedwick of inviting their (white) children to a frenzied (black) world of sex and liberation, even if he never spoke about sex, politics, or generational conflict.

Todd Storz usually didn't mind when parents and politicians expressed dismay over rock and roll and the wild and crazy style he had urged his deejays to cultivate. Storz loved a good public dust-up; it had to be good for ratings, he figured. But as the anti-rock backlash blossomed, Storz cast a concerned eye at the bottom line and decided that a few words to his announcers about their role might be in order. At a 1958 convention of deejays, Storz distributed a brochure reminding jocks that they were "invited guests in thousands of homes every day, and they owe their hosts and hostesses the consideration of Conduct Becoming a Gentleman." He urged deejays to speak against delinquency at schools and raise money for charities. In an ad on the cover of *Broadcasting* magazine, Storz called the deejay "The Man Closest to the People of America . . . , friend, companion, confidant. He is teacher, counselor, shopping guide. His audiences accept him as one of the family. They write him; they hang on his words. He has great responsibility. He lives up to it."[26]

But assurances from station owners did little to mollify adults who believed that radio was separating them from their children. Some white adults accused radio of mixing the races, exposing their children to exactly what had led those families to move out of the cities in the first place—the perceived threat of violence and sexuality that they associated with black America. The country had experienced the same sort of backlash soon after movies hit it big in the early years of the twentieth century. The sudden popularity of that new medium had sparked campaigns aimed at censoring films or even closing down movie theaters to halt the crime, delinquency, loose sexual mores, and race mixing that the movies were accused of fomenting. A similar backlash had greeted the dawn of the Jazz Age in the 1920s.

Now, Top 40 radio and rock music stood accused of alienating youth and poisoning their minds. America's new realities—the baby boom, the exodus to the suburbs, the paving of the nation, the decline of manufacturing, and the vast increase in leisure time—created a market for new distractions and inspirations, and radio, in large part because of the accidental vacuum created by television's arrival, delivered. The resulting face-off between young and old was so rattling that it led some parents to turn against their children's generation. The forces of tradition had one more big battle to stage, one last shot at stuffing the genie back into the bottle.

Chapter 4

✳ *BOOZE, BROADS, BRIBES, BEATLES*

Y OU DIDN'T GO on the radio to make a lot of money. You did it to be in showbiz, to get the girl, to be the guy everyone listened to, to have your voice recognized when you ordered lunch or took in your shirts. Hunter Hancock viewed radio as the way out of Texas, as his ticket to the swell scencs he'd heard from all those hotel ballrooms on long, hot

nights in San Antonio. So when Hancock found himself spinning records in Los Angeles near the end of World War II, the money was the last thing he cared about.

Until it came time to pay the rent and buy some wheels. Then it became clear: a deejay's pay would not do. Luckily, there was an easy answer. The record promoters who came around nearly every day had plenty of cash on them, and they were only too happy to help a struggling kid trying to make it in radio. Usually, the promoters started out with

ALAN FREED

(Courtesy alanfreed.com and Judith Fisher Freed)

a buck here, a fiver there, just a token of thanks for giving a couple of records a listen. Then, when the jocks started playing those records on the air, there might be a more regular payment, even a set fee for each spin.

Stations paid deejays by the commercial spot, so side deals with record guys didn't seem out of line. "In those days, I got $2 for a one-minute commercial and $1.50 for a half minute," Hancock said. Record promoters paid at least that well. Hancock started taking money from promoters in the mid-1940s. "You made your deal with the record companies, and you worked with a distributor, who had several lines. He would only push the best, so when he came to me with songs, I played them. I had a verbal contract with three or four distributors, I played their records, and at the end of the month, they'd give me a check. The smaller distributors might slip you something right away if you played their records. There was nothing wrong with being paid to play something on the air. It was no different from how we got paid by the radio station."

Record money accounted for at least half of Hancock's income in those years, and no one looked askance at the arrangement. After all, the deejay was master of his studio. What he liked, he played. And what he got paid to like, he played too. Records arrived at stations wrapped in cash. In big cities, some deejays even had rate cards that they handed to promoters: $100 buys a certain number of spins for your record. Most deejays insisted they wouldn't take money to play records they didn't like. With hundreds of new releases arriving at the station each week, there was always something that sounded good and came with cash.

Payola—gifts and payments to deejays made as inducement for playing records—wasn't illegal. Nor was payola new—in the heyday of sheet music, song pluggers handed out cash to get barroom pianists to play their tunes, and in the 1930s and '40s, promoters paid bandleaders to push their songs.[1] Although payola would become a symbol for those who accused radio of leading America's youth into cultural rot and degenerate behavior, it was never used to slip raunchy records onto the airwaves. What payola did was heighten the influence of deejays and win exposure for artists and songs that might otherwise have disappeared into stations' overflowing record bins. Even a classic such as Chuck Berry's "Maybellene" needed payola grease to get it started: after Leonard Chess of Chess Records offered New York deejay Alan Freed a songwriting credit on the tune, Freed played the song for two hours straight on his WINS show. "Maybellene" shot up to #1 on the charts and Freed raked in a share of the profits.

Hancock continued taking payola—money, gold cuff links, a gold record that a grateful Mercury Records gave him for helping to make the Platters' "Only You" a million-seller—until the practice turned into a scandal. "Then Uncle Sam came in and said, 'If you take money and play the record, it becomes a hit.' Baloney. You can't stuff music down people's throats. We had bombs and we had hits. All they did by ending payola was cut out about $15,000 a year, which was a huge amount then."

Federal prosecutors targeted Hancock for failing to report his payola earnings on his tax returns. "My stupid accountant said I could count that income as gift money and I didn't have to report it," Hancock said. But of course he did have to, and in 1962, he was found guilty of failing to own up to $18,000 of payola money between 1956 and 1958. He paid a fine and continued working on the air.

Hancock was no anomaly. Everybody took the money. Stations had open doors. "You could go from one station to the next," said George Michael, who worked for a distributor of Motown Records before launching his own career as a Top 40 deejay. "I'd go right to the disc jockeys. But at first, I didn't know anything about payola. I learned. Christmas 1960: I'm in college, working for the record company on the side. 'George, take this to the station,' the guy tells me. I took an envelope to one deejay. He opens it, says, 'Man, you gave me so-and-so's check.' So I go back to the boss and say, 'What am I doing?'

" 'You're taking around Christmas gifts,' he says."

By the time he got his own accounts, Michael knew payola was becoming controversial, so he found other ways to push his records— serving deejays as their gofer at record hops, getting them extra records. But payola was so routine that distributors who handed out the cash could get openly indignant if their commands were not obeyed. At New York's WINS, executive Rick Sklar was in the control room one evening when deejay Murray the K called in sick. A substitute host was found and Sklar stuck around to monitor the show. The phone rang in the control room, and when Sklar answered, a guttural voice demanded, "Where's my record?"

"I beg your pardon?"

"Where's my record?" came the angry response.

"I don't know what you mean."

"My deal with Murray is that he plays my record at 8:15. Where's my record?"

It was 8:24. "I don't know anything about your deal with Murray," Sklar replied. "Who is this?"

The phone went dead, and Sklar, curious, checked the station log. Sure enough, Murray had played the same song each night at 8:15 for six weeks.[2]

Cousin Bruce Morrow escaped the fate that more prominent deejays faced because he was just starting out when the scandal hit. Offered small amounts of money, he says he declined because "I thought it was wrong. I got a cherry pie once and I played the song. To this day, I feel guilty about it. But it was just dumb luck that I didn't get sucked into it. I was too small a fish."

The big fish in each town not only took money but became players across the music business. Promoters and record company executives were so desperate to win airplay for their acts that they offered top jocks a piece of the action—songwriting credit, part ownership of a band, even their own labels. Hunter Hancock started a record label in 1959 with his business partner, releasing singles by Big Jay McNeely, Joe Houston, and other R&B artists.[3]

By the end of the 1950s, the back scratching and palm greasing had become so widespread that some deejays complained it was turning their craft into a seedy underworld. In 1959, Todd Storz hosted the biggest, most raucous convention of deejays staged to date. The Americana Hotel in Miami Beach was the setting for a bacchanalia for twenty-five hundred deejays, with free bottles of liquor and prostitutes on call all week long. In one eight-hour party at the Americana featuring the Count Basie Orchestra, two thousand bottles of bourbon were consumed. Hired women were instructed to make themselves available to any deejay, with one proviso: at the height of the man's arousal, the prostitutes were to extract a promise that the jock would play the latest record being pushed by a particular company.[4]

But the deejays convention ended with an exposé in *The Miami Herald* headlined "Booze, Broads and Bribes." The convention couldn't have come at a worse time. Public grousing about deejays leading America's children astray was at its zenith. After vandalism and fights broke out at concerts put together by Freed and other deejays, city governments took to banning rock-and-roll shows. Church leaders and civic groups issued anti-rock statements. And in the New York offices of ASCAP, the organization of old-line composers and songwriters, the time seemed right for a final assault on BMI, the competitor that represented most rock and black artists. ASCAP lobbyists enlisted help from Frank Sinatra and other mainstream singers, who called for a congressional investigation into the dirty lyrics, payola, and phony songwriting credits that infested rock radio. The object was to break BMI, strip deejays of their power to decide what music got on the air, and roll back the rock revolution.[5]

ASCAP's campaign and the outrage sparked by news reports about rock-crazed kids and corrupt deejays prompted New York's district attorney and the Federal Trade Commission to launch investigations into how music reached the airwaves. But the main event in this attempt to restrain history was to be a good old Washington media extravaganza, a series of hearings before the House Special Subcommittee on Legislative Oversight. A nation that had spent the past decade alternately mesmerized and appalled by hearings exposing communist sympathizers in government and Hollywood, mobsters in business, and cheating in TV quiz shows geared up for another big show.

On February 8, 1960, Chairman Oren Harris, a Democrat from Arkansas, solemnly convened his committee. The congressman explained that this investigation had begun with a tip from one Max

Hess, owner of the Hess Brothers department store in Allentown, Pennsylvania, who was prepared to testify that it was "common practice" for his shop and others to make secret payments to radio stations in exchange for informal plugs on the air. Hess told the committee that the main factor in determining what music was played on radio was bribery, and those songs that deejays were paid to play were then forced upon the buying public.[6]

Some members of the committee used the hearings, which continued sporadically for much of that year, to rail against rock music as a pernicious assault on American values. Congressional hearings were a handy tool for those who sought to stymie the forces of cultural change. Just six years earlier, the Senate had taken on the comic book industry, challenging the insidious impact of those dramatic face-offs between superheroes and the archenemies of civilization. If nothing else, hearings guaranteed plenty of ink. The payola story produced bold 72-point headlines trumpeting revelations of free cars and mink coats: "DJs Admit Pay."

The star witness in the early hearings was a Boston deejay named Norman Prescott, who told the committee that he had quit his job at WBZ a few months earlier because "I became contaminated by the [payola] situation and was just so disgusted with myself and with the industry that I wanted to walk away from it. I think something happens to every man when he realizes somewhere in his life that he is no longer just an immature boy having a lot of fun, but he now has the responsibilities of a parent and he does not want to reflect in any way on his family some of the things that he is ashamed of."

Prescott's contrition and shame were a sham. His presence in front of the cameras was the result of a carefully managed campaign by federal investigators to flip the deejay. Committee staffers had confronted Prescott in Boston with photostats of canceled checks to the deejay from record distributors. "We were able—I do not like to use the word—in effect, to compel Mr. Prescott to testify the way he is doing this morning," said Robert Lishman, the committee's chief counsel.[7]

Between 1957 and 1959, Prescott had taken $9,955 from three record promoters in fifty-four checks; in addition, the record distributor made the payments on Prescott's new Mercury. In return, the dee-jay would drop by each week to pick up a stack of new records. Back at the station, he would play eight to ten songs from the stack each day, "anything that I wanted to play . . . , so long as it was represented by their distributorship," which handled deejay relations for about twenty-five record labels.

The way Prescott told it, radio was shot through with corruption. Salespeople at WBZ and his previous employer, WHDH, had re-quired him to follow each commercial for a new Hollywood movie musical with a song from that same movie. Deejays had been in-structed to play songs by the Lester Lanin big band in lieu of paying Lanin for coming to Boston to perform at a station promotional event.

But the main fraud that Prescott detailed was the one that hit hardest for most Americans: those Top 40 or Top 20 charts that dee-jays were forever yapping about were a complete fiction. They had lit-tle or nothing to do with popular taste and everything to do with payola. Other witnesses backed up Prescott. Deejay Bob Clayton of Boston's WHDH told the committee that the weekly Top 10 list he provided for publication in the *Boston Traveler* newspaper was based on no poll of any kind. "I make them up and send them in," he said. "It doesn't say 'Boston's Official Top 10,' it says 'Bob Clayton's Official Top 10.'"

But Representative John Mack checked the paper and found that it did indeed say "Boston's Top 10 Tunes."

Clayton mulled that over and responded: "It shouldn't."[8]

Prescott's litany of fraud continued for hours. The records on the survey sheets handed out at local supermarkets were hardly the most popular songs in town; rather, they were the ones that the rack jobber who paid for the surveys was stocking on the supermarket's record shelves. And those were the same songs that the deejays had been paid to spin on the radio. Even the songs played at high school record hops were part of the fix: promoters plied deejays with free records for give-aways at the hops, so of course the jocks gave heavy play to those songs.

Prescott detailed every kind of extracurricular compensation deejays indulged in. Jocks got shares in the profits of record companies whose songs they agreed to play on the air. They got residuals on songs on which they were listed as co-writers, even if they couldn't read a note of music. Station executives were in on the game too, Prescott said, describing how his bosses once sent him to New York to solicit hundreds of free records from labels based there.[9]

When committee members got their chance to grill their star witness, they moved quickly to the true target of their probe. "Do you think without payola that a lot of this so-called junk music, rock and roll stuff, would not be played?" asked Representative John Bennett, a Michigan Republican.

"Never get on the air," Prescott replied.

"Payola is responsible?"

"Yes, it keeps it on the air, because it fills pockets."

Prescott was a blockbuster star in the next day's papers. Radio executives knew the game was up. A few tried to argue that they'd been ignorant of the abuses. But as David Segal, the Denver-based owner of stations all over the West and South, told me, "Anybody tells you they didn't know is lying. My boys got lots of money and plenty of pussy. If it got to be too much, we tried to cut it out. My rule was they had to meet the promoters on the outside, not in the building. But these kids made their money on the side. It was wrong, making #1 hits out of shit records. But they could do it—you play it enough, these idiots will buy it. Of course, when it turned into a scandal, we had to shut that down."

With national publicity and congressional action bearing down on the industry, WBZ suspended two deejays who had taken money, clothing, and other gifts from promoters.[10] Other stations followed suit, but even as they began to clean house, station bosses could only cringe as the foundation of hit radio, the idea that the songs played on the air were the most popular in the land, cracked. Record distributors testified daily about how they dished out savings bonds, salad bowls, hot trays, suits, and cars to friendly deejays. They told of doctoring Top 40 survey results. One promoter, Harry Weiss, got deejays to give him station letterhead with their signatures already affixed. He would then type in the names of the songs he was promoting and send the report off to *Cashbox* and other trade magazines, which published the list as that station's hits of the week.

One sacked deejay, Stan Richards of WILD in Boston, argued that if payola was eradicated, the music on the radio would improve overnight. Stations would drop songs by unknowns whose promoters paid their way onto the airwaves. The nation could look forward to hearing more Perry Como, Pat Boone, Frank Sinatra, and Peggy Lee instead of rock acts no one had ever heard of. "The country will now enjoy—it will still be popular music, which will reflect the taste of Americans, but it will be of a better quality."[11]

Day after day, congressmen sought proof that payola was the cause of "bad" music and the social ills that accompanied it. Questioning George Paxton, owner of Coronation Music, Representative John Moss, a California Democrat, asked whether "we would have had the same outbreaking of rather peculiar music" if jocks hadn't been paid to spin those tunes.

"I don't think that has anything to do with it," Paxton replied.

"I have never heard of so many singers who cannot sing," the congressman complained.

"That I have to agree with you, 100 percent," Paxton said.

"You mean that would have occurred without payola?"

"I think so," Paxton said. "I think the youth of today called for it, desired it, wanted it. I don't think anything could have stopped it."

"If you ever got home early, you have heard this raucous sound in the middle of the afternoon," Moss said.

Paxton: "I make it, but I don't listen to it."[12]

The committee heard from record distributors, network executives, and deejays both shattered and defiant. But the two big names that dominated the headlines as the year went on were Dick Clark, whose *American Bandstand* TV show made him the face of the rock invasion, and Alan Freed, who had toiled long and hard to win his reputation as the man who brought rock and roll to white America. The congressmen dearly wanted to put Clark in the committee's hot seat. But the TV host, the most eye-opening example of a deejay who had taken a financial stake in the records he spun, joined with ABC and managed to outmaneuver the feds. Clark divested himself of his interests in record companies and swore to the committee that while he had accepted a color TV, a ring, and a fur stole for his wife, he had never taken money from promoters. Clark's company, Click, took fees from record companies for artists' appearances on *Bandstand,* and some on the committee called those fees "kickbacks," but the money was passed along to the performers, and the charge never gained traction. ABC successfully defused the committee's wrath by admitting that Clark's producer, Anthony Mammarella, had taken money from record companies. By forcing Mammarella to resign, ABC created a scapegoat and laid the groundwork for a defense of their star performer.[13]

It was clear to the committee staff that Clark was guilty of the same behavior that resulted in a nationwide purge of radio deejays. When the Crests' song "16 Candles" was released in September 1958, Clark had played it twice in two months even though it was not on the Top 100 chart. Then, in November, six days after the rights to the song were transferred to Clark, he played it twice more, and the song went from nowhere to #91. In December, he played "16 Candles" six more times and the song jumped to #25. The song made eight more appearances on *Bandstand* in the next eight weeks and finally catapulted to #2 in nationwide sales. George Paxton, the owner of Coronation, which originally bought the song from its authors, told the committee he assigned the rights to Clark "with the hopes that there would be plays, further plays or more plays, no doubt about that." Paxton and Clark split the profits on the song; it was Paxton's biggest hit ever, and it made Clark's company nearly $10,000.[14]

Ever the gentleman, Clark was able to assuage the committee. He politely insisted that he really did help write the songs on which he was listed as writer, claiming that he suggested the title of "At the Hop." He maintained that his show did not favor the songs he owned, even though an economist commissioned by Congress to study airplay on *Bandstand* concluded that it was "inescapable" that Clark "favored those records in which he had some interest."[15] No matter: the committee neither fined nor disciplined Clark. With the stalwart support of ABC—Clark's show was grossing $12 million a year for the network—and the savvy decision to get ahead of the story by divesting Clark's interests, plus the committee's calculation that it could be politically problematic to tear down young America's sweetheart, Clark salvaged his job and at least part of his reputation.

Alan Freed had no such luck. Less than a month after committee chairman Harris called Clark "a fine young man," Freed was arrested

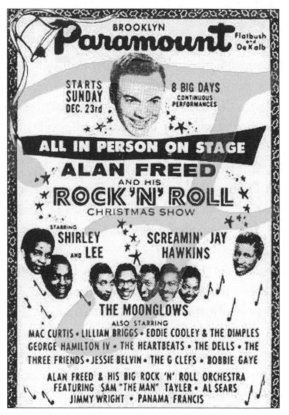

(Courtesy alanfreed.com and Judith Fisher Freed)

in connection with his receipt of more than $30,000 from five record companies. In 1962, he pleaded guilty to commercial bribery charges and received a suspended sentence. Unlike Clark, Freed refused to sign an affidavit saying he had never taken money for playing records. And unlike Clark, Freed, who also worked for ABC, found himself cut loose by his bosses. He was fired almost immediately after refusing to sign the affidavit.

Freed contended that he accepted money only after choosing on his own to play a tune. But he also bragged to friends that he had received so much from record companies that he should name rooms in his house in their honor. Two weeks after Freed refused to confess, his house was seized by the Internal Revenue Service.[16] Freed drifted to stations in Los Angeles and Miami but fell deeper into alcoholism and died in 1965. He was forty-three.

Years later, many of those who fell during the payola probe reestablished themselves as deejays or executives. Those who lived through the payola scandal came to see the purging of rock radio as the older generation's desperate effort to hold on to what they knew, to their ideas of how parents and children should relate to one another, to their concept of race in America, to their sense of respect and propriety. "The whole thing was about resentment of the music," said Steve Labunski, who ran Todd Storz's Top 40 station in Minneapolis. "If they were paying people to put Glenn Miller on the radio, they would never have stepped in. The payola scandal let people get off their chests their resentment of youth and their music, and blacks."

In New York, Hal Jackson had left his color-blind show on WMCA to do two shows a day on WLIB, a black station. There, he took record promoters' thank-you checks for $25 or $50. He also became more active in pressing for black rights. He appeared with Martin Luther King, Jr., and led pickets against construction sites that wouldn't hire black workers. Jackson was a folk hero in the city's black neighborhoods, making him a perfect target for publicity-hungry prosecutors. At the height of the payola investigations in 1960, Jackson was summoned by the Manhattan district attorney and arrested in front of a crowd of press photographers, charged with taking $10,000 from nine record companies. WLIB pulled him off the air, and the city erupted in protests, some of them led by Malcolm X and Adam Clayton Powell, the legendary congressman from Harlem. Pickets formed around WLIB's offices, and signs popped up all over Harlem: "No Hal Jackson, No WLIB! Turn Off Your Radio!"[17]

With no job and no money, Jackson could only watch as his life fell apart. It hardly mattered that his face still stared down from billboards onto the West Side Highway. The city's premier black deejay, perhaps the best-known black man in New York City, took a job cleaning office buildings at night. By day, he drove a cab. He and his wife separated. Several months later, prosecutors dropped all charges; they'd been unable to find any evidence that Jackson took money to play specific records. But WLIB's owner would not rehire the deejay. Jackson

(Courtesy alanfreed.com and Judith Fisher Freed)

struggled with menial jobs until his friend and fellow deejay Jocko Henderson found him a shift announcing classical music on an FM station in Philadelphia. Only after the payola scandals subsided did

Jackson return to the New York airwaves, starting over with an R&B show on a small station.

"I came back and my audience was loyal, and before long, I was on top again," Jackson said. "But Alan Freed was really destroyed. I visited him night after night and there was nothing left of him. He had made the careers of so many black performers, and the white establishment was really on him. They called him 'nigger lover' and he just kept putting the Shirelles and Dion and all the others on the air. They destroyed that man, totally."

The payola purge lasted about a year. The Federal Trade Commission investigated 255 deejays in fifty-six cities. Congress passed a bill making payola illegal, punishable by a prison term of up to a year. Stations cleaned house. Deejays quit in droves before they could be fired. Many left the business entirely; others moved across the country or changed their on-air names and started over. One record distributor in Pittsburgh put an ad in *Billboard* that said simply, "Effective immediately, payola will be discontinued until further notice."

But there would be no wave of prosecutions. And payola would never really go away; it merely changed direction. Now it was music directors and station managers, rather than deejays, who made deals with record companies and their distributors. The same free records poured into stations. The same influence was peddled. But stations slipped disclaimers onto the air at odd hours of the night: "Certain records heard or given away on KXOK were provided in consideration of cooperation by various record artists, manufacturers and distributors."[18] The payola scandal's main impact was to cut deejays out of decision making about the music that got on the air.

Stations tried to restore credibility to their hit surveys by adding a bit of science to the process, relying more on national sales figures than on the old system of ringing up a few local record stores. The result was the first big step away from the localism of the 1950s and toward a blandness that would come to characterize Top 40 through the 1960s. "It took away our freedom," said Hunter Hancock. "We went to a Top 20 format and all the deejays had to play from a tight playlist. It grated on our sensitivities. I had to say only what they wanted me to say, which was very difficult for a guy like me. Also, I had to spin a lot of records that I was frankly ashamed to play."

In the first years after the scandal, rock and roll and the radio format that delivered it to the nation seemed to stall. The soothing tones of Bert Kaempfert and the bubbly ballads of Lawrence Welk replaced Frankie Avalon and the Platters at the top of the charts. Chuck Berry went to jail on morals charges and Little Richard entered the ministry. Many stations dropped Top 40 and reverted to a more adult sound featuring middle-of-the-road crooners. Rock's tainted status opened the door to other formats—in the South, country stations blossomed as radio resegregated its music to appeal to both listeners and sponsors. The first all-talk stations went on the air, and in 1961, Gordon McLendon switched his powerful XTRA—which reached all of Southern California from a transmitter in Tijuana, Mexico—from Top 40 to all-news, the first experiment in that format.

The lessons of Top 40's success were beginning to seep in. The nation was no longer one, undifferentiated audience. If stations that devoted themselves to music programming for young people could so dominate the ratings, other stations might lure different groups of listeners with other types of programming. The old network model of appealing to the largest possible audience was slowly being replaced by a pitch to advertisers to buy smaller but well-defined audiences.

In many cities, only one Top 40 station was left standing, and with each passing year, those stations pared their playlists further, including only the biggest hits. For a while, those who had led the fight against payola could argue that rock and roll had had its moment, that decency was being restored to radio and American life. But the youth juggernaut would not be stopped. Chubby Checker's "Twist"—the record and the dance—became a cross-generational sensation. The Kennedy administration's emphasis on youth—the Peace Corps, the rhetoric of American optimism, the artful deployment of the president's vivacious family as symbol of the nation's hopes—connected with the freshness of the folk music craze and the pure fun of Top 10 hits such as "Monster Mash," "The Loco-Motion," and "Duke of Earl." Deejays may have been chomping at the bit to get back to their former freedoms, but as far as listeners could tell, everything, in the words of the Chiffons, was "so fine (do-lang do-lang do-lang)."

THEN CAME THE BEATLES. Early in 1963 at WABC, Cousin Brucie and the station's five other "All-American" deejays sat in their music meeting with managers and listened to test pressings of "I Want to Hold Your Hand," which was already a hit in Britain and Germany. "Thumbs down," "No way," and "Stupid name for a rock group" were the comments. The record did not air.[19]

For days after John Kennedy was assassinated in Dallas that November 22, radio stations put aside their usual music and instead aired remembrances of Kennedy. The nation sorely needed a respite. On December 29, deejay Jack Spector played "I Want to Hold Your Hand" on New York's Top 40 WMCA. "It got no reaction," said Ruth Meyer, the station's program director at the time. "We thought we could break the Beatles before they came to town, but people weren't interested."

The Beatles' breakthrough came on television; Ed Sullivan had signed a one-year contract giving his CBS variety hour exclusive rights to show the band in the United States, and when the moptops first appeared on February 9, 1964, the nation entered the era of instant, media-driven frenzies. Within a week, the Beatles had four songs in the *Billboard* Top 100, and that meant four songs in constant rotation on Top 40 stations. On February 22, the band made the cover of *Newsweek,* over the headline "Eeeeeeeee . . . eeeeeeeeeee . . . eeeeeeeeee!" In Miami, WQAM deejay Rick Shaw got his copy of "I Want to Hold Your Hand" in a special-delivery package from Capitol Records and put it on the air immediately. Thirty seconds into the song, "the phones explode," Shaw said. "They're all going, 'Who is that, what is the name of that group, where'd that come from?' That never happened before, it's never happened since."[20]

"All that business about folks putting down dirty old rock and roll went away, overnight," Ruth Meyer said. "The world went crazy. No one said anything more about the music making kids delinquents. Everybody just wanted a piece of this."

Still, it was by no means clear that the Beatles were more than a passing fad, like the Singing Nun just a few months before, or another variation on the rock theme, like Chubby Checker or the Beach Boys. "Look what's coming up the charts," Cousin Brucie thought in August of 1964: it was Dean Martin's "Everybody Loves Somebody." Now *that* was a surefire hit.[21] It would be another year before Morrow was finally persuaded that there was something elementally different about the Fab Four, something that made them the perfect crossover hit, appealing at once to the kids' passion for rebellion and their parents' yearning to stay young while being grown-up. "They were devilish without a hint of evil," Morrow said. "The Beatles were conscious excellence with absolutely no self-consciousness." Their primary sales vehicle was radio, the Top 40 stations that whipped the nation into a frenzy over the band and its hits.

At WABC, Morrow happily jumped on the bandwagon. The station dispatched Cousin Brucie to Carnegie Hall to meet the Beatles, and Ringo Starr told him his dream was to become a New York deejay. Morrow ran a contest asking listeners to vote on their favorite Beatle. When Morrow offered to give away two tickets to a Beatles appearance to the seventy-seventh caller, listeners blew out the phone lines between Manhattan and Queens, Brooklyn, and Staten Island. Angry Bell company executives visited the station the next morning and threatened to remove WABC's phone lines; to prevent future shutdowns, the company installed a choke system that cut off calls when the system overloaded.

Sponsors got the message quickly. "They had been resisting advertising on Top 40 radio even though we had such huge numbers, because they wondered if kids really bought their products," Meyer said. "The Beatles made it clear that this wasn't just a kid thing—everybody wanted to hear this stuff."

If sponsors were happy, stations were happy. No Beatles connection was too flimsy, no promotion too cheesy. In New York, WABC recorded all-new jingles, rechristening the station as "W-A-Beatles-

C." In nearly every city, some deejay laid claim to the title "Fifth Beatle," even if his only tie to the foursome was a thank-you note from their PR man. When WABC managed to snare the first copy of "Love Me Do," Morrow put it on the air with a "WABC exclusive" announcement spliced into the middle of the tune so competitors couldn't tape the song off the airwaves and use it themselves. He played the song twice an hour.

In New York, Beatlemania peaked in August 1965, when WABC rented a suite above the Beatles' rooms at the Warwick Hotel and set up a remote studio there. Morrow broadcast Beatles bulletins in advance of the band's concert at Shea Stadium. As ten thousand fans, many of them holding transistor radios, gathered on the street below, Morrow leaned out the eighth-floor window with program director Rick Sklar holding on to his belt. Deejay Dan Ingram interviewed Morrow by phone and the Cousin described each step in the Beatles' progress toward the hotel. "Well, here we are in the Warwick Hotel, Dan. Actually, I'm outside of the hotel, doing this report by the seat of my pants. Below me I can see a bevy of very beautiful Beatles fans. . . . This is your Cousin Brucie at the W-A-Beatles-C headquarters at the Warwick Hotel." Every sentence was punctuated by piercing shrieks of thousands of girls eight floors below.

Then, as the band arrived, someone swiped a gold St. Christopher's medallion off Ringo Starr's neck. Morrow, his usually frenetic delivery at near-hysterical pitch, reported the news: "Something terrible has happened, that I'm quite ashamed of. Somebody took a medallion off Ringo's neck in the excitement and I'm sure they didn't mean to do this." Morrow interviewed Ringo about the loss. The medal hadn't been off his neck in three years, he explained, and "it's sort of a keepsake, it's from me auntie and if anyone's got it . . ."

"Is it gold?" Morrow asked.

"It is gold—I only wear gold" came the reply.

Morrow and deejay Scott Muni turned the 50,000-watt signal of WABC into a combination lost-and-found and detective agency. They offered a meeting with Ringo himself to anyone who brought the medallion to the station's studios. The station broadcast nonstop appeals, and a few hours later, Angie McGowan's mother called in. Angie had come home with the gold piece and the news that whoever had it was supposed to call Cousin Brucie.

"Is she in trouble with the police?" Mrs. McGowan wanted to know. Assured that her daughter would not go to jail, the mom agreed to bring her daughter and the medallion to the Hilton Hotel, where

BRUCE MORROW INTERVIEWING THE BEATLES IN
THEIR NEW YORK HOTEL ROOM, 1965   *(Courtesy Bruce Morrow)*

WABC kept them hidden for more than twenty-four hours while the station's promotion machine went into overdrive. Every fifteen minutes, WABC broadcast appeals for the return of Ringo's gold. The mystery became a frenzy involving virtually the entire city. Finally, the next evening, at the top of Morrow's show, with news reporters on hand and cameras rolling, Cousin Brucie introduced Angie, brought Ringo into the room, and talked the shaken girl through her tale. She had reached for Paul McCartney's head "because I wanted to touch his hair, and then I saw Ringo. I wanted to kiss him more than any of the others, so I tried to get my arms around his neck to kiss him, and when the whole thing was over, I had the medallion in my hand." Ringo kissed Angie, while Morrow broadcast the event live to his own audience and to ABC affiliates nationwide.[22]

Cousin Brucie and WABC rode the Beatles wave for five years, maintaining massive audience numbers with playlists that were, by today's standards, tight in number but unimaginably eclectic in scope. Simon and Garfunkel, Nancy and Frank Sinatra, the Rolling Stones, the Supremes, Herb Alpert, Petula Clark—if it sold, Top 40 played it. "The Ballad of the Green Berets" could bump up against "Wild Thing," "Cherish" might follow "Paperback Writer"—it didn't matter, as long as the Top 40 machine kept chugging along with jingles, head-lines, spots, and always the jocks, seemingly talking faster with each passing year.

Todd Storz's creation was a more dominant force than he had ever imagined it could be, even if it had taken an unexpected turn. Top 40 had helped carve out a new foundation for popular culture. The huge number of Americans born in the postwar boom, the rise of TV, and the softening of racial barriers all pushed radio executives to loosen their hold on the dream of mass appeal and instead consider reaching out to a generation. Youth was now cherished by all ages, and espe-cially by American business. Storz's mass-appeal format was refined into a ratings machine aimed at giving young people the sense that they were something apart, something special.

As that machine made more and more money, the corporations raking in the bucks demanded tighter control over their product. Dee-jay excesses threatened the efficiency of the Top 40 profit engine. Beatlemania pushed audience levels to new highs, giving the compa-nies that controlled Top 40 an opportunity to squeeze stations of their rebellious, anarchic spirit.

Authentic, edgy voices such as Hunter Hancock, Alan Freed, and

Cousin Brucie were pushed aside in favor of sound-alike shouters who did little more than deliver the time and temperature. Kids who grew up with the thrill of hearing once-illicit black music on the radio were now searching for the next thing, trying to recapture that sense of rebellion that had been reined in by the payola scandal and rekindled by the Beatles, only to be lost again in the calcifying, stale sound of the aging Top 40 format.

In the mid-1960s, in San Francisco at KYA and then in Los Angeles at KHJ, programmer Bill Drake developed his Boss Radio format, trimming the playlist to thirty records, speeding up the stations' sound, shortening jingles to just a few seconds, editing songs down to their bare minimum, limiting deejays to one-liners. Drake monitored deejays' every word, every pause; deejays were no longer storytellers but part of a sleek system designed to snare listeners as much with pace as with content.

Once again, radio was ripe for revolution. Adults left at sea by the noise of Top 40 had started to retreat to a radio backwater, the FM band, where the classics and "beautiful music," the kind you heard at the barbershop or dentist's office, were available, static-free. Very few people had FM bands on their radios, but record companies were selling stereo albums that sounded nifty on the new hi-fi sets that came with two speakers. Then, in 1965, the FCC decided to pry open the frontier of FM by decreeing that stations could no longer simply simulcast programs on their AM and FM outlets; they had to come up with original programming on FM.

Radio once more banged up against a technological frontier with no plan, no direction. Once again, a combination of accident and inspiration would crack open a generational fault line. The result was an unsettling new sound, an invitation to rebellion delivered in story and song.

PART TWO

REBEL

JEAN SHEPHERD *(Courtesy Fred W. McDarrah)*

Chapter 5

✳ NIGHT PEOPLE

*If you maintain a force in the world
that comes into people's sleep,
you are exercising a meaningful power.*

—Don DeLillo in *Underworld*

THE DEEJAY WOULDN'T PLAY RECORDS. He'd tell a story and then, instead of introducing the next song, he'd spin right into his next tale, flitting from an embarrassing moment at his junior prom to a singular triumph of his little gang of misfits at the Warren G. Harding School in Hohman, Indiana, and on to the adventures of Flick and Schwartz and—oh, the lost opportunities!—Daphne Bigelow, she of the "pure, translucent alabaster skin." Why should he play a record—the *same* record that had been played on yesterday's show—when he could tell the story of Ralphie Parker's quest for the ultimate Christmas present, the Official Red Ryder Carbine Action 200-Shot Range Model Air Rifle?

The executives who ran WKRC in Cincinnati in those first years after World War II had hired Jean Shepherd, twenty-five-year-old Army veteran, refugee from small-town Indiana, to handle the early-morning popular music show. The job description of morning show host included nothing about telling long, winding stories of childhood, military service, or the inanities of a world in which people hired to talk on the radio are asked not to talk on the radio. When Shepherd refused to get with the program, the bosses affixed a red light to the studio control board. Anytime Shepherd spoke on the air for more than three minutes, the light would flash on.

Shepherd proceeded to deliver his message bathed in a red glow. "I'm this kid, see," he'd begin, and half an hour later, no record had been played. Shepherd was eventually fired for talking too much. He'd figured something like that would happen. His expectations of his chosen career were minimal. Back home in Hammond, Indiana— Hohman was the thin disguise he concocted for his stories—Shepherd had been a radio geek from early adolescence. He'd spent his "entire childhood in the basement, developing deathly pale complexions and abnormally high IQs. I was one of the first true Nerds." After his family moved up to Chicago, Shepherd would spend long afternoons haunting the surplus radio parts stores on State Street, communing with the cigar-chewing gnomes who manned the counters, "memorizing the serial number and specs of every known radio part going back to Marconi."[1] Like Todd Storz, Shepherd joined the Army Signal Corps during World War II, and after the war he remained a devoted amateur radio operator; from early childhood until old age, he was a ham, scouting the airwaves for an anonymous, ready audience.

But any illusions Shepherd might have had about the glories of radio were dashed early on. At seventeen, Shepherd volunteered for a station promotion at a local circus performance, agreeing to provide five-minute-long broadcast accounts of his experience every three hours as he was frozen in a block of ice. The station equipped the boy with a rubber suit, a feeding tube, and most essentially, a microphone. Shepherd had found his place and he was uncomfortable with it from the get-go.

Shepherd's second deejay job in Cincinnati, hosting a hillbilly music show from Shuller's Wigwam restaurant on WSAI, lasted longer. Shepherd actually played songs during that stint, from 1948 to 1951. But he also told stories, in an easy, gentle voice with a rollicking chuckle and an ability to capture the characters in everyone's lives—

the class bully, the sad nerd, the power-mad camp counselor, the hysterical mother, the stoic, always-defeated Old Man.

Shepherd found a place on Cincinnati TV as well—at the very end of the broadcast day (thus the name of his show, *Rear Bumper*). The program followed the late movie on the tube and went on for as much of the night as Shepherd cared to stay. One night, however, the movie, something about a jungle goddess and a plane crash, was so bad that Shepherd came on after his opening theme and said, "Look, anybody who enjoyed that movie is not going to enjoy anything that I'm going to do. And conversely, any man with taste has already left us. So let's just part friends." Whereupon the closing theme swelled and the broadcast day came to a close.

Comedian Steve Allen saw Shepherd delivering his rambling, mesmerizing TV monologues and recommended that NBC hire the young storyteller to succeed him as host of *The Tonight Show*. (The network brought Shepherd to New York but hired Jack Paar instead, because—as Shepherd would later explain—*The Tonight Show* was not for Night People who were just opening up, but for Day People who were shutting down.)

On the radio in the early 1950s, Shepherd was still cast as a deejay. That's the only term there was for a guy who peddled his off-center view of the world on the air. He spent a couple of years in Philadelphia, where he captivated a cult following of listeners and confounded his bosses—what were they to make of a deejay who went on the air and told the audience, "The avowed purpose of my program is not to please, but to begin trains of sequence, to begin trains of thought"?[2]

Shepherd's act developed enough of a following to win notice in New York, where executives at WOR recruited him in 1955. The art of storytelling had largely vanished from radio after TV came on the scene, and WOR didn't know quite what to do with Shepherd. After a few months of spinning tunes and squeezing in a quick story in the late afternoon, he persuaded the bosses to move him to the overnight shift. Everyone would be happier that way—management, Shepherd, listeners, and, goodness knows, the advertisers, who had no idea what to make of this show. Rather than lolling away the wee hours with a broadcast of sweet music, WOR would present listeners—if there were any at that time of night—with one man, talking, as he put it, "in a vacuum, in a closed, sealed room."[3]

The assumption in the industry was that the announcer's relationship to the audience ought to be remote and formal. In a 1935 study, social psychologists asserted that because of "the impersonality of the radio . . . , there can be no direct give and take between the radio performer and his audience."[4] Shepherd intended to show the audience that he knew that they knew that radio's standard ways of doing things were an utter crock.

But WOR managers saw no need to pay to open their studios overnight for one crazed deejay with a likely audience of next to nobody. So they sent Shepherd out to do the all-night show from the hut at the base of the transmitter tower in the swamp of the Meadowlands in Carteret, New Jersey. There, with only an engineer in the next room, Shepherd sat in the dark from 1: to 5:30 each morning, accompanied by his microphone and the eternal hum of 50,000 watts of power coursing up the antenna out back.

He'd play a few records, jazz of course, but mostly, he'd talk about whatever popped into his mind. He did so in a voice that was startlingly conversational and informal, as if he were hanging out in your kitchen with only the night-light breaking the black. Alone, in the quiet of night, the mind gone just a bit soft, the soul opened wider, Shepherd conjured in the imaginations of susceptible listeners a world of distant fathers and frazzled mothers, bullies and boors, and frustrated adolescents pining for happiness. In those years of the gray flannel suit and the march of the interstates, the can-do confidence of the Organization Man and the promise of the new Levittowns, America was nonetheless a nation of searchers. By day, the clean young men at IBM in their white oxford shirts and slim dark ties seemed an army of satisfaction. But at night, there were doubts, puzzles, questions you didn't admit to at the office or with the neighbors.

This was the time of Eisenhower and McCarthyism, Milton Berle and Lucille Ball, bigger cars and smaller radios, the American Century at its peak. But it was also the moment of *Mad* magazine and *Playboy,* James Dean and *Death of a Salesman,* poets dressed in black and punks with hair slicked back—images and ideas best reserved for the night.

"If we sit and talk in a dark room, words suddenly acquire new meanings and different textures," Marshall McLuhan said. "They become richer, even, than architecture. . . . All those gestural qualities that the printed page strips from language come back in the dark, and on the radio." Jean Shepherd, McLuhan said, was the author of "a new kind of novel that he writes nightly. The mike is his pen and paper."[5]

While radio stumbled about for new programming, while the nation sought meaning in the peace and prosperity of the postwar years, Shepherd connected with listeners as had no one before him. Even without playing music, Shepherd put jazz on the radio. He improvised with his life; he challenged listeners to stay up late with him and question the world around them. Sitting before the microphone, playing "I'm the Sheik of Araby" on the kazoo or the Jew's harp, he invented talk radio. He reclaimed the intimacy that had made the medium so revolutionary when voices first emerged from crystal sets a generation earlier. "Life can't be talked about by just words," he once said. "You've got to do it with silence, you have to do it with beat and tempo and rhythm."[6]

While Todd Storz sold his brand of rapid-fire rebellion to young people across the nation, Shepherd and a small coterie of deejays struck out against the bland sameness of the pop culture by stretching the language. Jocko Henderson invented a proto-rap delivery that had all of Philadelphia and later New York saying, "Oooh-papa-doo and how do you do / This is your ace from outer space / I will be on the moon real soon / On the greatest and the latest rocket ship show." The hip-talking Jazzbo (Al Collins) on New York's WNEW and later on KSFO in San Francisco evangelized on behalf of jazz from a place he called the Purple Grotto, a mythical subterranean studio with stalactites and a lake and nary a telephone to break the magical spell. Long before LSD was cool, Jazzbo took his audience on a phantasmic trip populated by Jukes, his swing-loving chameleon; Harrison the Tasmanian Owl, who pushed Dave Brubeck's cool jazz; and a flamingo who favored "music to fly by."[7]

In Los Angeles, the first shock jock, Jim Hawthorne, astounded the city from the mid-1940s into the '60s not with raunchy material, but by playing records backward, at the wrong speed, and under his own brand of patter, which involved replacing the final syllables of words with the suffix "-hogan." Long before the invention of the seven-second delay made it safe to put callers on the air, Hawthorne took calls, holding the receiver of the phone up to the microphone, trusting his listeners not to say naughty words because he knew they shared his lingo, and that was plenty cool enough.[8]

In Boston, two young announcers hired to fill the time slot right before Red Sox broadcasts used satirical takeoffs on soap operas, advice shows, and other standard radio fare to introduce a rebellious note in an otherwise safe environment. Bob Elliott and Ray Goulding—Bob and Ray—courageously invented Commissioner Carstairs, a growling buffoon of a politician whose furious and wrongheaded assaults on ordinary people mocked Senator Joseph McCarthy's Red-baiting crusade at the height of his abuse of power. Bob and Ray were deliciously subversive, snapping at the hands that fed them with send-ups of every manner of advertiser. (Their "sponsors" included Einbinder Flypaper, "the greatest name in flypaper"; the House of Toast, a fast-food chain that limits its offerings to toast and prune shakes; and Mushies, "the great new cereal that gets soggy even without milk or cream.") And they were silly, creating immortal characters such as Harlow . . . P. . . . Witcomb, president . . . of the . . . Slow . . . Talkers . . . of . . . America; Biff Burns, the hyperactive sportscaster; and the McBeebee Twins, who speak in a near-simultaneous lockstep that drives any listener to beg for fingernails on a blackboard.[9]

Shepherd was not as linguistically far out as some of the wilder deejays, but he too came from a different place. Each show began with a fanfare from the horse track, the clip-clop of hooves, and a frenzied orchestral overture by a lesser relation of the famous Strauss family. Shepherd would begin, sometimes mid-sentence, chuckling at his own remarks, so a listener might believe he was eavesdropping on a stream-of-consciousness monologue already in progress.

The show was Shepherd's voice alone, searching for meaning, bar-ing the pain of papered-over memories, poking fun at all of it. "Everybody on the radio is delivering a message," he said one night. "All believe it's a secret, important message." Long pause. "And there are no messages. Life goes on, the winds blow over the pyramids. King Tut's mummy is on the road now—it's playing Cleveland tonight."[10]

Deejaying was Shepherd's second job in radio; first, he was the play-by-play man for the minor-league Toledo Mud Hens. Baseball taught him about radio's intimacy, the idea that one man could deliver his version of a ballgame to an audience that wanted to know the score, yes, but was also invested in the announcer's stories, in the rhythms of his voice and the poetry he created out of silences, the crowd noise, a few well-chosen words of description, and the distant crack of a bat.

To that one-on-one intimacy, Shepherd added a wider world. He spoke to people like himself—people who chuckled at life even as they despaired over their place in it, wondering, as he did, just why it is that anyone eats escargots. Early in his WOR career, Shepherd urged his listeners to express themselves in unison, like a crowd of baseball fans. (He never forgot his baseball roots; I once heard him deliver a play-by-play of the Christians' battle against the lions.) In his most conspiratorial whisper, he coaxed listeners to their windows, had them set their radios on the sill, and then, on his command to turn the volume way high, he bellowed—and they joined in—"You filthy pragmatist, I'm going to get you!" Listeners were astonished to hear other voices in their own apartment building, or across the street, or down the alley, echoing with the same insane shout. They heard it night after night, as Shepherd announced another installment of his "Hurling Invectives" feature, leading his Night People in a cry of "Drop the tools—we gotcha covered!" or "You dirty slob! Why don't ya move outta the neighborhood?" or his standard "Excelsior, you fathead!"

"Put your radio on your windowsill now!" he commanded one night in 1957. "Do it now! Now! The loudspeaker pointed out—toward the neighborhood. . . . And when I give you the cue, turn that radio up as loudly as it will go. We're going to use a very special kind of invective tonight. This is known as the disquieting with a touch of morbid curiosity type. Which is Type 23A, and a very difficult type to use." Then he fell into a whisper: "Turn it up! Lights out! For heaven's sake, turn the lights out. Turn the radio up. Pretend you're looking at television. Pretend you're asleep. Okay." Then, very loudly: "Myrtle! This is the third time you've come home drunk again! What about the kids? What about the kids? I ask ya: How long is this gonna go on? How long?"[11]

The insomniacs and the fearful and the lonely of the great metropolis—and beyond, because WOR's signal fell over thirty-six states in the clear of the night—grew to adore his stories and cling to his words and love him for what he meant. Not long before she died, my grandmother urged me to write about the loneliness of the night, the hours that stretch through the darkness and the silence, with no end in sight. During those hours, she, like so many, turned on the radio, just for the company. Like many of us, she thought she was the only one crazy enough to be padding around an apartment, listening to a voice just for the sake of hearing words, a sign of another intelligence out there somewhere, a person saying, if nothing else, "You are not alone."

Imagine the shock, then, when Shepherd's listeners heard those midnight choruses echo across the apartment canyons of the city. "Excelsior! . . . -elsior, . . . -elsior." The scene, so startling and powerful, was reprised years later in the movie *Network*, in which the TV newscaster-turned-mad-prophet Howard Beale urges his viewers to their windows to shout together, "I'm mad as hell and I'm not going to take it anymore." They do, and a popular movement is born.

Together, Shepherd and his audience created a crazy quilt of protection against mindlessness—"creeping meatballism," he called it, and whether it was McCarthyism or commercialism, corporate suits or ragamuffin hippies, Shepherd dispatched all of the insidious conformity of contemporary society with a single word: *"Excelsior!"* Onward and upward he traveled each night, railing against those who didn't get it, even as he knew there was no way out. *"Excelsior!"*

Shepherd's program swam—as he once wrote of his home, the Midwest—"in a turgid sea of Futility. . . . Almost all of humor is of the school of Futility. Futility, and the usual triumph of evil over good. Which is another name for realism." He aimed to capture "the mind of

man in all of its silliness, all of its idiocy, all of its trivia, all of its wonder, all of its glory, all of its poor, sad, pitching us into the dark sea of
oblivion."

In one of those faceless New York apartments in the small of the
night, Paul Krassner, a young man who would grow up to run a magazine called *The Realist,* would listen to Shepherd, ideally not alone.
"My idea of a hot date would be to find a girl who also liked Shepherd
and lie in bed with her all night listening," he said. "I would fall asleep
and wake up at 3 A.M. and he would be talking about how to explain
to a Venutian what an amusement park was for, or how he knew a guy
who could take an ice cube and say what make of fridge it came
from."[12]

Shepherd told that story many times, about a man who would
stand at a bar and order a bowl of ice cubes. He would savor each one,
consider, and pronounce: "Ah, yes, that's a Kelvinator, a 1936, yes?"

"Nope."

"Well, a Kelvinator anyway, right? Kelvinator, Kelvinator, ah, Kelvinator *1939,* right?"

"Check-o."

And on he'd move to a Frigidaire, 1947. Because every cube has a
flavor all its own, and every man a particular skill, a particular place in
the universe.

Listeners came to believe that Shepherd knew their world, knew
them, that he was speaking directly to them when he sometimes halted
a story mid-paragraph and said: "*You.* The husband and wife driving
on the Garden State Parkway, *you* in Rahway, listening to the train
whistle while you're worrying about whether you left the gas on. *You.*"

I heard Shepherd through my pillow, from the transistor radio cradled in my palm. He told me my bedtime stories. I would stuff my face
into that pillow to muffle the laughter so my parents wouldn't hear
that I was still awake. I would stay up into the night because Shep was
revealing himself and I never knew what might come next. He invented a kind of radio voyeurism that commands you not to change
the station because you might miss a story that could change your life.
Everyone who followed Shepherd's path on the radio—and there is

hardly a creative soul in the medium who does not trace his work back to Shep's stories—was enraptured to discover that in the darkness and quiet of a windowless studio, one person could step inside an audience's imagination. From Shepherd's nightly, serialized stories, there is a direct line to the anguished soul-searching of Vietnam-era monologuists and on to the sexual confessions of Howard Stern and his many imitators today.

Shepherd's listeners thought he was talking especially to us—the old folks and the night workers, the New York transplants and the teenagers, especially the teenagers, who were, as *Life* magazine said in 1961, "hooked on sound," but tired of Top 40's repetition and predictability.[13] You heard Shepherd and you knew that he knew. "At a certain age in life," he said one night, "when you're—oh, I'd say roughly between fifteen and nineteen, possibly, although that, you know, is subject to change—you really believe you know what it's about. You really, seriously think you've got life by the you-know-what. . . . And then, as you get older, you begin to have faint inklings, faint inklings of what an ignoramus you have been up to this point in life. And it's just beginning to dawn on you what an unbelievable ignorant slob you are now."

He did not insult his audience, because he shared this dark place with them. Shep would even gather his Night People now and then. One night, at Shepherd's direction, for no special purpose, his listeners came together. He called it The Milling, and he issued instructions about when and where. Hundreds of listeners came to a dark street corner in lower Manhattan, and, as he told them to, they stood around, they *milled.* The police came and asked questions, and, as Shepherd had directed them, they declined, politely, to respond, and the police were mystified, and then, without further communication, the listeners quit milling. They went home. But while Shepherd billed these gatherings as an act of art, a milling without specific purpose, the events satisfied his deep need to see if his message was getting through. Especially when Shepherd was doing the all-night show, his bouts of doubt became overwhelming, and it was then that he would announce a milling, at a midtown bookstore or in Washington Square

Park. Listeners would come by the hundreds, and Shepherd would come to see them, and the next night he would return to his closed, sealed studio.

In 1956, Shepherd and his audience combined forces on their most ambitious project. It began that April with Shepherd's visit one day to the Doubleday Book Shop on Fifth Avenue. He asked the clerk for a book of scripts from the old radio drama *Vic and Sade*, a daily serial that billed itself as "an oasis of smiles amidst a sea of tears." It was the kind of writing Shepherd loved, as nostalgia piece, as ironic plaything, as plain old cracking good yarn. But the clerk told Shepherd that there was no such book, because it did not appear on any publisher's list.

That night on the radio, Shepherd could not get over the clerk's statement. He went off on a long riff about the hegemony of lists, about the sad specimens of humanity who defined their lives according to train schedules and appointment books and top-ten surveys and Best Picture lists. Clearly, some revenge was required against this Rule by List—and against this mindless bookshop clerk and all bookshop clerks.

"Let's all go to the local book stores tomorrow and ask for a book that we, the Night People, know doesn't exist," Shepherd said. For once, he opened the phones and asked the audience to help him dream up the perfect title and author for a book. Hundreds of calls later, at 4:30 A.M., a listener came up with *I, Libertine*. Shepherd contributed the author's name, Frederick R. Ewing, and together, Shep and the audience filled out Ewing's resume. A civil servant in Rhodesia, he was best known for his British Broadcasting Company radio talks on erotica of the eighteenth century. His novel had been published by Excelsior Press, an imprint of Cambridge University.

Today, their cover would be blown long before they could take action. But then, Shepherd had no doubt about trusting his listeners to keep the plan to themselves: "At 3 A.M., the people who believe in lists are asleep," he said. "Anyone still up at 3 A.M. secretly has some doubts."[14]

The next day, booksellers all over the Northeast told customers first that they had never heard of *I, Libertine*, and then, as the trickle of requests became a steady stream, that it was "on order" or "not quite out yet." Bookshops got on the horn to distributors, who in turn began pressing the publishers for information on the book that everyone wanted. Within days, libraries placed orders, and newspapers even listed *I, Libertine* among "recently published works." At parties, people pretended to have read the book and opined on its literary qualities. A student at Rutgers University taking a course called "The History of English Writing" wrote a term paper on the British historian F. R. Ewing, with footnotes and quotations from his famous BBC talks. The kid got a B+ and a note from the professor: "Superb research!" The Philadelphia Public Library opened a card file on Ewing. The Legion of Decency in Boston, as a matter of course, banned the book, which everyone said was quite bawdy. The *New York Post* gossip columnist Earl Wilson claimed in print to have "had lunch with Freddy Ewing yesterday"—an item planted by PR people who were Shepherd listeners.

At Ballantine Books, publisher Ian Ballantine, fascinated by the stories his salesmen told of customers clamoring for a book that appeared not to exist, tracked the story back to Shepherd and offered him a deal: Let's publish *I, Libertine.* Shepherd teamed with Theodore Sturgeon, a science fiction novelist, to write a novel set in England in the 1700s, telling the story of Lance Courtnay, a respectable figure by day who becomes a profligate rake by night. The cover, featuring a dashing and slightly winking English gentleman and drawn by an artist at *Mad* magazine, screamed, "Turbulent! Turgid! Tempestuous!" over the title. A caption under the gent read, " 'Gadzooks!' quoth I, 'but here's a saucy bawd!' "

A few weeks before the book's publication, a *Wall Street Journal* reporter sniffed out the whole story and wrote it onto the front page: "Night People's Hoax on Day People Makes Hit with Book Folks," the headline said.[15]

I, Libertine, with a huge initial press run of 130,000 copies, sold well for some years. Surviving copies today fetch $500 and more.

Alas, while Shepherd's listeners worshipped him, the overnight show failed to attract much in the way of paying sponsors, seeing as how account executives tended to be Day People and Shepherd himself could not be bothered with the glad-handing that stations asked of deejays. After only eight months of doing the all-night show, Shepherd was fired. Not enough sponsors, WOR management said.

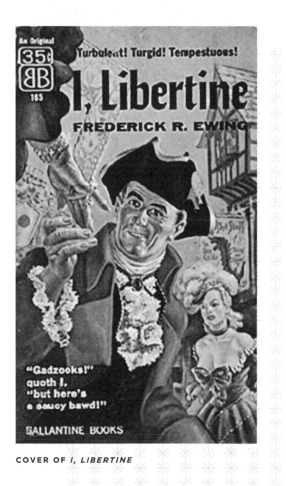

COVER OF *I, LIBERTINE*

"Four hundred followers of a nocturnal radio satirist who is about to be, as he put it, 'canned,' gathered in Manhattan last night 'in a final pitiful show of non-strength and disorganization,'" *The New York Times* reported on the day in 1956 after listeners learned of Shepherd's release. "They met out in front of the burned-out Wanamaker Building at Fourth Avenue and Eighth Street because they said they liked 'the Charles Addams feel of the thing.'"

McCandlish Phillips of the *Times* had a ball with his assignment. He had been sent to cover the oddest of demonstrations, the late-night gathering of "a quietly fanatic audience . . . of self-confessed eggheads, college students, artists, performers, semi-professional intellectuals." The *Times* didn't know quite what to make of this radio phenomenon, calling Shepherd "a spokesman for the Night People, who apparently are out of step with the whole order of things."

New York police herded the four hundred fans into a parking lot, where the subject of the protest addressed the crowd, railing against the mindless executives who had axed him. Radio, Shepherd said, was governed by the idea that "there is such a thing as an average man and that he's about 10 years old. They believe that nobody likes to hear talk. Putting on a pop record is the easy way out. It takes no ingenuity."[16] In passing, the *Times* mentioned that Shepherd was sacked because "he didn't sell soap."

After the protest and the press it received, WOR management gave Shepherd a one-week reprieve. Three nights into his return engagement, a listener called in to say that since the station believed Shepherd could not sell soap, each listener should go out and buy a bar of soap to prove WOR wrong. "After all, we Night People wash too," the caller said.

Shepherd loved the idea and batted it around with callers. They settled on Sweetheart Toilet Soap because it could use the exposure. Shepherd sang the praises of Sweetheart, then dispatched listeners to their local stores with instructions to buy a bar of the product, tell the shopkeeper that Shepherd sent them, and complete the transaction with the trademark Shepherd salutation, "Excelsior!"

Not that many minutes passed before station manager Bob Leder rang up the transmitter site in Carteret and ordered the engineer to pull Shepherd off the air. At 2:30 A.M., WOR switched to recorded music. The station announced once again that Shepherd was fired, this time because he "continually interjected unauthorized commercial material" into his program.

But fate again interceded on Shepherd's behalf. The makers of Sweetheart soap, touched by the display of affection for their product and by the sudden spike in sales, notified WOR that they would like to sponsor a radio program starring Jean Shepherd, nocturnal advocate for clean hands. WOR, knowing no shame, immediately agreed to the deal. But managers had one problem: they couldn't find Shepherd. Had he skipped town, or was he just playing hard to get? The station aired appeals to him to show his face. WOR placed ads in the New York newspapers in search of the missing minstrel of suds.

The station ordered Shepherd's replacement, an auctioneer and former vaudevillian from Parsippany, New Jersey, named Long John Nebel, to broadcast a plea for his predecessor to return.[17] That's how Shepherd, who had gone to Connecticut to make an educational film, heard that his mercurial employer had had another change of heart. The twice-fired talent signed on for a Sunday night program, sponsored by Sweetheart soap. Nebel kept the weekday overnight slot, where he hawked jewelry with mystical powers, introduced New Yorkers to a brash young man who called himself Malcolm X, and opened the airwaves to people who claimed they had been taken aboard UFOs. The passions of the night, as Shep had preached, knew no bounds.

AFTER MIDNIGHT—FREE FROM the tyranny of time and temp, news and ads—an individual intelligence on the radio finds listeners in cars and bars, tucked away in empty offices and wrinkled sheets. No focus groups or audience surveys govern the programming; ratings barely exist during those hours. Television has never made much of the overnight; the audiences just aren't large enough. The deep of the night is radio's time. In the same way that you speak to a friend more intimately on the phone than in person, for the same reason that Freud decided to have his patients face away from him, the oracles of overnight radio hold sway over an audience that can be frighteningly susceptible to suggestion.

From the first overnight show—Stan Shaw's *Milkman's Matinee* on WNEW in New York in 1935—it was clear that an audience was out there. At night, AM stations' signals carry with a cool-mint clarity, the great clear-channel, 50,000-watt sounds booming from the Northeast to the Midwest, from the Mississippi to the Potomac. The night brought far more than local audiences to Jean Shepherd, or to Herb Jepko, the genteel host of a far more reassuring program, *Nitecaps,* out of Salt Lake City's KSL. The Nitecappers were truckers, little old ladies, night clerks, and insomniacs who called Jepko's studio in Utah and chattered on about garden clubs, favorite recipes, and recent illnesses for five minutes each, at which point a gentle ring would interrupt, and Jepko would say, "I hear Tinker Bell," and it would be someone else's turn. From 1964 well into the 1980s, the show was the C-SPAN of all-night radio, but scrubbed clean of partisanship—a dispassionate forum for the anonymous, a collective expression of the insomniac's idle thoughts, fragments of daily experience flitting through the minds of too many people losing too many hours of sleep. Jepko—his voice an even, soothing, midwestern baritone—never judged, never criticized, never made fun. He didn't tell stories; he simply presided over a nonstop stream of verbal pitter-patter that sounded like a radio version of the quiet chuckles that passed for humor in the pages of *Reader's Digest.* Where C-SPAN blandly accepts every political view as equal and honorable, *Nitecaps* absorbed the night fears and frets of a restless people, smoothing out emotions twisted and exaggerated by the loneliness of the small hours. Like Shepherd's listeners, Nitecappers thought of themselves as members of a secret society. They held conventions of local chapters called Nitestands and published a magazine, *The Wick.* Long before the Internet, they invented a community that transcended geography.

They even shared an anthem: "We're the Nitecaps, nighty Nitecaps, and we hail from everywhere, but we meet and greet and reminisce when we broadcast over the air. . . . We love to hear each other chat, to hear each glad 'Hello!' But most of all we love to hear the voice of our own Herb Jepko. . . . On the quiet side, on the starry side, on the side where the moonbeams play, on the brand-new side of the day."

Jepko's quiet club reflected both the optimism and social repression of the country that produced Lawrence Welk and Billy Graham, Norman Vincent Peale and citizens band radio. No discussion of religion or politics was permitted ("I believe it is my obligation as a Nitecap not to carp and criticize," said the Nitecap Creed, which Nitecappers eagerly signed). That the host and chief Nitecapper was himself an alcoholic would never have been discussed on his program.

As welcoming as Jepko may have sounded, it was Long John Nebel, Shepherd's replacement in the overnight slot, who became king of the night. A former carnival huckster who once sold lucky numbers on the streets of downtown Washington, Nebel was above all a pitchman, and whether the product was vitamins, UFOs, mysterious sand dollars with healing powers, or vast conspiracies against President Kennedy, Nebel sold hard. He knew the night was darker than anything Jepko could countenance. He milked the fears of those who could not sleep. As long as they were up at one in the morning, they might as well stay up with him till five. Nebel transfixed generations of listeners with guests who were eyewitnesses to alien invasions, CIA mind control experiments, and the inventions of great American products. No topic served him as well as the JFK assassination; he returned to the theme literally hundreds of times, taking at face value any and every notion about conspirators, methods, and motives. He did this not simply because he was a showman but because he genuinely believed that if he put in all those hours and set his listeners to talking with his guests, they could make progress against the mysteries of the nation's darkest chapters. "I don't know, myself," he'd often say. "We're just exploring."

Nebel could explore—and pitch—parapsychology one minute and Chock Full o'Nuts doughnuts the next. He might spend four hours chatting up Malcolm X, then a solid half hour on the wonders of White Castle hamburgers. Whatever the topic, Nebel knew that to connect, he had only to intimate that there was something out there beyond what was already known. He sold the idea that someone was hiding something. It was information that John Q. Citizen did not have, but information that could be had right here on the radio, in the night, when the underbelly of a nation could be probed as it never could be by day.

Nebel stayed up all night with his listeners for a quarter of a century, first alone and in his later years with his wife, Candy Jones, a former model who claimed, with fairly persuasive evidence later borne out by a congressional investigation, to have been subjected to mind control experiments by U.S. intelligence agents. Nebel took listeners deep into the Twilight Zone, giving airtime to people who had been abducted and taken to Mars, to just about anyone who showed up at the studio. "The show was wide open," Nebel said. "We had sandwiches and people would just come up and not necessarily even get on the air." The door was unlocked; listeners could and did wander by.

If some of those people turned out to be less than credible, no matter—there was always another show the next night. For a long time, Nebel had a regular guest he billed as his science expert, Dr. Daniel Fry, an engineer at Aerojet Corporation. As Nebel told it, the man was a seminal figure in the history of air-conditioning technology. Only after many months of appearances on the show did Nebel learn that Dr. Fry was indeed in the air conditioning department of Aerojet: "He changed the filters." Nebel kept right on introducing the good doctor as his science expert. (Fry *was* an expert on explosives who was best known for his claim to have had contact with aliens in 1950.)

Until Nebel came along, telephone calls on the radio were usually one-way conversations. Because there was no way to ensure that the caller wouldn't curse, early talk hosts alone would listen to the call, entertain the audience with the occasional "Mmm-hmmm," and then paraphrase the comments. Nebel was one of several radio talkers and engineers who claimed to have invented the tape-delay machine that made it possible to put callers directly on the air; whoever deserves credit, Nebel was one of the first to build a show around listener calls.

But what he did best was sell. "People think I can pitch anything," he said. At the time, Nebel was selling space in a mausoleum. When fellow talk show host Barry Gray heard Nebel's pitch, he said, "He makes me want to move in for a weekend."

I spent a night in Nebel's studio during the final months of his life. Cancer had rendered him sleepless and gaunt, his voice diminished and soured. But when it came time to sell, he was once more the carny barker of old, the salesman who had discovered how night made listeners impressionable. "To sell mausoleums sounds like a big deal," Nebel told me and a fellow reporter.[18] "But it's going great." Whereupon he spent five minutes trying to sell us on the product. "A mausoleum is clean, neat. There's no connection with soil. There's no connection with a hole in the ground. There's no connection with water seeping in. It's easier on those you leave behind. It's not gruesome—it's very neat, a beautiful building. Digging a hole, putting a person in it . . ."

NEBEL HELD ON TO the all-night perch at WOR, but Shepherd remained on the station's schedule for twenty-one years, eventually relegated to a single hour each weeknight. Along the way, he did sell soap—but in a way that Madison Avenue wouldn't catch on to for many years. Shepherd's nightly command to his engineer to "hit the money button," his tendency to sing along lustily with the General Tires jingle (General owned WOR), and his frequent jabs at his own sponsors (after a beer spot, "Isn't it wonderful to be able to measure your happiness in empty flip-top cans?") foreshadowed the cynical self-mockery that would come to dominate advertising decades later.

Shepherd's improvised commercials winked and nudged at his listeners just as his stories did. In a 1965 spot for Miller beer, Shepherd scats along over a brassy big-band music bed and vamps his way through the ad, tossing the official copy aside: "Ooh, the glow of hospitality, the sparkle of friendship, those merry hiccoughs! These are the qualities that you pour with every glass of sparkling, flavorful, distinctive Miller High Life. Hoo-hoo! High Life, the *sham-pag-nee* of bottled beer, this beer . . . brewed for centuries in a musty old European castle. . . . You say *Wa-hoo!* when you pour Miller High Life." He sings along with the Miller theme and when the music cuts out, Shepherd sighs and adds, "Ah, right, we took care of that account, didn't we?" (Actually, Shepherd's playful approach to the Miller spots—"If you're gonna lay in a real trough full of genuine, vibrant suds, we can only recommend one"—were credited with establishing High Life, then new to the East Coast, as a top brand. "If you're gonna tie one on this weekend, tie it on in style. . . . You can get it in the magnificent champagne golden can, which makes a nice clink when it hits the sidewalk.")[19]

WOR never quite knew what to do with Shepherd; until the station finally let him go in 1977, he floated around the schedule with no connection to what aired before or after. Shepherd wasn't an easy fit anywhere. He appeared at nightclubs, in Carnegie Hall, in marathon monologue performances on college campuses. He published stories in *Playboy* and *Mad.* He hosted NBC's *Today* show for a week; a morning man he was not. He made two series of travelogues, *Jean Shepherd's America,* for public television. He was the model for the all-night radio talker in Jack Kerouac's *On the Road,* and for the Nightfly, the radio voice Steely Dan creator Donald Fagen wrote about in his song of that name, and for David Staebler, the Jack Nicholson character in the 1972 movie *The King of Marvin Gardens,* in which the Shepherd figure is a creepy loner who comes alive only when the red light switches on for his late-night radio talk show. You hear traces of Shepherd in Garrison Keillor's monologues about life in Lake Wobegon, Minnesota, and in Ira Glass's reporting on public radio's *This American Life.*

Shepherd collected his stories in several books, and in what has nearly displaced *It's a Wonderful Life* as the archetypal American holiday movie, *A Christmas Story,* which now airs to a cult following in twenty-four-hour marathons each December on the TBS cable channel. Shepherd wrote and narrated the movie, which threatens to become his only mass-market legacy; it tells the story of Ralphie Parker—Shepherd's middle name is Parker—a nine-year-old boy who is obsessed with acquiring the holy grail of Christmas gifts, an Official Red Ryder Carbine Action 200-Shot Range Model Air Rifle. "You'll shoot your eye out, kid," the entire world tells him. Shepherd's knowing narration adds enough grit to save the movie from falling entirely into sentimentality. But *A Christmas Story* is not the Shepherd known to the Night People.

Shepherd's rambling, mischievous ways, along with his baroque comic book vocabulary—"phantasmagoria," "gallimaufry"—and his never-ending reworkings of his childhood stories were the work of a jazz artist, a radio poet who did with words what Charlie Parker and Charles Mingus did with notes.[20]

Because of when he hit the scene and how he riffed, Shepherd is sometimes lumped with Lenny Bruce and the Beat poets, with the true rebels of the 1950s. But he shares with them only a love for the improvised life and a willingness to call his country's bluff. Stifled by society's conformist mask, poetry, the visual arts, comedy, and jazz all made a sharp turn in the late 1950s, becoming at once angrier and more cerebral. Bruce, Mort Sahl, Mike Nichols, and Elaine May appealed to a more educated elite; jazz's new avant-garde scorned the music's popular roots and veered into an academic alley. Even *Mad* magazine, where virtually everything in American life was "sick," hawked a version of America much darker than Shepherd's. Shep bought Jack Kerouac's celebration of "wild self-believing individuality," but he couldn't stomach Kerouac's lust for experiences beyond the norms of middle American existence.[21] For Shepherd, the great material and the great joys were hidden in plain view in a standard Indiana childhood, in the supposedly bland middle of the country, in the clash between the great American desire to conform and the greater American passion to stand out.

Shepherd never fit in. He married, had two children, and then walked away, ignoring his boy and girl for the rest of his life. He wouldn't talk about them with the people he worked with. Those who loved Shepherd's words often found that they had to ignore his deeds because he had little patience for anyone except his third wife and longtime producer, Leigh Brown. For all his insight into the lives of those in his stories, he steered clear of his own past except in fictionalized form, sweetened or soured for an audience he denigrated at every opportunity. Radio, Shepherd insisted, was an inferior art form, a commercial endeavor unworthy of a real writer. Yet radio provided Shepherd's greatest success, and in some elemental way, he knew it was his calling. In 1968, after seeing Samuel Beckett's play *Krapp's Last Tape,* about an old man who despairingly looks back at his years by reviewing his recorded musings, Shepherd told listeners that this "was the story of a man who tape-recorded things as he went along in life. Now that's very different from making a diary, you know. A lot of people keep diaries. And a diary is an incomplete record, because when you sit down to write—you're inhibited. The fact of writing itself inhibits most people. The most *natural* form of communication is the voice. . . .

"But *Krapp's Last Tape* was about a man who, every day, would record things on his little tape recorder. He'd sit there and he'd talk about his life. Now he didn't talk about the things that were happening, like, 'Today, Normandy was invaded.' When you talk into the tape recorder you do something else, see. You're very personal, generally. So he talked about the things that he was thinking about during the day. . . .

"And one of the things that fascinated me about *Krapp's Last Tape* is this is *definitely*, in a very real way, a play about the story of my life. . . . Not many people have recorded every day, forty-five minutes or so of their thoughts on life and existence and the passing scene."

Shepherd did. And the more his audience appreciated what he did, the more he seemed to retreat. Like his Old Man in his stories, Shep thrived on frustration and the frayed nerves of modern life—little failures were his oxygen, and when he succeeded, his instinct was not to dive into life or to share his happiness, but to go away, off to Alaska and later to an isolated spot on a Florida island, where he would die alone, considering himself a flop.

Shepherd succeeded on radio because he was neither elitist nor rebel. He knew that in life, there is little more powerful than the desire to belong, to be a part of something larger, something good. He could be vaguely anarchic, slightly dangerous, but his invitations to the fringe were always cloaked in an affectionate, affirming voice; his wildest lunges were always contained by the unyielding structure of the show, forty-five minutes, theme song to theme song. He was your odd uncle, an inspiration but never a danger.

He had no patience for those who sought only to tear down. "Most hippies come from affluent families," he told listeners one night in

1965. "They're trying to run away from their past." Another time he said of the radicals who were creating a counterculture: "I know these cats. They pad around the East Village. 'Legalize pot, race, war' and jazz like that. Deadly serious, like Nazis. I've met them down in the Cost and Accounting Department too, clean-shaven and in white collars. They can't see a damn thing ridiculous about themselves—only about you."[22]

Like the comic strip *Pogo,* another errant spring in the vinyl-slipcovered sofa of the 1950s, Shepherd found the soft spot between the fringe and the mass. He knew it was quintessentially American to scoff at the mass even as you were part of it. That's why *Playboy* chose Shepherd to conduct its interview of the Beatles—Shepherd was no rocker, but he would get that Americans desperately wanted to believe in the Fab Four, even as they watched the whole crazy phenomenon with one eyebrow arched.

"I began to feel special myself because they talked to me," Shepherd said of his encounter with the Beatles. "I said, 'What are you doing—this is a rock-and-roll group! What are you doing, Shepherd?' " He knew that even with his advanced degree in skepticism, he would do the American thing and cave to the power of celebrity, privately raging against the silliness of it all, but, when it came to the public moment itself, sheepishly submitting to authority and expectations, just as his Old Man did in his stories.

His fantasy was that his audience would come together in our conformity and loneliness. "Have you ever had the feeling the other people swing more than you do?" Shepherd asked in one of his live broadcasts from the Limelight, a Greenwich Village nightclub where he would take to the stage in black turtleneck, cords, and leather boots to deliver two-hour monologues to young couples out on dates. "That's part of that sense we all have of vaguely being cheated. *Other* guys meet the most fantastic chicks. Do you know, right here in this room, as I look down, I can see guys looking at chicks at other tables that are with guys who are looking at chicks at other tables! This gigantic chain of discontent!"

Late in the American night, when the commutes are over and there is a narrow window of calm, the lists are put away and the schedules empty out. In that space, Jean Shepherd discovered, radio could connect to the imagination as no medium had before. Shepherd created a new art form, finally putting to use the quiet hours in each spin of the planet. More important, he found a way into the souls of people in their beds and in their cars, those whom the *American Dictionary of Slang* credits Shepherd with dubbing "Night People."

"Every one of us," Shepherd said, "I don't care who he is, has a certain amount of Night People in him. Because no matter how many refrigerators you buy from [TV ad pitchman] Betty Furness, no matter how many 'custom' suits you buy, no matter how many cars with fins you buy, you're still an individual. And I'll say this: Once a guy starts thinking, once a guy starts laughing at the things he once thought were very real, once he starts laughing at TV commercials, once he starts getting a hoot out of movie trailers, once he begins to realize that just because a movie is wider or higher or longer doesn't make it a better movie, once a guy starts doing that, he's making the transition from Day People to Night People.

"And once this happens, he can never go back."[23]

IN HIS BUNK at a North Carolina military base, Robert Morton Fass, draftee late of Brooklyn, New York, starved for a bit more irony and wit than the United States Army's training programs provided, tucked his transistor radio under the pillow and tuned to WOR's powerhouse signal from New York City. Despite his exhaustion, Fass stayed up into the night listening to Jean Shepherd, marveling at his improvisational confidence, excited by the mystery, the impossibility of knowing what might come next.

Fass was, he told himself, an actor, a student of the theater. He had lived vicariously through the radio since boyhood. After listening to the stories on Ransom Sherman's *Club Matinee* program on NBC one day, Fass tried to copy one of Sherman's characters, who left the scene by smashing through a plate glass window. In his Brooklyn living room, the boy got a running start and hurled himself at the window. He did manage to put his hand through the glass.

Fass made a pretend radio with his Erector set and practiced speaking into the microphone for hours on end. He and his friends sat on the stoop at East Twenty-sixth Street and Avenue K and Bob introduced them to folk music. At Midwood High School, he got picked to make the announcements over the intercom system each morning and, his brother Dick recalled, "Bob felt like he was making a discovery about himself. He found that he could change himself and the people around him with his voice." Like Cousin Brucie, Bob was chosen to join New York's All City Radio Workshop, a daily adventure in radio theater for budding broadcasters and actors. At home, listening with his brother to Shepherd each night, Bob became enraptured with recording sound, capturing voices. At sixteen, he pleaded with his father for a wire recorder, the early version of the tape recorder.

Fass's father, an accountant, saw no reason why Bob should not proceed into the family business. Failing that, he was supposed to be a used-car dealer (his father, who did the books for car sellers, pictured them as the image of success). But Fass—tall, blond, with a golden voice and a gentle manner—was, despite his shyness, drawn to performance, to the anonymity of radio, and then to the nowhere-to-hide stage of the theater. Bob was embarrassed by attention from others, yet at the same time relished being at the center. He directed plays in the Army, then worked his way into off-Broadway and summer stock productions while stumbling from factory work to a job as copy boy at *Time* magazine. He wandered the downtown scene at night, frequenting the coffeehouses and folk music clubs that popped up in Greenwich Village as an escape from the frenetic commercialism of the rapidly suburbanizing Top 40 society. And when he got home, Fass turned to Shepherd, to those nightly glimpses of an opposing reality. Shepherd's message, Fass thought, was that you didn't have to accept the world as it was. You could insist on another version.

Fass's breakthrough came unexpectedly. In 1958, he met someone who was in a long-running play at the Theatre de Lys, a prestigeful off-Broadway address. They needed an actor to fill a minor role, and the previous occupant of the position had been a tall fellow, like Fass. "You fit the costume!" Fass was told, and suddenly he was Smith the Jailer in Brecht's *Threepenny Opera*. Fass spent nearly three years in the role and loved it. A life in the theater leaves days free for other pursuits, and Fass, through acting acquaintances, volunteered to read stories and novels at WBAI, an odd little FM radio station that aired literary readings, radio drama, classical music, jazz, the occasional academic lecture, and a program titled *Existentialism for Young People*.

Fass had been listening to the station for a few years, intrigued by its high-toned intellectual fare. When a job opened for a staff announcer, his fluid, deep voice seemed perfect. Plus, WBAI was paying $80 a week, a good bit more than a small part in an off-Broadway production paid. Fass took the job, which consisted largely of telling listeners "You are about to hear . . ." and "You have just heard . . ."

Like so many others in radio, Fass was shy and quiet off the air. But in the soundproof room, alone with the microphone, he imagined another place, where he and his friends could break free of the restrictions of a society that didn't know what to do with misfits and outcasts, with the kind of person who could really speak his mind only when he was alone in a dark room. It would take him years to figure out how to create that place on the radio, but when he did, Bob Fass and his *Radio Unnameable* would inspire a monsoon of musical, sexual, pharmacological, political, and social change. No one would shout "Excelsior!" but Bob Fass would grab hold of the spirit of Jean Shepherd, mix in the confidence and righteousness of a generation that had bonded over Top 40 and the Beatles, and create something entirely new.

Chapter 6

✳ THE JINGLE-JANGLE MORNING

M IDNIGHT ARRIVES IN SILENCE, just enough silence to induce mortal panic in any radio professional. The gap, only a few seconds, is long enough to encourage a quick-fingered listener to punch up a different station. But at exactly the moment when it seems as if this station perhaps has fallen off the air, a large man with a tiny ponytail leans into the microphone, inhales deeply and loudly, waits another long second, and, in a soft tone that seems impossibly restrained for a man of his bulk, says, "This is WBAI in New York City. Preceding program brought to you on recording. This is *Radio Unnameable*. My name's Bob Fass." Then, in barely more than a whisper, "Good morning, cabal."

And then another beat, and, depending on the night and the year, the next sound is Bob Dylan's first appearance on the radio (not as a singer, but as a comic actor, an improv specialist doing wicked parody of New York's Living Theater productions); or the first version of Arlo Guthrie's "Alice's Restaurant," which Bob Fass liked so much he played it over and over for the better part of five hours; or phone calls from Abbie and Anita Hoffman announcing that they've been sitting with friends and listening to Fass and they've decided to start a political party and they're going to call it the Youth International Party, the Yippies; or a Hare Krishna chant laid over a recording of a speech by

Adolf Hitler; or a live report from a WBAI newsman who has just been beaten by New York City police officers at a gathering of hippies in Grand Central Station; or a recitation by Marshall Efron of the

BOB FASS   *(Courtesy Robert Altman)*

"Poetry of Donald H. Rumsfeld," in which snippets of random thoughts from the secretary of defense's news briefings are connected to make him sound like a Beat poet.

Fass himself might not speak again for fifteen minutes, or for an

hour, or for the rest of the night. He might take phone calls from listeners, and he might put several of them on the air at once, asking them to "speak among yourselves."

Since 1962, *Radio Unnameable* has aired starting at midnight on WBAI-FM. For most of the 1960s and '70s, the show ran from midnight until at least 5 A.M., Monday through Friday. In recent years, Fass has been on the radio only one or two nights a week. From the start, the program had no format. It was an art piece, created anew each night, an improvised mélange of sound—live music, recorded speeches, random phone calls, eyewitness reports from war zones and urban conflicts, recitations of poetry and prose, solicitations for political causes eternal and evanescent, advertisements for illegal drugs, experiments with noise and beauty and silence.

Bob Fass recruited thousands of young people, many of them stoned, to join him at JFK Airport for a Fly-In. He lured them to the East Village to clean up the city's filthy streets—the Sweep-In. He invited them to Grand Central Station to confront the police and alert the city that it had a new force in its midst—the Yip-In. He did this not so much as a political activist or a Yippie prankster but as an actor developing a new kind of performance, a long-running play that continues to this day, long after most of its audience has aged beyond its ability to stay up even until midnight, let alone through to dawn.

FASS DIDN'T CLAIM to have anything particularly novel to offer when he asked the bosses at WBAI if he could expand his announcing job to include the hours after 1 A.M., when the station normally signed off before coming on again at sunrise. Sure, go ahead, came the response, and so he did. He thought he might play some music—he was a constant presence at the Greenwich Village coffeehouses where Phil Ochs and other emerging folkies were testing their new songs. Maybe he'd throw in some bits of theater, maybe spin some of the odd records he picked up at secondhand shops in the Village.

No one at the station cared much what Fass did on his show—after midnight, who was listening? So if Fass played a record called "How to

Teach Your Parakeet to Talk" just because he thought it was funny, no one complained. And if he took a tape recorder out to the coffeehouses and played the results on the radio, calling his show "Coffee Grounds," that was just fine. Fass's was the first radio show to feature a strange, falsetto-voiced singer who called himself Tiny Tim and sang songs that simultaneously paid tribute to the a cappella groups of the 1930s and spoofed the corporate music machine. On one of those first nights on the air, the stage manager of an off-Broadway show in which Fass was performing urged him to put a friend of his sister's on the radio, a guy named Bob Dylan who was a gifted parodist and, by the way, a singer too. Dylan came on and pretended to be the chief of a company that made clothing for folksingers.

Fass was, from the start, willing. "I tried to make it as unlike anything else as I could," he said. "I wanted to put my culture on the air— the Greenwich Village *cul-chah*—politics and exotic people. I'd put anyone on, because the idea was that if you didn't like what I was doing, three minutes later I'd be doing something else."

This, as the show's title suggested, was radio you could neither define nor name. It was the product of three turntables, one tape machine, and Fass's burgeoning library of tape—boxes piled in random stacks in his apartment on Cornelius Street in the Village and around the WBAI studios. Fass, like Jean Shepherd, insisted that his show reflect the moment, that it be improvised on the spot. The show was supposed to be as messy and wild as his apartment, a cornucopia of random possibility presenting itself as an alternative to a culture that valued order and certainty.

Fass had heard about another all-night show, out in Berkeley, where John Leonard's *Nightsounds* had evolved into a mix of jazz, poetry, political commentary, and satire bits. Fass did all that but added the sounds of the city he loved, collages of music and speech, a kind of radio free association. "When two pieces of information bump up against each other, something else occurs," Fass said. "Dylan sings 'While riding on a train going west,' and I juxtapose sounds of war and battle, and it creates a third thing, one commenting on the other."

"Everybody must get stoned," Dylan sang, and marijuana was a constant on *Radio Unnameable*, both as subject and as binding agent between host and guests and between host and audience. Station management officially didn't know and unofficially didn't much care—if Fass's idea of expanding horizons was to conduct his show in an altered state, that was cool. "Drugs were as much a part of Fass's show as coffee was for Arthur Godfrey," the genial morning man of 1940s and '50s radio, said Larry Josephson, who was WBAI's manager for a time in the 1970s. Memoirs of the 1960s are packed with references to heading over to BAI to get high and talk on Bob Fass's radio—folksingers and rockers, Yippies, gay activists, early feminists. Name the cause and its leaders were on the show, and often on something.

By being open about drugs, Fass built enormous credibility on the street. Callers often asked Fass about the quality of acid being sold at particular locations in the Village. When callers needed to be talked down from a bad acid trip—Fass always could tell by his phone calls when new acid had arrived in town—he would ring up Maggie Mandel, a psychiatrist in training, and she'd talk to the frightened listener on the air. If that didn't work, Fass would make house calls, signing WBAI off the air to visit a caller's house and calm a frightened soul.

But it was far more than drugs that inspired the nightly mix. "I was influenced by psychotherapy," Fass said, "by the idea of encouraging someone to talk—give them enough rope and you learn who they are." He brought in representatives of a group called Stamp Out Smut to rail against the profane comedy of Lenny Bruce—and then Fass rolled tape of Bruce's manic monologues. In 1963, Fass traveled to Washington to take part in the civil rights march at which Martin Luther King, Jr., made his celebrated "I Have a Dream" speech. Fass brought back tape and played it on the air. He recorded and aired everything.

Fass had no idea what to call this relationship he had created with his listeners. He asked his audience for help. "It was mainly to generate mail, to show the daytime people at BAI that there was an audience out there," he said. "I asked people to suggest a collective noun. Someone came up with *cabal*, and I thought, 'Very appropriate.' I looked it up and the dictionary said something like 'people who meet secretly, mostly at night, their identities unknown even to each other.' And here

we were, people talking to each other, the dishwasher talking to someone from the Harvard Club."

From that night on, Fass opened each program with the same
greeting: "Good morning, cabal."

AS RADIO BECAME A UTILITY, something you had on in the background
of life, Bob Fass became the nocturnal distortion of that omnipres-
ence. He was the opposite of Top 40. Fass was the guy who stopped
the clock and dared to broadcast the silence and the shouts of rage and
the bliss of altered consciousness. Fass was the voice of the new radio
and the counterculture—gentle, seductive, timeless. He was the vanguard of a revolution called FM.

From the beginning of AM radio, static was the big problem.
Lightning, electrical appliances, even streetlamps could render station
signals a staccato mess of spine-tingling noise. David Sarnoff, the
radio pioneer whose Radio Corporation of America gave birth to
NBC and eventually ABC as well, put his technical wizard, Edwin
Armstrong of Columbia University, to work on the problem in the
1920s. By 1933, Armstrong had developed the solution: frequency
modulation, or FM. The idea was to boost the bandwidth of the radio
signal and eliminate interference from other energy waves. By shifting
radio to very high frequencies and adding circuits that separated the
FM signal from most sources of interference, you could broadcast
music and voice with far superior sound fidelity. The only disadvantage
Armstrong could see was that FM signals carried only fifty miles or so.
Because FM signals don't bounce off the ionosphere as AM signals do,
they fall off Earth as the planet curves.

There was one other big downside to FM: no one owned radios capable of receiving it. The industry was concentrated on selling AM
sets. Sarnoff didn't want to switch gears and ask the American people
to buy entirely new kinds of radios. More interested in developing television than in hawking another flavor of radio, he shelved Armstrong's project.

The engineer would not give up. He devoted the rest of his life to selling the concept. It wouldn't be easy. Armstrong did persuade the Federal Communications Commission to award licenses for FM stations starting in 1940. But then came the war and all manufacture of radios ceased. After the war, the FCC moved the FM band to a new set of frequencies, rendering all prewar FM radios obsolete. (RCA pushed for that change to free up bandwidth for television. RCA also refused to pay royalties to Armstrong, who personally licensed the manufacture of all FM radios in the United States. Armstrong was so financially damaged and emotionally aggrieved that he sued his former employer. The legal battle would drag on for the rest of Armstrong's days.)[1]

Armstrong's political battle on behalf of his invention premiered FM's role as a renegade, anti-corporate, anti–mass medium. The radio industry, knowing that FM might eventually overtake the dominant AM technology, fought Armstrong to the end. His patents on FM expired in 1950. In 1954, financially ruined and in poor health, he jumped out of the thirteenth-story window of his Manhattan apartment.

Not long after Armstrong died, his estate won its case against RCA. Then the march of progress finally accomplished what Armstrong had not: the introduction of stereo records in 1957 fed a growing popular appetite for "hi-fi," top-quality sound systems that took advantage of the new 33⅓ rpm, long-playing discs, which generated much less noise and achieved finer reproduction than the old 78s. Veterans coming home from the military brought with them a new penchant for things technical. Magazines such as *Popular Mechanics* and *High Fidelity* won huge audiences; the popular press commiserated with female readers in articles such as "I Am a Hi-Fi Widow" and "The High Fidelity Wife, or a Fate Worse Than Deaf."[2]

In 1961, the FCC approved stereo broadcasting on FM; in 1963, FM car radios were introduced; and in 1964, the feds decreed that in big cities, AM stations that owned FMs had to cease simulcasting and put original programming on their FM stations for at least half of each day. The FCC gave owners until 1967 to comply, but the feds meant business: the AM band was full up with stations, while FM sat ready for an explosion of commerce. Station owners fought to hang on to the old ways. Todd Storz, believing always in mass audience rather than any appeal to special interests, never ventured into FM; Gordon McLendon lobbied Washington against the new order.[3] But while AM remained king, the nation's listeners were testing out a new dimension in sound, snapping up stereo novelty records (the sound of a Ping-Pong game, the ball bouncing from left speaker to right and back again; the roar of a car engine sweeping across the living room from one speaker to the other).

Slowly, radio makers started marketing AM-FM table radios and hi-fi sets equipped with stereo speakers and FM bands. Between 1960 and 1965, the number of FM sets in use soared from 6 million to 30 million. Five years after that, it was 93 million.[4]

In the early 1960s, FM remained the province of the privileged, appealing primarily to educated and affluent pockets in places such as New York, Washington, Boston, and San Francisco. FM meant the classics and Broadway show tunes—1961's top five bestselling LPs included two Broadway cast albums, *Camelot* and *The Sound of Music,* as well as the soundtrack to the movie *Never on Sunday*—which were rarely played on AM radio. AM listeners bought 45 rpm singles—period. FM also served up "beautiful music," the purportedly inoffensive background sounds designed to fill the silences in elevators and dental offices. In Houston, this was marketed as "The Velvet Touch" from KODA; in New York, as "The Sound of the Good Life" from WPIX's PIX Penthouse. None of this required much effort or any significant spending on talent. FM was a music service and that was that.

This did not sit well with the federal government. The FCC still regulated the architecture of broadcasting's content.[5] Television (*Bonanza! Gomer Pyle! Green Acres! Andy Griffith!*) mostly ignored the FCC's concept of the public interest. TV looked away from a nation that was hurtling down the road to a confrontation with its children, with black America, and with women. The TV networks offered an occasional documentary, but entertainment programming steered clear of the nation's fraying edges. AM radio had opened the door to a blending of the races and spoke at least superficially to a new generation's pace and identity. But AM also ignored that generation's political yearnings. The mass media offered hardly any outlet for the alienation and tough questions that were pushing their way to the surface. But the assassination of John Kennedy, the first battles of the civil rights movement, the initial cries of campus protest, the acid commentaries of comedians such as Lenny Bruce and Dick Gregory, and the sudden popularity of politically charged folk music called out for a place in the popular media.

FM radio stood empty and waiting.

THERE WERE NO GUARDS, no receptionists at WBAI's studios at midnight. As word spread about *Radio Unnameable*, Fass was rarely alone. People just walked in to watch, listen, share a joint, groove to the tunes. As Fass's crowd blossomed, his silences grew more daring, his content more challenging. "At this time, WBAI concludes another day of scaring people," Fass once signed off. He let his hair grow. The other guys at the station started seeing the same women return night after night to be with the man behind that seductive bass, and when daylight came, one of the "Fassbunnies," as his jealous colleagues dubbed them, would head home with the voice himself. Over time, Fass spoke less and less on the air; it was as if the show conducted itself, going where the spirit might take it. As Miles Davis once said of his own embrace of silence, Fass chose "not to play all the notes you could play, but to wait, hesitate, let space become a part of the configuration."

Fass developed regulars—artists, activists, and Village people who came by to pass the night. As Dylan became a folk hero, he made the show a regular habit, performing not only his comic monologues (his characters included Rory Grossman, Rumple Billy Burp, Elvis Bickel, and Frog Rugster) but his new songs. One night, Dylan fielded calls from listeners for a couple of hours. A starstruck high school student begged Dylan to endorse his decision to wear his hair long in violation of school rules. Nothing doing, the rebel replied—do as you're told. Dylan grew hungry and hijacked Fass's show to implore any and all cabbies who might be listening to bring food to the WBAI studios. (Several showed up.) The singer chastised a listener for tuning in to noncommercial radio "just to make yourself feel better." Throughout the night, Dylan cajoled the few female callers into describing their bodies in ever more glorious detail.

Richie Havens, Judy Collins, Arlo Guthrie, and others stopped by to sing and hang out. Guthrie developed "Alice's Restaurant" on the show, performing it in several versions over many months. After one performance in 1966, the listener reaction was so powerful, and Fass so taken by the number, that he repeated the tape all night, and kept playing it for weeks until crowds demanded it wherever Guthrie performed. *Radio Unnameable* listeners knew that "you can get anything you want at Alice's Restaurant," and they knew it long before the song was finally released commercially, eight months after premiering on WBAI.[6]

A few months after that visit by Guthrie, Jerry Jeff Walker dropped in with accompanist David Bromberg, and at about 4 A.M., they played a song about a down-and-out street dancer in New Orleans. A girl called Fass to say the song was "like not being alone anymore." Fass, captivated by the song, taped it and played it several times the next night, and the night after, and on and on, spinning it as if he were a Top 40 jock hyping a new tune on the super swinging survey. Immediately, record companies besieged WBAI with calls; they wanted to put that song on vinyl. A year later, "Mr. Bojangles" became a hit, and Walker credited Fass with creating the demand.

Fass's Village neighbors, Abbie Hoffman and his wife, Anita, saw *Radio Unnameable* as the perfect vehicle for their various causes. Hoffman was a civil rights activist who ran Liberty House, a Village crafts shop that sold items made by Southern blacks and used the profits to fund voter registration and literacy drives down South. Abbie and Anita would lie in their bed, covered with an American flag spread, listening to "Radio Bob," as Abbie called him, phoning in to talk politics, national and neighborhood.

Activists used the show to reveal themselves, turning politics into a catalogue of personal experiences. But Fass steadfastly kept his life to himself. He spoke through the music and the mix, but there would be no confessionals, no childhood stories. Unlike Shepherd's bottomless reservoir of allegories from the American Midwest, Fass saw no message, no art in his own family's journey from the fringes of the immigrant nation to mainstream success. Listeners had no idea that Fass came from a line of Jewish renegades who'd raised hell in the streets of New York. They heard nothing about Bob's brother the oncologist or his father the accountant. On the radio, Fass played a man who was at once rebellious, seductive, and soothing. He was no phony; his character was true to himself, but this was only a piece of Bob Fass. The other side of Fass, the shy, socially awkward boy from Brooklyn, remained safely off-mike.

In bedrooms all over the New York area, kids with new FM radios stumbled upon Fass and became addicted. Some of the voices that would break the last taboos in talk radio a generation later were in that audience—Howard Stern, Tom Leykis, and other future shock jocks—hearing things on FM they'd never heard on AM Top 40. Fass knew the city was changing; he could feel it every night. "Something cracked and America said, 'Wow, I don't have to be like that anymore. I can be' "—and Fass slipped into his buttery, groovy FM voice—" 'like this.' "

Lynne Tofte, one of those women who simply had to go down to the station to see who was behind this voice, was "wasting away on Staten Island, twelve years old and looking for folk music on the radio, and I found Bob. He brought me art, music, poetry, ways to think. He told me the Vietnam War was wrong, which nobody on Staten Island was saying. Night after night, he was my friend when I had no friends. I hardly went to high school because I would take No-Doz to stay up and listen to him and Abbie Hoffman and Marshall Efron. It was like they were planning a revolution and I heard it all."

When she was fourteen and visiting WBAI on an errand for a New Jersey radio station where she had volunteered, Tofte caught a glimpse of Fass through the studio glass. Nine years later, while working as an astrologer, she dropped by the station to get a closer look at the man she'd spent half her life listening to. "I got knocked over by the energy," she said. Like many of those who worked at the station, she managed to finagle a staff position mainly by hanging around. She became the record librarian and got to know her radio hero. They have lived together since the 1980s and were married in 1997.

By 1967, with protests against the Vietnam War bubbling up around the country, Fass moved more and more into politics. His friends Hoffman and radical essayist and comedian Paul Krassner were on the show often, and the combination of Hoffman's penchant for the theatrical, Krassner's puckish wit, Fass's hunger to be different, and their common passion for getting high combined to turn WBAI's *Radio Unnameable* into the birthing room of the counterculture.

THE STATION THAT GAVE itself over to Fass's all-night explorations was the hobby of an eccentric millionaire who owned patents on the paper used in the manufacture of tampons. Louis Schweitzer—who, as it turned out, also owned the Theatre de Lys, where Fass had made his off-Broadway acting debut—bought WBAI in 1955 because he wanted to hear more classical music and news of events *The New York Times* was not covering. Schweitzer picked WBAI because he could see its transmitter from his apartment at the Hotel Pierre.[7] This was entirely in keeping with Schweitzer's method of choosing his purchases: when he was unable to get his hair cut as he wished, he bought a barbershop and hired a barber named, legend has it, Louis Schweitzer. When his wife was frustrated in her efforts to hail a taxi, Schweitzer bought a Mercedes-Benz 190, paid $17,000 for a cab license and medallion, and hired a driver. Schweitzer's deal with the cabbie had him on call to the millionaire, but at other times, the driver was free to troll for passengers—if he gave the millionaire half the proceeds.[8]

Schweitzer's FM station, well stocked with the exotic programs he cherished—poetry readings, academic lectures, chamber music—failed to make much of a profit, which shocked no one. Schweitzer decided that profits and good radio were contradictory. He offered his station to the Pacifica Foundation, a California outfit that had been experimenting with asking listeners, rather than advertisers, to sponsor its programs.

Pacifica, which owned FM stations in Berkeley and Los Angeles, was the creation of Lewis Hill, a poet and pacifist who was assigned to clear trails in the Sierra Madre after he notified the military of his conscientious objection to armed force. When World War II ended, Hill—like Todd Storz and Jean Shepherd, a childhood ham radio buff—went into journalism as a radio newsman in the Maryland suburbs of Washington, D.C. Hill quickly grew frustrated by commercial radio's shallow stories and showbiz values. He was appalled to learn that the tests the big radio networks used to judge potential newsmen consisted of reading a few paragraphs of nonsense in different inflections. The idea was to measure a candidate's ability to communicate concern, gravity, humor, and so on, even without words. But Hill concluded that the test symbolized the artifice that permeated American radio; it was "especially designed to assure that nothing in the announcer's mind except the sound of his voice—no comprehension, no value, no choice and above all, no sense of responsibility—could possibly enter into what he said."[9]

Hill quit, went west, and launched the Pacifica Foundation, which proposed to create radio that would spurn all government and corporate support. Only listeners would pay for this station, which would promote peace and education with a heavy menu of classical music, lectures, and literary fare. After three years of fund-raising, Hill won FCC approval, putting KPFA on the air in 1949. The station became the darling of Berkeley's intellectual and bohemian elites. KPFA served up programs featuring film critic Pauline Kael, poet Allen Ginsberg, avant-garde composer John Cage, Communist Party diehard Dorothy Healy, future defense secretary Caspar Weinberger, Trotskyites and Buddhists, Beat poets and jazz hipsters. There were serious political debates and, one day, a show during which four panelists toked up to promote the benefits of marijuana (twenty-one members of the Pacifica board resigned in protest of that 1954 program).

Listeners did not prove eager to pay for such novel fare, and the station, chronically unable to meet its $4,000 monthly expenses, signed off just over a year after it had come to life. A flurry of donations got the station back on the air nine months later, and Ford Foundation money helped make the return feel a bit secure. But this was going to be a very messy form of media. The station seemed always to be torn by internal battles: What viewpoints should be presented? Who should decide? Hill found himself accused of dictatorship, and in 1953, the station's volunteer staff voted him out of power. A couple of coups later, Hill returned, frustrated and bitter about how his experiment in pacifism had become such a sniping institution. In 1957, Hill committed suicide, writing that he sought "peace and a kind of home." He was thirty-eight.[10]

By 1960, when Louis Schweitzer called to offer his New York City station as a gift to Pacifica—"to liberate a single element of mass media technology on behalf of the public," as he put it—the foundation also had a station in Los Angeles and a growing reputation as a tiny but courageous voice. The House Un-American Activities Committee that year accused the stations of promoting homosexuality and communism, both of which were indeed frequent topics of discussion on Pacifica talk shows. The probe led the FCC to delay renewing Pacifica's licenses for three years. But in 1964, in a case sparked by a Pacifica broadcast on which eight homosexuals spoke about their lives, the FCC would announce that it had no interest in censoring or screening sexually or politically "provocative" material because otherwise all programming would be reduced to "the wholly inoffensive, the bland." Pacifica was expanding the envelope.

LISTENERS COULD BE EXCUSED for thinking that Fass *was* WBAI and Pacifica, that he must have *lived* in the studio. People went to sleep with him on and woke up to find he was still going. But he did get out, and one evening in 1966, he visited some friends from an artists collective called USCO who were staging a multimedia show in an empty hangar at John F. Kennedy International Airport. On his way out, Fass stumbled upon a group of stoned hippies staring at the huge

Alexander Calder mobile installed in the International Arrivals Building. Hey, Fass thought, what a great place for a party. So he went on the air and invited his audience to show itself, to demonstrate just how many people were out there who liked this kind of music, who liked getting high and wanted nothing to do with AM radio and everything it stood for. Much as Jean Shepherd had asked his listeners to show up on a street corner and just mill about, Fass now wanted his audience to join him at a Fly-In.

Night after night, Fass talked up the idea, saturating his descriptions of the gathering with songs about flying and airplanes. Callers promised to round up friends and be there. On the appointed night, February 11, 1967, thousands of people showed up—some news accounts say three thousand, Fass says seven thousand—and proceeded to dance and sing, hand each other flowers and candy, smoke pot, and watch each other in the Arrivals Building at Kennedy. The Fly-In was little other than a chance for like-minded listeners to see and discover one another. But *The Village Voice* declared the event a "tribal" phenomenon, and Fass celebrated it on the air as "a colossal amount of human connection," an expression not merely of happiness "but ecstasy and joy. We're planning another one at your house."

Emboldened by the success of the Fly-In, Fass teamed up with Hoffman and Krassner and other minds broadened and bent by acid to build toward the next grandiose event. San Francisco's hippies had staged a huge Gathering of the Tribes, a Be-In in Golden Gate Park. Now, a group of Village activists, including Jim Fouratt, an actor who would soon play a key role in the city's first gay rights demonstration, and Paul Williams, editor of *Crawdaddy* magazine, organized a New York version of the event in Central Park's Sheep Meadow. On *Radio Unnameable*, Fouratt and Fass recruited listeners to join their Be-In. Thousands showed up to build bonfires, fly kites, smoke dope, chant "Love," trade flowers, and simply be there—with the radio tuned to WBAI, which fed back instant validation by covering the event live.

Two weeks later, Fass and Krassner produced their own tribal gathering, the Sweep-In. A woman had called in to the show to talk about her collapsing apartment, and Fass organized a posse of listeners to recruit carpenters and plumbers and rebuild the caller's place. Inspired by that good deed, Fass and Krassner decided to gather listeners on one filthy street of the Lower East Side "and clean it," as Fass said, "from one river to the other, with brooms and mops and brushes, until it was perfectly clean." They picked the street where Krassner lived and set a date, April 8. "We're gonna clean up New York City, physically," Fass told listeners. "We will begin to assemble with brooms, mops, dustpans, steel wool, anything that you can think of to clean with. There will be trucks to cart away the junk."[11]

Immediately, listeners started offering equipment. Mr. Clean himself volunteered to make an appearance and give away coupons. Word soon spread to the city government, which sensed an embarrassment in the making. Early on the morning before the Sweep-In, the Sanitation Department descended on Seventh Street for a total scrubdown, eliminating every possible bit of refuse that the assembled hippies of New York City might have swept up.

Undeterred, Fass and his following simply moved the Sweep-In down to Third Street. Writing in *The Village Voice,* Don McNeill, a young reporter who became the chronicler of Fass, Hoffman, and Krassner's exploits, described "a young father, his child strapped to his back like a papoose," walking down the street with a scrub brush and a stool. "At each No Parking sign, he stopped, climbed on the stool, and scrubbed the sign clean.

"Trucks of donated Ajax cleanser arrived, and the soap was passed out to hippies, housewives, and a few Bowery refugees who panhandled the cleanser around the corner for a dime. . . . Passing cars, stalled by the crowds, also got an enthusiastic scrub. . . . Participants passed out lunch, daffodils, incense and chanted the glory of the now-near-sacred banana."[12] They cleared out vacant lots, blasted the Beatles from their stereos, and on the wall of a tenement building painted "Because We Love."

Mayor John Lindsay pronounced himself delighted and praised the event on his weekly radio program as an excellent example of citizen participation. That was fine with Fass and his listeners. They knew what they were saying, and if the mayor wanted to hear what he wanted to hear, that was groovy too.

Fass knew that something bigger than "citizen participation" was happening here. "Everybody hated the Vietnam War and everybody hated being lied to," Fass said. "This was the first time they realized they weren't alone. There was nowhere else in the media that reflected this community of people."

The radio station became a kind of floating party. Fass's protégé Steve Post, who had a much darker sense of political possibility, gathered listeners for his own Central Park event, a Fat-In, at which the impossibly thin model Twiggy was burned in effigy, everyone wore horizontal stripes, and all manner of junk food was celebrated. Todd Storz would have been proud; WBAI's announcers would have gone into shock at the comparison, but these were classic radio stunts, bringing listeners together just as did Storz's treasure hunts of the 1950s.

Fass began summoning his audience to action almost nightly. They raised bail money for hippies who'd been arrested for sitting on the grass and playing instruments in Tompkins Square Park. They held a Milk-In to buy milk and other basics when the Visiting Mothers day care service on the Lower East Side ran out of money.[13] By the end of 1967, Fass's listeners were a street force.

Abbie Hoffman—a regular on the show from 1963 until his suicide in 1989—had spoken often on *Radio Unnameable* about the magic that might result if acidheads and political activists were to combine efforts. When Hoffman and Jerry Rubin attempted to exorcise the evil spirits inside the Pentagon by bringing thousands of hippies to Washington to levitate the military headquarters, Fass was elected to conduct the "prelevitation rite," in which the Pentagon would be surrounded with a sprinkled trail of cornmeal. Fass and a hippie known as Mountain Girl took the sacred meal to the capital, but just as they began to pour it, police stopped them mid-rite and held them for a few hours before concluding that no law prohibited spreading cornmeal on federal lands.[14]

Hoffman turned *Radio Unnameable* into the nightly bulletin board of this new force—"the verbal trenches from which we made war on plastic culture," as he put it. "Bob Fass was the secret weapon."[15] Hoffman would do almost anything to win TV and radio time, creating characters, wearing outrageous clothes, saying anything. But on Fass's show, he dropped the antics and talked strategy.[16] *Radio Unnameable* became the very public yet comfortably private gathering place for organizers of the anti-war movement.

On New Year's Eve at the dawn of 1968, at Hoffman's apartment, with everyone smoking Colombian marijuana, listening to Fass, and making elaborate plans for the future, the radicalization of the hippies was topic A. The Students for a Democratic Society and other intellectuals of the counterculture had grown far too self-important for this crowd.

Krassner decided the new force needed a name. "I'm going through ippie, bippie, dippie, hippie, I'm ready to give up, wippie, yippie. Yippie! It was so perfect I stopped there and didn't even get to zippie!"[17] By the end of the night, they were the Youth International Party, the Yippies, and Hoffman called Fass on the air and said, "Hey, we're Yippies now."[18]

A new political party needed a coming-out bash, and Fass joined with Hoffman and Rubin to plan and promote the Yip-In at Grand Central Station, a rehearsal for the demonstration the Yippies were planning for the Democratic National Convention in Chicago that summer. ("Why Grand Central?" a reporter asked at the Yippie press conference announcing the event. "It's central, man," a Yippie replied.)

Night after night, Fass played train songs to push the event. On March 21, 1968, "the usual suspects showed up," Fass said, "but so did more militant and anarchic people, and there were hundreds of police surrounding the station. Everyone was in a good mood until some people climbed up the information booth and tried to pull the hands off the big clock. They wanted to stop time." They did.

The police moved in and the results were not pretty. McNeill, the *Village Voice* reporter, was beaten bloody. Someone in the crowd exploded a couple of cherry bombs. Waves of police entered in wedge formation. Fifty-seven people were arrested; more than twenty were taken to hospitals. Fass had been taking calls at the station all night, with Krassner initially hailing the crowd for its loving behavior and Hoffman singing the praises of the police for their restraint. In those first hours, Fass was still playfully surrounding the calls with songs about trains (the Beatles' "Ticket to Ride," Dylan's "Freight Train Blues"). But soon callers started talking about firecrackers and police entering the building, and then the calls were punctuated by shrieks and shouts. Fass slapped on the Beatles' "Help!"

The calls only grew more frantic. Hoffman showed up at the studio after having his cuts treated at the hospital. Reporters arrived with tape of the melee. Fass stayed on the story through the night. He called police precinct houses to get on-air assurances that those arrested were being treated well. He listened for hours to phoned-in eyewitness accounts. *Radio Unnameable* stayed on until seven that morning. News organizations throughout the city turned to the show to find out what was going on.

Undaunted by the debacle at the train terminal, the Yippies pushed ahead with plans for an anti-war spectacle at the Chicago convention. Fass's role would be to host the rock concert the Yippies planned to mount in Lincoln Park. But when the day arrived and Fass took the stage, he found himself voiceless from having consumed massive amounts of a hash-oil and honey concoction stirred up by Hoffman and a fellow activist who went by the moniker Mad Scientist. By the time Fass managed to introduce the first band, Chicago police had pulled the plug on the concert.[19]

When federal prosecutors indicted Hoffman, Rubin, and the rest of the Chicago Seven for inciting a riot and a long list of other felonies, Fass and Krassner were not mentioned; apparently, the prosecutors considered them journalists and didn't want to complicate the case with free press issues. At a party on Hoffman's roof in Manhattan, the journo-Yippies sang, "We weren't indicted, we weren't indicted!" and danced in a conga line. Hoffman would call in to Fass's show every night of his conspiracy trial, but the party was changing course. The days of the Be-Ins were ending. The Yip-In and Chicago sucked the joy out of the tribe that had first come together via *Radio Unnameable.*

The audience gravitated toward the music, drugs, and other, more personal aspects of the counterculture. A few days after Woodstock in August 1969, Hoffman came on the show and snapped at callers who were talking excitedly about the already legendary rock festival.

"We got so much pleasure from giving the peace sign up at Woodstock," a caller said.

"I don't get pleasure from giving the peace sign anymore, because I'm not into peace and music," Hoffman said. "I'm into war and music." He urged the audience to adopt stronger slogans—"We're going forth from here and crush American culture" or "What you kids really ought to do when you go home is kill your parents."

"What? Kill our parents?" the caller replied, aghast.

"Well, that's an image, huh? If it's a new emerging culture, it's out to kill the old culture and what about the people who are running that culture and what about the government that runs it?"

The caller stammered, then blurted, "I'm not quite up to that yet, I don't think. Personally, I'm a little bit attached to my parents because they're really pretty cool, so I couldn't do anything like kill them."[20]

The audience for free-form radio was still growing, but in a new direction, inward, toward a supreme elevation of self that would eventually spread to the larger pop culture. "Politics is bullshit!" the singer David Crosby announced to a rally in San Francisco's Golden Gate Park in November 1969. By 1971, John Lennon was leaving the days of "Come Together" behind, pronouncing that "I just believe in me."[21]

ON *RADIO UNNAMEABLE,* Fass remained cloaked in darkness. "I never liked to speak personally," he said. "I never played with the self-indulgence the way the others did, Larry and Steve." Larry Josephson and Steve Post were WBAI's most popular hosts in the late 1960s. They talked politics and alternative culture, like Fass, but they were different. Their shows were mostly about themselves.

Post had a fierce case of Fass worship and terrible mike fright when he first went on the air at WBAI in 1965.[22] He had played radio as a kid growing up in the Bronx, and he was, of course, a Jean Shepherd fan. A speech therapist had recommended to his parents that they buy a tape recorder to help ease Steve's brother's stuttering, and the boys jumped at the chance to make up their own radio shows. Steve invented characters named Luke Warm and Paige Turner.

One of Post's first duties at WBAI was to substitute for Fass, and Post tried to duplicate the master's style—layering music, found sounds, and listener calls into a pastiche that sometimes had a theme and sometimes just meandered through the night. But once his initial anxiety about being on the air subsided, Post ventured into his own weekend overnight show, *The Outside*. Unlike Shepherd's stories of bullies and parents fretting over what the neighbors might think, Post's childhood tales were deeply personal, anguished chapters about guilt and repression, his racketeer cousin and his mother's cancer, the travails of life and the eternal search for a rent-controlled apartment.

WBAI's directors, the kind of people who had marathon discussions about the station's political underpinnings, were unnerved by Post's show—no, not show, *program*, Pacifica's ideologically proper leaders insisted—and by the station's anti–morning man, Larry Josephson. A lapsed IBM engineer who volunteered at WBAI because he was lonely and miserable in Cubicle America, Josephson was soon serving up his own mix of cranky humor, eclectic music, and startlingly personal confessions on *In the Beginning*. While Josephson quickly established himself as one of the station's most popular voices, Pacifica managers nonetheless complained that Josephson and Post were too personal. Too whiny. Too . . . popular.

Listener-sponsored stations know which programs bring in the money—all they have to do is tally the money collected during each show's pitch for donations—and Post's and Josephson's listeners contributed the most to WBAI. Listeners flocked to this confessional form of radio, far preferring it to the *Free Voice of Greece* and *News for Car Owners* and *Lesbian Nation* and *Hour of the Wolf* (hosted by a witch) and *Up Against the Wailing Wall* (hosted by a rabbi) and all the other balkanized programming of a station that deemed itself the alternative to bland, corporate culture. For a station that, as former WBAI manager Frank Millspaugh said, "engaged in unemployment insurance fraud on a wholesale basis, putting people on the payroll just long enough to qualify for unemployment and then off they went," anything that brought in some money was invaluable.

Most listeners associated WBAI with hard-core leftist politics, but Post and Josephson insisted on a different kind of radio—in the spirit of Shepherd's nightly cult meetings, but with an overlay of Jewish angst and comedy. Josephson opened his show with a wry "Greetings, war fans," and played plenty of anti–Vietnam War music ("One-two-three, what are we fighting for? Don't ask me, I don't give a damn, Next stop is Vietnam"). But he turned quickly from political to personal. He might devote fifteen minutes to a mad punning contest with a quick-witted friend; or play a hawkish right-wing commentary and then drown it out with a Bach organ piece; or identify the station as "Hippie Commie Fag Radio in New York, WBAI"; or talk to fourteen-year-old Lisa, who called in regularly to report on life in a Manhattan private school; or banter with Larry the Bagel Man, who delivered Josephson's breakfast; or shout to listeners as he searched the record library for a Janis Ian album ("Talk to your parents for a minute; I'll be right back. . . . I know it's here somewhere, I filed Janis Ian under 'Immature Rock.' . . . Oh, I can't find it, Mommy! I can't find it! I want my Janis Ian record!").

Free-form radio was necessarily anti-establishment and anti-authority, but it didn't have to be leftist or even overtly political. "I'm a non-ideological person," said Josephson, "and I was at this station with highly principled Quakers and Marxists, and I wasn't one of them. I was this Eisenhower liberal trying to mediate between idealistic crazy radicals, and I was angry at my mother and women and the world and I was trying to ventilate that through music and comedy and stories."

Where others heard a station bent on organizing the counterculture into a political force, Josephson saw a playground ("our 50,000-watt toy kit") where he could take what his heroes—Hawthorne, Bob and Ray, and Shepherd—had managed to do on commercial radio, and push deeper. "This was the vacant lot of media, and the kids were allowed to play," said Millspaugh, who as station manager let Fass, Josephson, and Post do their thing while he tried to expand WBAI's audience, even giving away FM radios. "Artists go into underutilized places and make them habitable. That's what these guys did with FM." At its peak, the station had thirty thousand subscribers; in the valleys, the number dropped below ten thousand.

The free-form approach spread beyond WBAI and Pacifica's California stations, and several college stations tried to mimic Fass's approach. But by the mid-1970s, listener-sponsored radio would be overtaken by a new approach, National Public Radio, which hired many of WBAI's programmers and captured some of its spirit. Going to NPR meant accepting a middle-class existence, a transition that was hard for some of Pacifica's more ideologically driven (and often trust-funded) people to make. "We had a lot of people who rejected their parents' lifestyle—and went home to have Mommy do the laundry," Josephson said. "And we had a big divide between the radio people and the politicals. I became politicized, hated the war, and yet I realized much of what was on the station was cant. But people like Fass would never admit to themselves that we are all capable of running a concentration camp."

Josephson kept up his morning confessions until 1972, when his young daughter died, leaving him for a time incapable of speaking on the radio. Post took his act to public radio, where he was the morning man on New York's WNYC, dispensing droll comments on the news between classical records until management decided that National Public Radio news would squeeze donations from listeners more efficiently than local programming.

There would come a time when it was no longer revolutionary for a voice on the radio to devote hours on end to his own sexual appetites and hang-ups. Larry Josephson's morning grumpiness would morph into Howard Stern's more explicit confessions, and commercial radio would find a way to capitalize on WBAI's adventures in ego.

In the deep of the night at WBAI, where no one would ever accuse him of using the radio to saddle listeners with tales of his own angst, Bob Fass would nonetheless carry on, layering sounds, piling callers atop each other, revealing himself in a very different way. After four decades, *Radio Unnameable* was no longer at the cutting edge of an emerging counterculture. But *Radio Unnameable* lingered, both as a reminder of long-ago possibilities and as what Fass had always wanted it to be, "a place where everyone could talk, where things happen, where something is diminished when you know what to expect."

A MOUND OF A MAN hustles into the studios of WBAI a few minutes before midnight, weighed down by bulging canvas bags brimming with CDs, tapes, and news clippings. He walks past a clot of young people in ratty T-shirts deeply engaged in debate with a couple of old West Indian gents about prophets and the future of the nation-state. An aging folksinger waits in the studio. A program about women's consciousness is ending: "We started out with the notion that we can awake within ourselves a passionate awareness of the molecules of emotion," the announcer says in a small, sleepy voice. A news report refers to the United States as "the occupying power" and to the chief executive as "President-Select Bush."

WBAI, once spread out in a building all its own on the East Side, later crammed into far less commodious West Side quarters, is incongruously located on Wall Street, on the tenth floor of an office building otherwise devoted to advancing the financial prowess of the ruling class. No one recognizes Bob Fass as he enters the station, a shaggy septuagenarian with a pinkish complexion and a sweet smile. He is not paid a salary, has not been for twenty years. He is, officially, a volunteer.

"BAI regards him as a relic of the sixties," Josephson said. "The racist Marxist Caribbean blacks who run BAI treat him like shit. They should give him a pension. He is an absolute idealist and an absolute truth teller."

The alternative culture had done its thing. After Vietnam and Watergate, the nation's young people turned away from politics and radio's sharp edge was dulled along with a pop culture that preferred to dance, dance, dance. In 1977, after Pacifica managers set a course toward a less provocative, more mainstream sound on the network's five stations, Fass and a small band of other WBAI staff members invaded the station's transmitter room atop the Empire State Building and locked themselves in, beginning a siege that knocked the station off the air for fifty days. In the opening hours of the action that February, Fass and the others gained control of the airwaves and played Dylan and Pete Seeger songs between announcements that the vast majority of WBAI's staff and volunteers had walked out to protest unilateral and drastic changes in programming. The station's new managers saw themselves as realistic: "We've been trying to be the voice of a non-existent movement," Pacifica Foundation vice president Peter Franck said then. "We're just broadcasting to more of a hard-core audience than we have to." WBAI's listener base had dropped by half since the early 1970s; listener contributions were way down too.

To make WBAI "more listenable," Pacifica's board hired managers intent on discarding the old white, liberal, Jewish audience and appealing instead to the new New York—Latins, blacks, and immigrants. The new program director, Pablo Yoruba Guzman, former minister of information for the Puerto Rican radical group the Young Lords, axed many long-standing programs and replaced them with music and talk aimed at the city's growing Hispanic and black populations. The old programming, Guzman said, was "so white-oriented it was shocking—a disgrace." The new station manager, Anna Kosof, derided the old WBAI staff as "a commune. It's a way of life of the '60s, and they haven't gotten out of that."[23]

Fass and other defenders of the status quo argued that the new managers intended to commercialize the station and discard its tradition of protecting free speech. Fass sat in the basement of the station for hours before the coup, smoking joint after joint with Guzman, trying to come to some understanding of the new reality. How could it be that Fass and the revolutionaries of the 1960s were now being called reactionaries standing in the way of the same blacks and Hispanics for whom they thought they'd been fighting? It was simple arithmetic, really—the 1960s were over, and the people who were still moving into the city, not fleeing to the suburbs, were taking over.

Fass didn't see it that way. His show was open to anyone, wasn't it? For thirty-five days, with the station off the air, Fass and a dozen or so others occupied the converted church on East Sixty-second Street that then served as the station's home. When police finally took back the building, the last five holdouts, Fass among them, were arrested and charged with criminal contempt.

The aftermath of the strike was devastating. The station lost listeners, struggled to pay its bills, and descended into a frenzied internal bickering that would continue for many years. Guzman quit, saying that the station staff was a festering sore of "racism and mediocrity." And Fass was banned from the station for the next five years. His nights stretched before him, empty and silent.

While Fass was fighting for the one place where he could come alive, most of his friends from the old days had moved on. Nearly twenty of his former WBAI colleagues ended up in public radio; several more went to the TV networks. Others went into filmmaking or teaching. Fass could have joined the exodus; he had offers, but not to do an all-night, free-form program. "I tried to do things for public radio," he said, "but I didn't like having to read something that had to last thirty-eight seconds exactly. I wasn't used to being vetted."

"Bob never compromised," Josephson said. His friends were forever begging Fass to double-park his ideals, just this once, and take whatever good deal was being offered at the moment. Nothing doing. Fass had always maintained his purity, no matter the cost. When WBAI was raising money to buy a building, managers courting a potentially large donor invited some program hosts to come in and schmooze the rich guy. Fass, the station honchos explained, is one of our great imaginations. Fass volunteered that he had an idea for raising money. "I think we should have a Fuckathon," he said, explaining that listeners would pledge money for each relationship consummated at the station, much as people give runners cash for each mile they cover in a charity race. Station leaders watched in silence as the mark, a millionaire real estate mogul, walked out of the room.

Banned from his radio home, Fass collected unemployment, and then he didn't. He acted in a couple of off-Broadway shows, and then he didn't. He made a couple of commercials as a voice-over announcer, and then he decided that wasn't quite right. He had a public access cable show on TV for a while, called *If I Can't Dance, You Can Keep Your Revolution*. He took a job doing telephone solicitations, selling tickets to productions at Lincoln Center. He hung out with the other Yippies and they planned their annual Marijuana March. For a long time, he really didn't do much of anything. He was, he said, very depressed.

"Bob alienated all of his friends," Josephson said. "None of us were pure enough for Bob."

At a low point a few years into his exile, Fass wondered whether anyone remembered who he'd been and what he'd done. He wondered if *Radio Unnameable* had had a lasting impact. Fass placed a tiny ad in *The Nation,* the left-liberal weekly: "Good morning cabal. If you ever listened until 'Bye-bye,' I wuv you, you are a member of the cabal. Where are you? What are you doing?" Fass got letters from all over the world.

"Ninety-nine of a hundred people who know Bob would say he smoked way too much dope and had a reputation for being spaced-out and uncontrollable," said Jon Kalish, who went through college glued to *Radio Unnameable* and ended up working as Fass's gofer, heading out to the streets to record interviews and sounds for the program. Kalish, who became an independent producer for public radio, believes Fass simply "never learned how to function in the straight world."

The absolute idealist lost his loft in Chelsea in 1988. He has never made more than $175 a week. WBAI paid him until 1977, if sporadically; since then, a long dry spell. For many years, he lived on Social Security and the salary his wife, Lynnie, earned as a researcher at a Manhattan law firm. (In 2005, after Lynnie lost her job and she and Bob hit a very rough patch financially, more than two hundred friends and listeners gathered at a restaurant in Tribeca to celebrate Bob's forty-third anniversary at WBAI. The event was a fund-raiser—at $100 per guest, it generated $22,000 to cover food and rent for Bob and Lynnie—but also a chance to show Fass what he had meant to the singers and musicians who got their big break on the show, to radicals who found an outlet in the night for their anger and their ideals, to listeners hungry for a program that felt like home. "Bob welcomed me as a sixteen-year-old near-runaway," said Jan Albert, who started out as a listener and eventually became a program host at WBAI, where Fass gave her children's show its name: *Candy from Strangers.* "Bob introduced me to Fats Waller, Allen Ginsberg, things I've been searching for ever since in media. I haven't found it again.")

Eventually, Fass got back on the air on WFMU, a college station in New Jersey that had essentially modeled its entire format on his program. But it wasn't the same. He was twice the age of many of the other programmers, and his community wasn't in New Jersey; the musicians, artists, and radicals who used to drop by the studio didn't happen by East Orange very often.

In 1982, new managers let Fass back on WBAI, but his show would never again air five nights a week. He had his following, and they still donated money to the station. The Yippies still used the show as their club megaphone, rallying supporters to their Marijuana Marches. Abbie Hoffman called in from his underground hideouts; his vasectomy was broadcast live on *Radio Unnameable.* And Fass still organized listeners into action; in the Reagan years, Fass launched a group called Homeless for Reagan, and before long, he got callers together to create a real organization to work on behalf of people displaced by gentrification.

But for a quarter of a century, Bob Fass has been something of a ghost at WBAI. He is the station's one link to its glory days. His friends from that time like to say that Bob is the only member of his generation still doing what he did in 1967. But six nights a week, he is not on the air. He is at home in the ramshackle house he and Lynnie bought across from an abandoned chocolate factory on Staten Island. The house is all they have. Thousands of tapes of his shows from five decades sit in teetering stacks in the living room, down the halls, into the bedrooms, boxes and boxes of them, hundreds upon hundreds of hours of archives that no one has ever listened to. Most of the tapes are not labeled. Ceiling tiles droop down onto towers of old tape decks and video players. Speaker wire crisscrosses the room, strung from one bookshelf to another, from the ceiling to the floor, a tangle of dozens of attempts to preserve the past. Rugs lie atop other rugs. Old sport jackets hang from a metal rod that was once a frame for ceiling tiles, now missing. And everywhere, cats slip in and out of rooms, nine cats, darting here, napping there. It's their house.

After midnight, after Lynnie goes to sleep, Fass often gets into his banged-up old Bonneville—118,000 miles on the odometer—and drives to Manhattan. There are still a few people, though not many, who can manage to keep his hours. He picks up his mail. He bombs up and down the avenues. He wants to be on the radio. He flips on WBAI and hears the other all-night shows, the Moorish Orthodox anarchists and the ravers and the son-of-free-form deejays whose efforts at humor are "about as deep as an oil slick." He knows what he could do with that airtime.

"Nostalgia means sickness for the past," he said. "I like now. Past, future—these are things that can be altered. But the moment—the immediate moment—that's what it's about." He's been writing about the past lately, about his grandmother, who knew Emma Goldman and who gave birth to Bob's father on a Manhattan street during rites for a rabbi whose funeral procession had come under attack by a rival sect.

Fass has never spoken of any of this on the air. He never saw the merits of the Me Obsession. "When I started the show, I was in therapy," he said. "I decided to save the personal stuff for the therapist. Figured I was paying for it."

It is finally Thursday night, his night on the radio. Five long seconds of silence, and then Fass leans in and his voice softens and he closes his eyes for a moment and says, "Good morning, cabal." If you're listening in bed somewhere, you hardly know what year it is. Fass has invited Eric Levine, a folksinger who has been coming on the show for twenty years, up to the studio, and Levine has brought along Gina Tlamsa, a Celtic flutist who started listening to Fass when she was a kid, babysitting in other people's apartments, and she's bubbling with excitement because this is her first time on the show. Levine will sing his "Ballad of the CIA," which has all the subtlety of a rocket-propelled grenade attack. There will be songs that blame landlords and lawyers for the miseries of the poor, and songs that compare George W. Bush to Richard Nixon.

And then, at 12:34, Fass interrupts Levine mid-tune. "There's a caller who says something important is happening," he says by way of explanation. He punches up line one with repeated jabs of his thick fingers; technical grace was never his strong point.

"I'm in the Fort Greene housing project in Brooklyn," the caller says, "and there's a riot situation. They have the block blocked off. They murdered a young man in the back."

"What's happening now?" Fass asks, and the caller describes police officers pointing guns and police helicopters circling overhead.

"I didn't know who else to call," the caller says, and Fass asks her to get a friend who's closer to the action and put her on the phone.

"Is there someone who can call us from the street?" he asks, and within a couple of minutes, four phone lines light up. Over the course of the next hour, Fass punches up one caller after another—jab, jab, jab on the buttons on the phone console—and slowly, he teases out the whole story, about how a plainclothes detective shot a man who he'd seen shoot another man on the street, about confrontations between residents and police, about the rage that's been pouring out all night long.

"You want a presence, people to witness what's going on?" Fass asks one caller, and now six lines light up, and listeners volunteer to go watch what the police are doing. Callers from all over the city talk about how it's become hard to afford to live even in the ghetto, and other callers relay eyewitness accounts of the original shooting, and now eight lines are flashing, and a caller, Maria, reads the real estate listings from *The New York Times* and says that addresses that used to be called Fort Greene—a black ghetto—are now being called Brooklyn Heights North, after the affluent white neighborhood nearby.

The callers are Caribbean and Hispanic and American black, and they are calling the seventy-year-old white Yippie radio artist who does this for nothing and knows how to do almost nothing else, and they thank him for being there and for listening, and he says nothing but "You're on the air." And he punches more buttons and puts callers on the radio alone and in pairs and in small groups. They debate the future of their city and talk about organizing a march, and their conversation shifts to how jobs are being sent to Bangladesh and India, and when you call American Express or America Online, the customer service person is halfway around the world because the wages are cheaper there, and now it is even harder to make it in the big city.

There'll be a few inches in the *Times* the next morning, under the headline "Police Kill Man They Say Had Just Killed Another." And in the *Post*, the headline will be "Narcs Gun Down Murderer," but neither paper will have a word about the fears in the night or the jobs gone overseas or the people who cannot afford to stay in their own apartments. On this night, forty years after he started, out there in the darkness, people are coming together because Bob Fass is on the air.

Chapter 7

✳ NO STATIC AT ALL

THE STORY APPEARED in the second issue of *Rolling Stone,* Jann Wenner's new paper for the rock generation, and it was more manifesto than news item. On November 23, 1967, under the headline "A Rotting Corpse, Stinking Up the Airwaves," Tom Donahue, radio revolutionary, put into scathing rhetoric exactly what many of the nation's young people had been thinking: Top 40 radio "has alienated its once-loyal army of listeners" by ignoring the new rock albums that were outselling 45 rpm singles. Top 40 insulted listeners with "absurd jingles" and "babbling, hysterical disc jockeys" who "do everything they can to offend the musical taste and common sense of everyone in their audience over twelve."[1]

THE WORLD'S BIGGEST DISC JOCKEY SHOW!

TOM DONAHUE
"OVER 400 POUNDS OF SOLID SOUNDS!"

NOON TO 4:00 PM TODAY AND EVERY DAY

RADIO KYA · DIAL 1260

TOM DONAHUE IN AN AD FOR KYA RADIO IN SAN FRANCISCO *(Courtesy Bay Area Radio Museum)*

What made this screed so powerful was that Tom Donahue, cultural rebel, was also Big Daddy Tom Donahue, one of the most successful of what he now described as those "happy, oh yes, always happy-sounding cretins who are poured from bottles every three hours" on Top 40 radio. Donahue had spent his thirties at stations such as WINX in the Maryland suburbs of Washington, D.C., WIBG in Philadelphia, and KYA in San Francisco, spinning the hits and putting his purring baritone and impressive girth to work pushing the manic impishness of the go, go, go hit radio formula. Without much exaggeration, KYA advertised his as "The World's Biggest Disc Jockey Show, Over 400 Pounds of Solid Sounds!"

"Big Daddy for the Boss of the Bay, Channel 1260, where good things are happening!" Donahue crooned on a typical broadcast in 1961. "Number one on the Swinging Sixties Survey, the Tokens, 'The Lion Sleeps Tonight'! That is a *hit*!" He hawked super-jackpot contests and sold discount wares ("Never have you bought so much with your dollar as you can at your 88-Cent Stores!"). He was, he promised the Bay Area, "the largest Big Daddy Tom Donahue anywhere," and he was always in a hurry—"got to keep it moving 'cause I've got to get to lots of hits."[2]

Donahue had become a household name hosting *Danceland*, Philadelphia's top pop music show. But he got embroiled in the payola scandal, caught having taken $1,650 from a record distributor between 1957 and 1959.[3] Donahue had to start over in Charleston, West Virginia, where he built himself once again into a dominating personality. On the air, he was friendly, cool, commanding—communicating just a touch of danger with his daily sign-on, "I'm here to clear up your face and mess with your mind."

Off-mike, Big Daddy was bored out of his mind, walking through his shifts paying only the slightest attention, driven only by his desire to go home, drop his work persona, get high, and sink into the music he really loved. Donahue could no longer stand the kind of radio Joni Mitchell described as "every song a one-night stand, genuine junk food for juveniles." In 1965, after one particularly deflating day when Donahue was broadcasting from San Francisco's Cow Palace arena and the kids who pressed their noses up against the remote studio window started flipping the deejay the bird, Big Daddy quit KYA. He went into business as a concert promoter (staging shows by the Rolling Stones and the Beatles—their last live performance, at Candlestick Park in 1966) and record producer (Sly Stone, Grace Slick's Great Society). But Donahue soon missed being on the air, being the voice, the star, the connection between the music and the kids. He'd gather with his radio friends at his apartment late at night, and they'd sit around getting stoned, listening to their favorite albums—Dylan, Aretha Franklin, Otis Redding—and complaining about what was on the radio—the Monkees, the Archies, the Association. Why "Windy" instead of "Blowin' in the Wind"? Why did every song on the radio have to be a maximum of three minutes long? Why did radio have to be so out of it?[4]

And then one night in 1967, Donahue was hanging with his fellow unemployed deejays when a friend, a promoter for Elektra Records, came over with a new release. "We had been ingesting some controlled substance," said Raechel Donahue, Tom's partner and later his wife, "and we were all playing pinochle, and all of a sudden we heard the same record over and over again because I'd forgotten to put the little arm down [on the record player], so it was just playing the size of a single, which turned out to be the last eleven minutes, which turned out to be 'The End' by the Doors. So we're hearing 'Father, I'm going to kill you' over and over, and Tom finally said, 'What *is* that?' "[5]

The record didn't have a title yet, only a catalogue number. But it was enough to impel Donahue into action. There had to be a way to get that on the radio. "We sit here every night and smoke dope and play records for each other," Tom Donahue said. "I wonder why nobody's done this on the radio?"[6]

The way to accomplish that was FM. "A friend of mine in L.A. kept talking about FM stereo, FM stereo," Donahue said, "and I didn't even have a goddamned FM radio. But I could see that was where it was going to go because I could see people buying stereos."[7] Thanks to the federal government, FM opened up to thousands of hours of new programming in 1967, just as long-playing albums were liberating musicians and record companies to produce songs that might not fit on a 45 single—or on Top 40 radio, where songs were often edited down to as little as two minutes to quicken the pace. Bob Dylan put out "Desolation Row" at eleven minutes; the Rolling Stones matched that length with "Going Home." The Doors' "Light My Fire" was six minutes and thirty seconds long; it became a Top 40 hit only in the three-minute version the group recorded especially for radio play.[8]

Donahue was intent on getting this new Doors song on the radio—the *complete* version. By the time Raechel woke the morning after the pinochle game, "Tom was already dressed—*that* was kind of frightening—and had the phone book open to the *K*'s. He let his fingers do the walking to the listing of radio stations and he dialed up one FM station after another until he found one whose phone was disconnected. Bingo. He said, 'Give me my power tie, blow-dry my hair, we're gonna go paint the sky blue for somebody.' "

Tom had found a troubled station called KMPX, which tried and failed to make a go of it renting out airtime to preachers from storefront churches and immigrants who produced foreign-language programs—Portuguese, Irish, Chinese. "The phone was out of order because they hadn't paid the bill," Tom recalled. "So I went over there and talked to the manager about taking over a four-hour period of time with the idea that if my programming was successful, we would go from there." Donahue tried to buy the nighttime hours, but the station manager wanted thousands of dollars that Donahue didn't have. A week later, KMPX's manager, sounding a bit desperate, called back and offered Donahue the time for free if he sold advertising and gave management half of the revenue.

On April 7, 1967, Donahue lumbered into the studio in a warehouse by the docks along San Francisco Bay, lugging bags full of his favorite albums. Big Daddy was back, but he was going underground, albeit in a thoroughly public forum. He was playing the stuff the corporate boys wouldn't touch, spinning records for a generation that had had enough hype. Still, from the start Donahue knew enough about the business not to go too far beyond the familiar. "I played a lot of blues, but I was edgy about losing people," he said. His Top 40 show-biz instinct led him to mix his favorite obscure music with tunes the audience already knew—Beatles, Stones, Dylan.

The response was instantaneous. Though FM radios were hardly common in 1967, KMPX's new sound found an audience among the children of the immigrants who tuned in to the station for its foreign-language programs. Within ten days of launching his show, Donahue had to add phone lines in the studio to handle the calls. Listeners seemed drawn to the station, literally. Four nights after Donahue went on the air, he recalled, "this fella and a girl came up. They brought me flowers and beads and a Vietcong pennant, which we put up on the wall." The first sponsor, a ski shop, called during the second week of broadcasting and bought time; three days later, the shop's owner phoned Donahue to tell him that fourteen people had come in on a spring weekend, "just rapping with him about how great it was that he bought time on this radio station."

When Donahue arrived at KMPX, he discovered that the station was already home to an overnight show hosted by Larry Miller, who played folk music, along with some rock. Miller, a musician, had launched a show of folk, cabaret, and poetry on a classical FM station in Detroit in 1966. When he moved to San Francisco, he persuaded KMPX to give him the overnight hours. He advertised his show with handbills he drew himself, and he called his music "folk-rock." He served up electric, eclectic sounds unavailable on AM radio—Grace Slick, the Grateful Dead, Joan Baez. When he spoke, it was over a background of sitar music, and his voice was soft—barely audible, really—and oh so groovy.

"I'm especially knocked out that you called to request that," he said one night in 1967, and he indeed sounded almost unconscious.[9] "You certainly are a nice bunch of people, you're doing all right as an audience." Just before three that morning, he turned a tad grouchy: "Do me a favor and don't call up and ask for Eric Burdon anymore because I think he's a phony. No depth to his work. There goes the Eric Burdon album over my shoulder. I don't like the Animals. I'm not going to lie to you or put you on, because you've had enough of that listening to the radio."

Miller had been on KMPX for two months when Donahue arrived; the two met when Donahue's evening air shift ended that first night in April. They believed they were creating something entirely new, something that fit like a puzzle piece into the jagged lives of the tuned in and the turned on of San Francisco. As it happened, something similar had already surfaced briefly in New York City. In July 1966, WOR, the AM powerhouse where Jean Shepherd worked, decided to comply with the FCC's order to stop simulcasting its AM programs on its FM station not by switching to beautiful music, as so many FM stations had, but by papering the city with psychedelic posters, playing the rock that didn't make it to Top 40, and hiring rebellious-sounding deejays (including Top 40 legend Murray the K and Rosko, the black jock later best known as the voice of CBS-TV sports). The station launched with the Troggs' "Wild Thing," eschewed jingles, limited commercials to a few per hour, and let deejays pick their own music. WOR-FM's pitch to advertisers was that the "kids are now the adults, and they have tired of Robot Radio, Hot Rod Radio, Slam Bang Radio and Trite Radio." But advertisers weren't buying, and WOR-FM's experiment with free-form rock radio lasted less than a year.[10]

Despite that failure, commercial radio was finally catching up with what young Americans played on their living room stereos, what a few college kids were trying out late at night on campus stations, and what Bob Fass and other pioneers at Pacifica had been doing for the past few years. Donahue and the other innovators at the first free-form FM rock stations knew what was missing from Top 40 radio. Now they had to figure out how to adapt the emerging counterculture to a mass medium. They asked Fass and other WBAI programmers for advice. In San Francisco, Tom and Raechel Donahue listened often to Pacifica's KPFA, the Berkeley station that was the voice of campus radicals, beatnik poets, and advocates of psychedelic drugs.

Donahue took "what KPFA was doing for the political arm of the left and added music to it," Raechel said. Donahue's listeners came not only for the music but for the whole mix, the reflection of what was happening in Haight-Ashbury, Berkeley, and wherever else young people gathered. "Pacifica would tell us when the marches were and we'd pass that along," Raechel said. "We were both on the same side.

But just because you like the music doesn't mean you have to go along with the politics."[11]

Donahue and the other deejays were eager to prove they were on the cutting edge: they played Elvis Presley, Mozart, and the music of an Italian group that made odd sounds with their lips. From a studio equipped with a "color organ," a device that projected splashes of red, green, yellow, and blue light onto the wall depending on the frequencies of music being spun, KMPX aired a musical blend that was about 60 percent rock and roll, 20 percent blues and R&B, and 20 percent jazz, electronic music, and poetry. Donahue and friends played Led Zeppelin's new album a month before its official release, and by the time the record hit the stores, KMPX listeners had placed a hundred thousand orders for it.[12] KMPX opened its airwaves to local bands and especially the Grateful Dead, whose members frequently dropped by the studios. Donahue's deejays played the work of a percussionist who put a block of ice on chicken wire and miked the random drips of water down into a fifty-five-gallon garbage can.[13]

The governing principle was to play music—any cut from an album, not just the song the record company designated as a single—as you would for your friends. Listeners dropped by with records they'd picked up in other cities. Deejays competed to create the coolest sets, segueing from one mandolin solo to another, from a lyric about rain at the end of one song to a lyric about rain at the start of another. Jocks took pride in building sets of songs that had something in common—a theme, an artist, a certain mood. Raechel Donahue started a set with Aretha Franklin's "Respect," which led to Otis Redding's "Respect," and on to Redding's "Satisfaction," the Stones' "Satisfaction," and the Stones' "Red Rooster," followed by Willie Dixon's "Red Rooster," after which the deejay worked her way back to Aretha. Only after the deejay listed every song she'd played and told a few stories about the artists—only then might KMPX slip in a commercial.

As KMPX pushed out its foreign-language programming and expanded to a twenty-four-hour rock operation, Donahue took the helm of the station, hiring deejays who above all loved the music—so much so that B. Mitchell Reed, another Top 40 jock known for his speedy delivery, took a $900 a week pay cut, from $1,000 to $100, for the chance to sit beneath the Vietcong pennant, speak in a normal, conversational tone, and even bask in the occasional silence. Deejays saw their work as Fass did, as an improvisation, a statement.

KMPX sounded unlike any other station on the dial, in part because it included the voices of women. Industry gospel said listeners wouldn't accept female voices as authoritative. Donahue, however, decided early on to hire "chick engineers" because the old male engineers were frustrating his attempts to give deejays control of the station. The engineers who sat across the glass from the jock were responsible for cueing up records and starting each song. The control room guys at KMPX neither understood nor approved of the long sets of music that the new jocks ordered up. If he brought women in to do the job, Donahue figured, the engineers would be less likely to challenge the deejays. "And come to think of it, they were all pretty too," Raechel Donahue recalled.

Before long, KMPX had seven "chick engineers," as the station's promotional material called them, and they were photographed together for print ads wearing floral dresses, gypsy gowns, and long silken nightshirts. But Dusty Street (her real name), Suzy Creamcheese (not), and some of the other engineers wanted their own turn on the air, and Donahue soon gave them a show, *The Chicks on Sunday.*[14] This passed for revolutionary.

Underground radio portrayed itself as a rejection of authority, commercialism, rules—everything once-rebellious Top 40 had come to stand for. (Donahue specifically banned Motown songs because that distinctive sound was so powerfully associated with Top 40 in listeners' minds.)[15] This was radio for a generation that was skeptical of anything concocted by their elders, but yearned to believe in something. San Francisco experienced its Summer of Love in 1967, and with the Grateful Dead and the Jefferson Airplane playing in Golden Gate Park, and Bob Dylan and Joan Baez singing of peace and a new generation, Jimi Hendrix getting airplay in England but not back home, and

Timothy Leary urging Americans to "turn on, tune in, drop out," KMPX sounded like love beads and long hair; it was threatening in a way that Top 40 had long since ceased to be.

Television had lost much of this generation; the network audience was graying, and the rare efforts to appeal to young viewers—ABC's *Shindig* and *Happening '68* and NBC's *Hullabaloo,* go-go-booted teen dance shows that became instant camp—were more clumsily square than anything AM radio ever perpetrated. FM, on the other hand, sounded like a different plane of consciousness. The clarity of FM's signal, the freshness of stereo sound, and the smooth calm of the new deejays' patter combined to attract the people President Richard Nixon derided: "They call themselves flower children," he said in 1968. "I call them spoiled rotten." Adult society had an inkling that something strange was happening on the FM dial, and the automatic response was to reject it: in *The New York Times,* critic Jack Gould sneered at how "stereophonic FM, which surrounds the listener with sound, is purposely raised in volume by the young so that they can physically sense the vibrations of the radio waves and emphasize what one college graduate characterized as the social schism between generations."[16]

KMPX embraced those kids, their music, their politics, their drugs. "Radio is the people," Tom Donahue said. The station had a lost-dog bulletin board, an innovation that grew out of Janis Joplin's propensity to lose her Great Dane, George, nearly every week. Instead of the predictable public service announcements that littered AM radio, KMPX donated airtime to the Berkeley Free Clinic, a venereal disease clinic. Like Fass, KMPX deejays rallied listeners to help each other: when a young man was arrested in Sausalito for violating the midnight curfew, he used his one phone call to ring up KMPX; the overnight jock took up a collection and station staffers went over to the jail to bail out the listener.[17]

The station bought the first full-page ad ever to appear in *Rolling Stone,* a swirling psychedelic poster featuring a drawing of Tom Donahue with a turntable spinning a record on his head; long, stringy images of Frank Zappa and the Jefferson Airplane; and the Beatles in their *Sgt. Pepper's* garb. Deejays started identifying the station as "Kilo

Mother Pot X-ray," and from the spacey, ethereal way the jocks spoke on the air, the audience could be excused for thinking their radio friends were stoned out of their minds.

In many cases, they were. Donahue himself set the tone, his deep, grooving voice accentuated by his huge barrel chest and smoker's rumble. On the air, Donahue used his show to push for a ballot initiative to legalize pot. Off the air, the studios were often a haze of marijuana smoke. Drugs were a positive good, many at the station believed: Donahue hired deejay Chandler Laughlin directly upon his release from prison on a marijuana conviction because Tom figured that "if he can sell pot, he can sell ad time."

Head shops and drug paraphernalia companies were among the major advertisers on KMPX and the other underground stations that started to bloom. At KMET in Los Angeles, a special room for pot smoking was built between the station's two record libraries, with its own ventilation duct.[18] In New York, WNEW's Rosko asked listeners to ride with him on "the mind excursion, the true diversion, the hippest of all trips."[19] At KMPX, deejays were so open about drug use that they would invite listeners to join them in Golden Gate Park to get high. Larry Miller signed off his air shift each night with "May each and every one of you find a little pot at the end of your rainbow."

KMPX even offered listeners a free drug testing service. California was spraying paraquat and other insecticides on marijuana crops, so the station told listeners that if they sent in a sample of their stash, KMPX would have it tested by a company called Pharm-Chem.

Although the jocks thought themselves free to push the envelope, there were limits to what was permitted on the air. When deejays played Steppenwolf's "The Pusher," station lawyers warned that lyrics glorifying drug use could get the company in hot water with federal regulators.

> *You know I've seen a lot of people*
> *Walking around with tombstones in their eyes,*
> *But the Pusher don't care if you live or if you die.*
> *(Chorus) Goddamn the Pusher*

"We pointed out that it was *damning* the pusher," Raechel Donahue said. "It was against heroin specifically. 'Goddamn the pusher.' And the attorney said, 'Yeah, but did he have to say it eighteen times?' "

Back in Washington, what seemed like an epidemic of song lyrics about drugs coincided with an explosion of heroin use and attendant crime problems. The Nixon administration, led by a president who had staked his political future on an appeal to a "silent majority" of Americans who were presumably appalled by the anti-establishment counterculture, decided to push back. In 1971, the FCC warned stations against broadcasting songs with lyrics that might "promote or glorify the use of illegal drugs."

The impact was immediate. Stations banned the Jefferson Airplane's "White Rabbit" ("Remember, feed your head"), songs from the musical *Jesus Christ Superstar* (the issue was sacrilege, not drugs), even "Puff the Magic Dragon." Songs intended as anti-drug were tossed out along with obvious tributes to altered consciousness.

Few stations were in the mood to jeopardize their licenses. In Philadelphia, when deejay Steve Leon played Arlo Guthrie's "Coming into Los Angeles" ("Bringing in a couple of keys / Don't touch my bags if you please / Mister Customs Man"), he was fired midsong—by the owner of WDAS-FM, Max Leon, the jock's father.[20] But in San Francisco, Donahue, undaunted, announced an All-Drug Weekend, playing back-to-back songs about getting high, interspersed with readings from the Bill of Rights.

ON TOM DONAHUE'S STATION, Richard Nixon's cut-and-spliced words droned on in an eerie proto-rap: "Expanding the war, ending the war, expanding the war, ending the war, the war, the war, the war, the war," and then the sound of a huge bomb explosion filled the background, and Buffalo Springfield sang, "What's that sound? Everybody look what's going down." The Gnus, the daily report of current events put together by Scoop Nisker, one of Donahue's off-the-street hires, was on the air.

Mixing politics and music was important to Donahue, even though he knew from both listener reaction and some early surveys that the audience really wanted their station to stick to music. But KMPX and its successor station, KSAN, had no intention of delivering news in the traditional manner. To create a newscast that would be as much of an alternative as KMPX's music offered, Donahue turned to Nisker, Peter Laufer, and other anti-war movement journalists who adopted Bob Fass's free-form approach and rejected the mainstream concept of ob-

TOM DONAHUE *(Courtesy Jim Marshall)*

jectivity. They cut up speeches by Nixon and other white men in suits, then spliced choice phrases together to create jarring juxtapositions and mocking mixes.

Nisker called it "the only news you can dance to."[21] His Gnuscast began one day like this: "The news today, friends, is obscene, dirty, immoral, filthy, smutty news. But if you cook it up in a brownie, it doesn't taste all that bad. Meanwhile, the Vietnam War is still going on, and man, that's obscene."[22]

Nisker's unscheduled, free-form newscasts and his Body Count Thursdays attracted attention from radical groups such as the Black Panthers, the Weather Underground, and a communist youth group in Chinatown, all of which used the station as a bulletin board, dropping by communiqués to be passed along to listeners. This might have seemed routine on noncommercial Pacifica radio, but it perked up plenty of ears on a commercial station. The FBI joined KSAN's audience to monitor the activities of radical groups it considered suspect. With Weather Underground members dropping by to rap about their plans to disrupt military installations, and later the Symbionese Liberation Army using the station as a conduit for its revolutionary messages, FBI agents became regular visitors, which led to frantic scenes of deejays vacuuming marijuana seeds off the KSAN carpet while G-men cooled their heels at the receptionist's desk.[23]

Nisker's Gnuscast was not alone in taking the news underground. In Los Angeles, Pacifica's KPFK featured the satire of Firesign Theatre, a troupe of writers fresh out of Yale who created a late-night "phone-in rap-time psyche-trip" called *Radio Free Oz*. Not far away, at KPPC, a station Tom Donahue took over to expand the underground sound to Southern California, the news came in the form of comedy from a trio called the Credibility Gap—featuring Harry Shearer, later the voice of many of the characters on *The Simpsons*.

If AM radio had spent the previous decade rebelling against the social, racial, and sexual strictures of adult America, FM was now asking basic questions about justice, authority, and the structure of society. "The radio was screaming 'Power to the People—Right On!'" as the gonzo journalist Hunter Thompson put it.[24] In a political and social movement that by its nature had no central headquarters, local radio spread the word and created invisible bonds among like-minded people (much as instant messaging and blogs would emerge as political tools a generation later). As Thompson wrote, "You could *afford* to get mixed up with wild strangers in those days—without fearing for your life, or your eyes, or your organs, or all of your money or even getting locked up in prison forever. There was a sense of *possibility*."[25]

That possibility in radio spread quickly. After the *Rolling Stone* manifesto hit the newsstands, Tom and Raechel Donahue took their show on the road, evangelizing on behalf of no-playlist, free-form radio. By late 1968, more than fifty commercial FM stations went underground in some form—playing album cuts, speaking about and under the influence of drugs, putting their politics on the air.

In Atlanta, WPLO program director Ed Shane laid out the format in a 1969 memo to his deejays. Part of what he said could have come straight from the Top 40 playbook: "Many stations have been confusing the intimate, conversational announcing style with non-professionalism. . . . There's no need to sound lost." But underground radio was very different from Top 40, and even someone trying to reduce it to a formula found himself out on the edge of society: Shane told his staff to avoid public service announcements for the military and read those for the Peace Corps or Biafra Relief instead. News, he said, must not be straight wire copy but should "argue a point." "Choose your music by taste rather than charts. . . . You're not there to sell records. The music you play must possess meaning and message." Don't play the Cowsills' prettified version of "Hair," play the Fifth Dimension's "Aquarius." Don't play Glen Campbell, play Donovan's "Atlantis," which "poses the question, 'Was Atlantis important in our own evolution?'"

At no other point in the history of radio would executives at commercial stations instruct their staffs, as Shane did, to "delve into the more obscure, like Ars Nova, Velvet Underground, and New York Rock and Roll Ensemble," or to air overtly political songs, including Buffy Sainte-Marie numbers that were "an eloquent protest of Indian conditions" and "a good lament of the war," or a Judy Collins song that "describes man's inhumanity to man." The object of this kind of radio, the memo said—and this came from a manager, a *salesman*—was to "relate as a human being."[26]

—

THE UNDERGROUND SOUND had its most immediate and powerful impact on college campuses. In 1967, most college stations were safely and quietly broadcasting classical music and occasional lectures. But over the next couple of years, a wave of transformation swept through those basement studios. At Georgetown University, radicals took over the operating board of WGTB-FM, dumping middle-of-the-road and Top 40 fare and even some of the Jesuits' beloved religious programming. They substituted progressive rock, far-out jazz, and plenty of politics, presented by a "news collective."[27]

At the University of Buffalo in New York, WBFO broadcast a respectable mix of jazz, classical, and academic programming until campus unrest and the inspiration of Bob Fass and Tom Donahue's underground FM combined to create something entirely new. The station hired a professional manager, Bill Siemering, who viewed radio not only as an extracurricular activity and an educational tool but as an art form and an essential cog in the machinery of democracy.

Siemering's polite, thoughtful manner masked a burning passion for social justice. He arrived in Buffalo to discover that listeners had no compelling reason to connect to WBFO. The station's sound captured little of the ferment of campus life in the late 1960s. "The station was a nothing, nothing at all," said Richard Siggelkow, a university vice president who hired Siemering, who had been his student in Wisconsin.

Siemering latched on to any idea that would make his station feel urgent, necessary, a happening place. He reached out to professors, artists, and students for programming ideas that would mirror the new times. In 1969, WBFO devoted twenty-eight hours to a broadcast of the ambient sound of the city of Buffalo. With live feeds from General Mills and Bethlehem Steel plants, from the campus and downtown, a composer altered and mixed the sounds, the zzzzz of steel being sliced and the clamor of workers at shift change, the moan of city buses and the clatter of a campus cafeteria. "It was a John Cage idea, that everything can be musical," Siemering said, "so you had this feeling of being connected to the city and its sounds." Radio, Siemering wrote that year, should be "on the frontier of the contemporary and help create new tastes."[28]

In Buffalo, the great divide was between the races, and when blacks rioted in the wave of violence following Martin Luther King Jr.'s assassination in 1968, Siemering urged student reporters to go out and cover stories in the ghetto. But when a white student reporter got roughed up at a community meeting in the black part of town, Siemering changed tactics. He told his reporters not to go back to the ghetto. He went himself. And when he asked people what was bothering them, he heard a stream of complaints from blacks who said they didn't feel comfortable confiding in naïve white kids from the college.

Determined to connect, Siemering set up Studio J, a storefront studio on Jefferson Avenue, in the heart of black Buffalo, about five miles from campus. WBFO turned over its weekend airtime to a neighborhood group that appointed its own programming chief. Weekends on WBFO sounded nothing like what aired Monday through Friday.

"We weren't represented in the news at all," said Ed Smith, a black theater director whom Siemering recruited to host a jazz program and interview local musicians. "We always complained because the black stations in town were just doing the top R&B thing, with no community focus. With this satellite studio, we could reach not just the black audience, but the whites too, who had never heard our perspective before."

Smith and others spread the word. They found a postal worker who wanted to produce a news show; a clerical worker, Bey Barlow, who had been waiting all her life to present a weekly history of the blues; and a housewife who had put her singing career aside to be a mother but now jumped at the chance to host a children's program. A one-legged Vietnam veteran walked in off the street and asked if he could do a show; his program of avant-garde jazz was the first of its kind in Buffalo. The weekends were mostly music but included a seven-week series on school busing, featuring interviews with both black and white parents, and a series on drug abuse narrated by addicts telling their life stories.

Siemering opened weekdays to new voices as well. Buffalo, a state college, fancied itself the Berkeley of the East—its president had come from the radical California campus, and Buffalo students had demonstrated their political bona fides by voting to eliminate their school's football program. As campus radicals became more demanding in their protests against the war in Vietnam, Siemering and his small band of student reporters decided to get serious about covering the news. They bought a few portable Sony reel-to-reel tape recorders and set out to "let everyone talk," as Ira Flatow put it. Flatow, an engineering student from Long Island who had grown up "never sleeping because I was listening to Jean Shepherd," relished Siemering's idea that WBFO could be the one place where you would hear the "why" of everyone's opinions.

In the spring of 1970—after the U.S. military incursion into Cambodia, but before the shootings at Kent State—Buffalo was the site of an early and dramatic face-off between student protesters and police. Hundreds of cops in riot gear, carrying shotguns and tear gas launchers, stormed the campus while protesters holed up in the student union refused to leave. When a cloud of tear gas reached the home of university vice president Warren Bennis, nearly a mile from campus, he and English professor Bruce Jackson drove over to the student union and immediately made for the WBFO studio on the second floor of the occupied building.

"Warren wanted to reach the students, and WBFO gave him an open mike and let him talk while the other media were reporting the police line, which was that nothing was going on," Jackson said.

WBFO stayed on the air deep into the night, staffers stuffing towels under the studio door to keep out the tear gas. While commercial stations focused on the damage to buildings and the cost of the riots, WBFO put radicals, campus administrators, and city officials on the air and let them have it out. "I interviewed the acting university president and the leader of the student strike," Siemering said. "The idea was that there is not a single truth here."

"This is, of course, grandiose, but to us, it was Ed Murrow broadcasting from the roof in London during the Blitz," said Bennis, who argued to protect the radio station when other administrators grew

frustrated because WBFO was giving voice to the student radicals.[29] "Most of the radio and TV stations were either not giving the news or it was very much anti-student."

The student journalists were determined to be the one outlet delivering every perspective. "We were long-haired-hippie-freak-looking guys," said Flatow, who became a reporter at National Public Radio and host of its *Science Friday* program. "But we knew we had to go in and interview the cops, even if they looked like they wanted to beat us up."

The riot coverage emboldened Siemering to bring even more change to the station. He launched a magazine show called *This Is Radio,* a mix of news, music, and interviews that would later evolve into two mainstays of public radio: *Fresh Air,* which has been hosted since its inception by *This Is Radio* veteran Terry Gross, and *All Things Considered,* National Public Radio's flagship program, which Siemering conceived and launched in 1971.[30]

From the storefront studio to the campus uprising, WBFO made radio vital to its community. Siemering was a dreamer and builder, and like Tom Donahue, he channeled his passions into a manifesto, a series

BILL SIEMERING (AT MICROPHONE, CENTER) IN STUDIO A AT WHA IN MADISON, WISCONSIN, IN A 1960s DRAMA PROGRAM

(Courtesy Current *newspaper)*

of papers every bit as harsh as Donahue's blast against Top 40 radio, and even more idealistic in their quest for a new kind of media culture. In essays and proposals written between 1969 and 1971, Siemering spelled out a vision of a nationwide web of stations, a new kind of American radio, a national public radio. "You couldn't be alive and not be aware of the cultural ferment," Siemering says of that time. "We weren't political radicals, but we were radicals for our medium. I was clearly seeing radio as an agent of social change."

TOM DONAHUE WAS INTO social change too, but in commercial radio, the bottom line was the bottom line. From the start, underground radio was a contradiction in terms. "It was very important to us that we sounded like 'the people,' and not like a bunch of sellouts," Raechel Donahue said.[31]

Underground station managers and deejays refused to air spots for advertisers they disapproved of. At KMPX, the rules were no Army, tampon, fast-food, gasoline, alcohol, or cigarette spots. ("If they had pot spots, we probably would have run them," Raechel said.) When they accepted ads from big companies like Coke or Pepsi, the stations often insisted on producing their own spots rather than accepting slickly produced tape from Madison Avenue.

Whatever misgivings the Donahues and others had about being perceived as part of the machinery of American consumerism, as underground radio caught on, the ratings and buzz attracted advertisers eager to reach young people. Enough ad money poured into KMPX in the spring of 1968 that owner Leon Crosby raised his bargain-basement advertising rates to the level charged by mainstream stations. That meant the station needed to reach beyond bed shops, head shops, and record stores and lure big-time accounts.

And that, Crosby said, would happen only if the station cleaned up its act. So he ordered Donahue's staff to halt illegal drug use at the station, ditch the long skirts and open-toed shoes, and start wearing ties and looking like real Americans. This did not go over well with Donahue and the gang, who after all were still adjourning to Tom's place

after hours to get high and rag on the establishment. It especially did not go over because Crosby's paychecks had a habit of bouncing. Donahue responded to the edict by resigning. The staff formed the Amalgamated American Federation of International FM Workers of the World, Ltd., North Beach Local 1, and the union announced it would stage a walkout if Crosby didn't bring back Donahue, give him total control, boost everyone's wages, and share the profits. And they wanted double pay on Halloween and, oh yes, the summer solstice as a paid holiday. This was, after all, the Great Hippie Strike.

At 1 A.M. on the night the strike would begin, deejay Bob McClay told his audience, "We've been talking about splitting and leaving and that's what's happening. We have all been enjoying a groovy thing here, [but] Tom Donahue quit last week. My head is in a strange place. The reason we're doing this is so there can be, oh, creative freedom, so there can be truth, be it in the music, in what we say, whatever. I hope you don't feel abandoned." And he played a rock version of "We Shall Overcome."

Later, a soft voice came on to say, "The Great Sphinx looks with scorn upon our station. It has watched while our motives were murdered and our talent wasted. To his mighty disgust, black sheep have been sacrificed to our sponsors." It went on like this for hours. Finally, just before 3 A.M., the Grateful Dead arrived in the studio and the deejays signed off. Moments later, a voice said, "Okay, this is now Radio Free San Francisco."

But it wasn't. KMPX was off the air. Silence followed. Back in New York, Bob Fass put Donahue on *Radio Unnameable* and provided live coverage of the strike's beginning. Concert promoter Bill Graham sent the striking jocks a truckful of food. Longshoremen offered to bust up any scabs the station might hire as replacement deejays. Bands such as the Dead and Creedence Clearwater Revival staged concerts in Golden Gate Park to support the strike. "They wanted to sell spots to Coca-Cola!" the strikers shouted to the crowd, which could hardly believe that such dastardly schemes had been afoot at their beloved station.[32]

With Donahue and his staff still on the street, Crosby signed his station back on the air with new deejays. But bands asked KMPX not to play their songs, sponsors pulled ads, and demonstrators picketed outside the studios. Then, after an eight-week standoff, the strike became moot: KSAN, a classical station with lousy ratings, had been playing some rock on Saturday nights, on a show called *Underground Sunshine.* The station's owners at Metromedia invited Donahue on the air to talk about the strike, and that appearance led to another, and soon Donahue and Metromedia were talking. In the end, Tom won permission to re-create the KMPX sound on KSAN, under corporate ownership and with most of his KMPX crew.

The new KSAN was a fast winner in the ratings. On this station, there were somehow fewer compunctions about selling out to the Man. Donahue, after all, knew what business he was in. "Radical community stations are supported by advertisers with money," he said. "If you get in bed with the devil, you better be prepared to fuck."[33] There were still spots for the free clinic and Donahue still ranted on the air against the "fat capitalists." KSAN salesmen purposely printed their business cards in psychedelic lettering on three-by-five stock so they wouldn't fit in a Rolodex.[34]

But when the Bank of America, which recently had suffered attacks by rock-throwing radicals at one of its branches, inquired about advertising on KSAN, it became clear that corporate America could do business with the underground. KSAN's Travis T. Hipp, a talk show host and ad salesman, suggested to the visiting bankers that their spots carry the slogan "There's a Bank of America a stone's throw from where you live." Hipp recalled that the bankers walked out after that one.[35] But the bankers overcame their hurt feelings, signed up with the station, and actually did use that slogan on some spots—proving once again the ability of American commerce to co-opt rebellion and rechannel it toward the glories of profit.

As FM became more popular, the pressure to produce ratings pushed underground stations to become more predictable, more like something that advertisers could feel comfortable buying. In the corridors of the fading radio networks in New York and at the offices of the corporations that controlled the Top 40 pop culture, the social forces that created underground radio had not gone unnoticed. Doubt crept into the most mundane business decisions—doubt and fear and a sense that everything was changing.

ON LATE-NIGHT AM RADIO in the late 1960s, listeners could close their eyes and hear a divided and pessimistic nation, at war abroad against its will, at war at home against itself. Talk shows focused on rebellious youth, murky conspiracy theories surrounding the JFK assassination, and the eerie mysteries of the night sky—whispers of aliens at home and above the clouds.

On FM, underground radio suffused itself in drugs and escaped in music that reached for a higher consciousness. But flower power and the Age of Aquarius could not camouflage the pain of a generation straining to assert itself, a generation that repeatedly poked its parents in the eye. After the assassinations of Martin Luther King, Jr., and Robert F. Kennedy, after the endless anguish of 1968 and a war that no one seemed capable of stopping, the music on FM seemed to lose its joy and focused instead on bad trips, pusher men, narcs, and the overwhelming sense that America was on the wrong track.

In Ann Arbor, Michigan, in October 1969, some University of Michigan students persuaded themselves that the end was near. A serial killer was on the loose. Radicals occupied the campus administration building. Someone torched the ROTC military training facility. And in the dormitories late at night, the real obsession, the question that had many people spooked, was whether Paul McCartney was dead.

Rumors about the prettiest Beatle had been bubbling, entirely by word of mouth, in a band of college campuses from Illinois to Michigan. Students had been collecting clues for several months, and when they got back to school that fall, a couple of them published articles in college newspapers laying out the evidence: On a cover of the Beatles' *Yesterday and Today* album that was quickly recalled by the record company, Paul looks like he's in a coffin. The song "Nowhere Man" is a reference to Paul's death. The cover of the *Sgt. Pepper's* album depicts a funeral with an arrangement of flowers that spell out "Paul?" And on and on, dozens of clues, traded at parties and in cafeteria conversations.

And then, one Sunday that October, Russ Gibb, a part-time deejay and concert promoter, was on the air at Keener-FM, Detroit's WKNR-FM, an underground rocker that specialized in eclectic music and spacey jocks. Gibb liked to take calls on the air, and on this night, he punched up a guy named Tom, a student at Eastern Michigan University in Ypsilanti.

"Hello, Tom, what's going down?"

"I was going to rap with you about McCartney being dead and what is this all about?" Gibb scoffed at the notion, but Tom persisted, suggesting that the deejay put "Revolution 9" on the turntable and play it backward to hear a coded message.[36]

Gibb did as he was told. "That's when I first heard the thing that everybody said sounded like 'Turn me on, dead man.' "[37] Instantly, Keener-FM's phones starting ringing off the hook. Everybody, it seemed, had another clue. Kids came down to the station and started banging on the windows out front, holding up album covers to demonstrate their various proofs. The station manager called Gibb from home with a blunt message to the deejay: whatever he was doing, "keep doing it."

Among Gibb's listeners that night were some students who wrote for *The Michigan Daily,* the state university's student newspaper. Fred LaBour had already been assigned to write a review of the Beatles' new album, *Abbey Road,* and, armed with the clues aired on Keener-FM, he quickly threw together a story, adding a whole slew of evidence that he picked up from other students, plus a few bits he made up himself after a careful study of *Abbey Road.*

"McCartney Dead; New Evidence Brought to Light," the headline read on October 14, and LaBour assumed that readers would be tipped to the fact that he was spoofing by the jocular tone of his writing and the ridiculous nature of some of his "evidence" (Paul was replaced by a look-alike named William Campbell—LaBour almost went with Glen Campbell, but figured that using a famous singer's name would be too much of a giveaway).[38]

If anyone did take the LaBour story as a joke, that reader has not yet surfaced. Back at Keener-FM, Gibb put LaBour on the air ("I don't know, there's so many coincidences," the student said. "It seems there has to be—something is up, I don't know"). The *Michigan Daily* story became the basis for an hour-long documentary that Gibb cobbled together with fellow deejays John Small and Dan Carlisle. *The Beatle Plot* begins with a voice-of-God announcer who invests each phrase with grave moment: "The subject is Paul McCartney. The theme is symbolism. The thesis is death. The proposition—coincidence. It began on a recent Sunday." In excruciating detail, the program spells out the clues—the lyrics, the photos on Beatles albums, the hidden messages in one song after another. Backward the songs play until reels the mind. Beatles tunes known and loved by millions become groaning, pulsing electronic mysteries. McCartney and Lennon sound like a growling stomach, an angry crowd, a dizzying, disturbing aural equivalent of paranoia.

The deejays buttressed their audio "evidence" with excerpts from forty hours of phone interviews they did in the rush to get their show on the air—Eric Clapton saying "I'm as convinced as anybody," one of Bob Dylan's managers describing how he'd seen John Lennon and Ringo Starr together without Paul. And Lennon, clearly annoyed, dismissing the entire premise as "rubbish, just insanity: I have no idea what records sound like backwards. I never play them backwards."

"Apple Records seems to want us to believe it's all a coincidence," the Keener show concludes. "But we don't."

Neither did hundreds of other deejays and newspaper reporters, who jumped on the story within hours after the Keener program hit the airwaves. Gibb and LaBour were invited to Hollywood to appear on a TV show in which celebrity defense lawyer F. Lee Bailey put the Paul Is Dead rumor on trial. In New York, WABC deejay Roby Yonge was yanked off the air in the middle of his show—at 2 A.M.—for breaking the Top 40 format and perpetuating the rumor by playing "Revolution 9" backward, over and over. Finally, a month after the rumor first found its way onto the radio in Michigan, *Life* magazine sent a reporter to McCartney's secluded farm in Scotland to confront Paul, who looked quite reasonably alive in the cover photograph. The picture of the Beatle with his family ran under the headline "Paul Is Still with Us."

If anything, the *Life* story served largely to extend the rumor to corners of the country where it had not yet aired. The Paul Is Dead episode was never about fact; it was about trust and the growing sense that there was no one truth, and that *Life* magazine and AM radio and the daily newspapers were not conveying the only version of reality that mattered.

Paul *was* dead, in a sense that meant something to many young people. "We never really said he was dead," Keener deejay John Small claimed years later.[39] "We implied certain things. I didn't think he was dead physically. I thought he was dead spiritually, in the group." The fact that the Beatles were in the process of breaking up was enough of a death to justify the Paul Is Dead hysteria, Small said. To young America, the loss of the Beatles was every bit as traumatic as the assassinations, riots, and images of war each night on TV. On FM, Buffalo Springfield sang Stephen Stills's anthem of pop revolution, "There's something happening here / What it is ain't exactly clear."

TOP 40 DIDN'T CARE ABOUT any political message in Stills's "For What It's Worth"; the tune was a hit and Top 40 still had a mass audience for whatever was hot and fresh. Adults still liked the mix of Motown, middle-of-the-road melodies, and rock and roll. Advertisers were still drawn to AM radio's powerhouse ratings. Anytime 20, 30, or 40 percent of the audience was listening, advertisers wanted to be there.

Top 40 also benefited from a backlash against the underground; just as Donahue's KMPX was making a name for itself, Top 40 found a huge hit in "An Open Letter to My Teenage Son," a message written by a Michigan advertising man and spoken over the "Battle Hymn of the Republic." "You ask my opinion of draft card burners," the narrator said. "I would answer this way. All past wars have been dirty, unfair, immoral, bloody and second-guessed. However, history has shown most of them necessary. If you doubt that our free enterprise system in the United States is worth protecting . . . , then it's doubtful that you belong here. . . . I love you too son, but I also love our country. And if you decide to burn your draft card, then burn your birth certificate at the same time. From that moment on, I have no son."[40]

But while one side in the nascent culture wars lined up against underground radio and another embraced the FM sound as its true voice, the vast majority of Americans were somewhere in the middle, including many deejays working in Top 40. At KYA in San Francisco, Johnny Holliday "could feel it closing in. The FM station played the longhair music and our boss said okay, we better start playing it." So KYA aired shortened versions of Janis Joplin and Jefferson Airplane songs between the jingles and contests. But FM had far better fidelity, and "me going to the Fillmore was like having Janis Joplin out to the country club," Holliday said. "I had no idea how to connect to those people, no idea."

Cousin Bruce Morrow watched as his bosses struggled over which songs on the Beatles' *Sgt. Pepper's* album should make the cut at WABC. "Little by little, we moved," he said, "but the kids on the streets were changing in big ways and we didn't see that. We stole from FM, we expanded our music list and added some album cuts." The station reduced commercials from eighteen minutes an hour to eleven and gave away albums and concert tickets in an attempt to be hip. But it was all show. By the time underground FM came along, Morrow was faking it. "I didn't know what the hell was going on," he said. "Listeners would call, newspaper people would ask me, where are you on the war? And we didn't talk about that on WABC. The young people found their new connection on FM, while on AM, we were still stuck in the mores of their parents."

Throughout his career, Cousin Brucie had based his success on his ability to get inside the heads of his young listeners. He knew instinctively what was worrying them, what they really wanted to say but couldn't. It was all about sex and hormones and that had been revolution enough. Not anymore. Young people cared about being sent off to war and about the gulf that separated them from their parents' concerns. And as Morrow felt more and more disconnected, his show hardened into predictability. His numbers slipped. He suffered a loss of faith.

"Sometimes I had to lie and say I was against the war, because that's what the majority was saying," Morrow recalled three decades later. "And I really felt uncomfortable, because really, I thought they were traitors. I believed that broadcasters should be neutral. I didn't understand. I was afraid. I'd go to parties and pretend to be doing all that stuff, but it offended me, the drugs, the politics, all of that. I was brought up to believe in waving the flag, not burning it."

When WABC sent Morrow to Woodstock, flying him in by helicopter, he felt lost, out of place. These were not his kids. "I was getting a pseudo," he said. "I was not a hippie, but I wanted to be accepted. I was physically uncomfortable and I thought, 'God damn it, it's because of these people that I'm uncomfortable.' "

But after watching state troopers arrest young pot smokers, Morrow became more sympathetic. He saw a connection between these kids and the ones who came to his shows at Palisades Amusement Park. "They were the same kids, just as nice," he said, "and I moved around and saw them helping each other, and the calmness came over me."

Years later, Morrow concluded that he had been wrong, that the kids "were right. They were prophets. I thought John Lennon was anti, but he was pro. Now I know we were lied to and cheated." But in the moment, all Morrow could see was that his time was over. Top 40's audience was so huge that it would take the better part of a decade to dissipate, but the course had been set.

LIKE TOM DONAHUE, Allen Shaw was a Top 40 veteran who carved out space on the radio to play the album cuts he loved. Shaw's success at breaking Top 40's rules and slipping in his own choices at stations in Albany and Chicago persuaded him there was big money to be made by tapping into the new youth culture. In 1968, after he heard Tom Donahue evangelize on behalf of free-form radio at an industry conference, Shaw wrote to network executives in New York, proposing that they swallow their skepticism and take the underground "above ground and into the light of day." If a network could strip out the negatives—the drugs, anti-establishment politics, and anti-Amerika attitude—and accentuate "the great new music, freedom of expression, brotherhood and LOVE," Shaw predicted that that network would find riches in a generation uniquely disposed to spend, spend, spend on a whole new lifestyle. The format would be called LOVE.[41]

"We'll be in the progressive rock bag, but the music is only an indicator of a more deeply rooted set of changes in our society," Shaw wrote. "LOVE is black and white, old and young, rich and poor, father and son, boy and girl, and country and nation. . . . The desire is to prove that black ink is beautiful." Shaw dismissed the purists' form of underground radio as boring and self-indulgent. He thought he could sell underground-inspired programming to a network eager to reach the rapidly swelling ranks of young America. Most networks quickly said no, thanks—CBS was high on its "Young Sound," featuring instrumental covers of hit songs; NBC was interested, but only for its AM stations; and Westinghouse, seeing no commercial future in FM, was selling off its stations. But executives at ABC saw that about one in four albums on the Top 100 were "progressive rock," the new, politically neutral term for the underground sound. If Shaw could pull off his program service on the cheap, ABC was willing to try it on the network's seven FM stations, which then played mostly classical music or show tunes.

Shaw decided that LOVE would be one long program with one hip voice, and that summer, while visiting Chicago, he heard what he would call "the voice from heaven." John Rydgren was a Lutheran minister who had a radio show called *Silhouette* on which he spun records between easy-to-swallow, scripture-free spiritual messages.

Shaw hired the velvet-toned minister and renamed him Brother John. LOVE would consist of progressive rock hits intercut with mini-sermons on love, war, drugs, and the new culture. A Procul Harem song would end and Brother John's mellifluous baritone would follow softly. "Have you ever been at the brink of understanding a concept?

Then for you, the concept is concrete—solid fact. Love—sounds terribly simple, doesn't it? But: Isn't it true that a concept becomes true for a person once a person becomes part of it? Love becomes a fact for a person."[42] A short silence, then a station identification jingle—more muted and slower than Top 40 jingles, but still a dissonant clash with Brother John's mellow groove. And then the music returned, and some listeners undoubtedly persuaded themselves that what Brother John had just said made sense, that it was, like, deep.

In a tape sent to potential advertisers, Brother John warned that "you'll hear things you may not like," but he assured the time buyers of corporate America that "LOVE is a feeling, an understanding and caring for humanity," and that the "eighteen-to-twenty-eight young adult can best be sold in the LOVE environment." After all, while they were thinking about "truth, beauty and love," these young people were also "establishing brand preferences, obtaining credit cards and starting new careers and families."

LOVE launched in February 1969, and the underground press critics laughed themselves silly over the format's corporate sound. But the public seemed to like it. WABC-FM, LOVE's New York affiliate, called itself "New York's medium with a message." ABC's FM stations got a boost in the ratings, and stations outside the network added the programming.

Shaw believed he was transmitting the drumbeat of the flower children to a broader audience. He thought Americans would embrace a positive message without the dark side of the counterculture. But in city after city, audiences sampled LOVE in impressive numbers and then drifted away. LOVE lost out to underground stations that delivered a locally created, authentic reflection of what was happening on the streets. San Francisco chose KSAN over LOVE, New York chose WNEW-FM over LOVE, and before long, Shaw was retooling, adding deejays and instructing them that it was okay to talk politics, to take a stand against the war, to mimic not only the flowery side of the underground but the whole package, downers and all.

Still, it didn't sell. By 1970, LOVE yielded to money, Shaw sent Brother John packing, and ABC converted its FM stations to a local, alternative-rock format, "totally involved in and a reflection of the American counterculture." This time, Shaw wanted the most radical jocks he could find; there were even talks with Bob Fass about leaving Pacifica to join the American Broadcasting Company. (Fass thought better of the idea, and so did ABC.) On the Fourth of July that year, ABC's FM stations aired a special called *Self-Evident Truths* that could have been a production of Tom Donahue's San Francisco underground station, except for its smoother sound. The program juxtaposed voice clips of Nixon, Vice President Spiro Agnew, and former president Lyndon Johnson defending the Vietnam War, and overlaid their tired rhetoric with searing rock sounds and righteous, rebellious quotations from the Constitution and American Revolutionary patriots.

Shaw cringed in his office, awaiting the inevitable bullet from his bosses. It never came. The company had bought in to the revolution— at least until the ratings books arrived. Deejays chose their own music and even got to weigh in on whether commercials were fit for their station's sound. ABC's only restrictions were that there be no obscenities or promotion of drug use. In "A Culture in Evolution," a memo written to calm the nerves of anxious advertisers, ABC noted that this was the most powerful young generation in the nation's history. ABC was bullish on the kids, noting with relief that "they do spend and would rather live well than die rich." (Whew.) After all, young people were buying $40 see-through shirts and $80 leather pants, $200 custom coats and unprecedented numbers of records, books, and cars.

With six in ten Americans under the age of thirty-four, "today's youth are spearheading the development of a LIFESTYLE uniquely their own. It reverses the cultural priorities of most Americans; it replaces competition of the marketplace with cooperation of the small, intimate peer group or commune."

What drew this generation together, ABC contended, was FM radio. "Pretty soon everybody is going to reject the plastic," the American Broadcasting Company assured Madison Avenue. "And then the United States will be reoriented as a group of thinking individuals rather than a 'homogeneous mass' "—a parting shot at the mass numbers Top 40 radio was still racking up.[43] The hippies were finding their capitalist groove, the capitalists were exploring a new bag, and radio fancied itself in the vanguard of the great cosmic convergence. Capitalism could be beautiful, man. Except that Americans still loved that hit music.

THERE WERE AT MOST FOUR Summers of Love. By 1971, managers insisted that deejays sound a bit livelier and a lot less stoned. "It wasn't funny to be the dope-smoking airhead on the radio anymore," Raechel Donahue said. At New York's underground WNEW, playlists tightened; whereas in 1967 the station played only two records from *Billboard*'s Hot 100, by 1969, that number was up to sixty-eight.[44] At ABC in 1971, the numbers showed that only 4 percent of the audience listened to free-form radio. ABC heard the silence; Allen Shaw announced, "We are out of the free-form thing entirely." Jocks could still determine the order in which songs were played each hour, but the song list was ordained by management.

Then, an FCC ruling against a free-form station sent a chill through the underground: raising the specter of payola, the agency said that the format "gives the announcer such control over the records to be played that it is inconsistent with the strict controls that the licensee must exercise to avoid questionable practices."[45] ABC and Metromedia immediately declared that their alternative stations were really "progressive," not free-form. While deejays had some leeway in deciding what tunes to play, management assured regulators that the adults were always monitoring the selections.

Despite the nation's endless fascination with the new, Top 40 radio still pulled in vastly more listeners than FM rock stations could even dream of. The radio business didn't yet have the research tools to know it, but they had discovered in underground FM a perfect niche, a demographic slice of the populace that shared an affection for one kind of programming. There was gold at the end of that rainbow, but it would take a rock-obsessed kid in Chicago to discover the treasure.

Chapter 8

✳ PLAYING THE NUMBERS

ON DECEMBER 12, 1963, Lee Abrams became a boy obsessed. His parents gave him his first transistor radio, and the eleven-year-old reacted as if he'd been granted a free pass to fly around the world. Lee listened constantly—under the covers, through his pillow, walking to school. He spent evenings scanning the nation's AM airwaves for new stations from faraway places. He set his alarm for the middle of the night to listen to distant deejays he'd come to admire. At home in Chicago, Lee listened for the jingle that announced the arrival of the big, bold voice that was his very favorite.

All across Mid-America
Goes the brightest sound around,
All across Mid-America
Comes WLS-Chicago!

When Lee was a teenager, the jingles blew by fast and furious on WLS, Chicago's dominant Top 40 station. Jingle singers crooned, "Don Phillips on the *East of Midnight* program, across the Great 48," and here came Don: "A little story out of Saigon today: Staff Sgt. Billy Hammontree is a very lucky guy. Stepped on a grenade booby trap that didn't work. Tripped another booby trap that also malfunctioned. All in one day. If it's like that over there, I'm glad I'm not over there."

Another singing jingle: "What's the weather for the weekend gonna be? Will it be hot, cold, rain, snow?"

Don was ready with the answer: "Well, we're having a super summer on 8-9-0." He sang along with the station ID jingle. Then: "This is Hannibal and the Headhunters."[1]

Lee couldn't get over the idea that Phillips's arch little stories were streaking through the night across the entire continent, carried from

LEE ABRAMS AS A TEENAGE BUDDING RADIO
EXECUTIVE IN CHICAGO, 1960s *(Courtesy Lee Abrams)*

Lee's hometown to more than thirty states via WLS's clear-channel signal (meaning no other stations used that frequency on the dial). Barely into his teens, Lee memorized jingles. (Quite some time went by before he realized that the little ditties were on tape, rather than performed live by the orchestra and chorus he'd conjured in his mind.) At fourteen, Lee attended radio industry conventions, read *Billboard* and other trade magazines, and exchanged letters with other radio freaks in cities from Miami to San Diego.

Lee took to dogging the deejays who hosted record hops at local schools and veterans halls. He would make himself useful, hauling records, fetching coffee, anything to catch a glimpse of the magic behind the microphone. At sixteen, he expanded his obsession from radio to music. He managed a cover band, the Dimensions of Thyme, and he figured that for them to succeed, they had to play the tunes kids wanted to hear. So Lee began what he called his "hitchhiking studies." He thumbed rides all over the city, to hops, concerts, radio station events, appearances by his band and others. At each stop, he conducted what one day would be called exit polls.

"On a one-to-ten scale, what do you think of these bands?" he'd ask, reeling off the names of one group after another. He wrote everything down, compiled the results, and called up stations to share his numbers. His room became a forest of questionnaires. Lee wrote down every new idea, every gimmick he gleaned from that data and from his listening. He collected them into a newsletter, which he typed up and sold, taking out ads in the trade papers offering "Better Ideas for Better Stations."

In 1969, when his family vacationed in Miami, Lee, then seventeen, wormed his way into the studios of WQAM and into the good graces of the guys who ran the station's FM sister, WMYQ. In exchange for an occasional gratuity from the station's News Tip of the Week kitty, Lee created WMYQ's music research department: He would call record stores and offer a trade—if the store let Lee know how its records were selling and which songs were hot, the station would give the store ten or twenty free copies of records it got from distributors. The store could then sell those records, keeping every penny as profit. There was one catch: Lee wanted more than sales numbers. He asked store managers to give bad information to any other station that called. Eager to get the free records, the stores happily played along. And Lee had an easy way to confirm that the shops lived up to their end of the bargain: He simply tuned in to the competition and heard them spin—and promote as "top hits"—records that were actually sitting unsold in store bins. This business was going to be fun.

Lee took his precocious plunge into radio research in the service of Top 40 stations, but his own taste was moving toward the album cuts that underground FM stations such as WLS-FM were playing. Yet as much as Lee loved the harder, more complex music on underground FM, he despised the stations that played it. They sounded unprofessional, sloppy, haphazard. To a young man who believed above all else in radio as craft, this was unforgivable. Lee cringed when he heard an underground deejay play two versions of "America," by the British rock band the Nice, simultaneously—the live version on the left channel of a stereo broadcast and the studio version on the right.

"It was such nonsense," Lee said. "Too cool for the room. They were blowing it. Music was everything to me, and here was this new kind of music that could be so perfect, so big, and these guys were talking to their friends on the radio. They were targeting such a small, elite audience, and they were so spacey." Lee knew he could fix this. All a station needed was the right set of information about what music to play, who the audience was, and what they wanted from radio and life.

Lee Abrams was not old enough to drink or vote, but he was well on his way toward reinventing radio and restructuring pop culture.

FROM THE DAWN OF commercial broadcasting, advertisers needed to know just what they were buying when they ponied up for a few seconds of airtime. The science of polling was in its infancy as radio became a mass medium, and pioneers such as George Gallup and Paul Lazarsfeld soon realized that the methods they developed for public opinion research had powerful potential as a marketing tool—and a source of profit.

In the 1930s, opinion research was crude—samples were small and not quite random, and questions were usually designed to capture basic information ("What shows did you listen to last night?") rather than to understand who was listening and why. But the radio industry desperately needed data, and the 1930s and '40s were a period of experimentation: CBS hired psychologists to watch listeners from behind curtains and record their behavior. C. E. Hooper created the Hooperatings, using random phone calls to count the audiences for specific programs (even though half the nation's households did not yet have telephones in the early 1940s). The Pulse ratings company visited listeners at home to interview them about their habits. A. C. Nielsen pushed a mechanized and more reliable approach starting in 1942, wiring its audimeters to home radios to record each turn of the dial.[2]

The rise of Top 40 and rock and roll created a need for more specific research: radio executives were eager to prove to hesitant advertisers that stations that obviously reached enormous numbers of young people were also listened to by people with jobs and checking accounts—adults. But in private, radio executives dismissed their own studies; they knew how flimsy their methods really were. Many surveys were based on quickie sidewalk interviews or a couple of hundred postcards popped in the mail.

The very idea of research was anathema to deejays and even to many of their bosses, who believed supremely in their own ability to pick hit songs. George Michael, one of the most music-savvy Top 40 jocks and a ratings powerhouse in Philadelphia and then New York, saw no need for survey data. "I went to every high school football and basketball game and the pep rallies and I'd hang around and talk and hear about the songs that were hot. I didn't need numbers. I could feel it."

But as surveys became more ambitious, both advertisers and radio executives came to see them as more meaningful. The first goal of radio research was getting one seemingly simple question answered: what were people listening to? By the 1960s, so much listening occurred in the car, at the park, and in the backyard that meters attached to home sets no longer did the trick. When radios moved into cars in a big way in the 1950s, Hooper sent pollsters out into intersections to collar drivers stopped at red lights and quiz them. Arbitron, the company that would come to dominate the industry, began issuing diaries in 1964—the method that still accounts for most radio ratings, despite its questionable reliance on listeners' memories, honesty, and diligence.

In 1960, WMCA in New York commissioned a psychological study of radio listeners, opening the door to the idea that audiences could be analyzed not only by basic characteristics such as age and sex, but by attitudes and desires: Exactly how did radio connect to them? What phrases made them feel part of a community? And who was that community?

By the end of the 1960s, the new tools of measurement showed that the era of a single mass pop culture was fading. A more crowded radio dial offered more narrowly focused choices. The days of one station holding on to 60 percent of the listeners in a market were over. Underground rock stations were chipping away at Top 40's audience. Specialization had arrived. If someone could harness that specialization, documenting exactly who was switching over to FM, the cultural landscape—and the business—would change dramatically.

One station owner, Stanley Kaplan of Charlotte, North Carolina, addressed his colleagues in 1968 with a radical notion: "As research becomes more sophisticated—and there is much evidence that this is already happening—the greatest economic success will go to the station that owns the audience under 25 and doesn't have a single soul over that age. In the next five years or so," he predicted, advertising agencies might say that "we are going to put 35 percent of our budget into 18–24 and 22 percent of our budget into 45–51, etc. . . . No one ever again in most markets can ever be a generalist."[3]

LEE ABRAMS REBELLED AGAINST REBELLION. He loved how radio made people feel like they were part of something bigger. And he loved how a new music—the rock that made him feel alive—was connecting to young people and shifting the culture. At Abrams's first job, in 1970, as music director of an FM Top 40 station in Miami, he itched to play progressive rock in a way that would reach out to all young people, not just hip stoners.

The youth culture of the 1970s did not belong only to the radicals who took over college campuses and burned draft cards and brassieres. The new, wider audience for FM rock was not just early adopters, turning on, tuning in, dropping out. Dick Nixon's silent majority grew into FM, graduating from transistor radios to the stereo console. These kids never made it to the Summer of Love or even to Woodstock, but they were Pepsi People Feelin' Free. They were affluent, assured, and acquisitive, and Abrams wanted radio to reflect their reality, not the stoned, antagonistic approach of the underground sound. Young people needed radio to offer them an escape. But that escape had to be familiar, unthreatening—it could not make listeners feel dumb or out of it.

"Familiar music works," Abrams said. Why play music that thousands of people like rather than music that millions like? "Sounds pretty obvious, but people continue to fight the idea."[4] Abrams looked at the ratings numbers and saw proof that FM was failing to capitalize on its potential. About one-third of radio listening was on FM, but FM accounted for less than 15 percent of radio's revenue.[5] To correct this imbalance, Abrams believed, was no sellout, but a business imperative. In 1971, Abrams merged the music of the FM frontier with the tried-and-true foundations of pop culture, writing a format for a rock station that would play familiar album cuts in a predictable, Top 40 formula, but with a cool, FM sound. Listeners would get the sense that they had graduated from AM to a more adult approach. This would be "progressive, album-oriented" rock rather than "underground." The focus would be on the music, not the deejay. And the music would be selected scientifically, with research done pretty much as young Lee Abrams had collected data on his hitchhiking tours of Chicago. Only now, Abrams would use record stores to distribute callback cards— postcard-sized entry blanks that would enroll shoppers in a music giveaway contest sponsored by the station, which then called the listeners and quizzed them about which songs they wanted to hear and which they hated. As Abrams predicted, listeners asked for the music they knew best. Abrams sold his format to WQDR in Raleigh, North Carolina, joining the station as a consultant. In one three-month ratings period, the station went from a 1 percent share of the market's listeners to an 11 percent share. He was on his way.

While Abrams and his consulting partner, Kent Burkhart, packaged their more commercial approach to FM radio, underground stations moved clumsily in that same direction of their own accord. The more money alternative stations made, the more owners and managers asserted themselves into the hippie haven of the broadcast studio. To attract advertisers and maximize return on these stations, managers made programming more predictable. Research was their tool of choice. Stations called up listeners and asked, "Which songs are you tired of? What do you want to hear whenever you turn on the radio?" Deejays suddenly had to play a certain number of hits per hour and choose from a short list of less familiar tunes. Rather than let deejays blather on about their parties the night before or their acid-enhanced proposals for the future of the planet, stations handed jocks liner cards instructing them to deliver station slogans after each set of music.

The listeners who first discovered the underground sound were growing older; they had spouses and houses and responsibilities now, and they didn't have the patience to sit through someone else's head trip. The war was winding down, the Nixon presidency was self-destructing, the divisions and discord of the 1960s were dissipating, and the sounds on the radio were more upbeat, familiar, assuring. It was a time for "Silly Love Songs," as Paul McCartney sensed. Where once there had been more than three hundred underground stations nationwide, by the mid-1970s only a couple of dozen remained.[6]

In their place, more specialized FM stations sprouted, designed by Abrams and other consultants to train listeners to believe they could get precisely the kind of music they wanted—"More music! Less talk!" "Your music!" "Music for the way you live!"—at the punch of a button. Abrams's format—which he called Superstars because the songs were all by the familiar artists whose names kept popping up in his calls to listeners—could be installed at any FM station, no matter its size or location. Stations no longer needed newscasts or public affairs programs; only the music mattered. Deejays were barely a factor; the stars were the groups—the Rolling Stones, the Eagles, Fleetwood Mac. By the mid-1970s, more than three hundred stations had bought Abrams's package.

In college dormitories, in the bedrooms of high school kids, in the rapidly increasing number of cars now equipped with FM, Superstars stations offered a new kind of cool, sounding mellow and free. Announcers sounded like adults, not hopped-up pseudo-adolescents. Just as the kids who leaped across the musical color line in the 1950s did not necessarily become civil rights activists or Beat poets, Abrams's listeners were not inclined to join the ranks of campus radicals. But they nonetheless felt themselves part of a movement, a collective of like-minded young people who shared not only a style of music but an approach to life. The medium that brought them together, that taught them the right attitudes, the cool tone of voice, and the happening catchphrases, was the new FM, the package created by Lee Abrams. He had captured just enough of the anti-establishment tone of the underground to sound authentic while purging alternative radio of its anarchic instincts and of the very unpredictability that Tom Donahue believed was at the core of radio as a creative art. Deejays who had worked at early FM rock stations were appalled. They felt wronged, abused. But Abrams's listeners knew little or nothing of that internecine battle. They felt as if they were on the inside, discovering new music, new experiences. The revolution had been co-opted and the ratings were terrific.

IN 1975, TOM DONAHUE, then KSAN's station manager, died of a massive heart attack. He was forty-six. In honor of Big Daddy, his station canceled all commercials for twenty-four hours. But KSAN would not survive its creative leader for very long. "They waited until he died and then they brought in people with pie charts and statistics," said Raechel Donahue, Big Daddy's widow.

Despite his hippie-dippie rhetoric, Tom Donahue, a radio pro, would have understood the consultants' approach. After all, Donahue had always imposed a certain structure on his free-form stations. KMPX and KSAN from the start issued general guidelines about the mix of music deejays should play, and Raechel kept lists of what each jock spun so that tunes were not accidentally repeated on the same day. There were even a few hard rules. You couldn't play Billie Holiday's "Strange Fruit" late at night because listeners on the edge might decide to jump off a bridge. But rules were minimal and enforcement was informal.

After Tom died, new managers responded to the pressure of competition from other FM rockers. In 1978, KSAN program director Bonnie Simmons made it clear that the days of free-form commercial radio were dwindling. She publicly denied using playlists, but the station did impose discipline on its deejays. "Everyone is giving much more thought in doing their shows not to alienate the audience," Simmons said. "I don't want a real hip, cultish radio station that no one listens to."[7] Management pushed the station to be "less exclusive," urging deejays to broaden their appeal by playing more familiar tunes and being, well, less weird.

That July, when KSAN fired deejay Norman Davis, managers put the reasons in writing: "You were discharged because you refused to follow instructions as to the type of music you were to play. As you had also received prior warnings about this, the discharge is considered to have been for misconduct."[8]

But tightening control over the music and bringing in consultants did not save KSAN from the dictates of the ratings. In 1980, KSAN dropped rock entirely and flipped to a country-and-western format.[9] Management had found a more profitable niche.

THOUGH THEY WERE STILL #1 in most markets, the big AM Top 40 stations knew the end was near, and they tried to change. At WABC in 1968, program director Rick Sklar banned his jocks from playing any pre-Beatles music. Deejays retaliated by relabeling every oldie in the record library, changing the dates on rock classics such as "Duke of Earl" and "Earth Angel" so that they were suddenly current songs. Sklar backed off.[10] Managers intent on maintaining ratings and profits placed ever stricter controls on deejays, clamping up personalities once encouraged to be wild and crazy. Bruce Morrow never let listeners in on his doubts and questions. That simply wasn't his style. He'd never told them much about his off-air life, even when he was king of New York's high school scene. But off the air, Cousin Brucie worried that everything he said and played was now irrelevant, corny. The Cousin worried that the kids might be laughing at him.

The Beatles broke up, and the ship of Top 40 drifted. While FM explored the new rock, AM carried on, head firmly in sand: between 1971 and 1973, Morrow noticed, the three most frequently played tunes on Top 40 radio were Three Dog Night's Pollyanna-ish "Joy to the World," Roberta Flack's simple love song "The First Time Ever I Saw Your Face," and Gilbert O'Sullivan's saccharine "Alone Again (Naturally)." Each "ignored the temperament of the country just as AM was trying to do."[11]

A few blocks from WABC's midtown studios, a rival network-owned station experimented with a late-life face-lift of AM's personality. The idea was to wipe off the bland smile of Top 40's heyday and add a sprinkle of naughtiness. WNBC hired Don Imus, a bad-boy deejay from Cleveland who sounded hung over (and often was) and teamed him with newsman Charles McCord to fill the spaces between pop hits with biting comedy bits savaging President Nixon, evangelists, TV newscasters, and those very tunes that management required Imus to play. Imus began a steady climb in the ratings, eating away at the massive audience of WABC's morning man, Harry Harrison, whose show consisted of nothing more than the hits, commercials, time and temperature, and the stentorian deejay repeatedly booming "Good morning!"

In 1973, WNBC hired the howling, mysterious Wolfman Jack to go head-to-head against Morrow. The upstart station arranged for a six-foot-tall tombstone engraved with the message "Cousin Brucie's Days Are Numbered" to be loaded onto the front steps of the ABC building. But while the Wolfman leered through the night, Cousin Brucie continued on his cheery, asexual way, still building his brand with visits to PTA meetings, supermarket openings, and Police Athletic League cookouts.[12] WABC executives took comfort that the old ways were not yet dead: Wolfman Jack's New York stay was over in less than a year. But rather than revel in his victory, Morrow in 1974 decided to accept WNBC's promises of more freedom to select his own music; Cousin Brucie stepped off his throne, taking a midday shift to play the hits for housewives. Morrow saw that Top 40 in its original incarnation was destined to crash; he figured that by jumping to WNBC, he might be able to leap onto the next train.

It was not to be. Miscast, bored, separated from the young audience that did homework to the rhythm of his show, Morrow would last only until 1977 in that role. Bob Pittman, the former Top 40 jock who had taken over WNBC in a last-ditch attempt to remake the format, called Cousin Brucie in and told him it was time to make room for younger guys.

The big AM Top 40 stations could still deliver 15 or 20 percent of listeners with a single buy, and advertisers weren't ready to give up on an audience of millions. So Top 40 soldiered on, even as listeners vanished by the hundreds of thousands. WABC replaced Cousin Brucie with George Michael, whose passion for the music was so infectious that he could make even casual listeners believe that pop singers were the ultimate poets of the human condition. Whether the song was a wild rocker or a sappy ballad, a funkilicious rump-shaker or a Hollywood tearjerker, Michael found the lyric that could tap into a listener's emotional memory and used that line to conjure a lead-in that made the song seem as if it had been written just for you.

Michael, who started out as a record promoter for Motown and later won massive audience shares as a jock in St. Louis and Philadelphia, routinely searched out songwriters to get their account of what inspired each song. He turned those stories into ad-libbed walk-ups spoken over the introductions to each song, masterfully timed so his mini-drama ended exactly as the song's vocal began.

"This song is Philadelphia," Michael said one night as a steady beat chugged beneath his rich baritone. "It's about Wildwood, it's about Ocean City, it's about Avalon, it's about meeting the most beautiful girl on the beach," and instantly, the Beach Boys sang "Little surfer, little one. . . ."

Or: "Lordy, baby, you go ahead, you chase that golden rainbow, but if you ever get lonely, you call, you know 'I'll Be Around,' " and the Spinners tune soared on the feelings Michael had set in motion.

Unlike Morrow, Michael sometimes used his own experience to find emotional hooks for his seven-second stories. When Michael's wife took off for Mexico, leaving him with three young children to care for while he worked in Philadelphia, those silly pop songs he played each evening suddenly struck him as more meaningful than ever before.

In twenty-eight seconds, an eternity for a song intro, Michael told his listeners his story: "This is when the woman I was married to took off with some guy that was eighteen years old and I was left with three kids. I used to play this song in my mind every night for her. Now I play it and say, 'Hey, good riddance, goodbye.' I say, bring on Harold Melvin, the Blue Notes, Kenny Gamble, the MFSB Orchestra. I can only tell you, it's the love I lost, at that time it was bon voyage, but the love I've got is the greatest love I have ever known." The music swelled, and Melvin and the Blue Notes sang: "The love I lost was a sweet love."

Despite the pure joy he loosed onto the airwaves, Michael, like Cousin Brucie, knew that playing all the hits made ever less sense. "You had a real dilemma in the '70s," he said. "Do I dare to play 'Ain't No Stoppin' Us Now' up against Jimi Hendrix? I'd go on and say, 'Do you want to get stoned and be in a purple haze or do you want to put your hands on the radio and feel something? Then this song is for you.' " And he'd spin the anthemic McFadden and Whitehead soul number.

But both Michael and his audience were confused, torn between two worlds. He wore a Beatles pageboy hairdo and Nehru suits, but he was adamant about not doing drugs (except for the time he interviewed the Rolling Stones and shared their hash, rendering his interview unusable). He was a grown kid who kept a jukebox at home and actually listened to the records he played (a relative rarity among jaded deejays), but he was also keenly aware that "we were about to become extinct."

In WABC's Manhattan studio each evening, Michael was "in my fantasy world. I might be thirteen years old when I play some song, and my eyes are closed and I'm seeing that beautiful girl, I'm off in another world." He was among the last of Top 40's artists, a precision craftsman who, decades later, keeps in the top drawer of his desk the chrome-plated stopwatch that he bought in St. Louis in October 1964 and used at work every day until he left WABC in 1979 to launch a new career as a TV sportscaster. On many songs, Michael didn't even need the stopwatch: with his eyes closed, Michael could sell the Real McCoy's "Come and Get Your Love" in the seven and three-quarters seconds before the vocal started, painting an image of a hooker he'd seen crossing Forty-second Street, beckoning across the avenue for a stranger to "come and get your love now."

But in the late 1970s, Michael found himself competing against stations devoted solely to progressive rock, hard rock, country, soul, or disco, each targeting a different demographic slice of society. It was time to say goodbye to everyone's song, to the idea that a vast nation could build its shared memory from one set of voices in the night. The music that had served through most of his career to unite was now being used to divide audiences by age, sex, class, and race. Michael put his stopwatch in the drawer.

AS LISTENERS SOUGHT THEIR PLACE in the new musical department store of the air, blacks found themselves in a familiar position—without many choices. Top 40 was no racial paradise, but the mix of music freely and comfortably crossed racial boundaries. Most Top 40 deejays were white, and the few black deejays were often racially "neutralized." Jocks such as the legendary Frankie Crocker, later a pioneer in black FM radio, were encouraged to speak "white" when they worked in Top 40. In some cities, black deejays' photos were left off the survey sheets that Top 40 stations distributed at record shops. But for twenty years, because of Top 40's racially mixed audience, radio had been the most integrated place in the pop culture.

FM changed that. Radio was resegregating, and blacks had but one place to go: back to the AM soul stations that had survived in the shadow of Top 40, sharing the Motown menu while spicing in funkier stuff that was "too black" for Top 40—James Brown, the Isley Brothers, and lesser-known groups with a bluesier sound. AM soul stations—most big cities had one—generally had poor signals and often were licensed to operate only during daylight hours. Almost without exception, they were owned by out-of-town whites who made sure that the stations played the hits and provided only the bare minimum of political discussion or black community news.

Soul stations survived the Top 40 era because, despite the edicts of white owners, radio was the only piece of the pop culture that blacks considered their own, with black deejays, artists, and music. The black press was in dire straits, and television resolutely ignored black America. Other ethnic radio stations had largely vanished as the audiences for programming in Italian, Greek, or Yiddish blended into the American melting pot. But blacks could not disappear into white society, and they stayed true to their stations, even if they were white-owned.

Soul radio operated on a strict formula: black deejays mimicked Top 40's style and sold advertisers on the one place in town that could deliver black consumers. Still, few owners saw much upside to the format. Black America listened to more radio than whites did, and blacks were more loyal to their favorite stations, but the assumption in the industry was that it just wasn't worthwhile to program for blacks—the ad rates were too low and the potential for backlash from white advertisers too high.

" 'Going black,' " David Segal recalled, "was the two dirtiest words in the business." Segal owned more than a dozen stations in the 1960s. After World War II, he had borrowed money from his mother and built a station in Texarkana, Texas. In the 1950s, he flew his private plane to small towns across the South and West, snapping up tiny AM stations at bargain prices. In 1965, he bought a failing station in his home city of Denver and, after a short-lived and hopeless attempt to beat the city's popular country station, Segal decided to venture where no one else would: in 1967, with riots ripping apart the nation's cities, Segal launched KDKO as Denver's first black-oriented radio station.

The music was R&B—Marvin Gaye, James Brown, the Jackson 5—the slogan was "Soul Power!" and most of the deejays were black, including characters such as Cosmo Harris, Dr. Daddy-O, Billy Soul, and the Nighthawk. Among the city's black population of eighty-five thousand, the station was widely known to be white-owned, and some ministers and activists denounced KDKO as a leech, sucking money out of black Denver. But the station reached out in ways that won respect—hiring an all-black sales staff, broadcasting obituaries collected from black mortuaries, peppering the steady diet of soul hits with newscasts from a black-run network in New York.

In 1968, when a confrontation between Denver police and Black Panther radicals threatened to set off the kind of rioting that had devastated many East and West Coast cities, Segal's station appealed for calm. Deejays, police, and city and church leaders urged blacks to stay off the streets. In the end, Denver avoided the wholesale violence that had charred so many other urban centers.

That experience persuaded local businesses that KDKO had such an influence on black Denver that they couldn't afford not to advertise. On the other hand, the charged racial climate only exacerbated staff resentment of the station's white owner. "The whole staff hated my guts," Segal said. "They were so angry. Every time I walked out of a meeting, they'd say, 'Fuck him.' But we owned the black community."

Segal had no illusions about lifting black Denver's economic or social status. He wanted to make money, and he would have flipped the format to something else in a second if he thought he could boost his profits.[13] "Radio is a fucking money machine," Segal said a quarter century after he sold KDKO. "I wasn't in it to win black friends. Our rates were a lot lower than on the white stations, but we made money. Enough so I'm sitting on my ass in Rancho Mirage."

Segal may be more open than most about his mercenary motives, but his bottom-line approach and racial callousness were typical of the white owners who ran nearly all black stations. Relations between owners and deejays were especially dicey at soul stations owned by Jewish businessmen, such as Segal and Egmont Sonderling, a New

Yorker who owned WWRL in his hometown, the legendary WDIA in Memphis, and WOL in Washington.

Sonderling came to radio from the record industry, where he ran Old Swing-Master, a prominent Chicago producer of race records in the 1940s. Blacks who worked at his stations gave Sonderling credit for letting them play the music they wanted to, but as riots tore cities apart in the late 1960s, radicals and not-so-radicals began demanding more black control. Publicizing toy giveaways and blood drives wouldn't cut it any longer.

Sonderling stations had long appealed to blacks with easy, cheap nods at racial identity. WOL jock Bob "Nighthawk" Terry would tell tall tales about his encounters with the "po-lice," then pause dramatically to take a long, vulgar slurp of his National Bohemian beer, exhale, and say, "Mmmm, them white folks sure make some good beer."[14] Such antics felt increasingly backward, even insulting to a generation of blacks intent on repelling stereotypes. The same accusations of insensitivity that Jewish (and later, Korean) shopkeepers in black ghettos heard were now leveled at white-owned radio stations.

But while activists could urge ghetto residents to spurn the corner store and "buy black," there was no such opportunity in the media. In the nation's capital, that changed with a single gift in 1971. Anticipating new federal rules that would prohibit newspaper companies from owning broadcasting outlets in the same city, *The Washington Post* donated its WTOP-FM to Howard University, the federally supported black college. The idea was that Howard would use the station to train black students to go into broadcasting. As a bonus, since the *Post* held a commercial license, the university could make money operating the station.

WHUR—Howard University Radio—went on the air on August 10, 1971, and suddenly black radio left behind jive-talking, proto-rapping deejays and obsessions over the latest dance craze. Washington, then almost three-quarters black, was home to a burgeoning black middle class as well as to thousands of students who were drawn to the black nationalist movement, the Black Panthers, the Nation of Islam, and other political groups that made the capital their base.

Deejays on Sonderling's WOL had taken to calling Washington "Chocolate City," a phrase that funkmaster George Clinton would later immortalize in an album of that title. The words reflected a new racial pride and determination to run the town. But while WOL urged Chocolate City to come together around the love and pride message of 1970s soul tunes, WHUR attempted something far more challenging. The station offered difficult jazz pieces, academic lectures, serious news programs, readings of folktales, and concerts of Delta blues shouters. While soul stations stuck to three-minute rip-and-read head-line summaries, WHUR hired full-time reporters and launched a nightly newscast called the *Daily Drum*.

With the slogan "360 Degrees of Black Experience," the station reached out to black communities that had never heard themselves on the radio—Caribbean immigrants, federal workers, professors at Howard. Hours-long programs spoke to Washington's large Caribbean population with music and news from reporters in several island na-tions. "All of a sudden, you had this radio station that wanted to be doing something other than socking that soul at the capital city," said Milton Coleman, a news reporter who came to WHUR in 1973 after several years in the black nationalist movement.

Kojo Nnamdi was managing the Drum and Spear bookstore, which specialized in black nationalist works, when WHUR debuted. "I'd never heard radio like this before—days-long discussions of the future of black people, hearings on government abuses, the entire score of *Ain't Supposed to Die a Natural Death*, the Broadway musical by Melvin Van Peebles," Nnamdi said, "and it affected me so much. The station had a strong black identity and it developed such a loyalty. I just felt drawn to it." Nnamdi landed a job as a reporter at WHUR.

The news staff was mostly veterans of the civil rights movement, with little experience in journalism, but plenty in organizing commu-nities and pressing their pet issues. Every cause was welcome—reports focused one day on the Panthers, the next on a back-to-Africa move-ment, and the next on Jesse Jackson. Reporters had beats covering African affairs, labor, and other issues with a special connection to black listeners. A public affairs program was titled *Ten Minutes Left*.

For a time in those first years, WHUR's daily news block was a three-hour stretch of evening drive time. "This was serious; this was something different and progressive, an alternative to R&B," said Coleman, who later moved from WHUR to *The Washington Post* and ultimately became the paper's deputy managing editor. "HUR was trying to appeal to a different part of the black community." Coleman lived then in suburban Prince George's County, part of a growing movement of black professionals out of Chocolate City and into the same suburban dream that had lured whites out of the cities.

WHUR's FM signal reached into the suburbs with far better fidelity than the weak AM soul stations, and FM was increasingly where young people—black and white—tuned for their music. But while WHUR built a loyal following in political and student circles, the station's managers increasingly grumbled that the emphasis on politics and jazz—and often, a way-out brand of the music, such as Ornette Coleman and late-period John Coltrane—prevented WHUR from reaching the broader black community.

"There was a lot of very experimental stuff on the station," said Jesse Fax, WHUR's music director through much of the 1970s and '80s. "I started to tighten things up, moving to the more melodic jazz and to a more contemporary sound—Al Jarreau and Herbie Hancock, as well as some more popular hits—the O'Jays and that sort. It didn't go over very well with some of the staff, but I knew that FM would eventually use whatever music philosophies had worked on AM."

Fax thought a three-hour news block was "crazy," a guaranteed turnoff to listeners. He lobbied to cut it back. WHUR still broke away from music to cover demonstrations on the National Mall against South African apartheid, but the station pushed ever harder to win ratings numbers against the growing roster of FM stations in Washington.

In 1974, a new general manager closed the door on WHUR's fringe politics and avant-garde music. Tom Jones introduced what he called the Ebony Lifestyle System, a format heavy on popular music and light on the news and public affairs programming of the station's first years. The Ebony System didn't last long, but the pivot had been made. "Black stations wanted us deejays to sound less black," said Jacquie Gales Webb, a longtime WHUR deejay. "They wanted to get away from the AM sound of the soul stations to attract the black middle class."

The person who perfected that appeal at WHUR, sales manager Cathy Hughes (then Liggins), used research to elevate black radio to a new sophistication. Hughes believed people used radio in different ways at different times of day. She undertook computer-assisted research to determine how listeners used radio to accompany their activities at each stage of the day. She massaged the station's sound to provide lots of information as listeners prepared for work in the morning, then switched to background music through the midday. Her psychographic research divided the clock into "dayparts," each with its own programming personality. Hughes's signature creation was her evening program, the *Quiet Storm*, hosted by Melvin Lindsey, a velvet-voiced former Howard student, and named for a Smokey Robinson song that was, as Hughes said, "all subliminal suggestion about oral sex."

Lindsey's magnificently cool voice and laid-back style combined with very long sets of love songs—Phyllis Hyman, Patti LaBelle, Sarah Vaughan, Luther Vandross, Barry White, Teddy Pendergrass— to attract the single, young black women Hughes knew were out there in the evening, sitting at home and thinking about their love lives. "Cathy's logic was that between seven and midnight, some guy is seducing some girl and he doesn't want to get up to change the record," Nnamdi said. *Quiet Storm* became a nightly feature in 1977, and in less than a year, it was #1 in its time slot. The station jumped from #20 to #3 in the D.C. market, becoming a substantial contributor to the university's bottom line.

WHUR maintained its hour-long newscast for years to come, and the news department accepted Hughes's psychographics and the *Quiet Storm* because, as Nnamdi said, "to inform people, you had to get them in the door. In other words, you had to pump the funk." But as each ratings point came to mean millions in potential profits, and research honed stations' sounds to the point that every song was subjected to audience testing and phone surveys, the hour-long *Daily Drum* came to be seen as a drag on the bottom line. The news show was gradually whittled down to a ten-minute recitation of headlines and a quick phone interview, usually on some lifestyle issue. By 2000, WHUR was telling potential advertisers on its website that "you never have to worry about your client's commercial being aired next to controversy."

But Hughes, long gone from WHUR by then, loved controversy. She also loved the idea of empowering blacks—and herself. After leaving WHUR, she married TV producer Dewey Hughes, and, in 1979, the couple bought WOL from Egmont Sonderling. Hughes dropped the station's soul sound to attempt something altogether new—a black talk format, with Hughes as star host. She became a firebrand, a rabble-rouser, and a defender of the race who took on the mayor, the big daily newspaper, the whites, the Jews, the Asians, and anyone else she thought was blocking the path toward black success. Hughes became Washington's angry black voice. Her station never won much in the way of ratings or profits, but it developed a fiercely loyal following. Listeners called themselves the "WOL family" and joined "Miss Cathy" on pilgrimages to Africa and protests in Washington. They lined up outside her storefront studio in the heart of black Washington to ask for favors and shower her with accolades.

Hughes parlayed her popularity into political influence. But her real aim had little to do with being a successful on-air personality and everything to do with amassing financial power. She began to expand her radio empire, one station at a time, first in Washington and then around the country. Her Radio One became the nation's largest owner of stations aimed at black audiences.

Few cities ever had a black FM station quite like WHUR in its early days, but black music formats spread to FM throughout the 1970s. Some stations duplicated the AM soul approach, while others sought a more adult sound, copying WHUR's *Quiet Storm* and mixing jazz and fusion with R&B hits. In the new environment of narrowly defined formats, "urban" was now the accepted euphemism for stations aimed at blacks. And radio once more became as segregated as it had ever been.

Radio remains one of the most racially divided institutions in American culture; in no other area of the entertainment world are the races as rigidly and openly separated. That separation, helped along by federal incentives, bumped up black ownership in broadcasting. In New York, Hal Jackson joined with Percy Sutton, the Manhattan borough president and a former lawyer for Malcolm X, to buy WLIB and its FM station, which became WBLS. But in many cities, black-owned stations struggled against white-owned outlets airing the same format, the same music. Black-owned stations competed by appealing to racial pride. Jackson said he opposed it, but his company aired promotional announcements letting listeners know that WBLS was "black-owned and -operated." One spot put it straight: "There are some radio stations out there that are faking the funk and are just the opposite, you know what I'm saying? If you know some brothers and sisters listening to those plantation stations, ask them: Who you gonna support? The people's new choice in '95—the Vibe, 107.5, WBLS."

"I always wanted a broad audience, not just blacks, and I thought that to get everyone, you had to play a broad variety of music," Jackson said. "But that's not how the consultants and the researchers do it, and they won the day. And we all went our separate ways."

LIKE TODD STORZ two decades earlier, Lee Abrams sold a recipe, a formula for ratings success. But new technologies that emerged in the 1970s gave Abrams and the new band of consultants an advantage Storz could not have imagined when he created Top 40. Thanks to computers, radio stations now could be fully automated robots of pop culture.

Just as Tom Donahue staked out empty acreage on the FM band to create underground radio, entrepreneurs aiming at an older audience used FM to serve up "beautiful music," the instrumentals that provided musical wallpaper for doctors' offices and coffee shops. No one listened closely to beautiful music; the stations were intended as background sound. Announcers had only to read off the names of tunes and the occasional weather report. A few companies began selling twenty-four hours a day of beautiful music at minimal cost, delivering a complete station on ten-inch reels of tape.

Beginning in the late 1960s, TM Productions in Dallas offered stations an early computer-driven automation system. All a local station had to do was slip in the occasional station identification and commercials. Listeners might hear an occasional beep signaling the computer to trigger the next tape, but otherwise, hardly anyone would know the station was unmanned. By the mid-1970s, about 15 percent of stations were computer-run.

If automation worked with beautiful music, why not with soft rock and country—with virtually any kind of music? "It was a one-announcer format, one voice on twenty-four hours a day, and he'd even tape your local IDs," said Don Hagen, a radio consultant and deejay who started out at TM in 1974. Prefab formats were cheap and easy. In an innovation later known as voice tracking, a deejay could tape a four-hour program in fifteen minutes; the computer would pop in his announcements between songs. Stations initially paid for these program services, but by the mid-1970s, they were available without charge; local stations agreed to run commercials that the program service sold and included on its tapes.

Hagen and the other architects of prefab formats assumed their approach would not work for Top 40 or album rock, formats that sought more of a listener's attention. But these early syndicated formats persuaded many owners that with the Top 40 era coming to an end, there was no need to spend money on talent, promotions, or news. To make money, all you needed was a niche. It hardly mattered how narrow that niche might be, as long as you kept costs extremely low. A radio station became something akin to a fragrance or a style of furniture, something you used to create a mood—a format sold with a simple slogan, "light rock," "relaxing classics," "music the whole family can listen to."

By 1980, FM listening had edged out AM in the country's ten largest markets. Abrams's album-oriented rock (AOR) format led the way in the fragmentation of FM programming into an alphabet soup of music formats—AOR, CHR (contemporary hit radio—a new twist on Top 40), MOR (middle of the road—Barbra Streisand, Herb

Alpert, Frank Sinatra), AC (adult contemporary—Neil Diamond, James Taylor, Barry Manilow), as well as golden oldies (hits from the 1950s and '60s), country, black, "beautiful music," and on and on.[15]

Advertisers loved the apparent precision of the more finely tuned formats. Almost overnight, an enormous industry—consultants, syndicators, research companies, ratings services, and newsletters—emerged to divide the audience into gradations of age, sex, income, ethnicity, and lifestyle. The trick was to define the precise mix of music and packaging that would pare away unwanted listeners and maximize the desired group. An advertiser looking for single white women in their late twenties and early thirties could buy time on a soft rock station; if their products were aimed at eighteen-to-twenty-five-year-old men, they might look toward the hard rocker.[16]

The explosion of new formats meant something had to go, and in many cities that meant the loss of the only stations that played classical, jazz, Broadway, big-band, or ethnic music. Listener rebellions—petitions, letters to newspapers, and complaints to Congress and the FCC—became common, but in 1981, the Supreme Court ruled that owners were free to program their stations as they wished, without regard to public taste.[17]

That same year, the FCC gave stations full command over programming. The commission's chairman during the Reagan administration, Mark Fowler, announced that "we are at the end of regulating broadcasting" as trustees for the public. "Whether you call it 'paternalism' or 'nannyism'—it is Big Brother, and it must cease. I believe in a marketplace approach. . . . The Commission should, as far as possible, defer to a broadcaster's judgment about how best to compete for viewers and listeners."[18] The FCC scrapped rules requiring stations to devote some portion of their airtime to news, public affairs, local, educational, political, and children's programming.[19]

Liberated, stations segmented the audience with a vengeance. The accidental genius of Top 40 had been to tap into the country's exploding youth market at a time when American business had not yet realized the transforming nature of the baby boom. Now, as boomers moved into adulthood, radio reached out to them with a more targeted appeal. Radio's new formats promised choices for listeners, while freeing economic power that had been locked up in Top 40's mass appeal.

A Top 40 station hawking a couple of brands of basic beer to one undifferentiated audience sold lots of beer. But a dozen stations reaching a dozen demographic groups with targeted programming could sell many varieties of beer—a strong beer for men on hard rock radio, a light beer for women on the soft rocker, an effete foreign beer on the progressive station, a beer with an ethnic or racial appeal on Hispanic or black radio. Increasingly, you were what you listened to: "What's your station?" replaced "Who's your favorite deejay?" or "What's your favorite song?" as questions that could place a stranger.

The mounds of statistics and demographic analysis that landed on managers' desks seemed to require action: if the choice of songs determined who listened, why spend big money on personalities, news reporting, or community events? "The emphasis switched from programming to management," said Ruth Meyer, a Todd Storz protégé who ran New York's Top 40 WMCA from her gut before she transformed herself into a consultant, selling the gospel of statistics. "Programmers lost their confidence and just did what the consultants told them to, and they had no idea why they were doing what they did."

"Music cost nothing and more commercials meant more revenue," said Bud Connell, another former Storz Top 40 program director who became a consultant. "Listeners began to control the medium through rapid station changing, seeking the better record moment to moment. After all, music was now all they had to listen for, and they took charge."[20]

Popular culture found itself with a chicken/egg question: did the music split into niches—lite rock, modern rock, active rock, adult alternative rock, hard rock—because radio divided itself so narrowly, or did radio merely adapt to changing listener demands? Before anyone could figure out the answer, new layers of consultancies bloomed. Psychographics researchers promised to determine scientifically the order in which songs should be played to maximize listener loyalty. Demographers used census data to predict that teen influence over music's direction would wane, so stations added oldies to cement their hold on the essential twenty-five-to-thirty-four age group.

Niche programming encouraged advertisers to extend their brands, specializing for each demographic group. More brands meant more ad dollars and a happy circle developed. But as the number of niches grew, stations' shares of the audience plummeted. Never again could a single station boast of controlling half or more of a region's listeners. Now, single-digit shares were just fine, even hailed as a roaring success. Tenths of a ratings point suddenly mattered—which drove program-

LEE ABRAMS
(Courtesy Lee Abrams)

mers back to the research even more slavishly. Success was redefined as dominating your niche.

Radio now offered Americans not a relationship between listener and deejay, but a commodity packaged on behalf of advertisers and sold along with consumer lifestyles. Lee Abrams became an airport vagabond, endlessly traversing the nation to turn stations into copies of each other. His stations made good money and played the songs people said they wanted to hear. The kid who nagged his way into radio studios was now the industry's most sought-after guru. But a generation of listeners who had grown up with radio as companion and friend grew less enchanted. Abrams himself started wondering what had gone wrong, why people didn't feel the same emotional bond anymore. In his low moments, he wondered: Had he sucked the life out of what he loved? Had he created a monster?

LEE ABRAMS NEVER CARED for disco. In fact, he hated the stuff. But without Abrams, the music might never have emerged from the urban club scene. FM radio, now rigidly segmented by music styles, came late to the disco party. The dial was sliced into such narrow niches that the new music didn't fit any existing category and therefore had nowhere to go.

Disco came up through gay clubs. In 1977, it leaped across the color line and into middle America's boom boxes and motel lounges, largely because of the movie *Saturday Night Fever*. Van McCoy's "The Hustle" and KC and the Sunshine Band's "Get Down Tonight" and "That's the Way (I Like It)" were the first disco hits to win big play on Top 40, back in 1975, but the Bee Gees' hits from the John Travolta vehicle—"Night Fever," "You Should Be Dancing," "How Deep Is Your Love"—really put disco front and center on Top 40 in 1977.

Yet the trimmed-down AM versions of those disco hits had to share Top 40 airtime with the likes of "Convoy," a trucker anthem by C. W. McCall; Barry Manilow's "I Write the Songs"; and Paul Simon's "50 Ways to Leave Your Lover." It was all too jarring to young listeners who spent ever more of their time on FM and expected to hear their kind of music served straight, no other styles, thanks.

Disco was an incessantly upbeat music that captured the desire of city dwellers to escape gas shortages, rampant inflation, and corrupt politics. Here was a music that transcended many of the ethnic and social divisions that radio had just spent years analyzing and embracing. But the business was so caught up in its categories that it saw only a gay fad that had morphed into a lower-class black and Hispanic street music.

One station changed that. In July 1978, under the guidance of Lee Abrams and Kent Burkhart, a New York FM station switched from Spanish-language to all-disco. Virtually overnight, WKTU (Disco 92) became the most popular station in the nation. Reaching huge numbers of blacks, Hispanics, and whites alike, KTU did the impossible, bumping the most successful Top 40 station in history, WABC, off its perch at the top of the ratings. Disco was silliness and sexual liberation, cocaine and commercialism, escape and excess—and radio had nearly missed the boat.

Abrams and Burkhart's research told them that the unusual ethnic mix in the nation's largest city would take to disco across color lines, so WKTU featured deejays with distinctively black, Hispanic, and white ethnic accents. "It's cold, cold, cold tonight," Disco 92's Paco Navarro ("Paco is my name, disco is my game") told his listeners one night, the constant beat pulsing behind his round Spanish-tinged vowels. "So get warm, baby, warm up"—his gravelly bass voice grew slower and deeper—"and put it together and dance, dance, dance, dance."

The music quickly radiated out from the big city to become a national sensation. In Los Angeles, Top 40 jock Rick Dees recorded a novelty record called "Disco Duck"; it sold 6 million copies. Black stations in most cities jumped on the disco bandwagon, offering a distinctive flavor of the faddish music.

At WABC, New York's #1 station for most of a generation, ratings fell two points in the first Arbitron book after Disco 92's debut—a stunning drop that shook the network brass. WABC program director Al Brady tried adding oldies, playing longer versions of songs, and freeing deejays to do more funny stuff. Hoping to find a new audience in the eighteen-to-thirty-four age range, he fired his stuffy old morning man, Harry Harrison, and his dynamo of an evening jock, George Michael.[21] He added more newscasts and New York Yankees baseball broadcasts. Nothing worked. By 1980, WABC had sunk to ninth place.

FM and its consultants with their research and statistics had won. In Chicago, Abrams and Burkhart were hired by WLUP-FM, a sagging rock station known as The Loop. Abrams, thrilled to program a rocker in his hometown, decided to spurn his usual research and do this one from his gut. He would play album cuts that he knew would score with working-class white Chicago guys. His deejays would be as Chicago as WKTU's were New York—this would be "Da Loop," emphasis on "Da." The station adopted a scantily clad, busty blond mascot named Lorelei. There was Loop beer, a heavily caffeinated Loop cola, a station logo written in graffiti style.

The same guys who pumped up disco as "the beat of New York" staked their success in Chicago on the virulence of anti-disco sentiment among white guys who wouldn't go near that fancy dancing. "We were smoking pot, and disco was cocktails and coke," Abrams said of his target audience. "We were long hair and jeans and a T-shirt; they were short hair and fashion and dressing to get in. Our station was going to be everything that was against disco."

And so Abrams had deejay Steve Dahl blow up a disco record every morning, starting up the beat and then ripping the needle across the record while punching up an explosive sound effect. Dahl's routine electrified his audience. Abrams and his promotions man, Dave Logan, decided to go for broke: they approached the Chicago White Sox and sold the pathetic team on a stunt.[22]

July 12, 1979, was Disco Demolition Night at Comiskey Park. For ninety-eight cents and one disco record, fans could enter the ballpark, see the White Sox face the Detroit Tigers, and watch Dahl explode a truckload of disco records. More than sixty thousand people crammed into the oversold stadium; thousands more stood outside. Between games of the doubleheader, Dahl ran onto the field carrying an American flag and a Loop banner. "In the name of rock and roll, stop this disco menace!" he shouted over the PA system. And then, with the crowd chanting "Disco sucks!" a countdown filled the scoreboard and a deep crackling boom echoed through the stands. Bits of vinyl cascaded over the outfield. The Loop had hit the big time.

Like WKTU, Da Loop shot up through the ratings like a cherry bomb on the Fourth of July—from nowhere to #1. "Man, that was community," Abrams exulted a generation later. Abrams happened to like the music on Da Loop. But that's not why he created it. "We were going after eighteen-to-thirty-four males," he said, "and this was the way to #1. We took it to our other clients and it worked everywhere."

The one format that was left out in the cold was the one that had sought to reach everyone. The suits at ABC decided WABC's Top 40 approach was no longer viable. Ingram, morning man Harry Harrison, midday jock Ron Lundy, and Cousin Brucie would all eventually make their way over to FM, to WCBS, the oldies station, where they played the same songs they always had, reminding listeners of long-ago days when the whole city listened to everything, together.

But nostalgia was just one more niche, a marketing device aimed at aging boomers—subcategory white, female, suburban, age thirty-five to fifty-four. For the next two decades, Bruce Morrow would spend only a couple of evenings a week on the radio, until the next generation of executives decided that oldies no longer reached the desired demographic, and then the Cousin was out.[23] The demise of Top 40 WABC finally persuaded Morrow that the money, influence, and action were now attached to Abrams's world. Morrow started buying up small stations, programming them not with the music he loved or the jocks he admired, but with the content the consultants recommended. It was financially rewarding, but Morrow was bored. He couldn't picture the kids who might grow attached to these stations. There had to be some other way. Radio was meant to insinuate itself into people's imaginations, into their love lives and their dreams—wasn't it?

On a May afternoon in 1982, Musicradio WABC finally stopped the music. After a few nostalgic speeches, Dan Ingram played Donna Summer's "Last Dance." It was the same song WKTU had chosen as its first disco record four years earlier. And then, for the perfect Top 40 sign-off, Ingram followed "Last Dance" with John Lennon's "Imagine." If you don't like one song, keep listening. Something for everybody. But there was no everybody anymore, only groups and subgroups, niches and slices.

After a second's pause, WABC signed on again, now as an all-talk station. AM radio had found its task in the newly specialized pop culture: chasing after men. The medium was ready to lead the culture into an era of piercingly partisan politics and relentless raunch.

PART THREE

NICHE PLAYER

TOM LEYKIS

Chapter 9

✳ SHOCK AND AWE

RENEE IS WAITING to talk to the guy on the radio. She's been listening, and it's hard to shock her, but she's heard this big mouth call women "sluts" and "bitches" and "sperm receptacles," and she's heard him advise one man after another to use women for sex and then dump them, and finally she's had enough. She phones in to the station.

"Who do you think is going to take care of you when you're old?" Renee asks when she gets her turn on the air. She's forty, and her husband respects her, she tells the audience—and the host of the program interjects, "Ugh, forty years old, we do *not* want to see *you.*"

Renee pushes on, telling the host that women won't stand for this kind of abuse, that women are loyal and true, whereas this show is a haven for haters. "You don't like children," she says. "You don't like women."

The host listens, then takes a deep breath. Exasperated, the man on the radio says, "You just proved to me why guys shouldn't have any respect for women." Then, angrily, "Who are you to be criticizing anybody, you slut? What kind of a goddamn pussy is your husband to tolerate your mouth and your behavior? Renee, the boys here and I have a song dedicated to your husband. The boys are going to sing along now."

Tom Leykis gives the engineer a signal, and the Meow Mix cat food jingle fills the airwaves ("Meow, meow, meow, meow"), and seven hundred drunken young men gathered at a bar to watch Leykis do his daily radio show join in, twisting their slurred baritones into whiny feline voices. "They're playing his song, Renee," Leykis cackles over the cacophony.

It's *The Tom Leykis Show*, where American men hear what's long since become unacceptable in the workplace, on campus, and even in many bars and living rooms. This is a universe in which women are, at best, "chicks," and often far worse. Here, you learn never to spend money on women whose purpose is merely to be "booty call." Eat dinner before you take her out; buy the cheapest dish on the menu. This is a public service radio program, Leykis says, designed to "give men their balls back."

The Leykis show became the highest-rated radio program for male listeners in Los Angeles and in many of the sixty or so other markets where it is heard. This is the pinnacle of success in talk radio, the crowning achievement of a career that started in a suburb of New York City with a barely pubescent boy who dreamed of becoming a Top 40 deejay like the go-go guys he heard on WABC.

TOM LEYKIS WANTED TO BE Dan Ingram, the wily wit of Top 40 radio, who splattered his commercial copy with acidic barbs and punned his way through the tiny spaces between hit songs. Ingram "had open contempt for the music he was playing, and he got away with it," Leykis said with raw admiration. As a boy, Leykis (like so many other young people in Ingram's audience) assumed he was one of the select few who knew that Ingram was really spoofing the entire adult world as much as he was sticking it to WABC's rigid Top 40 format.

Tom Leykis wanted to be Don Imus, the coked-up bad boy of New York Top 40, the renegade hired by WNBC to take on the fresh-faced All-Americans of WABC. In the early 1970s, when Leykis was growing up, Imus was changing the definition of Top 40, adding comedy routines, savaging the TV networks and the staid newscasts of the era. Imus, who fell into radio after working in a uranium mine and trying to make it as an R&B singer (he did a pretty fair impression of Fats

Domino), openly derided the music he was forced to play. He showed up late and hung over to his morning drive-time gig. He played a cash register's *ka-ching* at the start of commercial spots. He screamed *"Waaaaaaaaaake-uuuuuup!"* to listeners. He treated New York to his very own corrupt evangelist character, the Reverend Billy Sol Hargis, who preached the gospel of easy money, shouting, "Put your hands on the radio!" Imus was a wild man, a comic and satirist banging up against the confines of Top 40. Leykis wrote a letter to Imus, begging to be permitted to come watch the great deejay in action. Imus gave the green light, and Leykis made the pilgrimage to NBC's studios at Rockefeller Center, snapping Instamatic photos of everything from the newsman to the engineering board.

Tom Leykis wanted to be Jean Shepherd. Every night, Tom listened in bed, in the Bronx bedroom he shared with three siblings, as the master storyteller spun his forty-five-minute tales of boyhood mischief and adult alienation, every sentence building the tension, every strand of the story streaming out in odd directions until, finally, in the waning seconds of the program, everything came together in a crisp conclusion of such wisdom that the listener hungered for more. Leykis signed up to work on his high school newspaper for the sole purpose of covering a press conference at which Shepherd was to speak.

Tom Leykis was a pudgy kid with a piercing cackle who wanted to be on the radio. When his father, a production manager at the *New York Post,* moved the family to Long Island to escape the prospect of school busing in the Bronx, Tom was devastated. Torn away from the places and kids he knew, deposited into a school where no one else seemed to share his passions, he retreated into his dream. At fourteen, he entered and won a contest in which WBAB, an oldies and pop hits station in Babylon, Long Island, offered one hour of airtime to the teenager who wrote the best essay on why he should be a deejay.

The prize was the 8 A.M. hour on a Saturday morning. Tom prepared for days, carefully choosing the music he would play—far better stuff than anything the station's lame deejays had ever put on the air. Leykis packed his albums into a plastic Sam Goody record store bag, persuaded his skeptical parents to drive him twenty miles to Babylon

on a rainy Saturday, and arrived at the big A-frame house on Route 109 where WBAB had its studios. The building smelled like the tube test at Radio Shack. It smelled like heaven.

The kid walked in with his bag full of superior radio programming and was met by the poor sap who had drawn the early-morning weekend shift. The deejay handed the contest winner a stack of plastic cartridges containing the songs scheduled for the next hour, and a pile of index cards containing the lines the guest deejay was to recite after each song. "This is what you're gonna play," the professional told the novice, "and this is what you're gonna say."

The kid was crestfallen. But Tom Leykis was on the radio.

And he was invited back. He was a fourteen-year-old ninth grader pulling regular weekend air shifts on a genuine radio station. Over the next decade, Leykis would struggle constantly to poke his way onto the radio. He went to Fordham University and pushed, unsuccessfully, for a slot on the student station. He dropped out of college and bought time on a small, foreign-language FM station in Newark, New Jersey, paying $80 an hour to control the 3-to-5-A.M. slot three nights a week. Then he went out and sold advertising to garment shops on Kings Highway in Brooklyn to eke out a slim profit. Between hawking ads and spinning records, Leykis worked days as a telemarketer, drifting from one boiler room operation to another, selling HBO, subscriptions to the weekly *Jewish Press,* and time-shares in the Pocono Mountains. And he launched a cable access TV show on which he played characters, did voices, and generally tried to be like Imus, Ingram, and Shepherd, with some of good old Bob and Ray's sketch comedy mixed in. Leykis was a talk radio fanatic—he stayed up all night listening to Long John Nebel and Bob Fass, he made crank calls to talk shows, he imitated his heroes on his cable show.

All the while, Leykis made a pest of himself at stations in and around New York. FM stations in the 1970s featured increasingly interchangeable deejays; with music the sole focus of the programming, Leykis was able to snare a few fill-in gigs here and there, playing the tunes, naming the bands, impressing no one. In 1979, Leykis, then twenty-three, got it in his head that a morning rock deejay on WPIX was stealing comedy bits from Leykis's cable access TV show. Both Leykis and the deejay, Mark Simone, were doing Dial-a-Date, a shtick in which the host matched up listeners and probed their love lives for *Newlywed Game*–type embarrassments. Leykis wrote to WPIX with his accusation, which Simone vehemently denied, but the two agreed to meet, and when they did, Leykis talked his way onto the show. In short order, he became Simone's comic sidekick; persuaded that morning shows needed some "edge," managers wanted more and more of Leykis's specialty, double entendre. He simply moved his cable access characters over to the radio: he was "Hal Harris, aspiring disc jockey," calling in to look for work, and he was "Ben Dover, America's foremost male chauvinist pig," who spoke in a heavy Noo Yawk accent and said things like, "Hey, you know, there's no such thing as a woman who's intelligent."

Simone saw Leykis blending his comedy ideas with his deep knowledge of talk radio's past. "Tom listened to Long John Nebel and Bob Grant night after night," Simone recalled. "He knew talk, and he was much freer than the guys who'd come out of Top 40 because he didn't have all those rules drilled into his head." The critics, particularly Marvin Kitman of *Newsday*, thought this was comic genius. Leykis and Simone took their act on the road, appearing at nightclubs and discos on Long Island and in New Jersey, calling people up from the audience to be made fun of. Leykis played his misogynist, macho character, and the two deejays made phony phone calls onstage. The guys in the crowd ate it up. Leykis had found his calling.

The gig with Simone was part-time, a few moments of pseudocelebrity in the early morning, while Leykis toiled the rest of the week as a customer service agent, answering calls to Citibank's toll-free 800 lines. The radio comic lived in federally subsidized housing on Roosevelt Island. When WPIX flipped formats and Simone moved on, Leykis moved his act over to WBAI—to Bob Fass's studio—where, for no pay at all, he developed his characters and tried to be Ingram, Imus, and Shepherd all at once. Leykis could not have imagined that a latter-day version of Ben Dover would deliver him to big money, the best cars, a standing table at West Hollywood's finest restaurants, a seven-hundred-bottle wine cellar in his four-story Hollywood Hills spread, and capacity crowds at auditoriums all over the country, where men chanted "Ley-kis, Ley-kis!" while heavily endowed women pulled up their shirts and begged him to whip out his Sharpie and sign—literally *sign*—their breasts.

BY THE END OF the 1970s, radio sorely needed a dose of showbiz. The turn away from strong personalities on FM had rendered listeners fickle. Deejays had been muzzled by executives who worshipped at the altar of market research and consultants who preached the gospel of playing it safe. Consultants could tell you what records to play, but every station had the same consultants. Radio needed something different. To stand out in the ratings, it would be necessary once again to stand out on the air. The way to stand out was talk.

Talk shows had been around for decades, primarily late at night, when the nation's sleepless millions let their minds wander into mysteries of worlds beyond our own. A handful of daytime talk shows did well in big cities, tossing around local political issues and social questions—abortion, busing, affirmative action. In Los Angeles in the 1960s and New York in the 1970s, Joe Pyne and Bob Grant, respectively, won large, loyal audiences with acerbic telephone talk—"Go gargle with razor blades," Pyne told callers who dared to disagree; "Get off my phone!" Grant shouted at those who questioned his rants against "limousine liberals" and New York's "tower of jelly" mayor, John Lindsay.

Talk—radio's most expensive programming because talkmeisters generally earn more than deejays, and hosts are supported by producers and phone screeners—didn't emerge as a twenty-four-hour format until the late 1960s.[1] Talk about controversial issues was problematic. The FCC's fairness doctrine forced stations to steer clear of talk about electoral politics, for fear of having to keep records for regulators and, even worse, grant equal time to "opposing viewpoints." Advertisers, wary of controversy, considered the talk audience too old and too odd.

One of the few markets in which talk thrived was Miami, where an unusually old population was drawn to talk as a companion, a break from sticky tropical nights. The king of Miami talk in the 1980s was Neil Rogers, who billed himself as a "fat balding liberal Jewish atheist homosexual," railed against old folks as "yentas" and "prunes," hurled abuse at Cuban immigrants then pouring into South Florida, and consistently won huge ratings numbers. When Rogers jumped to a rival station, his employers searched for a new voice to throw against the king. They hired Tom Leykis.

A decade as a hanger-on and wannabe in New York finally had persuaded Leykis that he needed to head out to the boonies and work his way up. He started the 1980s at a tiny AM station in Staunton, Virginia, living in a boardinghouse and making $160 a week to recite death notices, spin records, and host a chat program for homemakers. "It was impressed upon me that the host is not to express an opinion," Leykis recalled. So he responded politely to callers who phoned in to ask how to remove stains from corduroy or to explain how it was that Hitler had gotten such a bad rap.

From Staunton, Leykis moved to Albany, New York, for an 80 percent raise and his first real talk show. The rest of the talkers on WQBK were gentle types who traded comforting conversation with their listeners. Leykis decided to make his mark fast. Every night, he lobbed Molotov cocktails at his audience: Albany was chockablock with military vets, so Leykis started off with "If they reinstate the draft, I'm not going. Let's go to the phones." He'd do anything to get the phones to light up: "I think funerals are bizarre rituals, don't you?" Moved from evenings to mornings after his initial success, Leykis would start the broadcast day by reading all the answers to the Jumble puzzle in the morning newspaper. The paper threatened to pull its advertising off WQBK because elderly subscribers were calling to say that the man on the radio had ruined their morning fun with the Jumble. Leykis took to mocking his old listeners' voices. Desperate to outrage, he announced that he was broadcasting totally nude.

"I'm a veteran," one caller said by way of introduction.

"Yeah, so what?" Leykis replied.

After two years of savaging the elderly, he was twenty-seven and ready for Miami. But the king of South Florida radio was lying in wait. Neil Rogers turned his show into a nonstop rip of the new kid, calling Leykis a "supermarket bag boy with a cocaine problem," obsessing over his new competition for hours each night. Leykis returned fire, reading the ratings on the air to prove that Rogers's audience was in decline, revealing Rogers's real name, even managing to get himself booked on Rogers's show as a phone-in guest who was an expert on practical jokes. The radio wars went on for months, drawing national press and boosting ratings. Leykis established himself as a talk commando, a liberal libertarian who was pro-abortion, pro–gun control, pro–affirmative action.

But he was bored. The callers were old and predictable. The issues were dull and repetitive. The one show each week that really juiced Leykis was his Saturday program. His contract required him to work six days, and Leykis resented the imposition on his weekends. So instead of sticking with his usual political and topical fare, he devoted Saturdays to "The Kinky Hour," taking calls about sex and relationships, the weirder the better. It was 1985 and you still couldn't say anything terribly explicit on the radio, but Leykis was eager to push the envelope. If twins wanted to meet twins, he gave them a forum. If a caller wanted to boast about his sexual prowess, Leykis let him. The callers on Saturdays, he noticed, were considerably younger than those who rang up during the week. And everyone craved that younger demographic.

But a nightly show about sex? Not possible. There were rules about that sort of thing. You could jeopardize the license.

JEFF CHRISTY NEVER set out to be a talk show host. All he wanted to do was spin the hits and be the big man in town, like his hero, the great Larry Lujack, Chicago's premier Top 40 jock. Christy was a journeyman deejay in the 1970s, a jovial fellow with an okay voice and some clever shtick. He had grown up listening to Lujack, so it was only natural that he adopted Lujack's signature line about his show "serving

humanity," as well as a bunch of Lujack's winkingly grandiose ges-
tures—sound effects, desk thumping, quick-stab jingles. Christy's
show was always coming to you "with Excellence in Broadcasting,"
from the "Bachelor Jeff Radio Network" or the "Jeff Christy Radio
Network." Christy also had a funny way of tossing in pseudo-British
pronunciations, such as "shed-ule" for *schedule.*

Like many Top 40 jocks in the late 1960s, Christy had had his
name assigned to him. The program director at "solid rockin' gold"
WIXZ, an AM station in McKeesport, Pennsylvania, made the deejay
check the White Pages to be certain there was no other Jeff Christy in
the area. Christy played whatever hits came down the pike. He was no
longhair—never wore blue jeans, never protested the Vietnam War.
He paid no attention to the lyrics of the songs he played over and
over.[2] He focused on perfecting his patter and his pacing. Radio was a
craft that demanded discipline, and Christy was a superb technician. If
he was political at all, he probably opposed much of what the rock
stars of the day were singing about. But really, "I was just oblivious to it
all, obsessed with being on the radio," he recalled. "I tried to sound just
like Larry Lujack and I was pretty good at it, but it stunted me for two
or three years. Then I became more comfortable with myself and I just
kept trying to push the envelope. I was just trying to be funny in those
Jeff Christy days. I was totally driven by ambition."

The best of Christy's comedy bits took a bite out of the feminist
movement. One morning in 1973, Christy came out of the song "Love
Can Make You Happy" with a quip: "Women's liberation theme song
there for you." He read a letter from a listener who wanted to know if
it was possible for a girl to become a deejay. "Time for the Christy
Quickie Deejay Course," the jock intoned, demonstrating how to cue
up a record and start a song under his announcement. Pause. "After
you have mastered those two techniques, girls, change your sex!" Ba-
dum-*dum*!

Like so many other boys, Christy got into radio through his own
fantasy broadcasts. He was twelve when his mother bought him a
Remco Caravelle, a blue plastic transmitter with a telescoping antenna.
"I'd play records and put the microphone up to the turntable speaker

and you could hear the broadcast anywhere in the house," he recalled decades later. He imitated his favorite baseball announcer, Harry Caray, and his beloved deejays, Lujack and St. Louis's Johnny Rabbit. "Almost everybody who is in any way a performer has always known they wanted to do it, to be the focus of attention, to be more than yourself outside yourself," he said.

As Christy shoehorned more and more satire bits between the hits, station managers grew nervous. The consultants flexed their muscles and program directors told Christy to read the lines written for him on index cards and otherwise keep his trap shut. "I thought this was the end," the muzzled deejay recalled. "How can I possibly stand out under those rules?"

Christy bounced from job to job and nothing got better. In 1979, he quit radio. He took a job with the Kansas City Royals as director of group sales and reverted to his birth name, Rush Hudson Limbaugh III.

Four years later, Limbaugh returned to radio, handling news and commentaries for a Kansas City station, only to be fired for getting too personal and partisan in his comments. Then, in 1984, a Sacramento station offered Limbaugh a talk program of his own. *The Rush Limbaugh Show* was a daily dicing of the solons of the California capital, spiced with Limbaugh's comedy bits, "news updates" packaged with popular music to create a fast-paced blend of monologues, listener calls, and plenty of self-promotion. This was Top 40–style talk. The callers were the songs and Limbaugh was the talk deejay, always pushing forward, railing against the political targets of the day, repeating catchphrases and sayings that loyal listeners could chant along with him.[3] In the pre-Limbaugh era, callers on talk shows rambled on and on. New York's Bob Grant would read the *Daily News* while callers babbled; occasionally, he'd hold a pitcher up to the microphone and pour water to signify that the caller was running on. But Limbaugh treated each call as a unit of entertainment, paring each one into a relevant, succinct bit that flowed quickly into the next segment. The show adhered to the Top 40 rule book—highly produced, predictable unpredictability. The program was a hit. Limbaugh was a star.

"I wanted to find out if people would listen to me just for me," he said. "Not the music, not the contests, just me. None of the dreaded consultants. No producer, no writers, no prompters, no meetings. Just one guy and the microphone. I'm it. A solo flyer. If I'm not here, there's nobody to cut away to."

Limbaugh's success in Sacramento came just as the barriers to talk were being stripped away. In the early 1980s, satellite technology made it possible to send the same program to many stations at a fraction of the cost of the telephone land lines that radio networks used in their heyday. Talk could indeed be cheap. And it turned out that contrary to industry gospel, talk did not have to focus on local issues—national politics, relationships, the celebrity world, and good old sex knew no local borders.

As technology changed the cost structure, the federal government was busy removing restrictions on content. The FCC stopped enforcing the fairness doctrine, which it said did more to stifle public debate than to promote it. Congress tried to reinstate the rules, but President Ronald Reagan vetoed that move.[4] A series of court rulings made it clear that any federal role in monitoring content was minimal at best.

All talk radio needed now was a juggernaut, a blockbuster show to demonstrate that the format could score big ratings and haul in profits. In 1988, ABC Radio offered Limbaugh a package deal including a local late-morning show on WABC in New York and a national early-afternoon show on whatever stations he could sell himself to. The EIB (Excellence in Broadcasting) Network premiered on fifty-six stations in August 1988.

Limbaugh was an almost instant phenomenon, filling the midday slot on talk stations that blossomed across the AM band in the late 1980s and early '90s. He made local station owners happy with his blend of controversy, showmanship, and sales skills. When Limbaugh railed against "feminazis," a station in California immediately got a call from one of its sponsors, Woody's Barbecue, saying it would not do business with a station that allowed a host to voice such a slur. Word got to Limbaugh about the problem, and he took it to the listeners:

"Ladies and gentlemen, I was informed last Friday that Woody's Barbecue in Santa Barbara, California, has decided to drop its Christmas advertising plan with its local station because I have used the word 'feminazi.' Now, there are two ways I could deal with this. I could cry about it and I could shout about how unfair it is for Woody to do this. Then I could petition the government to make up the $250 that the radio station will lose. . . . Or I could approach this the conservative way: I could face it squarely like a man and fix it.

"This is what I'd like you to do. If you have plans to go to lunch or dinner this week, go to Woody's Barbecue. I understand Woody's food is great and we need to show him that he's making a mistake by not being part of the EIB Network revolution. Do me a favor and tell him why you're there. Let's make it our goal that Woody runs out of food by this Thursday."[5]

Within days, Woody's was running ads in the local paper boasting that Rush Limbaugh had endorsed its ribs. Limbaugh had proven that you didn't have to be there to be local. He had shown that an opinionated, conservative program could flourish without fear of reproach from government regulators fretting about balance. And he had shown doubters in the industry that whatever political perspective he might advocate while filling the spaces between commercials, his first priority was turning a profit for his stations. He mastered the art of making his program sound as if it might well be coming from your local station, even though it emanated from midtown Manhattan. (Limbaugh quickly dropped the New York local show to concentrate on the nationally syndicated program.)

Limbaugh's critics seized on his right-wing politics as the explanation for his success, painting him as a grim voice of the angry white man, a populist crying out against the male loss of status as women entered the workforce en masse and manufacturing jobs headed overseas.[6] The press tended to portray talk radio as a refuge of the ignorant and the reactionary, but studies of the audience belied that image. Talk listeners were demographically indistinguishable from Americans as a whole; if anything, they were more knowledgeable and politically involved than non-listeners.[7]

From the start, Limbaugh was an entertainer who delighted in making fun of serious political shows, even as he involved apolitical Americans in the minutiae of congressional maneuvering. In later years, Limbaugh was hardly shy about taking advantage of his political prowess and access to Republican leaders, but he always put showbiz first. When Limbaugh's political opponents gleefully pounced on the news that he was under investigation for trafficking in prescription painkillers and had checked into a rehabilitation center after becoming addicted to the pills, the talk host seemed genuinely perplexed. Despite his role as the nation's premier voice of popular conservatism, he still saw himself as a performer on the radio, a jock who happened to take phone calls and recite monologues rather than play hit songs.

"My purpose is not to make America more like what I think it should be," Limbaugh said. "I simply want to be the best radio guy there is. This is a performance—'talent on loan from God.' Now, I wouldn't say that in someone's living room. But I can say it on the air because I am talking one-on-one to millions of people and I have credibility with them on both sides—serious and joking. If people change their minds or agree with me, that's a bonus. But my objective is always to do a better show than yesterday. I am governed by advertising and audience."

That essential truth got lost in the uproar over talk radio's—and Limbaugh's—political sway as the format exploded in the early 1990s. The number of stations devoted to talk quadrupled in the decade ending in 1994, as music almost entirely vanished from the AM band. It became so cheap to pull talk shows off the satellite that many stations found it possible to operate without a single local program—that is, with no on-air staff of their own.

Politics—especially red-meat conservatism—dominated talk radio. In 1988, talk hosts flexed their political muscles, encouraging listeners to blast-fax Congress and mail in mounds of tea bags to express rage against a 50 percent congressional pay hike. The groundswell of popular outrage killed the pay raise. In 1994, Limbaugh virtually teamed up with Newt Gingrich to sell the Contract with America, a Madison Avenue–inspired conservative platform that helped win a Republican majority in the House of Representatives and made Gingrich House Speaker.

Limbaugh's success—he would eventually be carried on 600 stations, reaching 15 million listeners—spawned legions of imitators, most of them conservatives and most of them ratings failures. Radio consultants recruited ex-politicians, campaign aides, and names ripped from the headlines of Washington scandals—for example, Oliver North (Iran-contra), G. Gordon Liddy (Watergate), and Joe Scarborough (Clinton impeachment)—to try the talk game. Talk radio became a key weapon in the Republican campaign arsenal.

At the GOP national convention in San Diego in 1996, you could blow a cannonball down Radio Row—thirty-odd tables along the mezzanine above the convention floor—and take out the leading edge of the Republican revolution. Conservative hosts from coast to coast lined up to lavish praise on Bob Dole's presidential campaign. Off-mike after a quick interview with Virginia's governor, George Allen, talk host Mary Matalin shook his hand and said, "That was terrific, and I mean it as a parent and a taxpayer." Republican organizers left Democrats in the dust when it came to the care and coddling of talk hosts. At one point when I visited Radio Row, seven of the fourteen hosts on the air wore Republican Party pins on their lapels.

But those who confused political loyalty with showbiz acumen were generally relegated to the fringes of talk radio. Those who made the big time have been, for the most part, refugees from Top 40. Scratch almost any successful radio talker, and you find an ex-deejay like Limbaugh who has repurposed his quick-tongued manner of dispensing shreds of meaning, switching from music to talk while still serving his twin masters—the clock and the spots. Content is secondary. Tom Leykis, Don Imus, Howard Stern, Don Geronimo, Glenn Beck, Tom Joyner—all were jocks who made their living spinning the hits, and all run talk shows deeply inspired by the Top 40 formula.[8] They move quickly from bit to bit, connecting with the essential minutiae of daily life, hitting listeners' emotional cores, never getting in too deep.[9] They might do politics or eschew it entirely, but the format stays the same. David Letterman—another former Top 40 jock

(Boss Radio 57 in Muncie, Indiana, 1969)—follows the same rules on his late-night TV show: a slam-bam torrent of bits and jingles, always promoting the next feature, with bursts of familiar music to introduce and end each item.[10]

The goal is ratings—"period," said Walt Sabo, the architect of hot talk, the industry name for the non-political, lifestyle- or sex-oriented material that Leykis and Howard Stern do. Talk isn't inherently conservative or liberal. "The job of a talk host is to get you riled up and establish absolutes, because only an absolute point of view produces phone calls, which are really hard to generate." The best talkers are good because they are storytellers and showmen. Their heroes are not Churchill, JFK, or Reagan but Shepherd, Lujack, and Ingram, the legendary voices they listened to as shy boys alone in their rooms.

Their goal is the same intimacy and community that Top 40 jocks built. At the peak of his popularity, Limbaugh watched his audience flock to him like the kids who once turned out to record hops to see their favorite deejays. They gathered in "Rush Rooms" at restaurants across the country, listening together as they ate lunch. Like Top 40, talk radio gave its audience an easy way to rebel quietly against the frustrations of the larger society. Talk, like Top 40, created an "us" that the listener could join against the "them" that ran the country or made the rules or failed to understand their lives. But the Rush Rooms did not survive because what talk radio does best is to connect with people in the privacy of their cars or headphones. A public gathering breaks the spell, robs the imagination. Talk thrives when it says what listeners dare not speak aloud at the office or at home.

SLOWLY BUT SURELY, Tom Leykis bumped up radio's crooked career ladder, from Miami to Phoenix to Los Angeles, as a topical talk host, a liberal counterpoint to Limbaugh, a useful slot-filler for program directors seeking political balance from a clever showman. But always, Leykis reserved for his Saturday shows something extra, an injection of rude humor and ever more explicit sexual content that simply wouldn't be accepted during the week, when the suits were listening.

In Los Angeles in the late 1980s, at AM talk station KFI, Leykis called his Saturday edition *The Hangover Show,* on the theory that many in the audience were suffering from the previous night's excesses and might relish the raw material. "I came in one day and said I was late because I was having sex this morning," Leykis recalled. "I decided to tell the truth, and, literally, I had four hours of people calling in, wigged-out because I'd said I was having sex."

During his vacations, Leykis would go to other cities to do fill-in work. That's what brought him to Chicago, where, in 1991, he substituted at WLUP, The Loop, which was experimenting with a loose, chatty format in which deejays played only a few songs each hour, devoting most of the time to banter about their own relationships and specifically what happened last night. The experience was an epiphany for Leykis. He'd heard Howard Stern and the Greaseman, two Washington, D.C., jocks whose confessional styles and overtly sexual content were winning notoriety. But actually doing this sort of radio made Leykis realize the political stuff was toast. The politically attuned population was an aging AM audience—a fading demographic clinging to yesterday's technology. Voter turnout was plummeting, and in the 1970s, the portion of the American public that paid close attention to public affairs fell from 72 percent to 56 percent.[11] Talk radio followed—and led—the people.

Back in L.A., Leykis made his Saturday shows more and more explicit. In response, the FCC slapped KFI with three fines. The first sanction came after Leykis played host to a guest from an organization called Hung Jury, whose membership was restricted to men with members eight inches or longer. Two thousand dollars, please.

The second resulted when a caller to the show described how she masturbated her dog. Leykis asked the woman whether the animal made a noise.

"Yeah," she said.

"Do the noise."

She made a gurgling sound. Two thousand dollars, please.

The final fine was levied after Leykis asked listeners to call in and name the grossest thing they had ever put in their mouths. The answers were uniformly revolting—bugs, gum off the sidewalk, and the one that won the FCC's ire, a most repulsive bodily excretion. Another two grand.

Talk radio, born from the federal requirement that stations devote some airtime to public affairs, had been liberated to deliver nothing but entertainment. Radio's devolution into tightly defined niche formats had created a need for different varieties of talk—a style to appeal to young men ("hot talk"), a brand for young women (relationship and family advice), and a product for a more mature audience (traditional political talk). Well more than half the listeners to stations airing Limbaugh's show were over age fifty. In contrast, stations featuring Stern and similar programs attracted audiences in which fewer than 10 percent of listeners were fifty or older. Advertisers took note.

Working at a family-owned FM hard rock station in Washington in the early 1980s, Stern shocked listeners and management alike with his utterly frank discussions of—and brutal jokes about—everything from his wife's miscarriage to the size of black men's penises to his desire to be serviced by strippers in the studio. "Are you aroused as we speak?" Stern would ask female callers. He jumped on every major tragedy in the news, leaving his audience slack-jawed as he searched for the limits of satire—and blew past them. He took on plane crash victims, mothers of murdered children, deformed children. Every outrage brought a new wave of publicity, which led to a larger audience, which emboldened Stern to be more outrageous. The combination of shock and Stern's often hilarious comedy bits—"Bestiality Dial-a-Date," "Guess Who's the Jew," and "Mystery Whiz," which challenged listeners to guess which member of the show's cast was at that very moment peeing—had the desired effect.[12]

The nature of Stern's shtick was to push the act until it grew too hot for his managers. In 1982, bucking against management anxieties, he jumped from Washington to New York and a big network station, WNBC. Executives there made a big show of wanting to push the limits—an attempt to prove that AM radio could still be hip. "If we weren't so bad, we wouldn't be so good," read the copy in a magazine ad featuring a photograph of Imus and Stern, WNBC's morning and afternoon drive-time deejays. The two were pictured in shoulder-length curls, wearing wide-lapeled, open-collar white shirts and nasty-boy scowls. The station did its best to package the two as the brash new sound of Top 40, but the truth was that Stern was just passing through. There was no way his shtick would fit in with Top 40's broad appeal or with playing frothy pop on the AM band. In fact, from the start, NBC had ordered Stern to refrain from any jokes dealing with sickness, death, personal tragedy, or "sexual topics in a lascivious manner."

But Howard Stern was not about to be Cousin Brucie. In 1985, when Stern described the Statue of Liberty pleasuring herself sexually, Lee Iacocca, the automaker who was also chief of the Statue of Liberty Foundation, threatened to take all of Chrysler's advertising off NBC. Stern was soon let go. He moved to a low-rated New York FM rock station, where he was free to be as bad as he wanted to be. He became the self-anointed King of All Media, syndicating his show nationwide. CBS Radio paid Stern the grand sum of $705,000 in 1985, and by 2001, the company was happy to sign him to a five-year, $58.8 million contract. Many stations that carried Stern were FM rockers, and as Stern's morning talk show greatly outperformed the music programming that filled the rest of the day, a market developed for more hot talk.

Once again, the key to innovation was the removal of government restrictions. Throughout the 1980s and '90s, the FCC and the courts had consistently moved away from regulating content.[13] Despite persistent complaints from listeners about indecent programming, the FCC declined to get involved. Regulators condoned a phone-in show called Kiss My Butt Day; a Stern routine in which he called other deejays "a bunch of dickheads" and made a farting noise while saying "butt-plug jerk-off"; a 1992 program in which Boston deejay Charles Laquidara apparently tried to get his eight-year-old daughter to say "Lick me" to another man; and a 1994 bit in which Stern told a woman caller that "I love you no matter what, as long as you still got a vagina."[14]

In a society that had lost the courage to say no and the capacity to

declare behavior out of bounds, shock jocks had every reason to go farther and farther. Stern's show devolved into a daily parade of professional strippers who got naked for the host and his sidekicks. Sure,
along the way there were occasional bouts of finger wagging and even
some fines. Over the course of the 1980s and early '90s, the FCC fined
Stern's employers nearly $2 million in various attempts to rein in his
"depictions of sexual or excretory activities or organs." In 1993, stations were fined after Stern quizzed actor Pat Cooper about his mas-
turbation habits, delivered a lengthy description of rectal bleeding, and
discussed Santa Claus's proclivity for fondling children. Management
was happy to pay the fines and collect the vastly larger profits.

The, in 2004, Janet Jackson displayed her breast on the national
TV broadcast of the Super Bowl halftime show. Under enormous public pressure to show some teeth on the decency issue, the FCC focused
on Stern and other shock jocks. Clear Channel Communications—
secure in the knowledge that only six of its twelve hundred stations
aired Stern's show—demonstrated its newfound concern over raunch
radio by throwing him off its airwaves. This time, the government
seemed serious. Panicked radio executives knew audiences loved the
raunch, but they also sensed a grassroots rebellion against explicit excesses. Talk radio lived on the fault line between society's private pleasures and its public expectations of itself. The history of talk taught
executives that a temporary retreat might be prudent.

The FCC wasn't exactly stripping stations of their licenses. The
agency took more than a year before it issued a minor fine against
WNEW-FM in New York, where the talk duo of Opie and Anthony
in 2002 held a contest rewarding listeners for having sex in public
places and a Virginia couple scored big points by having intercourse in
the vestibule of St. Patrick's Cathedral. (The jocks were fired, then
snapped up by XM Satellite Radio as an extra-naughty pay-radio exclusive—only to return to FM with a second, cleaner daily show.) Regulators similarly delivered only a slap on the wrist (a $27,500 fine) to
the Detroit hot talk duo of Deminski and Doyle, who devoted an afternoon drive-time show to extraordinarily explicit listener accounts of
"funky sex techniques" such as the Shocker ("It's with the fingers . . . ,

two in the pink, one in the stink"), the Rusty Trombone, and the Cleveland Tornado. "We have brought these into the mainstream," one of the hosts boasted on the show.

"You guys are classic," one caller said. "This is classic radio right here. I love it."[15]

Public pressure to get tough on shock jocks ran smack into the libertarianism of President George W. Bush's FCC chairman, Michael Powell, who said he "gets queasy" over the notion of taking action against radio programmers. But Congress heard the outcry following the Janet Jackson reveal and pushed the FCC to get on the decency bandwagon. The agency issued a $755,000 fine against Bubba the Love Sponge (Todd Clem), a Tampa, Florida, shock jock whose comedy bits included extremely graphic descriptions of masturbation and famous cartoon characters talking about their sex lives. Clear Channel, owner of Bubba's station, quickly fired its bad boy, who then migrated with Stern to satellite radio.

Was this crackdown merely a momentary response to a celebrated outrage? While Stern whined about being censored and then jumped to Sirius Satellite Radio for $500 million over five years, most radio executives said privately that their post-breast-scandal curbs on content would be temporary. FCC staffers seemed confident that the courts—liberal and conservative judges alike—would soon demand a return to the laissez-faire approach that governed before the CBS "wardrobe malfunction." For the first few years after the Jackson incident, the FCC fines and threats kept coming. The pendulum of tolerance seemed to be swinging back toward a more restrictive atmosphere. But even if the FM band was becoming less hospitable to radio raunch, shock had a new, wide-open outlet, on pay satellite radio. Listeners might have to pay for it, but the bottom line was that shock jocks would be free once again to push the boundaries as hard as they dared.

IN HIS DARK STUDIO at the Westwood One network in Culver City, Tom Leykis cackles with delight. "The definition of a man is that you've been with someone you haven't even told your friends about. Some awful, horrible woman—because you just had to go. Like you'd rather take a whiz at the Ritz-Carlton, but you're on the IRT and you simply had to go, so you peed on the third rail. And you don't care, you'll take the ticket."

"The Professor," as his audience calls him, is in. It's been nearly a decade since Leykis jettisoned politics and responsible discussion of government, switched from AM to FM, and turned up the volume on his old Saturday sex shows. He could hardly be happier, wealthier, or more popular. On KLSX in Los Angeles and a few dozen other stations, mostly in the West, Leykis leads a raucous daily symposium on the wily ways of women and the simple strategies men must employ to bed them while they're young and unattached.

"I was a bit of a pussy for a while, until I realized that what women really wanted was for us to pin them down and give them a good crack," he says.

Every show starts with a recitation of Leykis's mantra: "This is the show where America gets together to talk about the issues you really care about. This is the program that is not hosted by a right-wing wacko or convicted felon."

Leykis dispenses pearls of wisdom from his Leykis 101 Golden Rules for Men, such as "Don't speak to women you work with unless it's related directly to work . . . because you're a walking lawsuit waiting to happen," or "Successfully getting a woman into the sack involves some sort of chemical inducement. Alcohol is the preferred inducement."

The show charges on, blending the host's raucous remarks with calls from men seeking advice and women sputtering with outrage. The men who listen—and the women who make up more than a third of his audience—embrace his rules as the teachings of an honored guru. Hardly a day goes by on which he fails to receive e-mail from listeners who say they regard him as their "father."

Leykis usually works alone in a dark, hypercooled glass booth, a single spotlight trained on his stack of e-mail and news clippings, the host standing and rocking, his considerable belly bouncing against the table, his eyes hidden behind ever present Ray-Bans, his mouth caressing the hanging microphone. But on this afternoon, Leykis has traveled far from his studio, to Vancouver, British Columbia, to meet his people.[16] It's one of his regular listener events, a live performance of his show before more than seven hundred avid fans at Cheers, a huge bar in a working-class neighborhood below the city's dramatic crest of snowcapped mountains. Fans line up for hours before the show, big tough guys in leather jackets, hockey fans, and construction crews, but also architects and lawyers, teachers and bankers. Many are married, many are not. Outside, scalpers ask $200 for a ticket (they were distributed free by the local station that carried Leykis's show)—and people are paying. The scene inside promises everything the Leykis show is about: a cigar girl wearing only a black suit jacket moves around the room, rewarding those who purchase a stogie with a brief placement of her bare bottom on their lap.

"Society's been feminized, and Leykis is the rare voice who calls it for what it is," says Simon Collinge, a fan who owns an office equipment company and listens to the show by himself, in the car. "You ever listen to him when he talks some guy into dumping his girl and then he gets them both on the phone and he really dumps her? Man, that's good radio."

Preceded onstage by seven buxom models, Leykis wins lusty cheers and roars of approval when—just checking—he asks, "Nobody in this room has a problem with women being sluts, right, boys?"

For weeks before his arrival in town, Leykis has been taunting Lynn Colliar, the anchorwoman of a Canadian morning TV news program, offering to donate $50,000 to the charity of her choice if she will attend his Vancouver show, bare her breasts, and permit Tom to sign them with his black Sharpie.

Colliar has declined, noting that "my job is to deliver news, not to support his career." Now, Leykis ups the offer to $150,000 and, with no TV anchorwoman in the hall, he invites to the stage any other woman who might wish to take part in his trademark ritual.

A young woman named Maya Leigh steps forward. "I'm too shy," she says when she reaches center stage. "I'm freaking out now."

"You gotta give them what they want," Leykis tells her. "Everybody wants to see."

Slowly, she drops her jacket and pulls down her shirt.

"Okay, there we are," Leykis says. "Now, that wasn't hard, was it? Show the boys." He leads her toward the other end of the stage. "Don't forget the boys over here." And for the radio audience, he adds, "She's showing her considerable rackage." Leykis leans in and signs his name in a swirling two-inch-high cursive.

A grinding rock anthem fills the airwaves and *The Tom Leykis Show* breaks for nine minutes of commercials.

Leykis, who has been married four times, started signing racks in 1998. He's been holding listener events since 1995, when he dropped in on fans who gathered regularly at a Seattle hotel to listen, drink, and pick each other up. His Seattle fans loved Flash Fridays, Leykis's weekly shtick in which he encourages female listeners out on the highways to lift their shirts, entertaining the men on the road and demonstrating the show's reach. Flash Fridays, he says, are an homage to his boyhood idol, Jean Shepherd, a tribute to Shep's famous call to his listeners to flash their apartment lights to show each other how large their community really was. Leykis adapted the stunt to his suburban audience, asking them to flash their headlights on the highway to show each other how many people were listening to the show. Some women soon took matters into their own hands, displaying a bit more than a flash of light.

One fateful Friday in 1998, when Leykis was doing his show in front of his fans in a Seattle ballroom, a caller asked, "How do you like being with all those breasts?"

"The breasts are on the freeway, not here," the host replied. But just then, a woman ran up from the Seattle ballroom audience, exposed herself, and said, "Here." She asked Leykis to autograph her bosom. Within minutes, a queue of women waited to be signed.

Leykis explained the phenomenon as a symptom of the difference between men and women. "Women are always looking for male approval; they compete with each other for it," he said. No matter how coarsely Leykis attacks the women, they keep asking him to whip out his Sharpie and "sign me."

In Vancouver, Leykis focuses the crowd's attention on a woman in the audience. "That chick is a filling station, a depository, a human toilet," he says. Whereupon the woman he has dissed removes her shirt and begs him to autograph her chest.

Leykis, like other shock jocks, plays a character who has something in common with his off-air personality but is broader, more vulgar, and much less attractive. "I don't make up opinions," he said. "I really do believe this stuff, but there is an irony to it that, well, not all the listeners might appreciate."

Are there any limits to what he can do on the radio? "None. If you give it a moment's thought, you can find a way to get anything on the air." So he goes on the air and names the woman who accused NBA star Kobe Bryant of raping her, and Leykis revels in the outraged calls and e-mails from thousands of offended women. And he's not really so terribly miffed when it's reported that he himself was once arrested for domestic battery. His ex-wife told police that Tom "pushed her head into a brick fireplace" during an argument. It's all fodder for the show, feed for the ratings.

Leykis traces the roots of explicit radio not to the companies that sell it or the jocks who perform it but to the government that created the conditions for it to flourish: "We got shock radio because a bunch of Republicans wanted deregulation. When limits on how many stations a company could own were raised, the price of stations skyrocketed, and the only way anyone could ever make back what they'd paid for a station was to cut costs, boost ratings, and sell the station for even more. Cheap, ratings-proven, satellite-delivered programming lowered costs and guaranteed an audience.

"I'm a hit man," Leykis said. "People know they can put me on the air and get numbers, fast. And to keep that going, I have to go on the air and tell the audience I'm going to whip my dick out, because the company needs to get a faster return on their investment." Leykis defends his raunchy act as a mere reflection of society's true nature. "It's what people are really thinking. The whole society has gotten more explicit. And in radio, we've gotten beyond the idea that talk has to have this *purpose* beyond mere entertainment. Our topics are just a vehicle for me to make fun of the callers. People don't tune in to hear *topics*. They like the personality. They don't care if you're conservative or liberal. All this crap about talk radio being all conservative: I'm no conservative and I've had a total of seven months out of work since 1981."

To listen to the Leykis show, or to any of Stern's other offspring, is to accept talk radio as a corporate-sponsored outlaw striking out against the hegemony of political correctness, reaching frustrated Americans in the one place where they feel completely in charge: the driver's seat. "Most of the talk media—the TV shows, Regis, Montel—are aimed at women; they show men as incompetent jerks, deadbeat scum," Leykis said. "At work, guys can't say anything. Can't say 'You look nice' or 'My wife's a bitch.' On this show, they can hear that and it's a release. It's pop anthropology, that's all it is."

Leykis denies any pretension to artistry. "We're in the advertising business," he said. "They're paying me to feign intimacy and get as many people as possible listening. We sell spots. We are here to serve the shareholders. To do that, I am going to try to get away with whatever I can get away with, because whoever goes the farthest does the best."

Whatever happened to the kid who wanted to be Shepherd, Ingram, or Imus? He's become a ratings machine, going however low the common denominator takes him. He seems to love it, and he does tell stories, like Shepherd, and make wisecracks, like Ingram, and create a character who does winning shtick, like Imus. Tom Leykis is doing what he always wanted to do: he's breaking new ground.

TODAY'S NEW GROUND involves an extremely buxom woman named Gail, who, it is important to note, gave birth a few months ago. On yesterday's program, Gail's nineteen-year-old son, Graham, called in to complain that his mother regularly invited her boyfriend over and had sex with him while Graham was in the room. The son was appalled. Leykis, his moral sensibilities apparently ruffled, called the mother a "slut" and a "whore."

Now, both mother and son have shown up at the Vancouver bar. Gail, thirty-eight, says she was offended by Leykis's comments. So offended that she announces her own peculiar form of revenge: she intends to spray the talk show host with breast milk. After a bit of banter with the host onstage ("I smoke weed with my son when I'm horny," Mom says, giggling), and after a brief delay when Gail announces that "I have to drink more beer," the mother moves to the front of the stage, lowers her shirt, squeezes her nipple, and sprays a jet of milk onto the suddenly silenced crowd.

"I've never seen anything like this," Leykis says, and the audience erupts in a roar of approval.

"I can't look," says Graham, the son.

"Holy shit," an entire table of men chants just below the stage.

Gail squirts again, and again, at the crowd, into a cup, onto the flashing cameras. Graham looks down, to Leykis, anywhere but at his mother.

"I'm genuinely stunned," Leykis says. "We have never had a mother onstage to squirt breast milk before."

"I had no idea," Graham says.

Gail leans into the audience, lets several fans sign her breasts.

"It's like when they feed the fish," Leykis narrates for listeners at home. "She's squeezing breast milk into their mugs. These are unbelievable breasts, Gail. These are amazing breasts."

The music swells, the canned announcer notes that "*The Tom Leykis Show* may contain content of an adult nature," and the show breaks for eight minutes of commercials.

Later, Leykis calls Graham back onstage, and in an effort to ease his pain and make up to him for the humiliation of watching his mother shower chanting strangers with her milk, the talk host invites the son to lick the breasts of Katie, a slim, barely legal woman who has run up onstage to be signed.

"I'm here to help," Leykis says. "Graham, that'll teach you to call a talk show."

Just before the three-hour show ends, a caller named Theresa phones in to ask Leykis "why the men up there aren't dropping their drawers for the ladies in the audience."

"Let me tell you, Theresa," Leykis replies. "This is—say it along with me, boys—*talk radio for guys*. Why don't you call the station that plays the Céline Dion music and ask them to have a listener event for girls? You are not in my target demographic. These guys are getting action from naked chicks onstage."

Theresa is not mollified: "Sweetheart, you need to get off the bitter," she says.

"No, sweetheart," Leykis retorts, "you need to get off the air," and with the crowd's cheers virtually lifting him off the stage, Tom Leykis punches up a sound effect that explodes Theresa off his program, and the kid from Long Island who wanted to be on the radio wraps up another day at the office.[17]

Chapter **10**

✳ SCATTERING SEEDS

Bill Siemering believed in a different kind of shock. What he heard every day on the radio in 1969 was completely out of step with what he saw both at the University of Buffalo and in the city and nation beyond campus. From his office at the student radio station, Siemering wondered how it could be that while America's young people rebelled against their elders, and blacks rose up against the white power structure, and women confronted the sclerotic male way of doing things, radio's report on American reality still consisted of five-minute hourly network headlines and sixty-second bulletins shoehorned between the hits on Top 40. How could radio be the source of the music driving the cultural rebellion across the country, yet remain—especially on the news—so distant, so formal, so tone-deaf to the ferment of the day?

Siemering, the professional manager of the student voice at the university, presided over a station that was typical of what was then called educational radio. Like most college-owned FM stations at the extreme left end of the dial, WBFO was a refuge for people who turned their backs on the mass pop culture. From the birth of FM well into the 1970s, college- and community-owned noncommercial stations divvied up their hours without regard to which shows came next. The Irish show bumped into the polka hour, which ran into the gardening show, which gave way to choral music. No one was expected to listen to everything. No one gave much thought to ratings, money, or maximizing audience. Those were commercial radio's worries.

Siemering's academic mien, gentle voice, and midwestern modesty—the very qualities that had attracted university administrators to him—masked the fact that he was determined to change the status quo, to insist that listening to the radio not be a passive pursuit. On

BILL SIEMERING AT WBFO'S STOREFRONT STUDIO WITH MEMBERS OF THE STATION'S WEEKEND PROGRAMMING STAFF, CIRCA 1970
(Courtesy University of Buffalo Library Archives)

campus, he helped students cover anti–Vietnam War protests in a challenging, almost confrontational way. He reached out to the city's black ghetto to give voice to the unheard. He attacked exactly those areas of conflict from which most managers fled—race, class, the divisions between rich and poor, powerful and weak. The campus could not contain his ideas or ambition.

Siemering never had been one to shout. A former high school English and history teacher, he was a gracious, slightly proper man who knew from his own experience in Buffalo and from listening to the Canadian Broadcasting Corporation's news and documentaries that U.S. radio was capable of far more depth and purpose than it had shown. As American society bubbled over with anger and confrontation in 1969, Siemering sequestered himself with his typewriter and churned out an influential series of papers advocating a national public radio, stations that would gather news and "unite us in our common humanity" rather than "a common banality." Few could argue with Siemering's observation that the headlines that passed for news on commercial radio were obfuscating and obscure in their brevity. The times called for something more, for a predictable unpredictability, a system of surprises that would put women, blacks, the poor, the young, the old—the left-out—into the story told by the news.

Siemering was not alone in pining for something more than headlines. In 1967, Congress created the Corporation for Public Broadcasting, which in turn set up PBS, the publicly funded network that gave educational TV stations a mechanism to create more ambitious programming, such as *Sesame Street* and documentary and cultural fare. Radio was initially left out of the deal, but Siemering and other managers of college stations pushed for some of TV's leftovers, and in 1970, National Public Radio was born, albeit with less than 10 percent of public broadcasting's budget. The initial idea was for a few dozen stations—most of them college outlets experimenting with radical news and documentary programs—to trade programming.

Joe Gwathmey, who ran the University of Texas station in Austin and was a founding member of NPR's board, argued that public radio should have a radical agenda, that in a "society in the midst of a revolution," NPR could eliminate the traditional filters of journalism and let Americans speak directly to each other.[1] Siemering stopped short of calling for class warfare, but his demands were nonetheless radical. Chosen as NPR's first program director, he moved to Washington and set about erasing the stigma of "educational" broadcasting—snore-inducing lectures and snooty classical announcers with phony British accents. Instead, he wanted to hear the voices of artists and writers, farmers and philosophers, "scattering seeds" of knowledge across the land. "Martin Luther King was saying that 'we have to write our essays in the streets,' " Siemering recalled, "and we wanted to use radio to capture the vitality of what was happening and to show that there's not a single truth here. The idea was that social change was inevitable and we wanted to facilitate it—not as advocates for a cause, but as facilitators."

With federal money in hand, National Public Radio launched its first nationwide program, *All Things Considered,* on May 3, 1971— May Day, date of the largest anti–Vietnam War demonstration staged in Washington.

Robert Conley, a veteran of NBC News and *The New York Times,* opened the program in a quiet, conversational tone then unheard in radio news: "Rather than pulling in reports from all over town, we thought we might try to take you to the event, to get the feel, the texture of the sort of day it's been, through a mix of sounds and events." As young protesters clash with Washington police, listeners hear police helicopters beating the air and chants of "Stop the war now."

"We wanted to be authentic, on the streets," said Siemering. "Commercial radio was the white male voice of authority from New York." So on the first edition of *All Things Considered,* the first voice heard after Conley introduces himself is that of a black nurse talking about her addiction to heroin. "Once you start doin' the drug, often enough you get to the point where when you wake up in the morning, your nose is running and your stomach is cramping, and you know, you can't stand for someone to come in there and holler at you . . . , and you're spitting up from the bed to the toilet. You stink, and Harry has knocked at your door." An electronic musical theme rises beneath the addict's anguished voice, and Conley, in a calm, anti-announcer voice—obviously ad-libbing his way through the broadcast—says there will be a portrait of this addict later on, and a story about what barbers in Iowa are doing to stimulate business in this era of long-haired fashion. But first, a lengthy account of the day's demonstrations, as police carted off nearly seven thousand protesters to RFK Stadium to halt them from shutting down the city. A snippet of folk music starts off a long collage of sounds from the streets of Washington: NPR reporters' descriptions of the protests, police directives, angry confrontations, all blended as Bob Fass did it on WBAI, without narration, a story told in the live sounds of the people making the news.

"Here come the police, one two three four police on motor scooters"—reporter Jeff Kamen describes the events over the sounds of shouting protesters and the gunning motors of police scooters—"Anger now, anger of the young people"—more shouting, anguish, fear—"Here come more police"—a kid shouts, "Come on, people"—a clip of the chatter on the police radio—then Kamen again: "The police knock down a demonstrator"—a sergeant says, "Let me get an ambulance down here"—the reporter approaches a police officer: "Sergeant! Jeff Kamen, National Public Radio. Is that a technique where the men actually try to drive the bikes into the demonstrators?"—the officer replies: "Naw, that's no technique. We're trying to go down the road and the people get in front. What are you going to do? You don't stop on a dime."

And on and on, from an Independence Avenue choked in tear gas, stories of kids and office workers vomiting in the street, police talking about protesters attacking them with tear gas, protesters complaining about police "beating on us," a Washington police officer expressing sympathy for the demonstrator's cause, Kamen reporting that "today in the nation's capital, it is a crime to be young and have long hair"—in all, twenty-nine minutes of coverage taking listeners into the event in a seemingly unedited, direct manner, followed by a reading of poetry about war. This was something new, a form of storytelling unique to radio. This was Bill Siemering's vision.

THERE IS NO PHYSICAL PLACE called NPR America, but it is nonetheless a distinctive cultural landscape, a mental region of this country that shares common experiences and passions, humor and politics. People who find satisfaction and community in the serious approach to news on NPR's *Morning Edition* and *All Things Considered* are often the same people who find a smile and a sense of belonging in the stories and sketches on Garrison Keillor's *Prairie Home Companion* or the wisecracking auto mechanics on *Car Talk*. Millions of Americans left out of commercial radio's definition of the money demographic have found an audio accompaniment to their daily rounds that appeals to their sense of being different. Public radio listeners are older, more affluent, and better educated than the commercial audience.

But like millions of commercial radio listeners who wonder what happened to the music radio they used to love, public radio's fans have noticed that music is vanishing from their favorite stations, replaced by ever more news and talk programming, all designed to sound just like the news and talk shows they already listen to. Jazz, classical, Latin, and other non-pop forms of music once at the heart of public radio are being squeezed into a few late-night hours or silenced entirely.[2]

The loose network of stations funded by listeners and intended as an alternative to commercial radio has evolved into a web of contradictions, adopting a corporate model and growing ever more dependent on the big-business sponsorships it once spurned. (Public stations collected 18 percent of their money from businesses in 2006, more than twice the 1980 level.) A source of programming originally intended to break down barriers of class, income, race, and education has instead attracted a relatively homogeneous audience that is among the most demographically attractive in the country. (NPR's average listener earns almost twice the average national income.)[3] And a form of radio initially designed to showcase less popular kinds of music now shies away from music that its research says detracts from winning the largest possible audiences.

Public radio is only in young adulthood, but it has already settled down to a successful, suburban existence. It is still growing at a healthy clip, and public radio can still be a thorn in the nation's side, surprising listeners with provocative content. But its personality has evolved from its rebellious origins into something more mature, more predictable, and less challenging. Like the rest of radio, it has become more corporate, more cautious—demographically correct.

That transformation, however, has coincided with public radio's greatest popularity and most extraordinary growth as a news gathering organization. For a relatively small but culturally important portion of the generation that grew up with Top 40 and alternative FM, public radio was the fulfillment of radio's promise to unite a generation. Commercial radio was busy chasing that generation into as many narrow alleys of consumerism as consultants could carve out. But public radio's listeners form a tribe that crosses generational lines and creates a social and political force, an unseen community with a bond as powerful and intimate as any audience has shared in radio's history.[4]

RUSS RINGSAK, TRUCKER, lapsed architect, wise man, backs the forty-eight-foot Ryder rig into the loading dock and checks off another thousand-mile trek on a never-ending journey through the American imagination. Last week, St. Paul; this week, Austin; next week, Durango, Colorado. The truck arrives Thursday night, with Ringsak its only occupant. A weathered fellow with long, stringy gray hair, mischievous squinting eyes and an impressive tattoo of a wolf spread across his shoulder, the trucker is advance man and scout for this weekly vestige of live radio, Garrison Keillor's *Prairie Home Companion.*[5]

For more than a quarter century, Keillor has been reporting the news from Lake Wobegon, playing music you can't hear on the radio, and recalling for listeners the stories of the hometown they remember fondly, yet have never set foot in. Every spring, Keillor takes his public radio variety show to college auditoriums, faceless civic centers, and grand old theaters in small towns and big cities, to audiences of graying hippies and proper retirees, graduate students and young professionals. The tall, reluctant man whose tales have changed the way some parents tell their kids stories doesn't join his cast and crew until less than twenty-four hours before showtime. He stays home, deep in composition, the ingredients of each week's monologue shifting in his mind as the hours slip toward Saturday at five, the moment the satellite sends *Prairie Home* to more than five hundred stations and 4 million listeners.

It's Friday at four, and somewhere in the sky over Middle America,

Keillor writes furiously on a laptop. He's been thinking about his monologue since midweek, but nothing's jelled yet. In a way unique to radio, *Prairie Home* is the reflection of one imagination. The show is Keillor, a hesitant, sighing voice that ranges from a thin upper register to a baritone rumble. But in another way, it is a theatrical extravaganza. It takes seventeen people, a semi full of crates, five Oriental rugs, a cardboard box packed with gravel and coconut shells, and assorted bands, writers, producers, and stagehands to put *Prairie Home Companion* on the air each week.

The show, one of public radio's biggest moneymakers, lags behind only *Car Talk* and *Marketplace* in its ability to wrangle donations from listeners. It is a ratings powerhouse, with an audience comparable in size to that of Fox TV's Saturday baseball game of the week. *Prairie Home* is a stretch of the cultural landscape fenced off from the coarseness, cynicism, and irony of postmodern life. Keillor's America is one of jokes you can tell your kids; of camp songs, sing-alongs, and presentations of Talent from Towns Under Two Thousand; of fiddlers, polka dancers, rockabilly bands, jazz trios and classical cellists, poets and playwrights, accordionists and humorists.

Christine Tschida, the show's former producer, liked to make the show's distance from the commercial world clear in her instructions to freelance writers who hoped to get their material on the show: "Don't give us anything to do with pop culture because Garrison won't know who you're talking about. The man does not watch TV."

In Room 1402 of the Austin Marriott, at 7:35 P.M. on Friday, an hour after Keillor arrives in town, actor Tim Russell, sound effects man Tom Keith, bandleader Rich Dworsky, and assorted others gather for their first look at the sketches, ad parodies, and other bits Keillor has written on the plane. The host orders drinks and some hummus appetizers. Quickly, the actors try out the bits, including a sketch in which a renegade cowboy is executed by being locked in the outhouse with the works of Thomas Pynchon, an ad for ketchup in which a husband and wife rediscover love and the simple life by forsaking seven kinds of salsa and coming home to "ketchup on a piece of white bread," and an ad for Bebopareebop Rhubarb Pie in which Keith, the soundman, barks like a dog, screeches like a grackle, squeaks like a bat, yells like a mob of teenagers, and rumbles like a pack of Harley-Davidsons.

The rehearsal is over in thirty-five minutes. Keillor—who neither laughs nor smiles at his own scripts—offers water and appetizers, then adds, "Care for a social moment?" The cast stands about awkwardly for a few minutes, before Keith leads them in an effort to recite the word *spam* in the voices of as many animals as possible. Horse, bird, dog, whale, walrus . . . Now Keillor chuckles heartily. Before nine, they break up. "I might write something new," Keillor says as his guests file out.

Overnight, Keillor crafts his monologue. "The News from Lake Wobegon," a staple of the show's second hour, runs fifteen to twenty-five minutes and is delivered without script, just Keillor on a stool, facing the audience, occasionally closing his eyes to summon the story. He looks as if he is spinning the tale as he speaks, but in fact he has written the story out at least twice. It is the hardest part of the show, and the most important.

Keillor remains in love with radio. He cherishes memories of great radio humorists such as Bob and Ray, whose sketches, soap operas, and ad parodies inspired him, as did his 1974 visit to the Grand Ole Opry, which he wrote about for *The New Yorker*. "It struck me as noble and thrilling that people would do this, and do it live. It seemed like something that a person could do." The first broadcast of *Prairie Home* on Minnesota Public Radio came four months later.

A little less than an hour before airtime, with the host rumpled, unshaven, and mid-rehearsal, the stage is cleared and the auditorium opened. The Bass Performing Arts Center on the University of Texas campus sold out its three thousand seats almost instantly—typical for a Keillor show. Seats go for as much as $50, with Minnesota Public Radio claiming 60 percent of the take and the local station getting the rest.[6]

When the station releases about a hundred last-minute tickets midday Saturday, the queue for them is more than two hundred people long. Folks wait for hours, doing their bills, listening to books on tape, reading Fitzgerald, Michener, Sara Paretsky. An astonishing number of the hopefuls wear Birkenstock sandals.

Along the line is Steven Beebe, a professor of speech communication at Southwest Texas State University, where he uses Keillor's monologues in public speaking classes. "He can provide just enough detail to make us believe in Lake Wobegon, but not too much to make it seem just his," Beebe says. "He knows some of the same people I know, the potluck dinners, like when I was growing up on a farm in Missouri. He puts up the scaffolding; we have to put up the siding ourselves."

Keillor has heard this before. He knows about the academics who write of *Prairie Home* as a postmodern church, a weekly opportunity for Americans—urban, suburban, and rural alike—to become one with the great myths of thrift, civility, and selflessness. "People certainly crave communion and community," he concedes. "But it's not my intention to provide that." With a typical bit of Lake Wobegon self-deprecation, he often says, "The whole show is just a hobby that got out of hand."

Showtime. The curtain rises and Keillor, resplendent in trademark red tie, red socks, red sneakers, and black suit, steps off the front porch set. He looks out onto a sea of smiles. All it takes is the slightest wave of his hand and the crowd jumps in on "Deep in the Heart of Texas" and "God Bless America."

The show is a series of rituals: the sing-along, the parodies, the greetings—scraps of paper on which the live audience has scribbled birthday wishes and parental admonitions, such as this, to Ross in Chicago: "Please do not write any more letters to editors of alternative newspapers. The Lord and I are not amused. Love, Mom."

And then, while his musical guest plays, Keillor retreats to an empty vestibule, faces a blank concrete wall, pulls his monologue script from his jacket pocket, and leans over, as if in prayer. A few seconds before he must step back onstage, he walks past his producer and says, "Out at 0:45," meaning he will finish in exactly twenty-three minutes forty-nine seconds. He tucks the script back in his pocket, strolls on, lifts the red stool to the proscenium lip, and says in that soft, airy voice, "It's been a quiet week in Lake Wobegon, my hometown."

A wave of applause is rewarded with a story that weaves together the tale of a young girl desperate to move on, a pastor who just won recognition for "best sermon by a pastor from a town of under two thousand people," a prom date, a ne'er-do-well slow-pitch softball team, a beauty salon where the ladies sat under beehive dryers, and, always, "hope, hope."

Along the way, Keillor lists the four chief pleasures in life—walking through a field of fresh sweet corn, the love of learning, "the one you thought of first," and the "joy of following in the Lord's will." He brings listeners to love the story's protagonist, a girl named Kate who is determined to live near an ocean, where "everything will be different." "She felt good in her short, short hair," walking along, when suddenly she heard a great roar from the ballpark. A white baseball somehow landed at her feet, a pointless home run that turns into an omen of hope. You can hear sniffles and small sobs from all around the auditorium. And Keillor finishes precisely on time.

Keillor's monologues are the product of a single voice—a unity that has become rare in a pop culture dominated by the collaborative storytelling of film and TV. "A simple narrative has power," Keillor says. "That's when radio comes into its close-up."

The show ends and Keillor disappears backstage to change clothes while fans linger at the foot of the stage, hoping for an autograph. In an hour, the stage will be struck, and Russ Ringsak's semi will be packed, ready to roll on into the Rockies.

Many years ago, when he chose a 1974 country tune called "Hello Love" as *Prairie Home*'s theme, Keillor added a verse of his own to the song:

> *I've heard it said for oh so long*
> *Live radio is dead and gone . . .*
> *I've heard it so often I guess it's true,*
> *But here we are, and there are you.*

THE NPR SOUND is midwestern openness and New England purpose, a smiling lack of cynicism and an assumption that listeners and programmers share values of tolerance, curiosity, and rationalism. By the 1990s, public radio had developed what Lee Abrams, the godfather of consultant-heavy FM rock, called "the only consistent, absolute attitude in radio. Everything consistently has the NPR sound—the writing, the style, the sound bites. I find the NPR attitude stuffy and elitist, but it works."[7]

Public radio listeners proved to be satisfied customers, willing to add their dollars to the support stations received from Washington and from foundations. But as with most ventures born in the throes of cultural change, public radio found itself criticized by those who said it had sold out, turning away from its conception as a force for social change. When Joan Kroc, the widow of McDonald's magnate Ray Kroc, died in 2003 and left NPR $230 million, public radio was transformed as a news organization.

But through two decades of growth, as its news operation expanded to more than 350 journalists, NPR became a target of conservatives, from President Ronald Reagan in the 1980s to House Speaker Newt Gingrich in the 1990s and the George W. Bush administration in 2005. Public radio had to fend off political and financial crises in each of those decades, as conservatives in Congress pushed to zero out funding for public broadcasting because of its liberal worldview and reporting that seemed sympathetic to homosexuality, abortion, and other culture-war hot buttons. But public radio rallied its listeners to support their favorite stations, and Congress, impressed by the backlash, backed off. Still, stations felt ever more pressure to raise money from listeners and businesses rather than rely on federal grants. Government's share of public radio funding dropped from a third to barely more than 10 percent.

To win more listener donations, public radio adopted marketing and research methods used by commercial stations. At Minnesota Public Radio, executives parlayed the success of Keillor's *Prairie Home Companion* into a marketing bonanza, building up and then selling off—for more than $100 million—a mail-order catalogue business that hawked tapes, mugs, and all manner of doodads and knickknacks designed to appeal to the public radio lifestyle.

But public radio's new commercialism and its growing popularity—
the audience grew steadily, from 2 million listeners a week in the early
1980s to 25 million two decades later—helped create something of an
identity crisis. "Public radio was born in the anarchism of the 1970s,"
said Robert Siegel, the veteran host of *All Things Considered.* "It was
created to say, 'I have no idea how to cure the world, but I know we
have to hear from more voices.' That lives on, but something has
changed: the people who come to us now have grown up listening to
us. Those of us who came to public radio in the seventies came looking
for an alternative. We came precisely because this was not CBS News.
But now people come to us not because we are an alternative, but precisely because we're the equivalent of the CBS News that their parents
listened to."

Siegel came to NPR as a refugee from commercial radio, where
he'd started out at WGLI on Long Island as "Bob Charles." The program director asked him to adopt that name because while the station
owner "was of the Mosaic persuasion himself, we didn't want to offend
any of our listeners." Siegel handled the morning *Swap Shop* and a
call-in show, wrote and read the news, even played some records. But
the basic corruption of small-time radio—the host was required to invite guests on his talk show who just happened to be station sponsors—nagged at Siegel. "There would be a wig expert on the show,
who happened to own the Wig Wam in Wyandanch," he said. "Or
suddenly you'd heard an ad for a builder and you'd wonder who got a
new house."

Siegel soon fled to journalism school at Columbia, where he fell in
love with using the new cassette technology to capture the sound of
events and put them on the radio in a kind of storytelling that was immediate and intimate. He first tried out his ideas in 1971 at WRVR,
an FM radio station owned by New York's Riverside Church. There,
Siegel recalled, reporters got to produce long stories with "a fondness
for the underdog in a liberal-radical sort of way."

But in 1976, with WRVR failing as a commercial venture, the
church sold the station and Siegel found work at National Public
Radio as a newscaster. The distinctive personality NPR had developed

by the time Siegel joined was as much a matter of tone as of content. What felt different was the on-air informality, the serious yet conversational manner in which anchors and reporters told stories. Fans loved the daringly gentle pace, while critics derided the tone as precious and fey—"the sound of an undescended testicle," as Larry Josephson, the former Pacifica morning man, put it.

Bill Siemering thought that informal tone would attract listeners who had grown skeptical of the officious, phony authority of traditional radio news. To lift the barrier between announcer and listener, Siemering pushed reporters to attempt a more personal and revealing journalism, such as one of Siegel's first stories, in which he went shopping with a welfare recipient to demonstrate how the poor lived.

Such intimacy drew a loyal and large audience. At public appearances, Siegel and other program hosts were mobbed by people who would talk about how they had sat in their cars in their driveways, unable to open the door until a compelling story had finished. That audience wanted more of the same, leading public radio managers to make the news shows more reliable and less experimental, and to create new programs. First, *Morning Edition* joined the afternoon *All Things Considered.* Then, more news and talk shows were offered, nearly around the clock. Their success threatened to crowd out almost everything else that had made public radio an alternative.

THE INTERNAL DEBATE over public radio's heart and soul was personified in one man—David Giovannoni, a consultant who, depending on your worldview, was either public radio's savior or architect of its sellout.

Giovannoni, to the surprise of critics who saw him as an evil emissary from the world of commercial values, is a lifelong radio nut, a collector of old radios and recordings who grew up in California listening to the way-out programming on Pacifica. In 1979, he started NPR's research department and a few years later went out on his own, creating surveys and computer analyses of public radio's audience and programming. He started with a simple statement that would ruffle no feathers in the commercial world but seemed radical to many in public radio: "By definition, a program with no audience is not a public service. For years, we labored under the well-intentioned but misguided conception that we could for one or three hours a week serve a completely different audience—a jazz show followed by a chamber music show followed by a Spanish-language show. You can't do that."[8]

Giovannoni's research led station managers to jettison old schedules of shows appealing to lots of different audiences. Instead, public radio focused on NPR America, people who lock their radios on *Car Talk,* Keillor, *Morning Edition,* and *All Things Considered.* The idea is to measure new programs by their ability to appeal to those who give money to existing shows.

"The cost of risk is becoming more expensive," Giovannoni said. "I feel a loss when jazz disappears from a market, or when classical disappears. Public radio people see what ratings have done to commercial radio. But how do you survive in a political environment that's telling us we've got to become more self-sufficient?" The Republicans who took on public radio—Richard Nixon, Ronald Reagan, Newt Gingrich—"were really our best friends because they crystallized what we have to do—go out on our own and reach our audience with programming they value."

Giovannoni's prescriptions made so much sense to many managers that they pulled opera, jazz, and bluegrass programs off the air, replacing them with news and talk shows that the numbers said would generate more revenue.[9] Giovannoni sold the idea that "our network programming serves our local listeners better than our local programming does. . . . Listeners find a sense of community that resonates with their values, beliefs and attitudes. . . . When we define 'local' by the place our programming originates, we're pretty much missing the point."[10] Like the Internet, public radio would replace geography with cultural affinity as the defining aspect of community.

Many public radio pioneers saw Giovannoni and his statistics as a destructive force. Larry Josephson, who went on from his Pacifica morning show to produce programs for public radio, became a regular critic of Giovannoni's efforts to homogenize programming. "At Pacifica, we didn't give a fat fuck about ratings, about who listened,"

Josephson said. "We didn't care if three people listened. We would have a show on Holocaust victims followed by a program on the mechanics of gay sex. There was no flow, zero. We did things because we thought they ought to be done. WBAI was a 50,000-watt toy kit. And that's the history of art—doing what you need to do for yourselves. That's what every radio great has ever done. You don't sit down in a focus group and see what people want to hear. NPR has focus-grouped theme songs for their shows."

By accepting Giovannoni's emphasis on numbers over ideas, Josephson argued, public radio lost sight of its purpose. That in turn eased the way for managers to pay themselves vastly higher salaries (top managers at large stations can make between $200,000 and $400,000 a year), solicit corporate underwriting that makes hard-edged reporting on business less likely, and support programming that comforts listeners rather than challenging them. "Giovannoni singlehandedly destroyed the soul of public radio," Josephson said. "If you do what he wants, you will get grants and corporate underwriting. The result of all his focus groups is that there is now in public radio no place where someone like me could go on and talk about my marriages and my divorce and the death of my child. When 'Lady Madonna' came out, I played it over and over for two hours because it moved me spiritually. No one would dare do that now, but listeners loved it because it came from deep inside me."

As a child in Los Angeles, Josephson became fascinated by *The Rosary Hour*, a Catholic Church–sponsored program on KHJ on which the rosary was recited over and over. A secular Jewish child, Josephson nonetheless was hypnotized by the rhythm and beauty of the ritual. Six decades later, sitting in a café on Manhattan's Upper West Side, a lumpy, seventy-two-year-old Jewish man repeated to me the rosary as it was embedded in his mind all those years before. That was radio's power, now diminished by the pseudo-scientific selection of programming to fit what listeners think they want to hear.

"We are a nation of lonely people," Josephson said. "And radio is your friend. The magic, the mystery is that the connection happens without any physical presence. But it happens only if it's an honest friend."

Josephson and Giovannoni both saw public radio listeners as a distinct subculture. Josephson defined them as people who believe that "books, trees, music, kids are good. Guns, war, racism are bad." Public radio fans consider "the public good to be at least as important as the accumulation of property, money and audience. . . . Listeners give us money because they believe that we are honest and open and we are essentially uncapitalist—not *anti*capitalist, but *un*capitalist."[11] Josephson believed that such listeners must be offended by programming that has been scientifically packaged for their demographic cohort. Public radio, Josephson said, is supposed to be an oasis from the market-tested, focus-grouped, safety-first culture. Giovannoni agreed that no one likes to be thought of merely as a member of a demographic, but he defended his research tools as an accurate reflection of listeners' lives. Far from feeling abused by programming designed especially for them, he said, public radio listeners cling to such programs, which give them a sense of belonging.

IN SANTA MONICA, California, in a damp basement on the campus of Santa Monica College, Ruth Seymour runs one of the nation's most popular and successful public stations—while rejecting Giovannoni's teachings. Seymour, another Pacifica alumna, has created a station unlike any other: KCRW airs NPR's main news programs but fills the rest of its day with local news and cultural shows and its own brand of music—an aggressively eclectic mix of electronic, techno, dance, world, reggae, classical, jazz, and pop that sounds like Southern California and attracts a worldwide audience on the Internet.

Seymour clings to old notions: "Radio's greatest assets are that it is cheap, immediate, and local. The lure of taking [most programming from the network] in Washington has just captivated poor little public radio stations that see some sort of glory in sounding the same as every other station. Giovannoni offered public broadcasters, who tend to be insecure, so-called scientific analysis. But all he could ensure is what is already happening. He couldn't ensure what hasn't been imagined yet."

Seymour came to radio as a shy New Yorker, a literary type who could barely bring herself to speak on the air. When she moved to California in the early 1960s, friends led her to the Pacifica station, where she heard programs by film critic Pauline Kael, black civil rights leader Malcolm X, and conservative semanticist S. I. Hayakawa. Seymour started out at KPFK producing documentaries about French black poets and Ernest Hemingway, James Joyce, and Man Ray. Interviews went on for ninety minutes, programs were open-ended. "It was marvelously anarchic," Seymour said. In 1971, she became the station's program director and led KPFK through the anti-war years, sending a reporter to Vietnam and producing programming with a proudly radical bent.

Since Seymour moved to KCRW in 1977, she has pushed to include a wider variety of political views than are usually heard on public radio. Officially, most executives deny any liberal or left perspective in the reporting or story choices made on NPR programs. But Seymour accepts the conservative critique: "It's a real problem. At NPR, the liberal center has prevailed to the detriment of public radio. We are too one-sided, and too often, that's what our audience expects. When I first had [then conservative commentator] Arianna Huffington on KCRW, we got many calls from listeners saying 'I don't listen to hear those positions.' "

Seymour is determined not to let easy audience expectations determine what gets on her airwaves. Giovannoni has pushed her to eliminate the "seams" in the station—the places when one kind of program bumps up against another kind that appeals to a different audience. "But I told him, we only have seams, and people like seams," she recalls.

An elegant woman with Faye Dunaway cheekbones, calm green eyes, and a soft Bronx accent, Seymour tools around L.A. in a 1989 Honda Accord, runs her station from a crowded cellar, and snarls at the huge salaries public radio managers grant themselves. She earns $80,000, one-quarter what some of her counterparts make. Seymour still gives deejays total freedom to pick their music, even if she can be ruthless about axing programs she thinks are failing. She refuses to outsource fund-raising efforts to consultants; KCRW still relies on volunteers, more than a thousand of whom help out with each fund drive. "Radio is in danger of losing its sense of the street, losing a generation of young people," Seymour says. "This corporatization cannot last because it doesn't excite. It deadens the mind and spirit."

THE AVERAGE AGE of listeners to *This American Life,* public radio's hip hour of memoirs, essays, and reporting on the daily dreams and dilemmas of ordinary people, is forty-seven. By public radio standards, this is young. The newsmagazines' audience is just a touch older. The average listener to *Prairie Home Companion* is fifty-two. But all nine of the public radio shows that draw the oldest audiences are classical music shows, with average listener ages ranging from fifty-six to sixty-two.[12]

These facts create something of a panic in public radio. From the 1990s onward, stations' response, guided by David Giovannoni's statistics, has been to dumb down their classical programs, play shorter and less challenging bits of music, and, in an increasing number of cities, scrap classical altogether.[13]

Wyoming Public Radio killed its morning classical programming after a workshop with Giovannoni persuaded managers that splitting stations' time among classical music, news, and other music would not provide the "consistency of appeal" that listeners required.[14] In 1999, Washington, D.C.'s WETA scrapped its morning drive-time classical show to air *Morning Edition* at exactly the same time as its rival public station, WAMU, aired the same program (both stations happily put the goal of maximizing donations ahead of any concern that listeners might resent such a simulcast on their two public stations). Then, in 2005, WETA killed off classical entirely, leaving Washington with no music on public radio and two public stations pumping out all too familiar news and talk programming. NPR dropped much of its jazz programming and cut back on its classical shows because music has not been as successful as news and talk in generating audience and donations: "We are not the Arts Doctors, offering the medicine that will heal society," said Jay Kernis, the network's programming chief.[15]

Such cutbacks followed the trend among the three dozen or so remaining commercial classical stations. As corporate consolidation swept through the industry in the 1990s, classical stations died in Miami, Philadelphia, Detroit, and other cities. Yet classical listeners are among the most affluent and high-spending of all audiences, buying more airline tickets, books, luxury cars, and stocks than any other format's listeners.[16]

What gives? Philadelphia's WFLN turned a $5 million profit every year playing the classics. But when a station can be sold for $42 million, $5 million is just not enough. At public stations, when *All Things Considered* attracts a higher rate of donations from listeners than does the local classical show, it's only a matter of time before the classics are either silenced or sliced into bite-sized bits. At stations that do stick with the classics, research prompted many managers to ban all choral music and opera and most twentieth-century compositions, long pieces, and chamber works. Beyond that, music testing severely limits the pieces many public stations play.

The modal music testing developed by Giovannoni and his partner George Bailey brings one hundred or two hundred NPR news listeners into a room to listen to snippets of music—in pop parlance, the hook of a song—and judge each piece by turning a dial connected to a computer. The results let programmers know what kinds of classical music are likely to send news listeners scurrying off to another station, and what styles keep them tuned in. The tests lead to a playlist filled with pieces that have clear, singable melodies.[17] The third movement of Beethoven's Sixth Symphony (the *Pastoral*) scores a solid 96 percent satisfaction rating among one station's core news listeners; Mozart's "Eine Kleine Nachtmusik" does nearly as well, at 91 percent. But those same listeners nix Stravinsky and Strauss, with 18 percent approval ratings.

Armed with such numbers, consultants peddle the idea that classical is just too harsh a medicine to be consumed in its raw form. "When an NPR news listener says classical music, he or she means something that sounds like a Mozart symphony—a brighter, less lush sound," said Craig Curtis, a longtime public radio executive and classical program host in Los Angeles, Minneapolis, and Washington. "We know this from focus groups, auditorium testing, and hook testing. And we know that every time you venture away from listeners' expectations, you blow away part of your audience."

At commercial stations, the impact of research on music selection can be even more dramatic. When Miami's classical WTMI was sold for $100 million in 2000 (a hundred-fold increase in price over its previous sale twenty years earlier), the new owner flipped the station to electronic dance music and dubbed it Party 93.1. A Miami AM station jumped into the breach and switched to the classics—with a difference. The new entry, WKAT, restricted its playlist to lively overtures, light pops, and bright, quick movements plucked out of larger works. Sousa marches, Yanni's whining, and Neil Diamond with strings filled out the menu. "Mozart is boring," announced the host of the morning *Bach and Roll* show. Classical lite landed with a thud in the ratings, and within a year, the station retooled, adding some longer pieces and deleting the pops. The audience responded with a considerable boost in ratings.[18] Time and again, heavily researched stations make no big splash in the ratings, yet management's belief in the statistics remains firm.

"There's a constant desire on the part of the consultants to steer you away from this music, to eliminate the personality and just make everything soothing and easy—it's insulting, dismal, comical," said Dennis Owens, who spent more than three decades as the witty host of the morning show on WGMS, the commercial classical station in Washington. "They do their mall testing—four or five bars of Haydn and people say, 'Yeah, I like that,' and five bars of Gershwin and people say, 'That's too busy,' and all of a sudden, Haydn is in and Gershwin is out."

In public radio, that mentality is pervasive. As a program director, Erik Nycklemoe, then at Northern Arizona Public Radio, based his decisions almost wholly on audience research. "I believe in David Giovannoni's approach," he said at a convention of public radio programmers. "I have no training in classical music. With his work, I know when and where my listeners listen and why they tune out. Our approach is light, bright, and airy. Music proven to drive people away should not be played. It's a no-brainer. You can't be hurt by what you don't put on the air."

Classical music accounts for 3 percent of music purchases in this country. It will never challenge rock or rap for popularity. But that was supposed to be the purpose of public radio—serving narrow interests that the unfettered marketplace might not support. And just as testing and research push out all but the most inoffensive and easily accessible shows on commercial radio and TV, the same techniques in public radio ensure bland and banal programming.

For three decades, Robert J. Lurtsema was the gravel-voiced maestro of the morning on public stations around New England and New York. Lurtsema was an uncompromising lover of the classics, an evangelist for the music he picked, a teacher. Shortly before he died, he told me that his life's work may have been for naught. "Once public radio loses its uniqueness, what the hell are we doing here? We cannot follow the numbers and surveys because then we are mere followers. And if we accept that, we abdicate the role of leadership. Then we're the same as the Top 40 crowd. Then we're finished."

IT NEVER DAWNED on Bill Siemering that his idea for a street-level newsmagazine staffed by storytellers rather than headline readers would evolve a generation later into a highly professional twenty-four-hour news-talk format that crowded out the kind of programming he had pioneered in Buffalo—locally focused and aimed at minority interests. Siemering didn't stay long in Washington. He moved on to Minneapolis, where he commissioned an artist to produce *The News Program,* on which listeners called in from pay phones to report on whatever they saw happening in front of them—preparations for a wedding, travelers passing through an airport. At his next stop, in Philadelphia, Siemering experimented with dance on the radio (a choreographer describing how to create dance in your living room) and supported another former University of Buffalo radio voice, Terry Gross, in her quietly innovative interview show, *Fresh Air.*

But although Siemering kept trying to push the envelope, he saw much of public radio settle into its ways, retreating from its local mission and cutting programming aimed at small but dedicated audiences. "It is paradoxical that when we had a small audience, we didn't have much to lose, so we could be more playful and spirited," he said. "Public radio began to turn to focus groups for feedback, and a focus group is a rearview mirror. It leads you to value what was. It weeds our creativity, and your niche gets smaller and smaller."

While NPR became a player in the national news, a respected voice often mentioned in the same breath as *The New York Times* or *The Washington Post*, Siemering worried that his baby was no longer taking risks or challenging listeners. Increasingly, the father of public radio listened from afar: Siemering won a MacArthur genius grant and took his message about radio to Mozambique, Swaziland, and Mongolia, where he helped small communities create local radio stations that operated on just $8,000 a year, teaching listeners how to start small businesses and care for sick children, giving voice to local musicians, and providing on-air lessons to people who had no school. He was still scattering seeds, while, he fretted, NPR's soil was hardening over.

Chapter 11

✳ FULL OF SOUND AND FURY

The radio business is a cruel and shallow money
trench, a long plastic hallway where thieves and
pimps run free, and good men die like dogs.
There's also a negative side.

—Hunter S. Thompson

A WEEKDAY EVENING IN SUBURBIA, a Holiday Inn at happy hour. In the lobby, flight crews check in for the night while five people cluster around the TV set, watching the president of the United States address the nation. In meeting rooms just off the atrium, the J. Walter Thompson agency puts on a marketing presentation for managers from Domino's Pizza, and northern Virginia Realtors get pumped up at a sales pep rally. At the end of the corridor, behind a sign that says "Music Survey," fifty-four people take seats in rows of tables stocked with hard candies, Cokes, brownies, and palm-sized, black electronic gadgets labeled "Perception Analyzer."

There is no deejay in the room, no radio station's music director is here, but tonight, these fifty-four people—recruited by telemarketers and selected because they collectively mirror this station's audience by sex (twenty-nine women and twenty-five men), age (ranging from thirty-eight to fifty-two), race (every one of them is white), and musical preference (40 percent like oldies best)—will choose the playlist for the Washington, D.C., area's oldies station, WBIG. Each person in the room will be paid $65 for two and a half hours of time. They will spend those hours listening to seven-second snippets from seven hundred of the most familiar pop songs from their teenage and young adult lives. They aren't told which station has paid for this research, but most of them figure it out soon enough. They will hear the Beatles and Carly Simon, the Supremes and Fleetwood Mac, the girl groups and the British imports, Elvis and ABBA, more Beatles and more Motown, clip after clip after clip until they think they've heard every song ever recorded. They will be amazed that they recognize almost every one of those songs from just a few seconds' worth of music. They will spin the red-capped dials on their Perception Analyzers from zero to 100, thereby telling the station which songs they want to hear on the radio and which would drive them to punch up another station.

If they follow the thick clot of wires that extends out of the computer at the front of the meeting room, they might notice that the cables disappear under the divider into the next room, the one with the closed door, the one where executives from WBIG sit eating club sandwiches and staring at a giant screen that tracks every twist of those dials, collecting all fifty-four opinions on each song in the form of five lines inching their way up and down the screen like an EKG readout, each line tracking a different subgroup of the listeners next door, the whole graph mapping the taste of the American radio listener, captured in precise metrics.

WBIG, like many oldies stations, hires a company to conduct these tests twice each year. Another group of fifty-five or so people will come in the next night, at another hotel in another suburb, and the combined results will determine the station's song list. Stations that play current top hits do this more often. But just about every music station in any big city in the country uses auditorium or mall testing—as well as more frequent phone calls to listeners at home—to pick its playlist. Some of the results are obvious before the technician switches on the first clip (the industry calls them "hooks," and an enormous side business replete with psychometrics and statistical analysis goes into choosing which seven seconds of a song will be presented to the survey group). No matter who's here tonight, they will like Roy Orbison's "Pretty Woman" and Aretha Franklin's "Respect" and the Beatles' "Help!" If you compared the playlists of all the oldies stations in the land, pretty much the same core of about a hundred songs would be on every list. But beyond those obvious choices, there are decisions to be made about the next hundred tunes, and the people who run the stations do not trust themselves to make those decisions. They want to deliver precisely the songs their desired audience most wants, and they believe this technology makes that possible.

"These 110 people are effectively determining the musical tastes of Washington, D.C.," says Steve Allan, then the station's program director. "A very small group of people are deciding whether you hear 'We Gotta Get Out of This Place' by the Animals or Elvis's 'Hound Dog.'"[1] Except that that is an unfair choice, because the executives know that Elvis—like any music from his era—doesn't have a prayer. "If it's before 1964, it's got to test well with everybody in the room," Allan says. He is a child of the 1950s, putting him at the older end of the station's target audience, but even at his age, "Elvis and that stuff means nothing to me." Fact is, oldies are in crisis: the format was born in the 1970s as a way of reaching people in their twenties and thirties who remained loyal to the pop songs of their formative years—Elvis, doo-wop songs, the Beach Boys, the Beatles, and Motown. But as the decades passed, and the 1950s material dropped out of the oldies portfolio, the format got stuck.

The wisdom in the industry was that everyone loved the Top 40 tunes of the 1960s, the songs that bring us back to an era when virtually everyone listened to the same powerhouse pop stations. But starting in about 1995, the numbers began to show that that wasn't true anymore. People in their thirties didn't necessarily want to hear "Surfin' Safari" or "Sloop John B." That left oldies stations staring at what the past three decades of radio had wrought. Modernizing the oldies format wasn't a simple matter of deleting the early 1960s tunes and adding the hits of the next decade. By the time the mid-1970s rolled around, Top 40 was dying and young Americans headed off in all different directions, to underground FM rock, to hard rock, to soft folkie rock, to disco, and on and on. Now, when oldies stations tried to bring those listeners back together again, there were precious few unifying tunes.

The one abiding belief that nearly every radio manager holds dear is that when Americans whine about radio—complaining that they hear the same songs over and over ad nauseam—what they're really saying is that this station is playing someone else's favorite song, not theirs. To a man (and they are nearly all men), radio executives will tell you—and they will haul out reams of numbers to prove it—that listeners cannot get enough of their favorite songs and cannot stand even one spin of the songs they loathe.

So the science of choosing music has come down to this—five colored lines rising and falling on a computer monitor. "Just watch," Allan tells me as the test begins. "You'll see the shit that rises to the top is the same as ever." The test starts out with a few control questions, just to make sure that the right people are in the room. A few seconds of rap and the lines plummet to the bottom of the screen. Then Rod Stewart's "Young Turks" ("Young hearts, be free tonight") and the lines shoot back up again. A snippet of hard rock floors the lines again, and they soar on the Beatles' "Love Me Do." Okay, we're in the right place.

The songs just keep on coming: ABBA (way down), the Bee Gees' "How Deep Is Your Love" (decent score, but a big age split), Harry Chapin's "Taxi" (dives in all age groups), America's "Horse with No Name" (a winner across the board), the Fifth Dimension's "Stoned Soul Picnic." ("That song never tests," Allan mopes. "Too bad—I love it." So does he play it? I ask. "It doesn't test," he repeats. End of story.)

The easy part of the evening comes each time a Beatles tune streams through the speakers—"Strawberry Fields," "Back in the USSR," almost any Beatles number does the trick, which is why WBIG, like most oldies stations, plays two or three of the Fab Four's hits each hour. But move forward in time and the picking gets dicier. "The times and the music became more fragmented," Allan says, "so the commonality isn't there. There are some songs that work, but then you hit disco in '78 and that changed everything." Songs that even smack of disco are far too divisive to reach the consensus Allan seeks between forty- and fifty-year-olds. For example, white women want their oldies station to play the melodic disco anthems—"I Will Survive," "Last Dance"—but black women hate them, preferring the 1970s soft soul groups, the Spinners, the Stylistics, and the like.

Buried somewhere in that decade of song lie the hits that will offend few enough listeners to make them acceptable. The challenge is to find the songs that might bring in younger folks without chasing away older, core listeners. (The perfect 1970s song, at least according to this night's test, is Fleetwood Mac's "Don't Stop Thinking About Tomorrow," which sends the EKG lines straight up like nothing but a Beatles tune. Whatever Bill Clinton's real musical taste may be, his advisors certainly knew their music testing when they chose that tune as his 1992 campaign anthem.)

Allan's task is to push the average age of WBIG listeners down from forty-eight without losing overall audience. "We had to move to more seventies music because, sadly, in America, if your average age is over fifty, your money's no good here anymore," he says. "Oldies is kind of dying, not because people don't want to hear the music, but because once you hit forty-five, American business doesn't believe you're going to spend any money." WBIG is set at 45 percent seventies music, and this test isn't showing much tolerance for more than that. (Anything by the Carpenters: numbers fall off a cliff. Linda Ronstadt: every song tanks.)

To make matters even more difficult, something new is happening on this night, something that surprises even the experts. Every time the computer serves up a Motown song—*every* time, whether it's the Supremes, the other girl groups, Marvin Gaye, the Chi-Lites—the lines on the screen dive. "Maybe we ought to rethink Motown Mondays," a longtime staple at the station, says Bob Carson, WBIG's creative director. "They're really shooting down every one of those songs."

But as the managers watch their playlist evolve before their eyes, Carson hesitates: "Testing brings everything to a middle point—whatever's least offensive—and I wonder if we sometimes miss the highs. Those musicians couldn't have imagined forty years ago that someday researchers would be sitting in a hotel room rating seven seconds of their song. I got really angry because they stopped making my favorite conditioner because of someone's squiggly lines on a screen. I called L'Oréal and they said, 'Thank you for your input.' "

One set of fifty song clips ends, a quick break, and the survey group is seated for another set, sixteen sets in all. The Fifth Dimension's "Up, Up and Away" is down, down, and out. "Stand Tall" by Burton Cummings falls flat. Tony Orlando's "Knock Three Times" is met with silence.

Finally, the ordeal is over and the subjects are free to leave. But a dozen accept the invitation to stay on and become a focus group, discussing their evening's work. Those who linger plead for songs they can sing along with, songs that will "mellow me out," and, repeatedly, "my favorite songs." And then the same people complain that the stations they listen to play "the same songs over and over," that there are way too many commercials, and that they are sick to death of Motown.

"You hear 'My Girl' till it's running out of your ear," one man offers.

"Yeah, always the same Motown songs," says a prim businesswoman.

A hefty woman admonishes the researchers to "stop putting us in niches and do something different. Introduce something new. A lot of us bought these records way back when and we know there's a lot more out there than they play on the radio. We know what's on the flip side of those records."

Finally, Steve Allan ventures to the front and announces what nearly everyone has figured out, that the station conducting this survey is BIG 100. "You're the tastemakers," he says. "We want to play as many favorite songs as we can, as often as we can."

Instantly, they light into him. Why won't you play any Led Zeppelin? Why won't you play a greater variety of songs by the artists you do play? Give us something different.

"Could I really do what you're saying?" Allan asks. "All that music on one station, really?"

"Yes" come the shouted replies. "You could! Do it! Why not?"

"But would you *expect* me to play Zeppelin?" Allan responds. "Would you come to my station for that?"

Slowly, the enthusiasm leaks out of the focus group. "Guess not," one gent says. The others see Allan's point and realize they have just guaranteed themselves more of the same on their favorite station.

Except for one thing: "So Motown Monday's got to go, huh?" Allan asks.

Absolutely, the group confirms.

"Okay," the boss says, "we've been doing it a long time."[2]

TAKE THE RESULTS of evenings like that one in Virginia, add "perceptual studies," in which extremely narrow demographic groups are questioned in detail about their attitudes toward radio and music, and pretty soon, you have a pile of numbers telling oldies station managers not only which decade to emphasize but exactly which year—indeed, which tenth of which year. In the first three years of the twenty-first century, the average era of songs played on the nation's fifty largest oldies stations "evolved from 1965.7 to 1966.7," according to Coleman Research, a radio consulting firm in Research Triangle Park, North Carolina.[3] Coleman concludes that as oldies stations play more music from the seventies, they lose audience. Worse, they lose both older and younger listeners: older folks don't know or don't like the newer music, and younger folks, lacking the broad musical base that older boomers shared, mainly like the music they learned in a fragmented pop culture.

Coleman advises stations to play a mix of music with "between 17 percent and 18 percent seventies content," keeping the portion of rock songs below 11 percent. Program directors sit at computer terminals crunching numbers like these to determine which songs will fulfill the consultants' formulas. With a few mouse clicks, managers can document what time their listeners wake up in the morning (most popular response: 6:30), whether they start the day with radio or TV (about even), and whether they want their morning music interrupted by a newscast (yes, four minutes, please).

Software programs such as Selector automatically determine the order in which songs will be played—plotting programming weeks in advance—to maximize the chance that listeners will stay tuned. (When deejays take listener calls for requests, it is only so they can record the call and play it back when the computer decides it's time to pop in that particular song.) Selector does virtually everything deejays and station managers once did, from setting up the music to plugging in commercials and jingles. Other programs analyze audiences by zip code, income, and ethnicity, allowing stations to fine-tune formats into ever-narrower slices. Stations calling themselves "hot adult contemporary," "mainstream adult contemporary," Top 40, and country might all play the same song by the Dixie Chicks, but they are designed to reach audiences that differ just enough to attract separate advertisers for a media company that, in many cities, owns all four of those stations.

It's hard to find a radio executive who does not concede—privately, with the notebook closed—that radio has become boring and predictable, that stations sound the same no matter where you are, and that the consistent decline in the amount of time Americans spend listening to radio is disturbing. Steve Allan likes oldies just fine, but the songs he calls me into his office to hear are new tunes he's just heard about from a friend. "We've perfected our science, but we've lost an entire generation of listeners," he says. "The only thing we have left in broadcast radio is convenience. We're there in the car. Young people don't get their music from radio anymore. They download it."

Americans still listen to an average of 3.2 hours of radio a day, and more than three-quarters of the population listen every day. But the choices on the dial are indeed narrower, even as the number of stations has increased. About half of all stations offer one of three formats— talk, adult contemporary, and country. Add oldies and religion, and you've covered 71 percent of all stations. Yet electronic dance, classical, jazz, blues, movie and Broadway soundtracks, gospel, New Age, and children's recordings make up a third of CD sales, and the first years of the downloading revolution revealed a similar passion for a far greater variety of music than radio provides.[4]

Industry executives point to the increase in the number of music formats available in most big cities since 1996, but that's misleading because formats are being defined ever more narrowly. The number of different songs being played across those formats has diminished considerably. This is known as "format redundancy." While one market might have a "rhythmic hits" station and an "urban" station, fully three-quarters of the music played on those stations is identical. And while one city's dial might boast an "active rock" station and an "alternative" station, 58 percent of the music they play is the same.[5] Redundancy is so common that in more than five hundred cases across the country, the same company owns two stations in the same market with virtually identical formats.

Radio's reliance on research has created a logical dead end: the research says people don't really want the variety and surprise they claim to crave, so stations serve up the same old stuff. Advertisers want to reach a defined demographic group, so stations have no qualms about alienating people who fall outside their target audience. Todd Storz defined success as grabbing 30, 40, 50 percent of the audience. Cousin Brucie was thrilled with 12 or 15 percent shares. Today, a station can hit its profit goals with a 4 percent share.

IF RESEARCH MADE THIS KIND of groupthink possible, consolidation—the intense station buying and selling spree of the 1990s—made it obligatory. In 1990, no single company owned more than fourteen stations in the United States. A decade later, four companies controlled half of radio's revenue and audience. Over that period, the number of station owners dropped by more than a third. The motor behind this extraordinary transformation was the 1996 Telecommunications Act, which freed an owner to control as many as eight stations in any big-city market and a virtually unlimited number of stations across the country.

The new law, the culminating act of two decades of deregulation, was a Clinton administration initiative that grew out of the Reagan White House's desire to get government out of the way of broadcasters. In the 1980s, radio broadcasters suffered through a period of diminished profit margins as MTV and other cable TV channels sliced media usage into ever-finer cuts. Radio companies lobbied the FCC for change and got their way: regulators shelved public service and news requirements, tossed out the fairness doctrine, eased limits on the number of stations one company could own, and suspended rules that prevented owners from flipping stations for quick profits. Liberated to buy more stations, radio companies blossomed into media giants. Prices and profits ballooned too.

Brothers Tom and Steve Hicks owned a Dallas investment company that had already helped remake the modern face of radio by inventing the Local Marketing Agreement, a tool that let an owner sign over control of his station to another owner who already had a station in the same town. The Hicks companies would sign up several stations in a given market, allowing the brothers to offer advertisers a menu of different demographic groups reachable with one buy. The result was an end run around ownership restrictions, creating facts on the ground that led inexorably to the 1996 Telecom Act.

The new law set off the biggest shopping spree in broadcasting history. By the end of 1996, 2,157 stations changed hands. More than a thousand stations were sold in each of the next four years. Clear Channel Communications grew in enormous leaps as it acquired other companies—AMFM, Jacor, Evergreen, Tom Hicks's Chancellor, Steve Hicks's Capstar—each of which had already snapped up dozens, if not hundreds, of stations. When it was all over, Clear Channel—born in 1972 when Lowry Mays, a San Antonio investment banker, bought a single station—owned more than 1,200 stations in 190 markets. Starbucks, by comparison, is present in 150 markets. From 1991 to 2004, Clear Channel's sales mushroomed from $74 million to more than $9 billion. At the end of the sales rush, Clear Channel, Cumulus, Viacom, and Citadel together controlled 70 percent or more of almost every U.S. radio market.

The attractions of consolidation were obvious: by owning eight stations in a single market, a company could shut down seven facilities; create a unified sales, technical, and support staff; cut labor costs dramatically; and gain extraordinary control over advertising prices and policies. As these newly dominant companies extended their reach, they could cut costs even further, pumping the same programming up to the satellite and down to stations in small markets in every state. A deejay in Denver could do his own show there, another show in Dallas, and perhaps a third for distribution to dozens of small stations that previously lacked big-city talent.

The need to cut costs grew organically out of the buying frenzy. As prices soared and acquiring companies took on mountains of debt, managers had to slash spending so the parent corporation could make its payments. The need to produce predictable profits translated into increasing pressure to generate reliable ratings.

The new climate was too much for Lee Abrams. The man who had lived and breathed radio research as a boy finally got out of the consulting business in the late 1990s. "We kept being told, 'Don't get creative on us,'" he says. "Consolidation brought a whole new level of caution. Owners would say, 'Hey, I spent $60 million on this station—I can't take chances.' And on top of that, the big radio companies bought the research companies, and then the game was up. You couldn't do anything different." Abrams craved a place where he could play radio as he had when he was young, a place where serendipity and joy had a chance against the hard realities of statistical analysis and market research.

ONE OF THE FIRST CASUALTIES of this consolidated reality was the news. When the FCC said stations could go news-free, many music stations quickly did just that. Stations knew listeners wanted some rudimentary headlines, traffic, and weather, so they outsourced the job. Metro Networks, a company that provides short news and traffic reports from one central studio, often serves dozens of stations in a single market (its announcers use different names on competing stations so listeners don't catch on to the fact that the news all comes from one source). In weather emergencies, stations that once provided a twenty-four-hour lifeline to citizens who had lost electricity or phone service now relied on an outside company equipped mainly to provide quick, chatty run-downs written off National Weather Service reports.

In small and midsized cities, radio reporters no longer attended city council or school board meetings. In the 1970s, when Sam Litzinger was a teenager with a weekend deejay show on WTIV in Titusville, Pennsylvania, all on-air staffers had to know how to put together a news story. In between *The Yodelin' Shorty Show* and the *Trading Post* swap shop, the station featured five minutes an hour of news, as well as expanded newscasts in the morning and early evening. Every little station in the rural area had a news director who sat in on school board meetings and checked daily police reports at headquarters. "If someone liked or didn't like a particular story," Litzinger says, "we heard about it, either by phone or from someone on the next stool at the Thompson's Drug Store lunch counter."

A quarter century later, those little stations have hardly any local content. They air nationally syndicated talk shows, with a national newscast from CNN or CBS. For many hours each day, such stations are unmanned, fully automated.

For decades, surveys tracking how people find out about major events showed that radio was most Americans' first source of information, whether about the great Northeast blackout of 1965 or the Kennedy assassination or the Three Mile Island nuclear accident. But by 2001, radio was caught unable to react to the 9/11 attacks; on that traumatic morning, many music stations either gave their airwaves over to a simulcast of TV news coverage, or turned to deejays who could do little more than take phone calls and relay what they saw on TV.

In 1999, Chester Reiten, a wealthy North Dakota radio man, sold his three stations in Minot to Clear Channel. That gave Clear Channel control over all six stations in town. In 2002, when a train passing through Minot derailed, releasing a toxic cloud of anhydrous ammonia fertilizer, local police tried to reach someone at the stations to get word out about the danger. There was no one at the studios of KCJB, the area's designated emergency broadcaster.[6] The station was on automatic, running satellite-fed programming from Clear Channel. Even if there had been someone on duty, it's not clear how the station would have responded: among Clear Channel's six stations in Minot, there was only one full-time news staffer.[7]

IN RADIO'S NEW REALITY, you needn't be there to be local. From his rambling farmhouse on ten acres of rolling hillside an hour north of Baltimore, Brian Wilson could roll out of bed and become the instant host of your local talk show anywhere in the United States. Starting in 1994, Wilson marketed himself to stations as an entertaining, provocative host who could, thanks to the miracle of high-quality phone lines and broadband Internet access, sound like he was in downtown Boston, Denver, or New York. On a given day, Wilson might substitute for a vacationing talk host in Kansas City, do his regular shift on a station in San Francisco or Baltimore, even handle an emergency gig for a station in Charlotte or Minneapolis, all from the comfort of home.

On an hour's notice, Wilson—his business was called Vacation Relief—could bone up on any local issue that callers were likely to want to talk about. All he had to do was click on the website of the local newspaper. "You only need to know the names of a few restaurants, a couple of little nuances about the mayor, the basic sports headlines," he explains. "It's a patina, a dusting, enough to show I'm hip, I'm happening, let's move on."

Some stations wanted Wilson to hide his actual location from listeners; others were perfectly happy to let him say he was coming from Washington, "the logic-free zone" (though actually, he lived ninety minutes outside of the capital). But in the era of consolidation, Wilson provided a vital service—just enough local content to distinguish a station's offerings from the generic national sound of Rush Limbaugh and family advice talker Laura Schlessinger, at little expense.

Wilson came to radio by accident, reading the news and hosting folk music shows on rural stations to raise money to go to law school. He grew up in New Jersey listening to Jean Shepherd's bedtime stories, Dan Ingram's Top 40 patter, and Bob and Ray's comedy sketches, and when he had the chance to become a Top 40 jock, he put law school on hold. He was an ambitious self-promoter from the start: in 1978 in Atlanta, he made 413 personal appearances, at high schools, private parties, record stores, movie premieres, parades, TV shows, and hospitals. He deejayed so many parties and dance contests that year that he made $150,000 above his salary of $40,000.

When Top 40 died, Wilson easily made the transition to talk. He combined his rumbling, gravelly voice with equal doses of acid sarcasm and libertarian righteousness; the showmanship came naturally. Wilson had been mixing music and talk in the final days of WABC in New York, finding that his comedy routines worked well in either format. In fact, he quickly realized, talk and Top 40 were remarkably similar. "It's my World Wrestling Federation theory of radio," he says. "Yeah, it's all phony, but what the hell. It's a lot easier to do all heat and no light than to solve the problems of the world."

Two decades later, from his home studio equipped with a mixer board, two computers, and a program that identifies callers by location, topic, and name, Wilson is still talking. He depicts himself as living proof of how consolidation changed radio—reducing local content to a quick glance at a website. But Wilson is no apologist for what radio has become. He still harbors the classic radio fantasy of buying a rural station to play whatever he wants to—and in 2003, after losing his daily gig on the San Francisco station, he and his wife, Cassie, bought a small station in rural Chestertown on Maryland's Eastern Shore. The couple handled the morning show themselves, picking their own music (even if the rest of the broadcast day consisted of satellite-delivered "soft oldies" packaged by ABC Radio). "A backlash is coming against this fifty-two-song playlist, voice-tracking, computerized bullshit radio," Wilson says. "Radio is nothing but disembodied nothingness anymore, and people will rebel against that." Alas, Wilson couldn't stick around for the revolution—in 2004, he took a daily gig as an oldies jock at a Baltimore station, only to have the station switch formats on him a few months later, leaving him without a steady gig. Wilson revived his rent-a-talker business. His dream of reconnecting a small community through radio would have to wait.

—

TOM KELLY PERFORMED the music radio equivalent of Wilson's Wizard of Oz act. Through a process known as voice tracking, Kelly, a popular oldies deejay at WBIG in Washington, could finish up his live after-noon air shift, then move into another studio and, in ninety minutes, digitally record his four-hour late-night shift as J. J. Jackson, the oldies jock on KQQL in Minneapolis. (Kelly was "J. J. Jackson" in Min-neapolis because the station already had jingles made with that name.) Kelly had only to speak his part; the computer plugged in the music, weather forecasts, and commercials. And no one was the wiser— except, of course, Clear Channel, which owns both stations. Clear Channel did give Minnesota listeners a wink and a nudge on the KQQL website: "Actually, J.J. is perhaps the most 'there' overnight presence in Twin Cities FM radio." And: "Those who might say or think that J. J. Jackson is a show biz name have obviously never em-braced the whole idea of the Witness Relocation Program!"[8]

For a few hours a week of studio time, deejays like Kelly make an extra $4,000 to $6,000 a year. Clear Channel saves a deejay's salary and benefits at one—or several—of its smaller stations. The decisions about what music to play are often made by a regional manager for Clear Channel, based on corporate research.[9] Clear Channel defends this practice as a way of bringing big-market quality to small-market stations. But voice tracking is not limited to small markets. In Tucson, the morning deejays on the top-rated music stations tried hard to sound like they were right in town, but they actually performed their shows in Phoenix, Denver, and Indianapolis. In some cases, apparently live morning shows were recorded the previous day. The out-of-town deejays were even flown into Tucson a few times a year to make ap-pearances before their fans.[10] Company president Mark Mays says such economies of scale "increase the quality of local programming. If listeners don't like what they hear, they will turn the dial."[11] The com-pany says 80 percent of its programming is locally produced.

"The listeners don't know and the listeners don't care," says inde-pendent station owner David Segal, whose stations use satellite-delivered programming. "For $25,000, the machine is there every day. It doesn't come late, it doesn't call you a son of a bitch. It just plays and plays and plays and nobody knows the better. You play morons for morons."

CLEAR CHANNEL COMMUNICATIONS censored the Dixie Chicks, removing the country-rock group from playlists because the singers dared to criticize the war in Iraq. Clear Channel used its talk stations to promote its political perspective, staging pro-war rallies around the country. When Britney Spears and other pop stars decided against hiring the company's concert promotion business, Clear Channel barred the artists' songs from its stations. When Clear Channel takes a dominant position in a market, it quickly sacks the news reporters, pares down the local deejays, and fills the airwaves with formulaic pap imported by satellite from distant cities. Clear Channel cements its control over radio and entertainment in those markets by buying up businesses that promote musical acts on the radio, book their shows in local clubs and arenas, and advertise those performances on outdoor signs.

If even a few of these terrible things that critics say about Clear Channel are true, then the company's practices have had a corrosive, depressing effect on the popular culture and the quality of radio—all for the purpose of jacking up profits. But it is also true that during the period Clear Channel is supposed to have become the evil empire of broadcasting, the company has had mixed returns. The company continued to struggle under $6 billion in debt it assumed to buy up all those businesses. Clear Channel's stock has been no winner either, drifting downward year after year.

Still, there is enough truth in each of the assertions against Clear Channel to have turned the company into the symbol of all that is wrong with radio—and with the broader pop culture. Clear Channel did sponsor pro-war rallies, but they were the brainchild of Glenn Beck, one of the company's widely syndicated talk hosts, and they were staged only in cities where his show airs. And Clear Channel did block a coalition of anti-war groups from buying commercial time on the company's Chicago stations, even after the stations' salespeople had approved the spots.[12] But when Air America, the liberal alternative to conservative talk radio, spread beyond its initial handful of cities in 2004 and 2005, Clear Channel stations led the way in adopting the programming. Some Clear Channel stations did make a big public show of pulling Dixie Chicks songs off the air after the singers criticized President Bush, but many more of the company's stations did no such thing. (It was another company, Cumulus Media, that actually ordered its forty-two country stations to take the Chicks off the air— "out of deference to our listeners," the company's top executive said.)[13]

Clear Channel's concert arm—the nation's largest concert promotion business—does play hardball, according to pop artists who say the conglomerate demands they appear at concerts promoting Clear Channel stations or face an implicit threat that their recordings will not air on those stations. (The company denies any such quid pro quo, and in 2006, federal investigators closed out their examination of the company, filing no charges. But Clear Channel said it planned to spin off its live entertainment business.) Concerts aside, Clear Channel still plays a powerful role in deciding what music gets heard.

In many cities, Clear Channel controls several stations, allowing the company to cluster its ad sales. That puts owners of independent stations at a considerable disadvantage: if an advertiser can choose between having his message air on eight stations, each reaching a distinct demographic group, or taking a chance on a single station that hits only a piece of his target audience, which path is he likely to take?

The company that controls half the stations in town is also the dominant force on the music side of the business. Clear Channel's deals with promoters have brought the murky underworld of the radio business back into the public eye as it has not been since the payola scandals of the 1950s and '60s. Under the reforms that replaced the payola system, deejays lost control over what music gets on the air. In the supposedly reformed system, Clear Channel and other station owners contract with record promoters who visit stations to push the songs that labels want to get on the radio. These promoters pay a big-city station from $100,000 to $250,000 a year for the exclusive right to pitch songs to station managers. That certainly sounds like payola, but it's legal because the labels don't directly pay stations to play songs. Rather, the station, in theory, is being paid for access to its research and playlist. The promoter then passes this information along to record companies, which are eager to know how their products are playing on the airwaves. The fact that record companies pay promoters an annual lump sum rather than a fee for each song they get on the air is supposed to insulate the system from payola pressures.

Promoters say they push songs to station managers on the merits of the music, not just the say-so of record producers. But of course promoters are paid by those record companies, and the promoters pass that money along to radio stations. Who's kidding whom? Promoters never stopped plying deejays with favors. In the decades following the payola scandal, some promoters provided drugs and women instead of cash and cars. Others stuck to legal forms of persuasion. "I never gave a disc jockey money in my life," says Frank Falise, a promoter who worked the mid-Atlantic states for Universal, MCA, Capitol, and other record companies. "But you took care of those jocks very well. You made sure they got plenty of records, backstage meets with the artists, photos with the artists, great tickets. If they can take their listeners backstage to see Elton John, that builds their audience and helps them make more money at their station. There's no payola the way it was forty years ago, but the business was always based on relationships."

Forty years after Congress congratulated itself for scrubbing payola out of radio, executives at Arista Records won radio airplay for a single by one of their artists by paying $250 a week for a team of workers to call up rock stations and flood the phone lines with requests for the song. "Please be sure all callers are male, preferably under 25 (or sounding like it!) and that the bulk of the calls are made between 6 P.M. and midnight," said an e-mail from an Arista employee in New York to the coordinator of the phone team. The e-mail is part of the evidence obtained by New York State attorney general Eliot Spitzer in 2005 in an investigation into the new payola. To avoid prosecution, Sony BMG, the music arm of the electronics giant, agreed to pay

$10 million and stop making payments and awarding expensive gifts to radio stations and their employees in return for spins of records Sony wanted on the air.

The e-mails and letters Spitzer's investigators found show that payola is alive and well. In a memo from 2002, one Sony executive lays out a plan to promote a song called "A.D.I.D.A.S." by rapper Killer Mike. Deejays whose stations let them select their shows' music were to be asked for their shoe size and sent one Adidas sneaker. If the deejay could then demonstrate that he had spun the song at least ten times, he'd get the other shoe, autographed by the artist. The investigation found record companies giving station program directors and deejays airline tickets, digital cameras, trips to concerts, even a laptop computer. The quid pro quo was spelled out without shame: thirteen stations owned by Infinity Broadcasting agreed to play Céline Dion's song "Goodbyes" on the record's launch date, according to a memo from a vice president at Epic Records. Those stations were to receive a trip to Las Vegas for a Dion concert. A few weeks later, when Epic officials learned that some stations were playing the record after midnight just to rack up the free trip, the record label reacted angrily: "If a radio station got a flyaway to a Céline show in Las Vegas for the add, and they're playing the song all in overnights, they are not getting the flyaway."

One Sony executive complained that "it cost us over $4,000 to get Franz [Ferdinand] on WKSE" in Buffalo. The station's program director, Dave Universal, apparently didn't like the song but agreed to play it in exchange for trips to Miami, according to a Sony e-mail. Embarrassed by the disclosure, the station's owner, Entercom, fired Universal, who denied taking money in exchange for airplay.

Even before Spitzer's probe began, music critics, reporters, and listeners had come to see the promotion system as evidence of continuing corruption in the radio and music industries. Under pressure from the public, the press, and regulators, Clear Channel in 2002 announced it would streamline the process by working exclusively with just three promoters. Those promoters immediately jacked up by 20 to 100 percent the fees they assessed record companies to get a new song added to a station's playlist.[14] Los Angeles promoters started charging $2,000 for each song that one black hits station added to its list. Clear Channel, while protesting that it had no control over how much the promoters charged record companies, happily pocketed the extra cash.

Clear Channel insisted that its stations pick music based entirely on research, without regard to what promoters pitch. But promoters and station managers say Clear Channel persistently pushed for more lucrative deals with promoters so local station managers could boost their bottom line with money passed through from record labels. And Clear Channel has other ways to squeeze revenue from record companies: the radio chain charged record labels $5,000 per song to present their potential hits at meetings of Clear Channel's top program directors.[15]

Finally, with congressional investigators sniffing around, Clear Channel announced it would no longer deal with independent promoters, but would conduct business directly with record companies. "We want to make sure that there's not even a tinge of perception that there's pay for play," company president Mark Mays said.

Alfred Liggins, chief executive of Radio One, made a similar move and defends it as a more honest system than the payola of yore. "Record companies used to say, 'Here's $1,000—now do you like the record?' Now they use these third-party promoters and say, 'Go get these records on stations, we don't care how you do it.' If that's the game, okay, fine, we're not going to deal with your independent promoters. We'll only deal with our own, and we'll charge them to talk to us. We'll have one person of our choice, and the record company will pay them and they will pay us. It's like a lobbyist. We're like senators: we don't necessarily do what they want, but we listen and the lobbyist hopes to have some influence." There is, of course, a crucial difference between the new pay-for-play system and Washington lobbying: Politicians must publicly divulge contributions from lobbyists. Radio stations don't tell listeners about their payments from promoters.

What's ultimately saddest about pay-for-play is that the new approach makes commercial radio even more predictable and uniform than it already was. Without local promoters pitching new artists to local program directors, listeners hear the same music in every city. Frank Falise says that after Clear Channel and other large companies became such dominant forces, "the program directors started telling me straight out: 'What difference does it make if I listen to your record if Joe Blow in corporate is making the decisions about what goes on the air?' "

Despite the ugly underside of the promotion business, the old payola had a desirable result: a wider variety of music got on the air. A promoter really could push a new act to a station here, a station there. That wider variety of music still exists, but as Falise says, "it's all on the Internet. I can't go tell a music director what's happening on the street anymore because the street's already downloaded the album. Radio is beside the point."

EVERY TIME CLEAR CHANNEL plugs one hole in its image, several more burst open. Most complaints center on the sheer size of the company and the resulting loss in local content. For all its massive reach, Clear Channel is a lean machine. Lowry Mays and his sons, Randall and Mark, the top executives, together own about 5 percent of the public company. The family routinely puts a single manager in charge of two, three, or four stations in a given market. Program directors who formerly concentrated on a single station now juggle two or three.

That steep pyramid of power makes it far more likely that managers will stick to the tried and true, rather than develop new programs or talent. Even so, the company contends that its stations offer listeners more choices in programming than ever before. Clear Channel research claims Americans are satisfied with what's on the radio. (Yet Clear Channel launched a big ad campaign in 2005 to promote its decision to reduce the number of minutes of ads heard each hour on its stations.)

Radio companies boast publicly about the diversity of programming they offer; inside the business, they flaunt radio's lack of choice. In a presentation to advertisers, Interep, one of the industry's largest ad sales businesses, contrasts radio with other media, arguing that magazines and cable TV offer far too many choices, "making it difficult to reach any substantial number of consumers. . . . Comparatively, radio stations in a market are still relatively limited in number."[16] Similarly, a Clear Channel executive in New Hampshire explained that more stations with varied formats "is not the answer to good radio, just as cable TV is not the answer to good TV. Both just give you more choices of crap. Radio is categorized and it ought to be. Only a slim number of people would like to hear Ja Rule, Rusted Root, Barry Manilow, and Dwight Yoakum on the same radio station. If you are actually looking for a station that will play Norah Jones, B-Tribe, Ned Otter, etc., then look for your closest college radio station. Give them a good listen. I guarantee you that after 30 minutes of pure hell, you will switch back to a Clear Channel station, because we play the hits."[17]

Lowry Mays puts his company's philosophy succinctly: "We're not in the business of providing news and information. We're not in the business of providing well-researched music. We're simply in the business of selling our customers products."[18]

In Clear Channel's bottom-line world, playing the right hits attracts the right audience, which in turn draws the necessary advertising. End of story. "We are a healthier industry now," says Alfred Liggins of Radio One. "Is it tougher for the little guy, the independent owner? Yeah. But that little guy cannot provide the same level of talent and programming."

Liggins took over Radio One from his mother, Cathy Hughes, whose unwavering dedication to Washington's black community and visceral love of street-level activism turned her talk station into a political powerhouse. But a new generation and a new business model changed Radio One, and Liggins, now head of a publicly traded company, proudly announces, "We serve a broader constituency than just African Americans. People know the Cathy Hughes story, but it's not a banner we wave. 'Hey, we're black-owned!' That doesn't cut it anymore. I've seen too many black owners get crushed by Clear Channel because they didn't do the best research and find the best talent. Times have changed. We can vote now; I can live anywhere I want. The tactics that got us to this level are not as effective today. A sit-in was the

right tactic for getting served at a lunch counter. It's not right for getting the same advertising rates as white stations."

But two hundred miles north of Liggins's suburban Maryland
headquarters, in a Manhattan office tower, Hal Jackson, the last living
pioneer of black radio, calls that a sellout. Even at his WBLS, one of
New York's last independently owned stations, "my own people, my
own program director tells me, 'Don't stretch out with the music on
your show, pull in, play it safe.' That money, that Clear Channel
money, is infecting everything we do. I don't know how long we can
say no to that money. We're constantly being approached to sell. And
even if we don't sell, we act more like them every day. Everything is
narrower, researched. Doing something just to serve the community is
seen as poor business practices."

Sure enough, in a memo to station owners counseling them that it's
okay to back away from news gathering, a media consultant from Forrester Research argues that "public service should be publicly funded.
Face it: Media is a business. Public service ceased being a priority for
media outlets long ago."[19]

IN THE BURBANK STUDIOS of KIIS-FM, a Clear Channel pop hits station, Rick Dees, perpetual teenager, perpetrator of the 1970s novelty
tune "Disco Duck," veteran of three decades of waking up Southern
California, is counting down the "Top 9 at 9." After all these years of
waking long before dawn, he's still a passionate, fast-talking, omnipresent voice for a city that lives in the car.

Dees has survived four station owners, seven general managers, and
ten program directors. As radio changes, Dees adapts. He's voice-
tracking his weekly countdown show, which is syndicated to three
hundred stations. He has no say in the songs he plays on his morning
show. He spins the music, makes his funny phone calls, announces
contest results, and sells his sponsors' goods, all with cheer and excitement.

When Dees's mother died, his dedication to his morning show was
so profound that he took only three days off before hurrying back to

the studio. On that first program back on the air, he played a song for his mother—"You Sexy Thing," the 1970s hit by Hot Chocolate. Immediately, the hotline in the studio rang. A Clear Channel boss was on the line, livid. "You fuck," he growled at Dees. "This is my show, my show. That is not on the playlist. Your fucking mother."

On a winter morning a few months later, with Dees's ratings down a notch, the deejay got another call from the boss. After twenty-two years of waking up Southern California, Dees was out, to be replaced by TV game show and *American Idol* host Ryan Seacrest. That February morning in 2004, Dees went on the air as usual: "It has been decided that I will no longer be doing the daily morning show on KIIS-FM. . . . It's a new day; let's get going."

VIRTUALLY EVERYONE IN RADIO believes the medium has become less fun, less creative, and just plain less worth listening to than at any other point since its birth. As for listeners, it depends on who's asking. When the National Association of Broadcasters commissioned a survey, it found general satisfaction with radio; about two-thirds of those polled liked what they heard on the air. But when the Future of Music Coalition, a Washington lobby fighting against further deregulation of broadcasting, asked similar questions, it found radio listening on the decline, especially among younger people.

Less partial research confirms it: the Arbitron ratings service tracks the amount of time Americans spend listening to radio, and its numbers show a steady drop since 1993, particularly among listeners age twelve to twenty-four. Duncan's American Radio, an influential industry source of statistics (owned by Clear Channel), says listening is at its lowest point in the survey's history, dropping 17 percent in the first three years of the twenty-first century alone.

Will the public turn against corporate radio? Can a popular rebellion restore creativity and fun, pushing radio back to its local roots? Or will we simply adjust to the loss? What's happened in radio in the past decade also happened to bookstores, drugstores, supermarkets, and hardware stores. The mom-and-pop stores that once lined downtown streets have given way to Borders, Walgreens, Wal-Mart, and Home Depot. American consumers have voted with our feet and our dollars: as much as we may grumble about mega-companies or wax nostalgic for the lost community of the old ways, we cast our votes for the big boys.

Is radio any different? Rather than rebelling in protest, many Americans find music elsewhere: Internet radio, satellite radio, downloading, file sharing. Yet at the same time, a backlash against the sameness of commercial radio has begun. A slew of anti–Clear Channel websites appeared to rally listeners. Common Cause, MoveOn.org, and some big-name musicians campaigned against government efforts to further relax limits on station ownership. When the FCC asked for public reaction to that initiative, the agency received more than ten thousand comments, only about a dozen of which supported the government's proposals.

Stories about "why radio sucks" and "why radio stinks" popped up in the press. When Prince opened a concert at New York's Lincoln Center by asking, "How do y'all like your radio stations, New York City?" the crowd responded with a booming chorus of boos. At FCC meetings, activists favoring radio diversity dogged commissioners, urging them to defy the big corporations and return control of the airwaves to the public.

And on the radio, Tom Petty, recently inducted into the Rock and Roll Hall of Fame, sang "The Last DJ":

And there goes the last DJ
Who plays what he wants to play
And says what he wants to say

Petty expected to have to fight to get his song on the air. Many station managers were initially reluctant to play a tune that struck so openly against their way of doing business. But the song quickly became the most-added single on rock and adult alternative stations. Radio executives said the song was okay to play because it was about not just radio but all of business, that it was a commentary on American life as much as on the fall of radio. And that was fine, because the bottom line was that they put the song on the air, which is the ultimately American thing to do: swallow up the protest and the anger and work it into the product.

Chapter 12

✳ BACK TO THE FUTURE

A WET, GLOOMY NIGHT; a barren industrial zone in the nation's capital. In a former printing plant now housing a breathtakingly expensive experiment in popular culture, eight actors in stocking feet prepare a re-creation of one of early radio's most daring moments. At the helm of this Halloween Eve evocation of the heyday of live radio drama is Glenn Beck, the Philadelphia-based talk show host who normally spends his days fulminating against liberals on two hundred AM stations nationwide. But Beck—yet another former Top 40 deejay who transformed himself into a radio talker—has put aside his day job to fulfill a lifelong dream.

When he was eight, Beck received as a gift from his mother a recording of the original broadcast of *The War of the Worlds*, as produced and narrated by Orson Welles for CBS Radio. That 1938 broadcast on Halloween Eve—a surprise to jittery Americans trying to negotiate the storms of war in Europe and Depression at home—created mass hysteria over the apparent invasion of New Jersey by Martians.

Sixty-four years later, Beck seeks not to cause such a panic but to rekindle a passion for radio, a belief that listening can matter—both to the audience and to the people who produce programming. Beck's *War of the Worlds*, like the original, features realistic-sounding news bulletins reporting the arrival of Martian spacecraft in Grover's Mill, New Jersey. The story is a science fiction fantasy about the mysteries of infinite space, but it is also an enduring commentary on the media and our love-hate relationship with the machines we use to connect to the world around us. *War of the Worlds* debuted in 1938 on a new mass medium called radio. Now, Beck is sending up the same alert at the start of the next century on a new mass medium called satellite radio. The message is that the messenger can be at once a comfort and a disturbance. Beck couldn't very well break away from the effluvia of the daily news and stage an old radio drama on his talk show. But he could zip down to Washington to XM Satellite Radio, which is only too happy to offer this production.

GLENN BECK *(Courtesy Premiere Radio Networks)*

Upstairs from the studio where Beck and his crew of actors try their hand at producing radio magic, Lee Abrams sits in a cramped, over-stuffed office, supervising something he had never imagined possible in all his years of playing radio. Well into midlife, Abrams—the kid who fell in love with creating connections between listeners and radio, the young man who scorned the self-indulgence of radio artistes, the grown-up who helped homogenize the pop culture—felt a need to return to the passions of his youth. Years of consulting had paid off in material goods, but Abrams had developed a bit of a problem looking in the mirror. He had shown owners how their stations could select the music that would draw precisely the audience advertisers sought. But listeners grew disenchanted and cynical. When technology offered them an escape, they grabbed it, choosing to get their music elsewhere—on the computer, from CDs they burned at home and traded with friends. Radio was no longer the sole source for new music, and folks Abrams's age were tiring of the hits that had stood them in good stead for most of their lives.

Throughout the 1990s, a small group of gadget geeks had been working on technologies that would transform radio much as cable had remapped television. Using satellites launched into orbit above the planet, the engineers believed they could provide, for the first time, coast-to-coast audio service, a truly national radio. Radio would no longer be local in the traditional sense; instead, satellites would transmit a different lure—a huge array of channels, enough to satisfy cravings for almost any kind of music. When executives at CD Radio—later renamed, in a burst of marketing genius, XM Radio—approached Abrams about bringing his energies to a whole new form of radio, he leaped at the chance.

Abrams saw satellite as a way to create dozens of stations without slavishly hewing to advertisers' demographic cubbyholes. Here was a chance to hire deejays and let them use their knowledge of the music. Finally, Abrams—still a 1970s-looking guy with a woolly bush of hair and a belly born of too many airport waits for too many consulting trips—could marry his childhood desire to put his tunes on the air with his adult savvy about marketing. Abrams had developed an elaborate theory about how and why musical trends happen in American pop culture. He saw a pendulum swinging from experimentation with the avant-garde to the safety and security of standards and then back again as the nation moved through periods of unsettling change and relative calm. Now he could program for many points along that continuum, offering nostalgia on some channels (old-time radio dramas, classic comedy bits, Broadway tunes, big-band hits) and cutting-edge sounds (unsigned bands, dance music straight from the clubs, new jazz, even free-form mixes) on others.

As programming chief at XM Satellite Radio, one of two companies taking a $2 billion plunge to introduce a new concept to Americans hungry for real radio, Abrams presides over a techno-cool complex of eighty-two studios. The only rule Abrams drills into the skulls of every deejay he hires is, "If you sound like FM, you're fired."

When I first visited Abrams, XM was just getting started. Doubters said Americans wouldn't pay for radio, something that had always been free. But TV had been free too, and now the great majority of Americans shell out $40, $80, $150 a month for cable. Satellite radio charges about $13 a month, on top of an investment of $200 or so in equipment, for 150 channels of music and talk that you can't hear on the radio, or at least not easily. The sounds on XM and its slower-starting competitor, Sirius Satellite Radio, which is based in New York, are beamed up to satellites and then return to Earth via antennas atop your car or in your kitchen.[1]

The programming is designed in response to what ails contemporary radio: nearly every form of music ignored by commercial and public radio has its own full-time channel on XM and Sirius—several styles of jazz; dozens of subgenres of rock, pop, and urban; bluegrass, folk, reggae, world music, techno, disco, novelty tunes; entire stations devoted to the pop songs of one decade, each broadcasting in the style of radio stations of that era—the 1940s, '50s, '60s, '70s, and so on. Plus talk, news, sports, and yes, drama.

The start was slow, especially for Sirius, which attracted only a few tens of thousands of customers in its first couple of years and didn't really click with listeners until it paid Howard Stern half a billion dollars to jump to satellite. XM, in the meantime, had staked out an impressive initial lead, collecting its one millionth subscriber in less than two years. (It took cable TV twelve years to reach that milestone.) But from 2004 to 2006, the rivals both picked up steam, through word of mouth and a hopped-up marketing campaign touting high-priced contracts with big-name talent. NPR morning host Bob Edwards and

Major League Baseball went to XM and Stern and the National Football League signed with Sirius. The two companies' numbers shot through the roof. After five years in orbit, the satellite companies had signed up more than 10 million customers. (XM retained a strong but shrinking lead, as Sirius found an audience with sports, Stern, and somewhat more sophisticated music programming.) Still, both services remained far from breaking even. And while their sound fills many of the gaps on ordinary, or, as the satellite people say, "terrestrial" radio, XM and Sirius both suffer some of the same ills that infect corporate radio—an overdependence on technology and a canned, detached sound. Most channels are voice-tracked well in advance of broadcast, so there are few references to anything happening right now, and obviously nothing about what's going on in your hometown, because the signal goes out to the entire country. Satellite's boosters argue that the entire nation is their "local" audience, and already a thriving community of XM listeners can be found on fan sites such as www.xmfans .com and www.siriusbackstage.com. Abrams argues that satellite listeners, like Web users, form their own affinity communities, coalescing around Christian rock, bluegrass, or 1970s pop rather than around a station whose deejays know the local high schools and the intersections that get tricky in icy weather.

Within weeks of arriving at XM, Abrams assembled a staff of old pros who've once again found a place where they can play the music they love, where they can dare to lead an audience. Abrams worked up a persuasive patter about how he has turned his back on the research and marketing that emasculated commercial radio. Some of Abrams's colleagues may be forgiven if they are skeptical of his new shtick. After all, this is the guy who made himself wealthy by promising that demographically determined programming would make FM radio totally responsive to listeners' desires.

But with the vehemence of a convert, the consultant whose research changed the sound and direction of American radio now rails against the hegemony of the consultants. Amazingly, the object of jeers and derision from musicians and deejays in the 1970s and '80s is now cheered as the darling of the grassroots rebellion against Big Radio.

He even appears at conventions of radio activists, where the anti-corporate-radio crowds greet Abrams as a folk hero. The man who once stood for slick-sounding sameness is now a populist preacher, leading the flock in snarling at consultants who, he says, distorted his teachings, taking the gospel of research to an unholy extreme, sucking the fun and life out of radio.

Inside XM, Abrams preaches a careful mix of freedom and structure. "FM tightened music as far as you can go without alienating," Abrams writes in a memo to deejays at XM.[2] "XM loosens music as far as you can go without alienating." Spurning the auditorium testing that commercial radio uses to choose music, XM relies on a combination of sales figures and its staff's own taste and instincts. This is no return to the days of free-form radio—XM is a huge public corporation whose investors include not only major automakers but the dreaded Clear Channel itself. But satellite radio's business model allows it to reach beyond the anxiety of commercial stations and attract a bunch of different, smaller audiences that in theory will add up to mass. If Abrams's first revolution sliced Top 40's mass audience into a dozen demographic niches, his reaction to the hardening of those categories is to let a hundred flowers bloom. But these are genetically engineered flowers, each selected for its ability to appeal to a particular brand of listener. XM and Sirius talk a lot about individualism and giving deejays leeway, but Abrams is never without a template for understanding audience desires. He built XM's menu of channels around a matrix of psychological and demographic characteristics that he can scrawl from memory onto any convenient napkin or envelope.

Abrams charts the appeal of each channel, dividing them into categories such as Special Interest (blues, reggae—real music for real fans), Cartoon (a channel that plays 1960s pop should sound like stations sounded back then), Audio Valium (background music), Sick (radio that sounds young and smart), and Point of View (channels for cultural minorities: truckers, evangelicals, New Age types). Abrams wants to capture the spirit and rebellion of 1950s and '60s radio, but keep it in the controlled context of the '80s and '90s corporate environment. He loves sending jocks to the Web to listen to old recordings of the great Top 40 deejays, hoping they will pick up on the freewheeling, unscripted theater of those days. "Use sound, Morse code, radio dramas, phone, nature, sampled harp, bagpipes, activate your George Martin gene, use accents, whispers, foreign languages," he urges his deejays.

But in another memo, he makes clear that XM has boundaries, and that the lines are drawn at maintaining the essential appeal of each channel. "Don't surprise people," he writes to his music staff. "AC/DC on the Deep Tracks channel is like ketchup on pheasant under glass. An album cut on the '50s channel is like sushi at the Top Hat Diner."

Satellite radio is everything radio has become in the past twenty years—on steroids. Abrams has not forsaken the gospel of niche narrowcasting; rather, he has adapted that model to the vast bandwidth available with satellite technology. Under the guise of offering far more choices, he has pulled back on the industry's love affair with research, recognizing that listeners want to feel they are discovering something new, not simply receiving what they asked for. Satellite radio feels like a seductive whisper in the ear after too many years of stilted commercial radio. Still, something is lacking, something live, local, and unscripted.

Beck's *War of the Worlds* causes no panic. XM doesn't yet have enough listeners for a single program to spark a noticeable reaction in the overall populace. And the production airs on XM's drama channel, so there isn't much chance that anyone would be fooled by the play's pseudo-newscasts. But that isn't the intent. Beck means to pay homage to the past, to tap into some of the primal force that lends power to radio, and to have a whale of a time. When Beck's sound effects guy achieves a painfully realistic *thud* of a body falling to the ground by dropping onto the studio floor a heavy canvas bag filled with the actors' shoes, the blasé engineers on the other side of the glass look up from their digital recording board and mutter, "Wow. Cool."

This is not mere nostalgia. It is a passion for what's real. It is why Beck insists on performing this show live. It is why the actors come for little pay and even less recognition. It is how radio connects.

—

THE RADIO THAT OPENED a generation's hearts to novel flavors of music and new ideas about the world was itself an accident of history, a desperate reaction to the rise of a new and threatening technology. From Hunter Hancock's bold experiment in playing race music for white Los Angeles to Cousin Brucie's adolescent love affair with the transistor kids of greater New York, from Bob Fass's midnight ramblings to Tom Donahue's offers to take you on a trip and test your dope while you wait, radio was transformed by the rise of television into a much more local and immediate medium than it had ever been during the so-called Golden Age of network broadcasting.

But at the start of a new century, satellite technology, the Internet, and the aura of certainty that research offered to bottom-line-oriented executives have conspired to undermine the very concept of localism. American pop culture is evolving simultaneously in seemingly opposing directions: toward a single national entertainment stream that sweeps out local musicians, writers, and voices, and toward an infinite number of affinity groups who gather electronically in cyber-communities and trade passions by downloading from friends. In neither trend does physical geography matter much.

The new pop culture, driven largely by the structure and ease of the Web, lends power to the increasing number of Americans who are tired or resentful of prepackaged, predigested pap. In their search for music, news, or talk that feels authentic, that audience has turned away from corporate radio, craving programming that is less slick and more intimate. Music lovers have two great desires: to hear the music they know and love—the iPod beats radio cleanly there—and to discover new tunes. Radio's great remaining quality is serendipity.

Two new ways for radio to reconnect with young listeners have emerged from opposite directions, from the very newest technology and from radio's roots. Internet radio promised from its birth to be simultaneously local and global. As inexpensive as broadcast radio is, a Web radio station—a website that streams audio to your computer—is even cheaper to operate and far easier to start. No license required. Just a few hundred dollars' worth of equipment and you're up and running, providing programming to anyone with a sound card and speakers.

Low-power FM stations—microstations designed to reach an area no larger than your neighborhood—also promised to democratize radio. The idea was that the FCC would license church groups, political activists, neighborhood collectives, punks, hunters, any and all who want to operate their own little FM stations, broadcasting with such low wattage that they can be heard only in one section of a city or in one rural town, thereby posing no threat to big commercial stations. Low-power stations play local bands and less-widely loved forms of music; they provide discussion and news of community events not important enough to make the TV news or the metropolitan newspaper.

Both Internet radio and low-power FM got off to exciting starts in the late 1990s. Both were beaten down—or at least effectively coopted—by body slams from the federal government and corporate forces.

In May 2002, the Arbitron ratings service published a list of the seventy-five most-listened-to Internet radio stations. The list displayed the bright promise of Web radio—the top twenty stations included classical and jazz outlets from London, Berlin, Seattle, New York, and Washington, D.C.; stations featuring electronic dance music or 1980s rock; and some traditional radio stations streaming their standard rock, pop, and oldies over the Internet. The list showed that computer users sitting at their desks at work were scanning the globe for programming they couldn't hear on broadcast radio. Early adopters tuned in to the top pop hits as determined by Britain's Virgin Radio rather than their local Clear Channel station. They chose London's JazzFM, the classical sounds of *The New York Times*–owned WQXR, the eclectic music mix of Los Angeles's KCRW.[3]

From the first heady days of broadband, many, if not most, U.S. radio stations either put their broadcasts up on the Web or planned to. College radio stations could now provide far-flung alumni with coverage of campus sports, as well as the edgy music for which college deejays are renowned. Garage- and attic-based Internet stations blossomed. Web radio attracted entrepreneurs who thought their unique mix of programming—local music, talk about schools or environmental issues, bedtime stories for kids—might lure neighborhood advertisers.

Then, in 2002, the Librarian of Congress, under pressure from the commercial broadcasters lobby, the recording industry, and Congress, issued new rules requiring Internet stations to pay royalties to the music publishing cooperatives ASCAP and BMI. Commercial radio broadcasters have never had to pay those royalties, on the theory that airplay of musical recordings promotes record or CD sales.[4] Librarian of Congress James Billington knew his new fee scale would silence most Internet stations, which could not afford to pay the royalties. Sure enough, within hours, basement Web operations started switching off the music. Some small stations survived by pulling all commercially released music off their shelves and dedicating themselves entirely to local artists who have no recording contracts. But at hundreds of college stations and many more solo operations, the Internet stream simply went silent.

In a matter of months, Internet radio played through the same stages that broadcast radio itself had traveled over the previous seventy years, moving from an initial period of creativity and anarchy to rapid commercialization and investment by major corporations. By late 2003—only eighteen months after those early signs of flowering diversity—Arbitron's list of the top fifty Internet radio stations had changed dramatically. America Online had launched its Web radio stations—offerings that mimic commercial radio's formats almost exactly. The impact of the new copyright rules was clear: now, twelve of the top twenty Internet stations were AOL's (AOL Top Pop, AOL Top Country, AOL Smooth Jazz, AOL Lite Rock, and so on). Among the top thirty stations, only four were not run by huge corporations— two independent Christian music outlets, a Web-only oldies station, and WXPN, the University of Pennsylvania's acclaimed provider of acoustic rock, folk, and world music.[5] Arbitron eventually shut down its ratings service for online radio and started over with a service that measured the audiences of only the big three corporate Web radio providers—AOL, Yahoo! and MSN. The wild edges of Internet radio were left out of the mainstream.

Could smaller, softer voices nonetheless make themselves heard in a media landscape dominated by large companies? Could the next revolution take place on the radio itself, just as it did when the industry last grew anxious about its survival, back in the 1950s? Technology might seem to be radio's enemy, but radio fought back with its own innovations. Beginning in 2005, manufacturers started rolling out a new generation of radios that received digital signals, giving stations a chance to offer several different programs on the same frequency. Dubbed HD Radio (a nod to the allure of high-definition TV), digital broadcasting would let traditional stations offer many more varieties of programming, perhaps neutralizing the threat from satellite. A country station might add a channel of classic country hits and another of music by new artists. A news station might devote one channel to traffic and weather reports while putting talk shows on another of its program streams. It would be several years before digital radio's promise became clear; the sets were expensive and cumbersome at first, and asking consumers to replace all their radios would not be an easy sell. But for the first time since FM came along, radio was moving to expand its offerings. Stations found themselves mimicking satellite radio with their new digital programs—adding electronica on a news-talk public station in Washington, all-comedy on a pop station in Indianapolis, indie rock on a hard rocker in Detroit, all of it commercial-free, at least for the technology's first eighteen months.

The radio business embraced digital out of panic, but a few years earlier, when the government proposed another way to add new voices to the dial, the industry was much less welcoming. Reacting to the popular outcry against corporate consolidation, the FCC proposed in the late 1990s to allow churches, community groups, and individuals to set up FM stations of such low power (100 watts maximum) that their signal could carry at most three or four miles. The FCC would keep big companies off these frequencies by forbidding any entity from owning two microstations within seven miles of each other. Bill

Kennard, the FCC chairman under President Clinton and a deejay back in his college days, declared low-power FM (or LPFM) "the antidote to consolidation." His ideological opponent, Michael Powell, President Bush's first-term FCC chief, also endorsed low power as a democratizing check against big corporate radio. Within months after the FCC invited applications for low-power licenses, political radicals, evangelicals, radio activists, and lovers of music such as Cajun, gospel, folk, and bluegrass inundated the agency with thirty thousand expressions of interest.

But an unlikely alliance of big broadcasting companies and National Public Radio opposed low-power FM. Each feared competition but couched their objections in technical terms—they were simply trying to protect their stations against signal interference from the little upstarts. A fierce lobbying effort in Washington produced the desired result: Congress increased the amount of space the FCC had to leave on the dial between existing stations and any new signal, thereby reducing LPFM's potential from thousands of stations sprinkled throughout the nation to perhaps a few hundred stations, mainly in rural areas. With one deft legislative slash, the big boys cut the number of potential stations by 75 percent.

Nonetheless, applications poured in—from florists in Gainesville, Georgia; Hmong immigrants in Minneapolis; zydeco lovers in Opelousas, Louisiana; radio history buffs in Bellingham, Washington. A lucky few won approval and found out how easy it is to get on the air. In Georgetown, California, the American River Folk Society got its micro–radio station up and running for just $7,000, using donated equipment, volunteers, and word of mouth to build KFOK. Broadcasting from behind Eldon's Barbershop on Main Street in a little town in the foothills of the Sierra mountains, KFOK plays everything from blues to folk, Broadway tunes to classical, as well as shows such as *Trolling for Trout*, which host Gary Oswald calls "a music program submerged in a fishy emulsion based on a redneck/hippy/hillbilly perspective and laced with a dose of fishy information like local fish plant sites, local fishing reports and anything else that reeks of fish."[6] KFOK serves up children's stories right after school lets out. The weekly schedule also includes an old-fashioned swap shop called *Radio Tradio*, *Horse Talk*, *Garden Thyme*, *Mrs. Webb's Sunday Morning Soul Call* gospel show, and *Free Mountain Air*, a morning program of local news and commentary.

On the Eastern Shore of Maryland, citizens who initially banded together to combat sprawl-minded developers started WRYR, a low-power station designed to give folk artists and storytellers a way to preserve their community and remind listeners why huge new housing developments might threaten traditional ways of living along the Chesapeake Bay. It costs but $600 a month to keep the station going—the programs are staffed by volunteers and expenses are picked up by local businesses and individual donors. The result: thousands of listeners hear programs such as *Sandy Stromberg, A Neighbor*, in which the aforementioned fellow plays classical music from his collection and reads from Colonial-era newspaper reports about the Maryland shore. Or there's *Chesapeake Moon*, the mystical adventures of Carol Bennett, who left a career at NASA to shoot into the noetic sciences, the study of the supernatural in a place free of the constraints of time and space. Or *RadioActivism*, a weekly hour dedicated to discussing nuclear power and other environmental issues.[7]

These stations don't get on the air solely by submitting an application. They hack through the thicket of federal bureaucracy with help from renegade anarchists who have seen the wisdom of working the system. Almost every month, the pied piper of micro-radio, a long-haired, woolly-bearded gent who goes by the pseudonym Pete Tridish, piles a few fellow radio radicals into Hedy Lamarr, his aging Ford Escort wagon, and drives through the night to a low-power FM radio barn raising. Tridish—his real name is Dylan Wrynn—is a former radio pirate, instigator of an illegal broadcasting operation in Philadelphia, who tired of fighting the FCC's enforcement officers and put his energies into launching new stations legally. His Prometheus Radio Project helps micro-stations find cheap equipment and cope with the FCC's love of paperwork. To his own surprise, Pete has found himself transformed from angry radical to someone who sits in conference rooms at Washington law firms, hammering out proposed language for federal regulations. Pete is a regular at the FCC's D.C. headquarters, fighting against right-wing religious groups that try to acquire low-power licenses to string together a nationwide network of evangelical stations—subverting low power's local purpose.[8]

For the better part of a decade, this curious, scraggly hero has wandered the back roads of America, an alternative minstrel preaching the gospel of radio for the people. His mission is to return radio to the true owners of the airwaves. It's an idealistic and classically American attempt to break through ideological barriers and give the individual a voice. It's a throwback to an idea of community that may seem quaint in an era in which jobs last but a few years, families move frequently, and neighbors are often strangers. But there is nothing cute about the desire people have to hear one another, or about radio's capacity to forge those bonds. New technologies come along and alter the media of the previous generation. But dire scenarios about the inevitable death of the old media rarely come to fruition. Rather, such predictions of doom tend to fade, much like the most florid promises about the peace, happiness, or togetherness that the new media will create.

Radio survived TV's rise, albeit in a whole new incarnation, because it served a convenient role in our daily lives and because it helped us believe in the American myths of mobility, individuality, and can-do savvy. Radio isn't what it used to be, but it never really was. Despite its troubles, radio is as much about the future as it is about the past. That future lies where Todd Storz, Hunter Hancock, Hal Jackson, Cousin Brucie, Jean Shepherd, Bob Fass, Tom Donahue, Lee Abrams, and so many others found their inspiration—in the voices of those who open their souls into a microphone, and in the imaginations of those who feel compelled to listen. In the villages where Pete Tridish works, but also in the big suburbs and cities where most Americans reside, there are still places on the dial where radio reaches into people's lives and captures our fancy. Those places, whether at a ballpark in California, a studio in Virginia, or a salty beach town in New York, are where the next radio generation will find its way.

✳ MAGIC

WHERE JON MILLER GREW UP, Giants baseball was on the radio, every game, every day, all summer. At the beach, along Fisherman's Wharf, in the schoolyard, the game was on. Miller had listened to the

JON MILLER (right) WITH JOE MORGAN IN THE
ESPN BROADCAST BOOTH *(Courtesy ESPN)*

Giants on the radio long before his father first took him to Candlestick Park on a Tuesday night in April 1962. The Giants rewarded their ten-year-old fan with three home runs, and though Jon Miller was happy, something was missing: "Where's 'Bye-bye, baby'?" he wondered. "The home runs were over the fence and the fans cheered, but where was the 'Bye-bye, baby'?" the radio call that Giants announcer Russ Hodges made famous. "That was the home run to me."

Four decades later, Jon Miller's own velvet baritone means Giants baseball to kids and grown-ups all over the San Francisco Bay area. Miller, who could live handsomely off his announcing for ESPN television, nonetheless chooses to be the night-in, night-out play-by-play man for Giants radio. Miller does this because he is in love with the idea that you can best see the action on the field in your mind, and because there are few places in American life in which radio—poor old tinny AM radio—still reigns supreme, and baseball is one of them.

Amid the sound-alike music and talk stations that clutter the dial, some of the best radio manages to survive in the belly of the beast— rich, quirky American voices that jump out from the corporate sameness and make us pull over to the side of the road to catch the end of a compelling story. Jon Miller is one of those voices.

He spent his youth sneaking his transistor set under the pillow, listening to the Giants and the 49ers, college basketball and Top 40 on KSFO, Johnny Holliday spinning the hits on KYA, and a young Don Imus doing guest shots as a deejay in San Francisco. Starting in 1968, Miller and a friend would buy bleachers tickets at the Oakland Coliseum, sit way up high, and—using statistics from the Sunday paper and phony commercials that Miller had written in advance—"broadcast" the A's game into Miller's big reel-to-reel tape recorder.

In college, he was a classical deejay, handled play-by-play on the football broadcasts, and freelanced news stories in the early days of National Public Radio (one of his first reports included the sound of a harpoon being shot off the last whaling ship in San Francisco Bay— how very NPR). But Miller's mission was to tell the stories of baseball, and he got to do that because he had a voice like pumpkin butter— thick, rich, smooth, with a smidge of sugar—and because he understood radio and the American imagination.

In 1981, when Miller was broadcasting Boston Red Sox games, a players strike interrupted the season. Stations were anxious about losing their sponsors, so when Miller and veteran Red Sox announcer

Ken Coleman decided to continue the broadcasts even without games, executives were wary but willing. Miller and Coleman decided to play the Red Sox' regular schedule on the Strat-O-Matic board game, a statistics- and dice-based effort to replicate what might happen if real teams met on a real field. It made for perfect radio: Miller imitated the voices of stadium public address announcers, local celebrities came on the air as managers of the teams, and Miller added sound effects culled from old broadcasts. Miller and Coleman even went back in time, using Strat-O-Matic's historic player cards to re-create games from the 1940s, complete with stories about hotels and restaurants from that era. The make-believe went on for thirty-two games; listeners loved it. Inevitably, some even called in to ask when the strike had ended.

"It got kind of ludicrous, which is the beauty of radio—it's all in the mind," Miller says. "We could tell a story about a player's house in Scottsdale, Arizona, and on the radio, the listener goes to that house. On television, you tell that story and you don't go anywhere, because you see things that don't match the story—the third base coach flashing signs, the pitcher getting ready. On TV, I caption what's being shown. On the radio, it's my story. As Ernie Harwell says, on TV, you get the movie version. The game on the radio is the novel."[1]

WHEN RADIO WORKS, it grabs hold of one person at a time and creates a bond between the unseen voice and the listener. And as that one-on-one relationship grows more intimate, the listener gains a sense of belonging to something larger. The act of listening connects us to others even when we cannot see them. And it connects us to something deep inside, a private place. TV memories are mainly nostalgic, the VH1 documentaries of our lives. Radio memories, because they are incomplete, lacking images fixed in time and place, reach into our hearts. They are the collective call of the eternal night.

In a nation of lonely people, when we hear music that moves us, or a political argument that sways us, or simply another human voice that tells us a story, we find company. And as we imagine the rest of the audience out there listening with us, a lone figure in a dark, windowless studio is also dreaming, conjuring a community of people who, astonishingly, inconceivably, are tuned in to *him.*

"There's no greater feeling in the world than being in a radio station alone, and all this stuff's going out to people and you're all by yourself," says Don Geronimo, whose syndicated *Don and Mike Show* with Mike O'Meara is a bunch of guys hanging around doing stunts, cracking jokes, and telling stories. Geronimo was so fascinated by radio as a boy in Rockville, Maryland, that he kept charts documenting how many minutes elapsed between spins of hit records on his favorite station. "The first time I was on WLS in Chicago, my dream come true, I put on 'Stairway to Heaven' and just walked around the building and said, 'I made it, I'm here, inside. This is my board. This is my cart machine. These are my jingles.' It's the lowest level of show business, but it's the only one where it's just you, making a crack in a dark room and somewhere out there, there's a hundred guys saying 'Hey, that's what I'd like to say to my wife.' "

Despite the success of Geronimo's Virginia-based show, he knows the medium he loves has hit a brick wall, that much of the emotional bond between station and listener has been lost. Geronimo looks at his college-age son and the eclectic range of music he listens to, and the Top 40 veteran wonders why radio cannot return to a time when it had the courage to let one voice present a mix of music that challenges, delights, surprises, and comforts. "If radio just tried, if they played the #1 rap song and the #1 rock song and then the #1 adult contemporary song, that station would do gangbusters," Geronimo says. "Oh, they'll be horrified and say, 'That's a car wreck,' playing different kinds of music on the same station, but that's why you have a jingle—that's what separates Dolly Parton from Quiet Riot. Because someone out there likes both of them, and even if you don't, you stick around, because you know that in three minutes, there'll be something you do like. What a simple idea, and they screwed it up." Although Geronimo's show traffics in talk, its packaging and spirit are defined by its Top 40 roots, and sometimes, when he's feeling nostalgic for what radio was and could be, Geronimo will take an hour of his show and play hit songs like it was 1973 once again. Geronimo, like an uncanny number of big-name radio successes, has a dream that he'll give up his gig, buy a small station down at the shore, and play Top 40. "I'll play everything, with no research," he says. "I'll hire young guys and give them zany names and let them talk and take them out on the van and have them do crazy things and give away money. No consultant would ever let you do it, but no consultant has ever proven that it wouldn't work."

It does work. The concept of creating community through radio works so well that just as blogs rose from the bedrooms of millions of American homes to tell professional journalists that they have no God-given right to determine what's news, thousands of people now use their computers to challenge the corporate version of radio. They are making their own radio programs—podcasts—and putting them on the Web, available free to anyone who might like to download the show and play it back on an iPod or any of the other digital devices that are challenging CDs and radio as the primary tools for listening to music. With remarkable speed following the technology's launch in 2003, thousands of people who could not find the music they loved on the radio reinvented themselves as podcasters. Here's a Dutch priest in Rome playing his favorite rock songs between expressions of the daily joys of prayer—with bonus news briefs from the Vatican (Father Roderick Vonhogen at www.catholicinsider.com). Here's *Eye on Wisconsin*, a ninety-minute mix of rock, local news, and highly opinionated punditry on matters local and national. Just as an earlier generation used the latest technology to make cassette tapes of their favorite tunes and pass them around to friends, podcasters rely on word of mouth and search engines to bring them an audience. As happens with so many new technologies, the first wave of success for podcasts carried along all manner of hyperbole about how this liberation from the time constraints of mass broadcasting would translate into the death of radio. "Wave Goodbye to Radio," said the headline in the *Portland Tribune* over an article about an Oregon man, Tim Germer, whose *Northwest Noise* program offers news about politics, food, local musicians, and beer.

Podcasting—first conceived in 2000 by a French blogger and executed in 2004 by a former MTV veejay named Adam Curry, whose own show mixes music and amiable chatter about technology—combines the garage band ease of Internet radio with the go-anywhere convenience of an iPod. Podcasting started out more as a hobby than a business, but Curry proved an effective evangelist for his creation, and soon hundreds of thousands of podcasts vied for an audience. The first

PAUL SIDNEY AT HOME IN BROOKLYN, PLAYING RADIO AT AGE NINE
(Courtesy Paul Sidney)

popular programs were talk shows, especially about technology and media; diaries of relationships, essentially aural blogs; and music programs, though these were limited, once again, by the fact that hardly any podcasters had paid for licenses to use copyrighted music. But with unprecedented speed, the major media companies grabbed hold of the new thing: within a year of the technology's launch, more than a third of the most popular podcasts were programs regularly heard on

National Public Radio or the BBC, and the big commercial broadcasters were soon making their programs available as well. Listeners seemed most interested in using podcasting as a tool to time-shift their favorite radio shows, listening when they chose to rather than when their local station told them to.

But music lovers and people with stories to tell were undeterred. They loaded their podcasts onto the Web, waiting to see who might listen. Podcasts proved once more the human passion to share culture through sound. In an atomized society in which personalized media technologies seem to narrow the possibility of a mass, shared experience, people of all ages still gravitate toward the corners of the media landscape that offer serendipity and community.

PAUL SIDNEY HAS BEEN PLAYING radio since he was five. His family didn't have a TV in their house in Brooklyn, so when Paul was in kindergarten, he'd slip up to his room to listen to John Gambling's chatty morning show on WOR. Back home each evening, Paul, an only child, was the announcer on the radio station in his mind. He had a microphone in his room, and a Victrola, and even a professional Telechron clock to time each segment of his program. While other boys on the block played stickball in the waning light, Paul remained inside, introducing records, narrating his life.

He loved to play radio, but Paul was ashamed to be the only one who sat indoors. Windows stayed open in those days before air-conditioning, and Paul could hear the cheers and shouts of the other kids running down the sidewalk. He wanted to be there and soon realized that his microphone might win him entrée to the games on the block. He carried his mike out onto the stoop and invited ballplaying children to be interviewed on his first remote broadcast. Everyone wanted to be on the radio.

A framed black-and-white photo of little Paul on the street in front of his house, taping that first program, sits in a place of prominence in the office just off the main studio at WLNG, the Sag Harbor, New York, FM station where Paul Sidney is president, owner, program director, weekend deejay, and host of 250 remote broadcasts each year. "That guy is on the radio all day, every day, for my entire life," is how the man at Schiavoni's IGA Market describes Sidney when I ask about the voice on WLNG.

It's a Sunday afternoon on the East End of Long Island, late spring, and neither the investment bankers nor the young clubbers from Manhattan have made their annual pilgrimage to the pricey beaches quite yet. The people who build the beachfront manses and serve the $43 bluefish specials and farm the land that hasn't yet been sold to developers still have the East End to themselves. Harried New Yorkers who consider the Hamptons their playground have their own glitzy weekly newspapers and even their own la-ti-da public radio station with its BBC News and gentle jazz, but the people who actually live on this sandbar between Long Island Sound and the Atlantic Ocean have their own voice too, and it is WLNG.

It is permanently 1963 on Paul Sidney's station, a land of swinging a cappella jingles ("Who's got the Beatles? *We've* got the Beatles! WLNG!") and singing time and temperature announcements. There are commercials in which local owners of hardware shops and family restaurants shout about their latest sale ("Call Fred Fisher, the East End's only attorney devoted solely to criminal defense; dial 877-KEEPMEOUT"), remote broadcasts from the doughnut shop and the fire station, Dionne Warwick and the Four Freshmen, Beatlemania and loud, boisterous deejays—deejays who ring cowbells, shout out greetings to callers, cover high school football, and spend an hour each morning moderating a *Swap and Shop* phone-in show on which callers do not hesitate to give out their home phone numbers.

WLNG is a low-fidelity, monaural FM station with more than two thousand jingles on tape, decades-old equipment, waterfront studios, a boat, and a bus. The station is firmly stuck in the analog age and absolutely committed to the huge, echo-chamber reverb that meant Top 40 radio to those who grew up in the 1950s and '60s.

"Sandwiches, pasta, they supply everything you can want for the boat, they'll do it for you at Dreesen's," Sidney says in an impromptu riff about a local deli that regularly invites him in to do Sunday morning remote broadcasts. It's a commercial, but no one could possibly find the borderline between paid advertisement and personal testimonial. Sidney pops in a jingle—a sweet soprano crooning that "It's smooooth sailing with the highly successful sound of WLNG"—and then moves on to the WLNG Tide Report. An organizer of a local art festival phones in details of the show at the American Legion Hall, and then the Fisherman's Restaurant offers a singing commercial ("Italian specialties, pizza and more, lots of good things that come from the shore") before the Summertime Safety Watch offers tips courtesy of Walsh Air Conditioning. Back at Dreesen's, Sidney interviews a man and his son who just wandered in for breakfast. "A lot of people say, 'Ah, the second-home owners never heard of LNG Radio,' but you listen all the time, right?"

"I've got you on a button in the car—just push the button and you're always there," the man replies.

It often seems that way on the East End. Four hours after that remote, WLNG—Sidney at the mike, of course—is on the road again, broadcasting from a bus, the kind that chugs along city streets, a 1978 GMC Motorhouse on which all but a couple of seats have been torn out, replaced by a broadcast console, a huge wooden desk, and bins and bins full of the old plastic tape cartridges that were the industry standard back in the 1970s, each tape containing a single song, jingle, or commercial.

On the air, Sidney, a garrulous lump of a man with dancing blue eyes, drooping ears, and a husky voice still firmly rooted in Brooklyn, says, "We'll be back with you in five or six minutes—gotta move the antenna," as if you're his neighbor and he has to get the phone before you can resume talking about those Yankees. He slaps on a jingle ("Live and local, twenty-four hours a day"), and while a song plays, Sidney hoists himself up from the broadcast chair and shambles outside to find a better position for the remote antenna. Then, he's back: "This diet today. I had seafood for lunch, seafood last night for supper. Gotta skip that cherry pie for dessert tonight," and before you realize what's he's just done, on comes the song "Cherry Pie," a doo-wop number from the fifties.

Shortly after I climb aboard to talk to Sidney, he thrusts a mike in my hand and waves at me—we're on the air! "Go ahead, interview me," Sidney says, and I toss out a question, but there can be no follow-up. Sidney is off and rambling, talking straight through the 3 P.M. news ("That's all right, there'll be more news at four," he tells listeners), telling stories about other stations, where big, faceless companies "are fooling the people, broadcasting from empty studios. It's not the real thing anymore, there's no one there. Here, we have fun, one to one."

For four decades, Sidney, a bit of a loner who has never married ("I'm married to radio—less interference"), has lived on WLNG. He's grown warmer and larger in the way radio people do, yet always sounds like a kid who cannot believe he has been permitted to speak on the radio. He looks like a guy who sits up at the front desk at the diner, spiking the sales checks, rarely rising from the chair, always ready with an opinion on the president, the war, the weather, the ball club. He looks even more Brooklyn than he sounds, unruly remnants of his sandy hair standing every which way on his smooth scalp, his pants in need of hitching up, his billowing Hawaiian shirts almost as loud as he is on the air.

Sidney flies through an hour on the radio like a Broadway dancer, each step following the last in moves so practiced, it would look awkward for them to cease. With less than a minute before the news, Sidney, in the bus with an unsynchronized clock and no direct phone connection to the main studio, talks up to the top of the hour. "Ah those oldies. Back in a few minutes. We've had such bad news, hope this is good news coming. WLNG, Sag Harbor." At that second, the CNN headlines kick in. Sidney hits it on the mark. David Cone, the baseball pitcher, once watched Sidney handle a remote broadcast from a car dealership and asked how the deejay hit his cues so precisely.

"Hey, a pitched ball, how do you do that?" Sidney replied. "I have a feel for when it's coming. I close my eyes and talk."

The station pays next to nothing, ads can be had for a song, but the deejays stay forever. Chuck Mackin, the overnight man, has been on

LNG for more than twenty years; Rusty Potz, the bell-clanging after-noon jock, for more than three decades. Sidney himself arrived in 1964 and worked his way up, finally buying WLNG in 1992. There are those in the industry who say the LNG deejays stay because, as one New York City jock put it, "they are unemployable anywhere else, every last one of them." But in fact, several have turned down work elsewhere, and a couple have gone to other, larger stations and re-turned to LNG for the stability and the lifestyle, for the freedom to do anything they please on the air. And yes, some didn't make it in the big city.

"Sometimes, when I'm not on the air, I freeze up," Sidney tells me. He's feeling a bit guilty about having had me interview him on the air, but he's not sorry: he knows himself only too well. He punches up a song and flips off the mike, and suddenly he is nervous, cautious, eyes darting about. A hitch creeps into his voice. With a sheepish grin, he says, "I'm better when I have a hot mike."

Sidney closes his eyes and thinks about the only other place where he is truly comfortable. There is a wooden bench outside the Variety five-and-dime store on Main Street in Sag Harbor, and that's where I go at night when I want to find Paul Sidney.

He talks about that place. "I sit there on the bench and find out everything that's going on. People stop and talk. Or I just listen. I've always wanted to do a show from the bench on Main Street. I once did an anywhere-everywhere remote—we just landed anywhere, went into places with a wireless microphone. A party in the woods in East Hampton where people were touch dancing. People loved it. But the bench would be the best place. It's quiet, but everyone passes by there."

Remotes take Sidney into other people's lives. Remotes build the expectation that if something important happens, WLNG will be there. Sidney was broadcasting from a carnival in Jamesport one day, interviewing firemen when they suddenly scrambled to leave. On in-stinct, Sidney followed them, and in a few minutes found himself in Moriches, at the crash of TWA Flight 800, the mysterious disaster that struck off Long Island in 1996. WLNG stayed on the air all night from the investigation site, taking calls from listeners who described watching the plane turn into a fireball and drop into the sea. The result was riveting radio, a community pulling together on the air.

Much of what airs on WLNG is not riveting. The newscasts sound like a recitation of the police blotter; the newsman reads off the full addresses of all nine Dairy Barn stores robbed by John Muller of Ronkonkoma in a weeklong spree. The morning death announcements include not only the names of the deceased but the time and location of the funerals and the details about when families will receive visitors.

This is the ultimate small-town station, and for many years, it was the only sound around. "When I moved here in '56, there was no radio station," says Dan Rattiner, who started his weekly newspaper, *Dan's Papers,* in the Hamptons four decades ago. "You could get a couple of New York City stations, very scratchy, and something from Connecticut. Paul came in and just kept doing what he does. It's weird, but people know LNG will be there. When hurricanes come through, the water washes over the dock out behind the station and into the studios and Paul is up to his knees in water, and everybody listening knows he is risking everything for them. And the rest of the time, you take it for granted. You hear it on in a store and it's comforting: I hear some song that reminds me of some girl I danced with and it's a private thing. I don't tune to it particularly; I'm just glad it's there."

People who live within reach of the WLNG transmitter share an insider's smile as Sidney creates a fantasy of a bustling, big station with the world's largest collection of jingles and a bulging roster of sponsors that advertise in a person-to-person style that went out of fashion half a century ago. People buy into Sidney's make-believe because it allows them to think of the place where they live as a collection of people who listen to the same old songs, care about each other's lost cats and dying grandmothers, and hang out at the same all-you-can-eat shrimp dinners. "Big sound, big staff, over three hundred people bringing you the music—well, between twenty-five and thirty, anyway, to bring you the big sound on the Sound," Sidney booms one afternoon.

The music changes hardly at all from year to year, the voices on the commercials are the same shopkeepers who've been selling on WLNG for most of the lives of most listeners. Is anybody listening? The village police log is littered with crimes solved because someone heard a description of a hit-and-run driver or a shoplifter on LNG's police report.

In the villages of Long Island's East End, WLNG and Paul Sidney are part of the aural wallpaper, along with the traffic on the Montauk Highway, the ocean waves, and the call of the gulls.[2] The station doesn't sound slick, doesn't even sound particularly professional. But something about that sound is compelling even to people who don't live on Long Island. Of 816 oldies stations around the world featured

PAUL SIDNEY ON WLNG'S BUS, DOING A REMOTE BROADCAST IN 2004 *(Courtesy WLNG)*

on the Internet radio site Live 365, WLNG, one of the smallest stations in the directory, ranked #7.

"Do we bomb? Absolutely," Sidney says. "But the people who tell you it's so awful, so many ads, you talk too much, well, they must be listening or how would they know? We're successful because everything the consultants say to do, I do the opposite. I don't narrowcast anything. Everybody likes Tony Bennett. You play 'I Left My Heart in San Francisco,' then play Billy Joel. Why is that so bad?"

For a society to work, Edmund Burke said, its people must recognize what it is they have in common. Those bonds can be big concepts such as liberty and democracy, but they can also be small things, single voices that remind us of who we are and what we care about.

Out on Main Street, on Paul Sidney's bench, the sun has set and the air grows chilly. A few people are out for after-dinner strolls, and they pass by the balding guy with his arms sprawled over the back of the bench. Almost invariably, they stop to ask Sidney what's going on. They listen to him; he's part of their daily routine. They feel they know him. He runs the only station on the radio that sounds like this place, and whether they like his show or not, the mere fact that they listen makes them part of this place too, and that is a richness beyond words.

ACKNOWLEDGMENTS

THIS BOOK IS the product of a passion that stretches back to sixth grade at the elegantly named P.S. 9 at J.H.S. 141 in the Bronx, where Charlie Varon, Mickey Richards, and I produced live coverage of the mini-riots that took place after school on the hill on West 237th Street. Equipped with our bulky new cassette recorders and a solid command of every cliché of broadcast newswriting we'd ever heard on New York's all-news outlets, we narrated the hair pulling and body checks for our own private station, WRIV. We were in love with the sounds of our own voices, and with the idea that we could tell stories, even if no one else was listening.

Other voices carried me through adolescence and beyond. I spent too many nights drifting off to the sounds of Long John Nebel, Barry Farber, and Bill Watson, and countless hours studying under the tutelage of Bob and Ray, Don Imus, George Michael, Bob Grant, Robert Lurtsema, and the Scooter, Phil Rizzuto. I tip my antenna to all of them, and to China Valles and Neil Rogers in Miami, Jon Miller in Baltimore, and the late Jerry Washington and Dennis Owens in Washington.

At the WBAI church in New York, Marty Goldensohn, Celeste Wesson, and Peggy Farber taught a radio rookie how to splice tape and tell stories. At WPRB in Princeton, John Shyer and Rob Forman were my teachers; the cast on my all-night *Magic of Radio* program— Alex Wolff, David Remnick, and Jason Meyer, as well as Gus Gil, Roger Mendes, and Joe Valentine—helped keep dawn at bay. Garth Ancier introduced me to the wider world of radio through his *Focus on*

Youth program, which turned out to be perfect training for a nascent media mogul.

I thank these editors who helped shape the book by commissioning pieces for their magazines and newspapers: Rem Rieder at *American Journalism Review,* Jacob Weisberg at *Slate,* and John Pancake, Peter Kaufman, Mike Cavna, Steve Mufson, and Tom Shroder at *The Washington Post.*

My editors at the *Post,* Jo-Ann Armao, Bob Barnes, Bob McCartney, and R. B. Brenner, were generous with their patience and support. I thank Len Downie, Steve Coll, and Phil Bennett for running the *Post* on the theory that a great newspaper will generate worthy books—and vice versa. In the Style section, where David Von Drehle humored my obsession and let me write the paper's radio column, I was lucky to have Janet Duckworth, Deb Heard, and Joel Garreau as editors. Frank Ahrens, my successor on the column, always shared his reporting and ideas.

Radio researchers and historians who generously opened their archives and insights to me included Dick Fatherley, Peter Kanze, Alan Sniffen, and Carolyn Travis.

Mike Freedman was kind to take me in as a visiting scholar at George Washington University, where Al May was my gracious host at the School of Media and Public Affairs. At Princeton University, Carol Rigolot, David Kasunic, and the staff of the Council of the Humanities made me feel very much at home during my time as Ferris Professor of Journalism. At the University of Maryland's invaluable Library of American Broadcasting, special thanks to Michael Henry for digging out relevant materials and giving me a base of operations. The Museum of Radio and Television in New York showed me hospitality as well.

My agent, Amanda Urban, adopted the initial idea for this book more than a decade ago and kept at me with her dynamic enthusiasm until the right structure evolved. At Random House, my first editor, Jonathan Karp, pushed me to reach beyond the obvious story; his successor, Jonathan Jao, helped to hone and polish the manuscript. I appreciate production editor Beth Pearson's dedication to the best possible presentation.

I wrote part of this book during a difficult passage in our family's journey, and our many friends demonstrated a love and devotion that can never be repaid. I especially thank Joel Achenbach and Mary Stapp, Nancy and Lanny Breuer, Jill and Dick Meyer, Laurie Davis and Joe Sellers, Nick and Hortensia Goodman, Cynthia Hogan and Mark Katz, Sherry Sprague and Gary Guzy, and Sue Turner.

My soul mate in all things radio and beyond, Charlie Varon, knows the roots of nearly every sentence in this volume; we have each other's books in our heads. He, Steve Reiss, and Christopher Sterling, a stellar historian of radio at George Washington University, read drafts of the book and made it better.

My parents, Helene and Harwood Fisher, taught me to listen to the world around me for meaning, purpose, and pleasure. They are present in every chapter.

I cannot conceive of a greater love than that of my wife, Jody, my first and most valued reader on every write-through. We are blessed with two children whose minds I admire, whose humor tickles me no end, and whose spirit lifts me at every turn. This book is for Aaron and Julia, who know that listening well is the path to one's own voice.

BIBLIOGRAPHY

Aᴌᴌ ǫᴜᴏᴛᴀᴛɪᴏɴꜱ ᴀʀᴇ ꜰʀᴏᴍ ɪɴᴛᴇʀᴠɪᴇᴡꜱ by the author except as indicated in the endnotes. Almost all of the interviews listed below were conducted expressly for this book; a handful were part of my reporting for articles published in *The Washington Post* or *American Journalism Review.*

The passage in Chapter 10 on Garrison Keillor previously appeared in different form in an article in *The Washington Post.*

INTERVIEWS

Abrams, Lee, Washington, D.C.

Adams, Bill, Rosslyn, Va.

Allan, Steve, Rockville, Md.

Allen, Randy, Alexandria, Va.

Armstrong, Bill, phone.

Beck, Glenn, Washington, D.C.,
  and phone.

Bell, Art, Pahrump, Nev.

Bennis, Warren, phone.

Boyce, Phil, New York City.

Breen, Julian, New York City.

Cohen, Arthur, Shirlington, Va.

Coleman, Milton, Washington, D.C.

Connell, Bud, phone.

Cooke, Holland, phone and e-mail.

Curtis, Craig, Shirlington, Va.

Dees, Rick, Burbank, Calif.

Dennis, George, New York City.

DeVany, Dan, Shirlington, Va.

Donahue, Rachael, phone and e-mail.

Elshami, Nadeam, e-mail.

Falise, Frank, Bethesda, Md.

Farley, Jim, Washington, D.C.

Fass, Bob, New York City.

Fatherley, Richard, phone.

Fax, Jesse, Kettering, Md.

Flatow, Ira, phone.

Freedman, Michael, Washington, D.C.

Gales Webb, Jacquie, Washington, D.C.

Gallaher, Eddie, Silver Spring, Md.

Geronimo, Don, Fairfax, Va.

Giovannoni, David, Washington, D.C.

Glass, Ira, Chicago and Princeton, N.J.

Hagen, Don, Washington, D.C.

Hancock, Hunter, Los Angeles.

Harvey, Paul, Chicago.

Harwell, Ernie, Tiger Stadium, Detroit,
  and Washington, D.C.

Hollander, Cynthia, Rockville, Md.

Holliday, Johnny, Chevy Chase, Md.

Hughes, Cathy, Washington, D.C.

Jackson, Bruce, phone.

Jackson, Hal, New York City.

Josephson, Larry, New York City.

Kalish, Jon, phone.

Kanze, Peter, White Plains, N.Y.

Keillor, Garrison, phone and Austin, Tex.

Klose, Kevin, Washington, D.C.

Kurman, David, phone.

Labunski, Steve, New York City.

Levey, Bob, Washington, D.C.

Leyden, Andrew, Washington, D.C.

Leykis, Tom, Los Angeles and Vancouver.

Liggins, Alfred, Washington, D.C., and
   Lanham, Md.

Limbaugh, Rush, phone and e-mail.

Litzinger, Sam, Washington, D.C., and
   phone and e-mail.

Love, Justine, Lanham, Md.

Lurtsema, Robert J., Los Angeles.

Meyer, Jason, phone.

Meyer, Ruth, phone.

Michael, George, Washington, D.C.

Miller, Jon, San Francisco and Baltimore.

Millspaugh, Frank, New York City.

Morrow, Bruce, New York City.

Moudy, Dale, phone.

Mueller, Ken, New York City.

Nebel, Long John, New York City
   (with Charlie Varon).

Nnamdi, Kojo, Washington, D.C.

Owens, Dennis, Washington, D.C.

Parr, Russ, Lanham, Md.

Post, Steve, New York City.

Rattiner, Dan, phone.

Ronneburger, Sue, New York City.

Rothman, Mark, phone.

Sabo, Walter, phone, New York City.

Schoberg, Tommy, Bethesda, Md.

Scott, Pat, Washington, D.C.

Scott, Willard, Washington, D.C.

Segal, David, phone.

Seymour, Ruth, Santa Monica, Calif.

Shearer, Harry, Santa Monica, Calif.

Sidney, Paul, Sag Harbor, N.Y.

Siegel, Robert, Washington, D.C.

Siemering, Bill, Washington, D.C., and
   e-mail and phone.

Siggelkow, Richard, phone.

Simone, Mark, phone.

Slade, Jim, e-mail.

Slowes, Charlie, Viera, Fla., and
   Washington, D.C.

Smith, Ed, phone.

Sniffen, Allan, New York City.

Spivak, Joel, Washington, D.C.

Travis, Carolyn, Washington, D.C.

Tridish, Pete, Madison, Wisc.

Walker, Ed, Washington, D.C.

West, Randy, phone.

Wilson, Brian, Baltimore, Md.

Zier, Bennett, Silver Spring, Md.

BOOKS

Bain, Donald, *The Control of Candy Jones,* Playboy Press, 1976.

———, *Long John Nebel,* Macmillan, 1974.

Barlow, William, *Voice Over: The Making of Black Radio,* Temple University Press, 1998.

Barnouw, Erik, *A Tower in Babel: History of Broadcasting in the United States, to 1933,* Oxford University Press, 1966.

———, *The Golden Web: A History of Broadcasting in the United States, 1933–1953,* Oxford University Press, 1968.

———, *The Image Empire: A History of Broadcasting in the United States, from 1953,* Oxford University Press, 1970.

Bergmann, Eugene, *Excelsior, You Fathead!,* Applause Theatre and Cinema Books, 2004.

Boorstin, Daniel, *The Image,* Vintage, 1961.

Brewster, Bill, and Frank Broughton, *Last Night a DJ Saved My Life: The History of the Disc Jockey,* Grove Press, 2000.

Cantor, Louis, *Wheelin' on Beale,* Pharos, 1992.

Cantril, Hadley, and Gordon Allport, *The Psychology of Radio,* Ayer Company, 1986 reprint of Harper & Brothers edition, 1935.

Colford, Paul, *Howard Stern: King of All Media,* St. Martin's Press, 1996.

Conan, Neal, *Play by Play: Baseball, Radio and Life in the Last Chance League,* Crown, 2002.

Dawidoff, Nicholas, *In the Country of Country,* Pantheon, 1997.

Delong, Thomas, *The Mighty Music Box,* Amber Crest Books, 1980.

Douglas, Susan, *Listening In: Radio and the American Imagination,* Times Books, 2000.

Eberly, Philip, *Music in the Air,* Hastings House, 1982.

Elliott, Bob, and Ray Goulding, *Write If You Get Work: The Best of Bob and Ray,* Random House, 1975.

Fisher, David, and Marshall Jon Fisher, *Tube: The Invention of Television,* Counterpoint, 1996.

Flammang, James, *100 Years of the American Auto,* Publications International, 1999.

Fong-Torres, Ben, *The Hits Just Keep On Coming,* Miller Freeman Books, 1999.

Fornatale, Peter, and Joshua Mills, *Radio in the Television Age,* Viking, 1980.

Fowler, Gene, and Bob Crawford, *Border Radio,* University of Texas Press, 2002.

Gabler, Neal, *Life: The Movie,* Knopf, 1998.

Gitlin, Todd, *The Sixties: Years of Hope, Days of Rage,* Bantam Books, 1987.

Harper, Laurie, *Don Sherwood: The Life and Times of the World's Greatest Disk Jockey,* Writers Club Press, 1989.

Hilmes, Michele, and Jason Loviglio (eds.), *Radio Reader: Essays in the Cultural History of Radio,* Routledge, 2001.

Hoffman, Abbie, *Soon to Be a Major Motion Picture,* Perigee Books, 1980.

Jackson, Hal, *The House That Jack Built,* Amistad Press, 2001.

Jackson, John, *Big Beat Heat: Alan Freed and the Early Years of Rock & Roll,* Schirmer Books, 2000.

Jezer, Marty, *Abbie Hoffman: American Rebel,* Rutgers University Press, 1992.

Kaiser, Charles, *1968 in America: Music, Politics, Chaos, Counterculture, and the Shaping of a Generation,* Weidenfeld & Nicolson, 1988.

Keith, Michael, *Talking Radio: An Oral History of American Radio in the Television Age,* M. E. Sharpe, 2000.

———, *Voices in the Purple Haze,* Praeger, 1997.

Kerouac, Jack, *On the Road,* Signet, 1957.

Ladd, Jim, *Radio Waves: Life and Revolution on the FM Dial,* St. Martin's Press, 1991.

Laufer, Peter, *Inside Talk Radio: America's Voice or Just Hot Air?* Birch Lane Press, 1995.

Lazarsfeld, Paul, and Frank Stanton (eds.), *Radio Research 1941,* Duell, Sloan and Pearce, 1941.

Limbaugh, Rush, *The Way Things Ought to Be,* Pocket Books, 1992.

McLuhan, Marshall, *Understanding Media,* Mentor, 1964.

———, and Quintin Fiore, *The Medium Is the Massage,* Bantam, 1967.

McNeill, Don, *Moving Through Here,* Alfred A. Knopf, 1970.

Mendelsohn, Harold, *Mass Entertainment,* College and University Press, 1966.

Miller, James, *Flowers in the Dustbin: The Rise of Rock and Roll, 1947–1977,* Fireside, 2000.

———, *Democracy Is in the Streets,* Simon and Schuster, 1987.

Minor, Dale, *The Information War,* Hawthorn Books, 1970.

Morrow, Bruce, *Cousin Brucie: My Life in Rock 'n' Roll,* Beech Tree Books, 1987.

Neer, Richard, *FM: The Rise and Fall of Rock Radio,* Villard, 2001.

Passman, Arnold, *The Deejays,* Macmillan, 1971.

Peck, Abe, *Uncovering the Sixties: The Life and Times of the Underground Press,* Pantheon, 1985.

Pollak, Richard (ed.), *Stop the Presses, I Want to Get Off!* Random House, 1975.

Post, Steve, *Playing in the FM Band*, Viking Press, 1974.

Postman, Neil, *Amusing Ourselves to Death: Public Discourse in the Age of Show Business*, Viking, 1986.

Putnam, Robert, *Bowling Alone*, Touchstone, 2000.

Schiffer, Michael, *The Portable Radio in American Life*, University of Arizona Press, 1991.

Shepherd, Jean, *Wanda Hickey's Night of Golden Memories and Other Disasters*, Doubleday, 1976 (reissue).

———, *In God We Trust: All Others Pay Cash*, Doubleday, 1966.

———, *The Ferrari in the Bedroom*, Doubleday, 1991 (reissue).

Sklar, Rick, *Rocking America*, St. Martin's Press, 1984.

Sloman, Larry, *Steal This Dream: Abbie Hoffman and the Countercultural Revolution in America*, Doubleday, 1998.

Smith, Wes, *The Pied Pipers of Rock 'n' Roll*, Longstreet Press, 1989.

Smulyan, Susan, *Selling Radio: The Commercialization of American Broadcasting, 1920–1934*, Smithsonian Institution Press, 1994.

Stokes, Geoffrey (ed.), *The Village Voice Anthology (1956–1980)*, William Morrow and Company, 1982.

Thompson, Hunter S., *Kingdom of Fear: Loathsome Secrets of a Star-Crossed Child in the Final Days of the American Century*, Simon and Schuster, 2003.

U.S. House of Representatives, 86th Congress, Second Session, *Responsibilities of Broadcasting Licensees and Station Personnel*, Hearings on Payola and Other Deceptive Practices, Subcommittee of the Committee on Interstate and Foreign Commerce, Jan.–Aug., 1960. Government Printing Office, 1960.

Viorst, Milton, *Fire in the Streets: America in the 1960s*, Simon and Schuster, 1979.

Walker, Jesse, *Rebels on the Air: An Alternative History of Radio in America*, New York University Press, 2001.

ARTICLES AND DISSERTATIONS

Abrams, Lee, memos to programming staff, XM Satellite Radio, 2000–2003.

Ahrens, Frank, "Why Radio Stinks," *Washington Post Magazine*, Jan. 19, 2003.

Balliett, Whitney, "Their Own Gravity," *New Yorker*, Sept. 24, 1973.

Behrens, Steve, "Jazzcasters Try Music Testing to Pick Cuts," *Current*, Sept. 2, 1996.

Blackburn, Dick, "Dee Jay Jive-O-Rama," www.wfmu.org/LCD/21/djjive.html.

Blackwell, M. I., "And Radio Was Never the Same Again," *Dallas Morning News,* Sept. 21, 1986, 1C.

Brady, Al, "Comments," www.musicradio77.com/albrady.html.

Braudy, Susan, "A Radio Station with Real Hair, Sweat and Body Odor," *New York Times Magazine,* Sept. 17, 1972, 10–11, 53–58.

Chen, Christine, "The Bad Boys of Radio," *Fortune,* March 3, 2003, pp. 118+.

Coleman, Jon, "Oldies Insights Winter 2003: Is Newer Music Helping or Hurting?" Coleman Music, www.colemaninsights.com

Conciatore, Jacqueline, "Radio Sharpens Formats to Keep CPB Grants," *Current,* March 17, 1997, 1.

Connell, Bud, "The Radio Generation and the Origin of Top 40," www.broadcast.net/pipermail/broadcast-airchex/2001-December/041786.html.

Corliss, Richard, "That Old Feeling: Shepherd and His Flock," *Time,* July 22, 2001.

Donahue, Tom, "A Rotting Corpse, Stinking Up the Airwaves," *Rolling Stone,* Nov. 23, 1967, pp. 14+.

Fatherley, Richard, "Radio's Revolution and the World's Happiest Broadcasters" (book in progress).

"F.C.C. Warning on Drug Lyrics Brings Sharp Reaction," *New York Times,* April 11, 1971, 50.

Fraser, C. Gerald, "Occupation at WBAI-FM Ended with Arrest of Five for Contempt," *New York Times,* March 19, 1977, 34.

———, "WBAI Head Says Takeover Recalls 60's 'Commune,'" *New York Times,* Feb. 22, 1977, 62.

Future of Music Coalition, "Radio Deregulation," Washington, D.C., Nov. 2002.

Giovannoni, David, "Programming Defines Community," speech, Sept. 18, 1998, www.aranet.com.

Grossman, Edward, "Jean Shepherd: Radio's Noble Savage," *Harper's,* Jan. 1966.

Hall, Claude, "Requiem for a Heavyweight," *Billboard,* Oct. 28, 1967.

Hardy, Charles, III, "Authoring in Sound: An Eccentric Essay on Aural History, Radio and Media Convergence," West Chester University, Jan. 1999.

Harrington, Richard, "WHFS: The End of the Rainbow," *Washington Post,* Jan. 16, 1983, G1.

Hentoff, Nat, "All That Jazz—Where Did It Go?" *Wall Street Journal,* Sept. 25, 2002.

Hill, Lewis, "The Theory of Listener-Sponsored Radio," 1951, www.hourwolf.com/listenersponsored.html.

Janssen, Mike, "Triple-A Strikes Chord with Disenchanted Listeners," *Current*, Jan. 27, 2003, 1.

Johnson, Lawrence, "WKAT's Style Has Classical Fans Howling," *Sun-Sentinel* (Fort Lauderdale, Fla.), Oct. 20, 2002, 1G.

————, "A Year Later, Classical Station Aims Higher," *Sun-Sentinel*, Sept. 7, 2003, 1G.

Josephson, Larry, and David Giovannoni, "Picasso vs. Giovannoni," *Current*, June 17, 1996.

Kaye, Bob, "The Story of 'I, Libertine,' " www.bobkaye.com/ilibertine.html.

"King of Giveaway," *Time*, June 4, 1955, p. 100.

Koch, Christopher, "Pacifica," 1968, www.radio4all.org/fp/koch.txt.

Krasnow, Erwin, "The Public Interest Standard: The Elusive Search for the Holy Grail," Advisory Committee on Public Interest Obligations of Digital Television Broadcasters, Oct. 22, 1997, www.ntia.doc.gov/pubintadvcom/octmtg/krasnow.htm.

Land, Herman, "The Storz Bombshell," *Television*, May 1957.

Lee, Jennifer, "On Minot, N.D., Radio, a Single Corporate Voice," *New York Times*, March 31, 2003, C7.

MacFarland, David, "The Development of the Top 40 Radio Format," dissertation, University of Wisconsin, 1972.

Mailer, Norman, "The White Negro," *Dissent*, Summer 1957.

Mann, Charles C., "The Resurrection of Indie Radio," *Wired*, March 2005, 103.

Mathews, Anna Wilde, "From a Distance: A Giant Radio Chain Is Perfecting the Art of Seeming Local," *Wall Street Journal*, Feb. 25, 2002, A1.

Maxwell, Cyndee, "Creativity Is a Way of Life for Brutus," *Radio and Records*, Jan. 10, 1997, 70.

Mayeux, Peter, "Todd Storz: New Dimensions of a Radio Pioneer's Influence," University of Nebraska–Lincoln, 2001.

Mayor, Alfred, "Radio Free New York," *Atlantic*, May 1968.

McBride, Sarah, "As Sponsorship Sales Blossom, Public Radio Walks a Fine Line," *Wall Street Journal*, March 17, 2006, A1.

McClay, Bob, "Murray the K on WOR-FM: They Screwed It Up," *Rolling Stone*, Nov. 9, 1967, 10.

McFadden, Robert, "Insurgent Staff Members Take Over WBAI in a Coup," *New York Times*, Feb. 12, 1977, 1, 44.

Morgan, Thomas, "Station Break: WOL and the Sound of Change," *Washington Post*, Dec. 9, 1980, B1.

Newsome, Melba, "Radio Activist," *Los Angeles Magazine*, July 1998, 50.

Philips, Chuck, "Clear Channel's Radio Pacts Irk Labels," *Los Angeles Times,* Sept. 5, 2002.

Phillips, McCandlish, "400 Hold a Wake for Radio Cult," *New York Times,* Aug. 13, 1956.

Rashbaum, William, "Police Kill Man They Say Had Just Killed Another," *New York Times,* May 2, 2003, B3.

Raz, Guy, "Radio Free Georgetown," *Washington City Paper,* Jan. 29, 1999.

Remnick, David, "The Accidental Anarchist," *New Yorker,* March 10, 1997, 56+.

Rivera-Sanchez, Milagros, "How Far Is Too Far? The Line Between 'Offensive' and 'Indecent' Speech," Indiana University Law School, www.law.indiana .edu/rivera-s.html.

Russell, Ron, "KCRW's Fiery Radio Warrior," *Los Angeles Times,* May 21, 1995, A1.

Rutenberg, Jim, "Fewer Media Owners, More Media Choices," *New York Times,* Dec. 2, 2002, C1.

Sand, Jay, "The Radio Waves Unnameable," senior thesis in American history, University of Pennsylvania, Nov. 26, 1995, www.wbaifree.org/fass/index .html#toc.

Schwartz, John, and Geraldine Fabrikant, "War Puts Radio Giant on the Defensive," *New York Times,* March 31, 2003, C1.

Sculatti, Gene, "Jazzbo on the Radio: Lives of the Hipster Saints," www.wfmu .org/LCD/20/jazzbo.html.

Shanley, J. P., "Night People's Friend," *New York Times,* Aug. 19, 1956.

Shepherd, Jean, "The Night People vs. Creeping Meatballism," *Mad,* March–April 1957.

Siemering, William, "Public Broadcasting: Some Essential Ingredients," Educational/Instructional Broadcasting, Nov. 1969.

———, "The Air Waves Belong to the People: A Report on the WBFO Satellite Project in the Nonwhite Community of Buffalo, N.Y.," Corporation for Public Broadcasting, Jan. 1971.

———, "Some Things to Consider About Audience Building," paper for NPR Audience Building Task Force, 1986.

Smith, R. J., "Radio Head," *Los Angeles Magazine,* Dec. 1, 2002, 98.

Sniffen, Allan, numerous articles and essays on www.musicradio77.com.

Steinberg, Jacques, "Money Changes Everything," *New York Times,* March 19, 2006.

Stevens, Joann, "WHUR Rocks with More Than Sweet Music," *Washington Post,* Aug. 16, 1979, DC1.

Trescott, Jacqueline, "Changing Their Tunes," *Washington Post,* Dec. 27, 1984, B1.

"Tucson Radio Making Waves," *Tucson Citizen,* May 3, 2002.

Weigle, Ed, "Porky Chedwick: Radio's Most Ignored Pioneer," www.440int .com.

RECORDINGS, FILMS, AND WEBSITES

www.440int.com, website featuring histories of radio disc jockeys and stations.

www.amandfmmorningside.com/splash.html, tribute site for WPGC Washington.

www.bossradioforever.com, devoted to KHJ Los Angeles and Drake radio stations.

www.famous56.com, tribute site for WFIL Philadelphia.

www.flicklives.com, detailing the history of Jean Shepherd's radio programs and other creations.

www.keener13.com, tribute site for WKNR in Detroit.

www.keener13.com/history/keener_kills_paul.htm, on WKNR and the beginning of the Paul Is Dead rumors.

www.manfrommars.com, archive of airchecks.

www.musicradio77.com, tribute site for WABC New York.

www.musicradiowls.musicpage.com, tribute site for WLS Chicago.

www.ncf.ca/beatles/trivia.html, Ottawa Beatles site, with airchecks of original Paul Is Dead documentary on WKNR-FM.

www.nitecaps.org, history of Herb Jepko's *Nitecaps* program on KSL Salt Lake City.

www.radio411.com/tributes.htm, a listing of radio station tribute sites.

http://radio-info.com/format/, archive of airchecks of station format changes.

www.radiothrills.com/jive95, history of KSAN and KMPX in San Francisco.

www.reelradio.com, vast collection of airchecks from throughout the Top 40 era.

Cruisin', series of discs featuring radio deejays and the music they played, K-Tel Records, 1990–95.

Eszterhas, Joe, *Telling Lies in America* (film), 1997.

Fatherley, Richard, *Radio's Revolution and the World's Happiest Broadcasters* (radio program), 1998.

Gales Webb, Jacquie, and Wesley Horner, *Black Radio: Telling It Like It Was* (radio documentary series), Radio Smithsonian, 1995.

Giovannoni, David, "Programming Defines Community," "Know the Audience," and other papers and speeches, 1998–2002, Audience Research Analysis, www.aranet.com.

The Golden Age of Underground Radio, DCC Compact Classics, 1989.

Hancock, Hunter, radio programs, 1951, Museum of Radio and Television, New York.

Lockwood, Roy, *Jamboree* (film), 1957.

Lucas, George, *American Graffiti* (film), 1973.

Scott, Willard, and Ed Walker, *Joy Boys* radio shows, 1965 recordings in Library of Congress, Recorded Sound Division, and various recordings, private collection of Greg Patenaude, Washington, D.C.

Shearer, Harry, *A Voice in the Night: A Tribute to Jean Shepherd* (radio program), www.kcrw.org/specials/JeanShepherd.html, 2000.

Shepherd, Jean, various airchecks of radio shows, catalogue at http://www .keyflux.com/shep/info.htm

Travis, Carolyn, *Rock Radio Revolution* (video), Travisty Productions, 2000.

——, *Rock Jocks: The FM Revolution* (video), Travisty Productions, 2003, and outtakes of interviews for that video, provided courtesy of Carolyn Travis.

NOTES

SIGN-ON: *THE MAGIC OF RADIO*

1. White, "Battle of the Century."
2. Eberly, *Music in the Air*, 34.
3. Keith, *Talking Radio*, 3.
4. Douglas, *Listening In*, 24.
5. Postman, *Amusing Ourselves*, 18.
6. Lee Abrams, memo to staff, Sept. 7, 2000.

CHAPTER 1: *OMAHA MORNING*

1. MacFarland, "Development," 158.
2. Fatherley, "Radio's Revolution," 7.
3. Ibid., 286.
4. The suits in New York wouldn't realize this till much later; not until 1956 did a report written for NBC, "Future of Radio," note the "paradox that the less people pay attention to radio, the more useful it becomes." Quoted in *Broadcasting*, Jan. 16, 1956, 86.
5. Land, "The Storz Bombshell," 3–4.
6. Miller, *Flowers*, 55.
7. Mendelsohn, *Mass Entertainment*, 88.
8. Land, "The Storz Bombshell," 4.
9. Miller, *Flowers*, 55.
10. Eberly, *Music in the Air*, 270.
11. Ibid., 76.
12. Barnouw, *A Tower in Babel*, 217.
13. Eberly, *Music in the Air*, 273.
14. Land, "The Storz Bombshell," 4.
15. Eberly, *Music in the Air*, 175.
16. "King of Giveaway," *Time*.
17. Fatherley, "Radio's Revolution."

18. Ibid.
19. Quoted in Travis, "Rock Radio Revolution."
20. MacFarland, "Development," 206–9.
21. Blackwell, "And Radio Was," 1C.
22. A most public expression of radio's hold over the popular imagination came each summer when the sounds of baseball wafted over city streets. In Brooklyn in the 1940s, Red Barber's voice echoed from shops, houses, and cars. In Pittsburgh, virtually everyone could perform Rosey Rosewell's home run call along with the Pirates announcer: "Open the window, Aunt Minnie, here it comes!" Which he followed with a sound effect of shattering glass. In the Midwest, Jack Buck's Cardinals coverage on St. Louis's KMOX from 1954 to 2001 became such a constant of summer life that when Buck's casket was placed in Busch Stadium on a June afternoon in 2002, thousands of fans waited up to five hours for the chance to doff their caps to the man who had taken them to distant ball-parks for so many years.
23. Eberly, *Music in the Air*, 207.
24. MacFarland, "Development," 405.
25. Fornatale and Mills, *Radio*, 27.
26. *Broadcasting*, April 14, 1958.
27. Quoted in MacFarland, "Development," 245.
28. Quoted in ibid., 271. Speech delivered Sept. 6, 1962.
29. Kerouac, *On the Road*, 148.

CHAPTER 2: *HARLEM MATINEE*

1. Mailer, "The White Negro."
2. Hancock died in 2004 in Claremont, California.
3. Cooper story based on Barlow, *Voice Over*, 50–56.
4. "The Jives of Doctor Hepcat" can be purchased from Antone's Records, 2928 Guadalupe, Austin, TX, 78705, phone 512-322-0660.
5. Cantor, *Wheelin' on Beale*, 19.
6. Ibid., 12.
7. Ibid., 87.
8. Ibid., 5.
9. Ibid., 82.
10. Travis, *Rock Radio*.
11. Miller, *Flowers*, 72.

12. The Haley tune got a big boost from its role in the opening scene of the movie *Blackboard Jungle,* in which a teacher brings his cherished collection of jazz 78s into class, only to have the kids fling them across the room, trashing them, while the movie soundtrack transitions into their weapon—rock and roll. "A drama of teenage terror!" the movie publicity shouted. "They turned a school into a jungle!" Miller, *Flowers,* 88.

13. Eberly, *Music in the Air,* 214.

14. Quoted in ibid., 214. Mitch Miller's path to his tirade is spelled out in Donald Clarke's *The Rise and Fall of Popular Music,* chapter 15, at www.musicweb.uk.net/RiseandFall/15.htm.

15. Filmed statement by council spokesman, in Travis, *Rock Radio.*

16. Jackson, *House,* 95.

17. But radio was not always a force for calm: in the Watts riots in 1965, crowds of blacks who were lighting fire to the city's shops chanted the catchphrase popularized by Los Angeles's top black deejay, Magnificent Montague: "Burn, baby, burn." That same Magnificent Montague crisscrossed the nation in the late 1950s as an agent of integration, pressing for federal action to force Southern states to comply with the Supreme Court ruling integrating public schools.

18. Miller, *Flowers,* 59, 84–85.

CHAPTER 3: *THE TRANSISTOR UNDER THE PILLOW*

1. Sklar, *Rocking America,* 174.

2. Morrow, *Cousin Brucie,* 18.

3. Ibid., 66.

4. Morrow has told this story in several variations. This version is based on my interview with him, as well as the account in his autobiography, *Cousin Brucie,* and the telling in Travis, *Rock Radio.*

5. Schiffer, *Portable Radio,* 174.

6. Ibid., 178.

7. Ibid., 213.

8. Ibid., 213–19. By 1963, no American company was even trying to compete; they had ceded the transistor radio market to the Japanese. Radio proved to be the first step toward Japan's near-total dominance of the U.S. electronics market; Sony exported its first televisions to America in 1960.

9. Morrow, *Cousin Brucie,* 16.

10. Travis, *Rock Radio.*

11. Flammang, *100 Years*, inter alia.

12. MacFarland, "Development," 37.

13. Douglas, *Listening In*, 253.

14. Quoted in MacFarland, "Development," 27.

15. Bud Connell, who worked at various times for both Storz and Gordon McLendon, summed up Top 40's appeal: "The context was always predictable and the content was entirely unpredictable."

16. Ken Nordine, a radio poet and master ad man, quoted in Passman, *The Deejays*, 291.

17. Morrow, *Cousin Brucie*, 64.

18. Ibid., 113.

19. Harper, *Don Sherwood*, 123–29.

20. MacFarland, "Development," 435, 460.

21. WABC's jocks were so popular that they once landed the #14 spot in the ratings—in Pittsburgh, 320 miles away from their station's transmitter.

22. Sklar, in interview on WBAI in New York, August 1984, available at musicradio.computer.net/Sklar.html.

23. Sklar, *Rocking America*, 86.

24. "My targeting plan was to go after everyone," said Rick Sklar, who ran WABC from 1963 to 1977. "I decided to build ratings on a coalition of audiences. I wanted the black urbanite and white suburbanite, the rich and the poor, and everyone in between, the young children, the teenager, the parents, and even the over-49s. I wanted all of them to think of WABC as *their* station." Sklar's formula was deceptively simple: play songs that made both kids and adults feel like they—and they alone— were part of the party, and hire jocks who understood how to blend radio's intimacy with the collective consciousness of a generation— deejays who made you feel they were talking directly to you, even as they made you feel part of the cool crowd. Sklar, *Rocking America*, 92.

25. Ingramisms—these and many more—are collected by many of Ingram's most dedicated fans on the Big Dan Kemosabe message board at musicradio.computer.net.

26. Quoted in MacFarland, "Development," 550–52.

CHAPTER 4: *BOOZE, BROADS, BRIBES, BEATLES*

1. "Few [band]leaders play a song solely because they think it's good," bandleader Artie Shaw said in 1939. "They play it only when a publisher

assures them it will be the firm's #1 tune—the tune the publisher is going to work on and put money behind." Quoted in Lazarsfeld and Stanton, *Radio Research*, 95.

2. Sklar, *Rocking America*, 53.

3. After the payola scandal, Hancock still played records from his own label, but only after getting approval from station management.

4. Testimony of Edward Eicher, convention manager at Americana Hotel, U.S. House of Representatives, *Responsibilities of Broadcasting Licensees*, 235.

5. Fornatale and Mills, *Radio*, 49–52.

6. U.S. House, *Responsibilities*, Feb. 8, 1960, 1–2.

7. Ibid., 6–17.

8. Ibid., 617, 624.

9. Ibid., 9–30. Prescott left radio and moved to Hollywood, where he became an executive in a company that made Saturday morning cartoons for television and animated films.

10. Ibid., 47–53.

11. Ibid., 250.

12. Ibid., 868–70.

13. Ibid., 816.

14. Ibid., 845–65.

15. Ibid., 1013.

16. Travis, *Rock Radio*.

17. Jackson, *House*, 129–57, and interview.

18. *Stinky Shafer Show*, KXOK, 1962, aircheck at www.reelradio.com.

19. Morrow, *Cousin Brucie*, 149.

20. Travis, *Rock Radio*.

21. Morrow, *Cousin Brucie*, 149.

22. Ibid., 157, and interview.

CHAPTER 5: NIGHT PEOPLE

1. Shepherd, Jean, "Remembrance of Things Past," *The Age of Videography*, out-of-print journal, 1996, possibly Shepherd's last published essay before his death. Available in scanned form at www.flicklives.com/Books/videography/videography.htm.

2. Quoted in Bergmann, *Excelsior*, 76.

3. From 1966 broadcast, quoted in ibid., 103.

4. Cantril and Allport, *Psychology of Radio*, 11.

5. McLuhan, *Understanding Media*, 264.

6. From a 1968 TV appearance, quoted in Bergmann, *Excelsior*, 195.

7. Sculatti, "Jazzbo on the Radio," 3.

8. "Hawthorne's fans were hip, smart, alienated people in the context of the repressive, sexually dead Eisenhower miasma," said Larry Josephson, who grew up listening to Hawthorne and later carried his spirit into a new form of radio rebellion on WBAI in New York in the 1960s.

9. Their approach to spoofery lives on in the work of some of their most avid admirers, including Keith Olbermann, David Letterman, and Garrison Keillor.

10. This and other quotations from Shepherd radio programs not otherwise attributed are from airchecks available from Shepherd collectors Max Schmid and Jim Sadur at http://www.keyflux.com/shep/info.htm, or from Shearer, *Voice in the Night*.

11. Quoted in Bergmann, *Excelsior*, 210–11.

12. Quoted in Shearer, *Voice in the Night*.

13. Quoted in Douglas, *Listening In*, 18.

14. Quoted from Shepherd appearance on Long John Nebel show, WOR, January 1968, transcribed by Bob Kaye and cited at www.bobkaye.com/ilibertine.html.

15. Henderson, Carter, "Night People's Hoax on Day People Makes Hit with Book Folks," *Wall Street Journal*, Aug. 1, 1956.

16. Phillips, "400 Hold a Wake for Radio Cult."

17. Shanley, "Night People's Friend."

18. I visited Nebel with Charlie Varon, my comrade in radio studies and a journalist turned playwright and performer.

19. Bergmann, *Excelsior*, 14, 306.

20. Shepherd appears with Mingus on a classic jazz recording, "The Clown," with Shep narrating a piece that smashes all concepts of category.

21. Quoted in Gitlin, *The Sixties*, 56.

22. Quoted in Grossman, "Jean Shepherd."

23. Shepherd, "The Night People."

CHAPTER 6: *THE JINGLE-JANGLE MORNING*

1. FM history sources include Eberly, *Music in the Air*; Douglas, *Listening In*; Barnouw, *Golden Web*; and Schiffer, *Portable Radio*.

2. *McCall's* and *Harper's*, respectively, cited in Douglas, *Listening In*, 265.

3. Fornatale and Mills, *Radio*, 127.

4. The most astonishing leap wouldn't come until the 1970s; the number of FM sets in use skyrocketed from 160 million to 240 million between 1973 and 1976 alone. Eberly, *Music in the Air*, 230.

5. U.S. House, *Responsibilities*, 684–85.

6. Post, *Playing in the FM Band*, 68; Sand, *Radio Waves*; Kaiser, *1968*, 40–41.

7. Post, *Playing in the FM Band*, 13.

8. Koch, "Pacifica," 16.

9. Quoted in Walker, *Rebels*, 45.

10. Koch, "Pacifica," 12–15; Walker, *Rebels*, 65.

11. Quoted in Sand, *Radio Waves*, chapter 7.

12. McNeill, *Moving Through Here*, 13.

13. Ibid., 90–98, 106–9.

14. Sand, *Radio Waves*, chapter 7.

15. Theirs was a mutual admiration society: when Hoffman's son america was born, Fass played Kate Smith's "God Bless America" all through the night. Hoffman, *Soon to Be a Major Motion Picture*, 120.

16. Jezer, *Abbie Hoffman*, 75, 87.

17. Sloman, *Steal This Dream*, 108.

18. Viorst, *Fire*, 431.

19. Sand, *Radio Waves*, chapter 7; Krassner and Fass interviews.

20. From *Radio Unnameable*, Aug. 19, 1969, quoted in Sloman, *Steal This Dream*, 179.

21. Gitlin, *The Sixties*, 428–29.

22. To make the switch from working at a Quaker peace group to announcing at WBAI, Post had to take a salary cut, from $65 a week to $45.

23. Fraser, "WBAI Head"; McFadden, "Insurgent Staff Members."

CHAPTER 7: *NO STATIC AT ALL*

1. Donahue, "Rotting Corpse," 14–15.

2. Aircheck at www.americantop40.com, Dec. 1961 on KYA San Francisco.

3. U.S. House, *Responsibilities*, 1039, 1157.

4. "I believe that music should not be treated as a group of objects to be sorted out like eggs with each category kept rigidly apart from one another," Tom Donahue said. In his *Rolling Stone* manifesto, he wrote, "The

music has matured, the audience has matured, but radio has apparently proven to be a retarded child." *Rolling Stone* founder Jann Wenner had been one of the guys who would hang around at Donahue's place listening to music. When Donahue suggested writing his manifesto, Wenner was only too pleased to publish it (Raechel Donahue, interview).

5. Quotations in this chapter from Raechel Donahue are from my interviews with her or from outtakes of a videotaped interview by Carolyn Travis in 2002. This quotation is from the Travis tapes.

6. Quoted in Eberly, *Music in the Air,* 236.

7. Unless otherwise noted, quotations in this chapter from Tom Donahue are from a radio interview at http://www.radiothrills.com/jive95/kmpx .htm.

8. Fornatale and Mills, *Radio,* 128.

9. Aircheck at http://www.radiothrills.com/jive95/kmpx.htm.

10. Claude Hall, "Requiem for a Heavyweight," *Billboard,* Oct. 28, 1967, and Bob McClay, "Murray the K on WOR-FM: They Screwed It Up," *Rolling Stone,* Nov. 9, 1967, 10.

11. Raechel Donahue, interview.

12. Ibid.

13. Raechel Donahue, Travis tapes.

14. Keith, *Talking Radio,* 124. KMPX's experiment with putting women on the air was copied by a few underground stations around the country, but women did not make significant gains in on-air jobs until after 1971, when the FCC began requiring stations to report on their affirmative action efforts.

15. Raechel Donahue, interview.

16. Gould, *New York Times,* May 20, 1970, quoted in Fornatale and Mills, *Radio,* 130. Gould's observations came a couple of years late—by the time he wrote, underground radio was already starting to die out.

17. Raechel Donahue, Travis tapes.

18. Keith, *Purple Haze,* 146.

19. Quoted in Douglas, *Listening In,* 274.

20. "F.C.C. Warning," *New York Times,* April 11, 1971, 50.

21. Quoted in Travis, *Rock Jocks.*

22. "The Golden Age of Underground Radio," 1989 release of 1969 recording.

23. Raechel Donahue, Travis tapes. The Donahues cooperated with the FBI probe of the Symbionese Liberation Army kidnapping of Patricia Hearst, passing the SLA's audiotapes to the authorities.

24. Quoted in Keith, *Purple Haze*, 51.

25. Thompson, *Kingdom of Fear*.

26. Memo appears in Keith, *Purple Haze*, 80–90.

27. Raz, "Radio Free Georgetown." After years of complaints by listeners about obscene lyrics, the students' refusal to broadcast the school's basketball games, and the students' insistence on running public service announcements for an abortion referral service, Georgetown University finally shut the station down and in 1979 gave the license to Washington's public college, the University of the District of Columbia. UDC ran it as a jazz station until 1997, when a congressionally imposed financial control board forced the college to sell the station to C-SPAN, which uses it to rebroadcast its television programs.

28. Siemering, "Public Broadcasting," Nov. 1969.

29. Bennis resigned from his position at Buffalo that spring after the acting president of the university ordered him to tell students and the public that the police would not be coming onto the campus, even though the university had actually arranged for the police presence.

30. *This Is Radio* included a number of the forms of journalism that *All Things Considered* and other public radio programs use to this day. For example, instead of airing a thirty-second snippet from a city council meeting, WBFO would put the reporter on the air and have an anchorman debrief him about what had happened that day.

31. Travis tapes.

32. Travis tapes.

33. Quoted in Fornatale and Mills, *Radio*, 140.

34. Keith, *Purple Haze*, 99.

35. Ibid., 96.

36. Quotations from WKNR-FM's programs are from recordings of the original broadcasts, available at www.ncf.ca/beatles/trivia.html. The genealogy of the Paul Is Dead rumor is hotly debated. A deejay at WOIA in Ann Arbor, Larry Monroe, has written that he took calls on the air about the rumor four days before Russ Gibb took the call from Ypsilanti, and that students from Eastern Michigan University dominated Monroe's show—until a mysterious power outage darkened the dormitory from which most of the students were calling.

37. Gibb, interviewed by Scott Westerman in 2002, www.keener13.com/jocks/russ_gibb.htm.

38. LaBour is a musician who became guitarist for the group Riders in the Sky.

39.   Interviewed by John Marsden of CFNY-FM in Ottawa, Oct. 1978, aircheck at www.ncf.ca/beatles/trivia.html.

40.   Victor Lundgren and Robert Thompson, quoted in *Rolling Stone,* Nov. 23, 1967.

41.   This and other quotations from Shaw's memos are from Keith, *Purple Haze,* 41–49, 111–17.

42.   Brother John, undated 1969 aircheck recorded from WABC-FM, from Aaron Mintz collection.

43.   Memo text in Keith, *Purple Haze,* 118–23.

44.   Eberly, *Music in the Air,* 238.

45.   Post, *Playing in the FM Band,* 181.

CHAPTER 8: *PLAYING THE NUMBERS*

1.   Aircheck from April 29, 1967, available at http://user.pa.net/~ejjeff/wlsac.html.

2.   Fornatale and Mills, *Radio,* 61–66; Douglas, *Listening In,* 125–30.

3.   Stanley Kaplan, owner of WAYS in Charlotte, speech to National Association of Broadcasters, quoted in MacFarland, "Development," 573.

4.   Abrams memos, 1998, 2002.

5.   *Broadcasting,* Oct. 1974, quoted in Douglas, *Listening In,* 276.

6.   Fornatale and Mills, *Radio,* 143.

7.   Quoted in *Radio and Records,* June 1978.

8.   Memos archived at www.jive95.com.

9.   Country didn't last either. KSAN today is known as The Bone and plays "classic rock" hits of the 1960s, '70s, and '80s—Rolling Stones, Led Zeppelin, the Doors, Bad Company.

10.   Morrow, *Cousin Brucie,* 167.

11.   Ibid., 212.

12.   Ibid., 218.

13.   In 1988, a subsequent owner of KDKO sold the station to a partnership led by one of the black deejays who had worked for Segal from the start, Jim "Dr. Daddy-O" Walker. Walker in turn sold KDKO—for a 300 percent profit—in 2001 to a white-owned company that ended thirty-four years of black-oriented programming and adopted a talk format. Denver's only black-oriented station at this writing is a hip-hop outlet owned by Clear Channel.

14.   Nnamdi, interview.

15. The most explosive growth in the 1970s came in the country format. Although some stations in the South had been playing hillbilly music since the 1920s, few owners had been willing to commit to a twenty-four-hour country format for fear that advertisers—assuming such listeners to be poor and uneducated—would steer clear. But from 1974 to 1977, the number of country stations doubled, in part because of a successful campaign by the Country Music Association to sponsor research showing advertisers that country listeners, while a bit less educated and considerably less affluent than other Americans, were entirely as likely to buy plenty of consumer goods. Study by Arbitron for the Country Music Association quoted in Eberly, *Music in the Air,* 267.

16. FM's niched version of Top 40, contemporary hit radio, featured jingles, fast-talking deejays, and pop music, but this was a wholly new animal. It was not designed to attract a huge and varied audience by playing the top-selling records. Rather, like the other new formats, it was crafted through research, with songs selected for their appeal to eighteen- to thirty-four-year-olds. Armed with research-proven music, programmers instructed deejays to limit their comments to one-liners provided on index cards. Deejay Don Geronimo, whose real name is Michael Sorce, moved from station to station as managers pushed to minimize the role of deejays in the 1970s. Geronimo insisted on taking listener calls and developing the games and bits that would one day turn him into one of radio's most inventive talk hosts. "That time was so frustrating, just an everyday battle," Geronimo recalled. "We also did incredible amounts of drugs in those years." At WPGC in Washington in 1980, Geronimo was ordered to limit his chatter between songs to ten seconds. Adamant that his station would be known exclusively for its music, the program director went out and bought a real traffic light and set it to turn yellow and then red ten seconds after the deejay's microphone was opened. Red light meant your mike had just been cut off. Geronimo soon left for Los Angeles.

17. The court ruled in the case of New York City classical station WNCN, which in 1974 was flipped to a quadraphonic rock format, sparking a listener rebellion, boycott, and lawsuit. The public pressure eventually resulted in WNCN's owner selling the station to a company that promised to and did restore the classical format. But after a lengthy legal battle, the Supreme Court concluded that the listening public has no recourse to the FCC in the event of a format switch. Station owners license the fre-

quency from the government and essentially may do with it as they wish. WNCN's new owner eventually succumbed to the demand for a higher return, and another flip followed in 1993, this time to a rock format. The station is now classic rock WAXQ, owned by Clear Channel. New York no longer has a serious classical station, only a classical pops commercial station owned by *The New York Times* and a public station that is steadily reducing its music programming in favor of news and talk.

18.   Mark Fowler, "The Public Interest," *Federal Bar Journal,* v. 213, 1982.
19.   The FCC deregulation of radio programming was completed in 1981, though the changes had been in the works for several years and reflected both the Reagan administration's belief in unfettered markets and the evolution of programming that had taken place since FM's rise to popularity.
20.   Connell, "The Radio Generation and the Origin of Top 40."
21.   Al Brady's account of his last-ditch efforts to save WABC are at www .musicradio77.com/albrady.html.
22.   Ahrens, "Why Radio Stinks."
23.   In 2005, WCBS-FM switched from oldies to a new format designed to appeal to young people who listened to a broad variety of music on their iPods and other MP3 players. Morrow and all of the station's other deejays were let go. He quickly signed with Sirius Satellite Radio to do an oldies show.

CHAPTER 9: SHOCK AND AWE

1.   In 1973, there were fewer than twenty talk stations in the country. Fornatale and Mills, *Radio,* 83. KABC in Los Angeles went to an all-talk format in 1966, and in 1970, WMCA became New York's first all-talk station, ending twenty years of Top 40 programming with an ad campaign that said, "WMCA brings you the voice you love to hear. Your own."
2.   "Given what I believe now, I'm surprised I openly played those songs and didn't object to them," he told me. "I was so young."
3.   "Two minutes of a boring caller is the same as playing a song nobody likes," Limbaugh once wrote.
4.   Douglas, *Listening In,* 299–300.
5.   Limbaugh, *The Way Things Ought to Be,* 16.
6.   The best example of the standard academic argument against Limbaugh

and conservative talk radio is Susan Douglas's *Listening In*, which contends that talk radio is "all about challenging and overthrowing . . . feminism" (289). But prior to Limbaugh's success, talk radio was dominated by female hosts of relationship programs—Dr. Ruth Westheimer, Dr. Toni Grant, Joy Browne, and a slew of other such purveyors of psychobabble. Laura Schlessinger's advice program, though preaching a conservative approach to family life, was the only AM talk show to challenge Limbaugh's audience figures in the 1990s. The key distinction here is that station managers seek different demographics at different times of day, and Schlessinger was enormously effective at attracting women eighteen to forty-nine, while Limbaugh excelled at winning the male audience.

7.   The results of a 1996 study by the Annenberg School of Communications at the University of Pennsylvania have been confirmed in several subsequent surveys by academics and industry groups alike.

8.   For the fun of it, Don Geronimo, co-host with Mike O'Meara of the syndicated, Washington-based *Don and Mike Show*, still occasionally takes an hour from his daily four-hour program to play Top 40 deejay, just spinning records, punching up jingles, and doing quick shtick. His talk show, which is as much about radio as it is about sex, guys, and pop culture, is heavily informed by the old rules of Top 40, and Geronimo keeps a count of the (remarkably large) number of times his jingles and announcements recite the station's call letters during each commercial break.

9.   Limbaugh's show is so true to Top 40 pacing that Top 40 loyalist Don Geronimo tapes the Limbaugh program to analyze the show's techniques, the name shouts (the "Rush Limbaugh!" jingle), rock bumpers (the music that bookends each segment of the show), and teases (Limbaugh's constant reminders of what's coming up next). "Top 40 was a fucking steam engine and that's what America wants," Geronimo says.

10.   A clip of Letterman's wacky stunts from 1969 is available at www .reelradio.com/tc/index.html#dlwago69.

11.   Statistics from studies by the Committee for the Study of the American Electorate, quoted in *Atlantic Monthly*, Nov. 2002, 48–49.

12.   Remnick, "The Accidental Anarchist"; Travis, *Rock Jocks;* Douglas, *Listening In*, 303–7.

13.   In 1978, the Supreme Court limited the broadcast—except late at night—of the naughty words in comedian George Carlin's "Seven Dirty

Words" monologue, which had been aired on Bob Fass's WBAI. Hardly any shock jock dared use those words, which were not actually banned; in fact, stations were essentially instructed that they could air such language at hours when children were less likely to be listening, namely, 10 P.M. to 6 A.M. The words in the Carlin case were *shit, piss, fuck, cunt, cocksucker, motherfucker,* and *tits.* In recent years, the FCC has dismissed complaints against stations that aired many of those words, sometimes because they were part of legitimate news coverage, sometimes because they were part of a comedy routine. Rivera-Sanchez, "How Far Is Too Far?"

14. To understand the FCC's definition of indecency, Rivera-Sanchez examined thirty-one complaints against radio stations filed between 1989 and 1995. In twenty-eight of those cases, regulators dismissed the complaints because the language was "not actionably indecent."

15. Transcript on file at Federal Communications Commission, WKRK-FM, Detroit, Jan. 9, 2002.

16. In June 2003, although Leykis's show was the highest-rated program on Mojo Radio, the Vancouver station pulled the program off the air, saying it had to do so to appease the Canadian Radio-Television and Telecommunications Commission, which has a strict code governing content. Mojo had tried editing the Leykis programs to eliminate offensive language, but that was not sufficient for the regulators. Leykis was replaced by sports talk from ESPN.

17. Following Tom Leykis is an unenviable task for any broadcaster. On KLSX, the next show opens with a caller denouncing another listener as an "effin' A-hole." The host guffaws and introduces the first bit of the evening: "Translate Jesse Jackson," in which callers compete to decipher an audio clip of the civil rights leader:

> "Was it 'the Koreatown Vicks report on Friday'?"
> "Sorry," the host says. "Next?"
> "Um, 'to pre-empt Hans Blix's report by Friday'?"
> "Very close!"

CHAPTER 10: SCATTERING SEEDS

1. Quoted in Hilmes and Loviglio, *Radio Reader,* 412–14.

2. When NPR's *Morning Edition* broadcast its annual Holiday CD Gift Guide, it featured music by jazz balladeer Eva Cassidy, folk rocker Joni Mitchell, jazz saxophonist Paquito D'Rivera, and the new wave surf band

Big Lazy, as well as a compilation of African rock. That none of the music could be heard on commercial radio goes without saying, but it is also true that public radio, which once reliably played all of those genres, now has ever less room for any of them, except in fifteen-second clips on NPR news programs (*Morning Edition,* Nov. 24, 2002).

3. The mean income of NPR listeners is $78,216, their average age is about fifty, and about 90 percent of them are non-Hispanic whites, according to NPR research.

4. "It's a tribal thing, the public radio audience," former NPR reporter Deborah Amos wrote in the online *Transom Review* (www.transom.org), Feb. 8, 2002. "They have imagined every place I've been with a tape recorder. They have imagined what it smelled like and what the people ate for dinner. And when the situation was dangerous, they imagined the danger and they worried. . . . Listeners are our co-authors, our co-conspirators, they engage, they imagine and participate with us. It helps to explain those 'wait in the driveway until the story is over' moments."

5. Much of this passage on Keillor's program appeared in somewhat different form in my "Constant Companion," *Washington Post,* June 14, 1998, F1.

6. Local public stations operate independently and pay National Public Radio, Public Radio International, American Public Media, and other program providers for the shows they air. While local public stations once produced most of their own programming, most now rely on NPR and other national program sources for the bulk of their broadcast material.

7. Abrams, memo to XM Radio staff, Oct. 3, 2000.

8. Giovannoni was also instrumental in bringing about changes in programming at Pacifica's five stations across the country, pushing the fiercely independent stations to air more national programming and move away from Pacifica's tradition of building program schedules with shows appealing to dozens of narrow interests, from radical feminism to gay liberation, from organic foods to Caribbean music. When station volunteers and listeners rebelled against Pacifica's efforts to force its stations to accept national programming in the late 1990s, the result was a series of confrontations—in court, in rhetorical battle on websites and petitions, and in actual fisticuffs as Pacifica hired armed guards and removed some program hosts from stations. In 2000, Giovannoni praised Pacifica's "enlightened leaders" for "applying proven broadcasting practices." Two years later, most of the managers who had followed Giovan-

noni's advice were forced out and listener groups regained control of the stations.

9. In 1997, the Corporation for Public Broadcasting made it far harder for public radio stations to resist Giovannoni's path, setting performance standards that require stations to hit audience size or listener donation targets in order to remain eligible for federal grants. The new rules forced many stations to kill programming that appealed to smaller, narrower audiences: stations dropped ethnic programs, big-band and 1940s jazz shows, and other local programs, picking up national shows that research indicated would draw larger audiences. Conciatore, "Radio Sharpens Formats to Keep CPB Grants."

10. Giovannoni, "Programming Defines Community," speech to Public Radio Program Directors Conference, Sept. 18, 1998, www.aranet.com.

11. Josephson at debate with Giovannoni before the Public Radio Conference, May 1996, quoted in *Current*, June 17, 1996.

12. Radio Research Consortium estimates based on Arbitron ratings, fall 2000.

13. Between 1994 and 2002, while the portion of nationwide public radio airtime devoted to news and talk jumped from 27 percent to 32 percent, the amount of time dedicated to classical music fell from 35 percent to 30 percent. Data compiled by NPR Audience and Corporate Research, reported in *Current*, Jan. 27, 2003.

14. Janssen, "Triple A Strikes Chord."

15. Quoted in Hentoff, "All That Jazz."

16. Scarborough Research study, Oct. 23, 2002.

17. Behrens, "Jazzcasters."

18. Johnson, "A Year Later."

CHAPTER 11: FULL OF SOUND AND FURY

1. Allan was forced out at WBIG in September 2003, six months after this music test and a decade after he took over the station, which remained one of the three most popular stations in Washington among the thirty-five-to-fifty-four demographic throughout those years. He became a consultant to WBIG and other stations and ran an oldies station in Detroit.

2. The changes contemplated at that focus group session turned out to be not nearly enough to lower the average age of WBIG's listeners. In 2006, the station, owned by Clear Channel, dropped oldies, replacing the format with a classic rock approach, focused on hit songs of the 1970s.

3. Coleman, "Oldies Insights," 16–17. The top-rated oldies stations in the country played songs whose average year of origin is 1967, while the bottom-rated oldies stations' playlists have an average year of origin of 1968.2, the study found.

4. XM Radio, Annual Report 2003, 4.

5. Future of Music Coalition, "Radio Deregulation," 55–61.

6. Lee, "On Minot, N.D. Radio."

7. Clear Channel reacted to the debacle by equipping its local technicians with cell phones and beepers.

8. In 2006, WBIG dropped its oldies format and fired its deejays, including Kelly. The Minneapolis station also dropped "Jackson."

9. Mathews, "From a Distance."

10. *Tucson Citizen,* May 3, 2002.

11. Statement to FCC, Richmond, Va., hearing, Feb. 27, 2003.

12. Two members of Congress, Jan Schakowsky and Danny Davis, recorded the anti-war spots after a group called Chicagoans Against War on Iraq raised $7,000 to pay for the radio time. The ads were initially approved by sales managers at WNUA and four other Chicago stations. But on March 11, 2003, a WNUA employee called Rep. Schakowsky's office to inform the congresswoman that the deal was off and that Clear Channel corporate headquarters had nixed the arrangement because it had decided not to accept any spots related to the war. This account was provided by Nadeam Elshami of Schakowsky's Washington staff.

13. Schwartz and Fabrikant, "War Puts Radio Giant on the Defensive."

14. Philips, "Clear Channel's Radio Pact Irks Labels."

15. Ibid.

16. Interep Research Division, "Fragmentation," 1998.

17. Steve Smith, imaging director, Clear Channel, Lebanon, N.H., in a letter to *Entertainment Weekly,* July 8, 2002, quoted in Future of Music Coalition, "Radio Deregulation."

18. Quoted in "The Bad Boys of Radio," *Fortune,* March 3, 2003.

19. Forrester Research, June 2, 2003.

CHAPTER 12: *BACK TO THE FUTURE*

1. The only interruptions in service I have experienced with XM Radio have been while driving alongside tall mountains or in deep hollows, and occasionally in some downtown office canyons where XM has not pro-

vided the repeater transmitters intended to overcome interference by tall buildings.

2. Abrams, internal XM Radio memo, June 5, 2002.

3. To some extent, that early list also reflected the geography of early adopters. Ten of the top thirty stations were located in Seattle; Washington, D.C.; San Francisco; and Boston—home to the most affluent and highly educated populations in the country and therefore to the group most likely to have access to broadband Internet connections. Arbitron Webcast Channel Ratings Report, May 2002.

4. Traditional broadcast stations pay royalties only to the writers and publishers of songs they play, while Web stations now must pay those fees plus extra royalties to the record companies and performers of the music. Billington accepted the recording industry's argument that traditional radio's exemption from those fees is justified because airplay promotes sales of the music.

5. Arbitron Internet Broadcast Stations Weekly Top 50, Nov. 13, 2003, www.arbitron.com/newsroom/archive/WCR11_13_03.htm.

6. See www.kfok.org.

7. See www.wryr.org.

8. About half of the first two hundred low-power licenses granted were given to religious groups. Paul Riismandel, "Radio by and for the Public," in Hilmes and Loviglio, *Radio Reader*, 445.

SIGN-OFF: MAGIC

1. On the fortieth anniversary of Dodger Stadium, fans in Los Angeles were asked to name their favorite Dodger of all time. The winner, by a healthy margin, was Vin Scully, the team's radio play-by-play man for fifty-four years.

2. In 2005, Sidney suffered two strokes and was off the air for a time. The next year, he came back to WLNG, which he's carried on virtually unchanged. While his memory is not clear, he occasionally appears on the air. Somehow, when he's on a hot microphone, flashes of his old self return.

Numbers in *italics* refer to illustrations.

MARC FISHER, whose column appears in *The Washington Post* three times each week, reports and writes about local, national, and personal issues. His blog, "Raw Fisher," and his online chat program, "Potomac Confidential," appear on washingtonpost.com. He also writes "The Listener," a radio column in the *Post*'s Sunday Arts section. Fisher is author of *After the Wall: Germany, the Germans and the Burdens of History*. Fisher has worked at *The Washington Post* since 1987 and served as the paper's Berlin bureau chief from 1989 to 1993. He has won numerous journalism awards, including the 2001 Associated Press award for best column writing, an Overseas Press Club award for best interpretation of foreign news, and a Society of Professional Journalists award for best magazine writing. A graduate of Princeton University, Fisher lives in Washington with his wife and their two children.

This book was set in Caslon, a typeface first designed in 1722 by William Caslon. Its widespread use by most English printers in the early eighteenth century soon supplanted the Dutch typefaces that had formerly prevailed. The roman is considered a "workhorse" typeface due to its pleasant, open appearance, while the italic is exceedingly decorative.